The Principal Na Voyages, Traffi Discoveries of the English Nation — Volume 05 Central and Southern Europe

Richard Hakluyt

Alpha Editions

This edition published in 2024

ISBN 9789362510044

Design and Setting By
Alpha Editions
www.alphaedis.com
Email - info@alphaedis.com

Contents

VOL. V

CENTRAL AND SOUTHERN EUROPE.

Nauigations, Voyages, Traffiques and Discoveries IN

CENTRAL AND SOUTHERN EUROPE.

A Catalogue of the great Masters of the Order of the Dutch knights, commonly called the Hospitalaries of Ierusalem: and what great exploites euery of the saide Masters hath atchieued either in conquering the land of Prussia, or in taming and subduing the Infidels, or els in keeping them vnder their obedience and subiection, taken out of Munster.

The order of the Dutch knights had their first original at Ierusalem in the yere of our Lorde 1190. within the Hospitall of the blessed Virgine: and the first Master of the saide order was called Henrie of Walpot, vnder whome many good things, and much wealth and riches were throughout all Germanie and Italie procured vnto the order: and the saide Hospitall was remoued from Ierusalem vnto Ptolemais, otherwise called Acon, and the foresaid Order grew and mightily increased, whereof I will hereafter discourse more at large in my Treatise of Syria. Henrie of Walpot deceased in the yeere of Christ 1200. The 2. Master was Otto of Kerpen, and he continued Master of the Order for the space of sixe yeeres. The 3. was Hermannus Bart a godly and deuout person, who deceased in the yeere 1210. being interred at Acon, as his predecessors were. The 4. was Hermannus de Saltza, who thirtie yeeres together gouerned the saide Order, and managed the first expedition of warre against the Infidels of Prussia, and ordained another Master also in Prussia to bee his Deputie in the same region. [Sidenote: Ensiferi fratres.] In the yeere 1239. the knights of the sword, who trauailed into Liuonia to conuert the inhabitants thereof vnto Christ, seeing they were not of sufficient force to performe that enterprise, and that their enemies increased on all sides, they vnited themselues vnto the famous Order of the Dutch knights in Prussia, that their worthie attempt might bee defended and promoted by the aide and assistance of the saide Dutch knights. [Sidenote: The first war moued against the Prussian infidels, anno dom. 1239.] At the very same time the ensigne of the crosse was exalted throughout all Germanie against the Prussians, and a great armie of souldiers was gathered together, the Burgraue of Meidenburg being generall of the armie, who combining themselues vnto the Dutch knights, ioyned battell with the Infidels, and slew about fiue hundred Gentiles, who beforetime had made horrible inuasions and in-roades into the dominions of Christians wasting all with fire and sword, but especially the land of Colm, and Lubonia, which were the Prouinces of Conradus Duke of Massouia. Nowe, the foresaide knights hauing made so huge a slaughter, built the castle of Reden, betweene Pomerania and the land of Colm, and so by degrees they gotte footing in the lande, and daylie erected more castles, as namely, Crutzburg, Wissenburg, Resil, Bartenstein, Brunsburg, and Heilsburg, and furnished them all with garrisons. The fift Master of the Order was Conradus Landgrauius, the brother of Lodouick, which was husband vnto Ladie Elizabeth. This, Conradus, by his fathers inheritance, gaue great riches and possessions vnto the Order, and caused Ladie Elizabeth to be interred at Marpurg, within the religious house of his saide Order. Vnder the gouernment of this Master, Acon in the lande of Palestina was subdued vnto the Saracens. Moreouer, in the yeere 1254. there was another great armie of Souldiers prepared against Prussia, by the Princes of Germanie. For Octacer, alias Odoacer king of Bohemia, Otto Marques of Brandeburg, the Duke of Austria, the Marques of Morauia, the Bishops of Colen and of Olmutz came marching on with great strength of their Nobles and common Souldiers, and inuading the lande of Prussia in the Winter season, they constrained the inhabitants thereof to receiue the Christian faith, and to become obedient vnto the knights. After which exploite, by the aduise and assistance of king Odoacer, there was a castle built vpon a certaine hill of Samogitia, which immediately after grewe to be a great citie, being at this day the seate of the Prince of Prussia: and it was called by Odoacer Kunigsburg, that is to say, Kings Mount, or Mount royall, being finished in the yeere 1255. Out of this fort, the knights did bridle and restraine the furie of the Infidels on all sides, and compelled them to obedience. The sixt Master was called Boppo ab Osterna, vnder whom the citie of Kunigsberg was built. [Sidenote: The Prussians abandon Christianitie.] At the very same instant the knights beeing occupied about the warre of Curland, the Prussians conspiring together, and abandoning the Christian faith, in furious maner armed themselues against the Christian, defaced and burnt down Churches, slew Priests, and to the vtmost of their abilitie, banished all faithful people. The report of which misdemeanour being published throughout all Germanie, an huge armie was leuied and sent for the defence and succour of the knights, which marching into the land of Natan, made many slaughters, and through the inconstancie of fortune sometimes woonne, and sometimes lost the victorie. Also the Infidels besieged these three castles, namely, Barstenstein, Crutzberg and Kunigsberg, and brought extreame famine vpon the Christians contained within the saide fortes. Againe, in the yeere of our Lord 1262. the Earle of Iuliers, with other Princes and great chiualrie came downe, and giuing charge vpon the Prussians, put three thousand of them to the edge of the sworde. Afterward the Prussians banding themselues together, were determined to spoile the castle of Kunigsberg, but their confederacie being disclosed, they had the repulse. And when the knightes had preuailed against them, they laide in pledges, and yet for all that were not afraid to breake their fidelitie. For vpon a certaine time, after they had giuen diuers pledges, they slewe two noble knights of the Order, and so by that meanes incensed the principall of the saide order, insomuch that they caused two paire of gallons to be set vp besides the castle, and thirtie of the Prussians pledges to be hanged therupon. Which seueritie so vexed and prouoked the Prussians, that in reuenge of the said iniury, they renewed bloody and cruel warres, slew many Christians, yea, and put 40. knights with the master of the Order, and the Marshal, vnto the edge of the sword. There was at the same instant in Pomerania a Duke called Suandepolcus, professing the Christian faith, but being ioyned in league with the Prussians, he indeuoured for many yeeres, not onely to expell the knights, but all Christians whatsoeuer out of the lande of Prussia, in which warre the foresaide knights of the Order suffered many abuses. For they lost almost all their castles, and a great number of themselues also were slaine. This Suandepolcus put in practise many lewde attempts against religion. For albeit he was baptised, he did more mischiefe then the very Infidels themselues, vntill such time as the knights being assisted by the Princes of Germanie, brought the saide Duke and the Prussians also into such straights, that (maugre their heads) they were constrained to sue for peace. Afterward Swandepolcus lying at the point of death, admonished his sonnes that they should not doe any iniurie vnto the knights of the order, affirming that himselfe neuer prospered so long as he vrged warre against them. Howbeit his sonnes for a certaine time obserued not their fathers counsel, vntill at length one of them named Warteslaus, was created one the Order, and the other called Samborus bestowed by legacie his goods and possessions vpon the saide Order, receiuing maintenance and exhibition from the saide Order, during the terme of his life. It fortuned also vnder the gouernment of the foresayde Master Boppo, that one Syr Martine a Golin beeing accompanied with another knight, went into the countrey to see howe the Prussians were imployed. And meeting with three Prussians, they slew two, and the thirde they reserued to guide them the directest way. But this guide betrayed them into their enemies handes. Which when they perceiued, they slewe the Traytour. Then fiue Prussian horsemen came riding and tooke them, deliuering them bounde to the custodie of two. And the other three pursued the horses of the two, which broke loose in the time of the fraye. And they tarying somewhat long, the other two woulde haue beheaded the two Knightes in the meane season. [Sidenote: A memorable stratageme.] And as one of them was striking with his drawen sworde, at the neck of Sir Martine, hee said vnto them: Sirs, you doe vnwisely in that you take not off my garment before it bee defiled with blood. They therefore loosing the Cordes wherewith hee was bounde, to take off his garment, set his armes more at libertie. Which Syr Martine well perceiuing reached his keeper such a boxe, that his sworde fell to the grounde. Which hee with all speede taking vp, slewe both the keepers and vnbounde his fellowe Knight. Moreouer, seeing the other three Prussians comming furiously vpon them with stoute couragious hearts they made towarde the saide Prussians, and slew them, and so escaped the danger of death. The seuenth great Master was Hanno de Sangershusen, who deceased in the yeere one thousand two hundreth seuentie fiue. The eight was Hartmannus ab Heldringen who deceased in the yeere 1282. The ninth was Burckardus a Schuuenden beeing afterwarde made knight of the order of Saint Iohns. The tenth was Conradus a Feuchtuuang: vnder this man the Citie of Acon in Palestina was sacked by the Soldan, and manie people were slayne. The Templars which were therein returned home out of Fraunce, where they had great reuenewes. The Knightes of Saint Iohn, who also had an Hospitall at Acon, changed their place, and went into the Isle of Cyprus, and from thence departing vnto Rhodes, they subdued that Islande vnto themselues. Nowe the Dutch Knights abounded with wealth and possessions throughout all Germanie, beeing Lordes of a good port of Prussia, Liuonia, and Curland, whose chiefe house was then at Marpurg, til such time as it was remooued vnto Marieburg, a Towne of Prussia. The eleuenth great Master was Godfrey Earle of Hohenloe. Vnder this man the knights sustained a great ouerthrow in Liuonia: but hauing strengthned their armie, they slewe neere vnto Rye foure thousande of their enemies. The twelfth Master was Sifridus a Feuchtuuang. Vnder this man, the principall house of the Order was translated from Marpurg to Marieburg, which in the beginning was established at Acon, and from thence was remooued vnto Venice, and from Venice vnto Marpurg. This Sifridus deceased in the yeere 1341. The thirteenth Master was called Charles Beffart of Triers. This man built a fort vpon the riuer of Mimmel, and it was named Christmimmel. The foureteenth was Warnerus ab Orsele, whome a certaine knight of the Order slewe with his sworde. The 15. was Ludolphus Duke of Brunswick, who built the Towne of Ylgenburg, and deceased 1352. The sixteenth was Theodoricus Earle of Aldenborg, and hee built the Towne of Bartenstein. The seuenteenth was Ludolphus sirnamed King. The eighteenth was Henrie a Tusimer. The nineteenth Winricus a Knoppenrodt In this mans time the knights took the king of the Lithuanians named Kinstut captiue, and kept him prisoner in Marieburg halfe a yeere, but by the helpe of a seruaunt, hauing broken out of the Castle, hee escaped away by night. But fearing that hee was layde waite for in all places, hee left his horse, and went on foote through vnknowen pathes. In the day time hee hidde himselfe in secrete places, and in the night hee continued his iourney vntil hee came vnto Massouia. But all the Knightes ioye was turned into sorrowe, after they had lost so great an enemie. The twentieth grand Master was Conradus Zolnerof Rotenstein. The one and twentieth Conradus Walenrod. [Sidenote: This man sent an ambassage to Richard the Second.] The two and twentieth Conradus a Iungingen, who deceased in the yeere one thousand foure hundreth and seuen. The three and twentieth Vlricus a Iungingen. This man dyed in battell in the yeere one thousand foure hundreth and tenne: which battell was fought against Vladislaus Father of Casimire. Both partes had leuied mightie and huge forces: vnto the Polonians the Lithuanians and the Tartars had ioyned themselues, ouer whome one Vitoldas was captaine: the Dutch Knights had taken vp Souldiers out of all Germanie. And when eache armie had encamped themselues one within twentie furlongs of another, (hoping for victorie and impatient of delay) the great Master of the Prussians sent an Herault to denounce warre vnto the King, and immediately (alarme beeing giuen) it is reported that there were in both armies, fourtie thousand horsemen in a readinesse. Vladislaus commaunded the Lithuanians and the Tartars to giue the first onsette, and placed the Polonians in the rerewarde of the battell: on the contrarie side, the Prussians regarded least of all to reserue any strong troupes behinde, which might rescue such as were wearie, and renewe the fight, if neede shoulde require, but set forwarde the flower and chiualrie of all his Souldiers in the verie forefront of the battell. The charge beeing giuen certaine vnarmed Tartars and Lithuanians were slaine handsmooth: howbeit the multitude pressed on, neither durst the fearefull Polonians turne their backes, and so a cruell battell was fought vpon the heapes of dead carkases. The combate continued a long time, terrible slaughters were committed, and the Lithuanians and Tartars were slaine like sheepe. But when newe and fresh enemies continually issued foorth, the Dutch knights being wearied, began to fight more faintly. Which Vladislaus no sooner perceiued, but in all haste hee sends forwarde his mightie and well armed bande of Polonians, who suddenly breaking in renewed the skirmish. The Dutch were not able to withstand the furie of the fresh troupes (great oddes there is betweene the wearied Souldier and him that comes in a fresh) insomuch that the knights with their people were constrained to flee. The master of the Order seeing his souldiers giue way vnto the enemie, gathered a companie together, and withstoode him in the face, howbeit himselfe was slaine for his labour, the flight of his people proued greater and more dishonourable, neither did the Dutch cease to flee, so long as the Polonian continued the chase. There fell on the Knights partie manie thousands of men, and the Polonians gotte not the victorie without great spoile and damage. This battell was foughten in regard of the bounds of regions in the yeere 1410. All Prussia following the happie successe of the Polonian king (except Marieburg onely) yeelded themselues vnto him being Conquerour. Howbeit the Emperour Sigismund taking vp the quarell, peace was ordained between the knights and Polonia, and a league concluded, certaine summes of money also were paide vnto the Polonian, Prussia was restored vnto the knights, neither was the saide order disturbed in the possession of their lands vntill the time of Friderick. The 24. Master was Henrie Earle of Plaen. This man being deposed by the

Chapter, was 7. yeres holden prisoner at Dantzik. The 25. Master was Michael Kuchenmeister, that is, master of the Cookes of Sternberg. The 26. was Paulus a Russdorff. The 27. Conradus ab Ellerichshausen. This man, after diuers and sundry conflicts betweene the Dutch knights, and the king of Polonia, concluded a perpetuall league with the saide king. Howbeit the citizens of Dantzig secretely going about to obteyne their freedome, that the foresaide Order might haue no dominion ouer them, made sute vnto the Polonian king to be their Protector. This Conradus died in the yeere 1450. The 28. was Lewis ab Ellerichshausen. Vnder this man there arose a dangerous sedition in Prussia betweene the chiefe cities and the knights of the Order. The citizens demanded libertie, complaining that they were oppressed with diuers molestations. Whereupon they primly made sute vnto Casimir then king of Polonia. The Master of the Order seeing what would come to passe began to expostulate with the king, that he kept not the peace which had bene concluded betweene them to last for euer. Also Frederick the Emperour commaunded the Prussians to returne vnto the obedience of the knights, who by the dint of their swordes had released that prouince out of the hands of Infidels, and had bought it with the shedding of much blood. Notwithstanding the popular sort persisting stil in their stubborne determination, proceeded at length to open warre. The cities adhearing vnto the king vsurped diuers Castles belonging to the Master, tooke certain Commanders and knights, yea, and some they slewe also. Fiftie and fiue townes conspired together in that rebellion: but thinking their estate and strength not sure enough against their own gouernors without forrein aide, they chose king Casimir to be their lord. Heereupon the Polonian king marched into Prussia with a great armie, taking possession of such cities as yeelded themselues vnto him, and proceeding forward against Marieburg, besieged the castle and the towne. [Sidenote: The great master ouercommeth the king of Polonia.] In the meane season the Master hauing hired an armie of Germane souldiers, suddenly surprised the king at vnawares in his tents, and slewe about 300. Polonians, tooke prisoners 136. noblemen, spoiled their tents, tooke away their horses, victuals, and armour, insomuch that the king himselfe hardly escaped vpon one horse. These things came to passe in the yeere 1455. The Master hauing thus obtained the victorie, sent his armie into the countrey, and recouered the castles and cities which he had lost, to the number of 80. putting many of his enemies also vnto the sword. Moreouer, he recouered Kunigsberg being one of the foure principall cities, which are by name Thorne, Elburg, Kunigsberg, and Gdanum, that is to say, Dantzig. [Sidenote: The king by treason ouerthroweth the Master.] And when the warre was longer protracted then the Master could well beare, and a whole yeres wages was vnpaid vnto his captains, those captaines which were in the garrison of Marieburg conspired against the Master, and for a great summe of money betrayed the castle of Marieburg vnto the king. Which practise beeing knowen, the Master fled to Kunigsberg, and newe warre was begunne, and great spoile and desolation was wrought on both sides: vntill at length, after composition made, the king retayned Pomerella, and all the castles and townes therein, together with Marieburg and Elburg: and the master inioyed Samaitia, Kunigsberg, &c. This composition was concluded in the yere 1466. The 29. Master was Henrie Reuss, first being deputie, and afterwarde Master of Prussia. The 30. was Henrie a Richtenberg, who deceased in the yeere 1477. The 31. called Martine Truchses died in the yeere 1489. The 32. Iohn a Tieflen died in the yeere 1500. The 33. being Duke of Saxonie, and marques of Misn, deceased in the yeere 1510. This man began to call in question, whether the foresaid composition concluded betweene the king of Polonia, and the Order, were to bee obserued or no? especially sithence [Footnote: Since, from *siththan*, SAX. But, fair Fidessa, *sithens* fortune's guile, Or enimies power hath now captiv'd thee. SPENS. *Faerie Queene*, I., IV., 57.] it conteined certaine articles against equitie and reason. Whereupon he appealed vnto the Bishop of Rome, vnto the Emperor, vnto the princes and electors of Germany, and preuailed with them so farre forth, that there was a day of hearing appointed at Posna in Polonia. And the Legates of both parts meeting heard complaints and excuses, and dispatched no other businesse. In the meane time Prince Frederick deceased in the tenth yeere of his gouernment. The 34. Master was Albertus marques of Brandenburg, [Footnote: Albrecht of Anspach and Baireuth, a scion of the Hohenzollerns. He was a man of will and capacity, who reinvigorated the order of the Teuton knights by renouncing Roman Catholicism and embracing Lutheranism, while he consolidated its influence by erecting Prussia into a Duchy, whose crown he placed on his own brow in 1525. After a prosperous reign he died in 1550, and his son, having lost his reason, the elector John Sigismund of Hohenzollern obtained the ducal crown in right of his wife Anna, daughter of Duke Albert.] whom the King of Polonia did so grieuously molest with war, and oppressed all Prussia with such extreme rigour, that the Prince of the countrey was constrained to make a league of foure yeeres with him, and to yeeld vnto such conditions, as turned to the vtter ouerthrowe of the whole Order. And amongst other conditions are these which follow. Sithence that the originall of all discorde betweene Polonia and the order doeth from hence arise, for that hitherto in Prussia, no lawfull heyre and successor hath borne rule and authority, but diuers and sundry haue had the gouernment thereof, by whose meanes the nations haue bene prouoked one against another, much Christian blood hath bin shed, the lands and inhabitants grieuously spoiled, and many widowes and Orphans made: the Popes, Emperors, and Princes being often solicited for the establishing of that perpetual league, which Casimir hath heretofore concluded &c. Sithence also that the truce which hath bene agreed vpon of both parties is in short time to be expired; and that it is to bee feared, that bloody warres will then be renewed, and that all things will proue worse and worse, vnlesse some lawfull composition be made, and some good and wholesome deuise be put in practise, as well for the benefit of the King and of his posteritie, as for the commoditie of the whole common weale of Prussia, especially considering that Albertus the Marques refuseth not to submitte himselfe to the Councell of the King, &c.

* * * * *

The Oration or speech of the Ambassadours sent from Conradus de Zolner
  Master generall of the land of Prussia, vnto Richard the second, King of England, and France, &c.

The messengers which are sent from the Master generall of the land of Prussia, doe propound and declare the affaires and negotiations vnderwritten.

[Sidenote: The ancient assistance of the kings of England against infidels.] Whereas it is apparant, that diuers and sundrie times heeretofore, your famous progenitours and predecessours the kings of England haue alwaies bene gratious promoters and speciall friends vnto the generall Masters of the land of Prussia, and of the whole order: whereas also they haue vouchsafed, by their Barons, Knights, and other their nobles of the kingdome of England, vnto the Masters and order aforesaide, sundry and manifolde fauourable assistance in the conquest of the Infidels (in whose steppes your excellent Maiestie insisting, haue, in these your dayes shewed your selfe in like sort right graciously affected vnto the Master generall which nowe is, and vnto his famous Predecessour) in due consideration of the premisses, and in regard also of diuers other affaires, which are at this present to be propounded vnto your Highnes, the foresaid Master general which now is hath caused vs his messengers to be sent with letters of credence vnto your Maiestie: humbly praying, and earnestly beseeching your roial clemency, that in times to come, the said Master general, his successors, and our whole Order may of your bounty most graciously obtaine the same fauour, beneuolence, and stedfast amity and friendship, which hath bin continued from the times of your foresaid predecessors: in regard whereof, we do offer the said Master of ours, and our whole company, vnto your highnes, as your perpetual and deuote friends. Notwithstanding (most souereigne Prince) certaine other things we haue to propound vnto your Grace, in the name and behalfe of our saide Master and Order, by way of complaint, namely, that at certaine times past, and especially within the space of x. yeeres last expired, his subiects and marchants haue sustained sundry damages and ablations of their goods, by diuers subiects and inhabitants of your realme of England, and that very often both by sea and land: the which, for the behalf, and by the appointment of the Master general aforesaid, and of his predecessor, are put downe in registers, and recorded in the writings of his cities in the land of Prussia. [Sidenote: Edward the 3.] Of which parties damnified, some haue obtained letters from the Master general that now is, and also from his predecessor, vnto your renoumed grandfather K. Edward of famous memory, and sundry times vnto your highnes also, to haue restitution made for their goods taken from them: whereby they haue nothing at al preuailed, but heaping losse vpon losse haue misspent their time and their charges: both because they were not permitted to propound and exhibit their complaints and letters before your maiesty, and also for diuers other impediments. Certain of them also considering how others of their countriemen had laboured in vain, and fearing the like successe, haue troubled the Master general very often with grieuous and sundry complaints, crauing and humbly beseeching at his hands, that he would vouchsafe graciously to prouide for them as his faithful and loial subiects, as touching the restitution of their losses: especially seeing that so much wealth of the English marchants was euery yeere to be found in Prussia, as being arrested, they might obtaine some reasonable satisfaction for their losses. Which thing the Master general aforesaid and his predecessor also haue deferred vnto this present (albeit to the great losse of their subiects) therby hauing meere and principal respect vnto those special curtesies and fauours which your excellent Maiesty and your worthy progenitors haue right gratiously vouchsafed vpon our Masters and Order: neither yet for the iniuries aforesaid, was there euer any maner of offence, or molestation offered vnto any of your subiects noble or ignoble whatsoeuer. Moreouer, in the name and behalfe of our foresad Master general we do propound vnto your excellency by way of complaint, that in the yere last past, 6 dayes after the feast of the Ascension, certain persons of your realm of England, with their ships and captains comming vnto the port of Flanders, named Swen, and finding there, amongst sundry other, 6 ships of Prussia resident, which had there arriued with diuers goods and marchandises: and being informed that they were of Prussia, and their friends, they caused them and their ships to remain next vnto their owne ships, protesting vnto them, that they should in no sort be molested of damnified by themselues or by any other of their company, and that they would faithfully defend them, as if they were their own people, from the hands of their aduersaries: and for their farther security and trust, they deliuered some of their own men and their standerds into our mens ships: howbeit a while after being stirred vp, and bent far otherwise, they took out of the foresaid ships al kind of armors, wherwith they were to gard and defend themselues from pirats, and they deteined the masters of those ships, not suffring them to return vnto their own ships and companies, one also of the said ships (hauing taken al the goods out of her) they consumed with fire. And within 3. daies after they came with one accord vnto the abouenamed ships, and tooke away from them all goods and marchandises which they could find, and all the armour and weapons of the said ships, the chestes also of the marchants, of the ship-masters, and of other persons they brake open, taking out money, iewels, garments, and diuers other commodities: and so they inflicted vpon them irrecouerable losses and vnkind grieuances. And departing out of the foresaid hauen, they caried 2. of the Prussian ship-masters with them, as their captiues vnto an hauen of England called Sandwich. Who, being afterward released were compelled to sweare, that they should not declare the iniuries offred vnto them, either before your roiall maiesty, or your hon. Councell, or your chancelor: neither, were they permitted to come on shore. And being offred such hard measure, when they made pitiful mones and complaints vnto your foresaide subiects, amongst other matters they spake on this wise vnto them: Do you complain of iniuries and losses offered vnto you? Loe, in your own countrey of Prussia there are English marchants, and goods sufficient, go your waies home therfore, and recouer your losses, taking two for one: and in this maner they were left, and so departed. Afterward returning vnto the land of Prussia, they and their friends repaired vnto the Master general, iointly and with one consent making their complaint vnto him of the losses which had bin inflicted vpon them by your subiects. And prostrating themselues at his feet, they all and euery of them made their humble sutes, yet he would haue compassion on them, as vpon his poore subiects, regarding themselues, their wiues, and children, and pitying their distres, and penury, and that he would graciously procure some redresse for them. And when he offred his letters vnto them, wishing them to prosecute their cause before your highnes, they answered that they were no way able to defray the expenses, and that others, who were in like sort damnified, had laboured that way altogether in vain and to no purpose: beseeching him again and again, that he would by another kind of means, namely by arresting of your marchants and their goods procure them restitution of their losses. [Sidenote: The arresting of the English goods and marchants.] At length the Master general being moued by so many and so great complaints, and by the molestation of his subiects, caused (albeeit full sore against his will) a certaine portion of English marchants goods to be laid hold on, and to be arrested, in his cities of Elburg and Dantzik, and to be bestowed in sure places, vntil such time as he might conueniently by his messengers propound and exhibit all and singular the premisses vnto your highnes. And forasmuch as the foresaid Master general and our Order do know no iust occasion, wherby they haue deserued your maiesties indignation, but are firmely and most vndoubtedly perswaded, to finde all curtesie, fauour, and friendship at your Highnesse, according to your wonted clemencie: the said Master generall therefore maketh no doubt, that al the aboue written damages and molestations, being in such sort, against God and iustice, offred vnto his subiects by yours, be altogether vnknown vnto your magnificence, and committed against your mind: wherfore presently vpon the foresaid arrest of your marchants goods, he dispatched his messengers vnto your roial maiesty. Wherof one deceased by the way, namely, in the territory of Holland: and the other remained sick in those parts, for a long season: and so that ambassage took none effect. Wherefore the said master general was desirous to send vs now the second time also vnto your Highnes. We do make our humble sute therfore, in the name and behalf of our master and Order aforesaid, vnto your kingly supremacy, that, hauing God and iustice before your eies, and also the dutifull and obsequious demeanor of the said master, and order towards you, you would vouchsafe to extend your gracious clemency, for the redresse of the premisses: wherby the foresaid losses may be restored and repaied vnto our subiects. All which notwithstanding, that it would please you of your wisedome and prouidence to procure so absolute a remedy, by meanes whereof, in time to come, such dealings and inconueniences may be auoided on both parts, and finally that your marchants may quietly be possessed of their goods arrested in Prussia, and our marchants may be admitted vnto the possession of their commodities attached in England, to conuert and apply them vnto such vses, as to themselues shal seem most conuenient. Howbeit (most gracious prince and lord) we are to sollicite your Highnesse, not onely about the articles to be propounded concerning the losses aforesaide, but more principally, for certain sinister reports and superstituous slanders, wherwith certaine of your subiects, not seeking for peace, haue falsly informed your maiesty, and your most honorable and discreete Councel: affirming that at the time of the aforesaid arrest your marchants were barbarously intreated, that they were cast into lothsom prisons, drenched in myre and water vp to the neck, restrained from al conference and company of men, and also that their meat was thrown vnto them, as a bone to a dog, with many other enormities, which they haue most slanderously deuised concerning the master general aforesaid, and his people, and haue published them in these dominions: vpon the occasion of which falshoods certain marchants of our parts, and of other regions of Alemain (who, of your special beneuolence, were indued with certaine priuileges and fauours in your citie of London, and in other places) were, as malefactors, apprehended and caried to prison, vntil such time as the trueth was more apparant. Whereupon, the foresaide master generall propoundeth his humble sute vnto your maiestie, that such enemies of trueth and concord, your Maiesty woulde vouchsafe in such sort to chastise, that they may be an example vnto others presuming to doe the like.

Moreouer, (high and mighty Prince and lord) it was reported vnto our Master general, that his former Legats required of your maiesty safe conduct freely to come into your highnesse Realme. Which when hee heard, he was exceedingly offended therat, sithence vndoubtedly they did not this at his commaundement or direction. We therefore humbly beseech your Grace, as touching this ouersight, to holde the Master generall excused, because there is no need of safeconduct, between so speciall friends.

Furthermore, sundry damages and complaints of the foresaid general Master, and his subiects are briefly exhibited, and put downe in the billes following. Also all and singular damnified persons, besides other proofes, were compelled to verifie their losses by their formall othes, taken vpon the holy Bible.

Lastly, we doe make our humble suite and petition vnto the prouidence and discretion of your Highnes, and of your honorable Councell, that concerning the premisses, and all other matters propounded, or to be propounded vnto your Maiesty, we may obtaine a speedy answere, and an effectuall end. For it would redound vnto our great charges and losse to make any long delayes.

* * * * *

An agreement made by the Ambassadors of England and Prussia, confirmed by king Richard the second.

Richard by the grace of God, king of England, and France, and lorde of Ireland. To all, vnto whom these present letters shall come, greeting. We haue seene and considered the composition, ordination, concord, and treatie, betweene our welbeloued clearke, master Nicholas Stocket, licentiat in both lawes, Walter Sibel, and Thomas Graa, citizens of our cities of London and York, our messengers and ambassadors on the one part: and the honourable and religious personages, Conradus de Walrode, great commander, Sifridus Walpode de Bassenheim, chiefe hospitalary commander in Elburg, and Vlricus Hachenberg Treasurer, the messengers and ambassadors of the right reuerend and religious lord, lord Conradus Zolner de Rothenstein, master generail of the knightly order of the Dutch hospital of Saint Mary at Ierusalem on the other part, lately concluded and agreed vpon in these words. In the name of the supreame and indiuisible Trinitie, the Father, the Sonne, and holy Ghost, Amen. Forasmuch as the author of peace will haue peacemakers to be the sons of blessednes, and the execrable enemie of peace to be expelled out of the dominions of

Christians: therefore for the perpetuall memorie of the thing, be it knowen vnto all men who shall see or heare the tenour of these presents: that there being matter of dissension and discord bred betweene the most renowmed prince and king, Richard by the grace of God king of England and France, and lord of Ireland, and his subiects on the one part: and the right reuerend and religious lord, lord Conradus Zolner de Rothinstein, Master generall of the knightly order of the Dutch hospitall of S. Marie at Ierusalem, and his land of Prussia, and his subiects also, on the other part: the foresaid lord and generall master, vpon mature counsell and deliberation had, sent his honourable ambassadours towards England vnto the forenamed most soueraigne prince and king, to propound and make their complaint vnto him of violence and iniuries offered (as it is sayd) by the English vnto the Prussians: in consideration whereof certaine goods of the marchants of England were arrested in the land of Prussia. Whose complaint the foresayd most gracious prince did courteously and friendly admit, receiue, and accept, and after many speeches vttered in this treaty, louingly dismissed them vnto their owne countrey againe, promising by his letters vnto the foresayd reuerend Master generall, that hee would dispatch his ambassadours vnto the land of Prussia. [Sidenote: 1388.] Whereupon, in the yeere 1388. he sent the hono: and reuerend personages Master Nicholas Stocket licentiate of both lawes, Thomas Graa, and Walter Sibill, citizens of London and Yorke, with sufficient authority and full commandement, to handle, discusse, and finally to determine the foresaid busines, and with letters of credence vnto the right reuerend lord and master generall aforesayd. Which ambassadours, together with Iohn Beuis of London their informer, and the letters aforesaid, and their ambassage, the said right reuerend lord and Master generall, at his castle of Marienburgh, the 28. of Iuly, in the yeare aforesaid, reuerently and honourably receiued and enterteined; and in his minde esteemed them worthy to treate and decide the causes aforesayd; and so vnto the sayd ambassadours he ioyned in commission on his behalfe, three of his owne counsellors, namely the honourable and religious personages Conradus de Walrode great commander, Seiffridus Walpode de Bassenheim chiefe hospitalary and commander in Elburg, Wolricus Hachenberger treasurer, being all of the order aforesaid. Which ambassadors so entreating about the premisses, and sundry conferences and consultations hauing passed between them, friendly and with one consent, concluded an agreement and concord in manner following: That is to say:

[Sidenote: 1.] First, that all arrestments, reprisals, and impignorations of whatsoeuer goods and marchandises in England and Prussia, made before the date of these presents, are from henceforth quiet, free, and released, without all fraud and dissimulation: insomuch that the damages, charges and expenses occasioned on both parts by reason of the foresayd goods arrested, are in no case hereafter to be required or chalenged by any man: but the demaunds of any man whatsoeuer propounded in this regard, are and ought to be altogether frustrate and voide, and all actions which may or shall be commenced by occasion of the sayd goods arrested, are to be extinct and of none effect.

[Sidenote: 2.] Moreouer, it is secondly concluded and agreed, that all and singuler Prussians pretending themselues to be iniuried by the English at the Porte of Swen, or elsewhere, howsoeuer, and whensoeuer, before the date of these presents, hauing receiued the letters of the foresaide right reuerende lord and Master generall, and of the cities of their abode, are to repayre towards England, vnto the sayd hon: embassadours, who are to assist them, and to propound and exhibite their complaintes, into the forenamed lord and king. The most gracious prince is bounde to doe his indeuor, that the parties damnified may haue restitution of their goods made vnto them, or at least complete iustice and iudgement without delay. Also in like manner all English men affirming themselues to haue bene endamaged by Prussians, wheresoeuer, howsoeuer, and whensoeuer, are to haue recourse vnto the often forenamed right reuerend lorde the Master generall, with the letters of their king and of the cities of their aboad, propounding their complaints and causes vnto him. Who likewise is bound to doe his indeuour that the sayd losses and damages may be restored, or at the least that speedie iudgement may be, without all delayes, executed. This caueat being premised in each clause, that it may and shall be freely granted and permitted vnto euery man that will ciuilly make his suite and complaint, to doe it either by himselfe, or by his procurator or procurators.

[Sidenote: 3.] Also thirdly it is agreed, that whosoeuer of Prussia is determined criminally to propound his criminal complaints in England: namely that his brother or kinseman hath beene slaine, wounded, or maimed, by English men, the same partie is to repayre vnto the citie of London in England, and into the sayd ambassadors, bringing with him the letters of the said right reuerend lord and master generall, and of the cities of their abode: which ambassadors are to haue free and full authority, according to the complaints of the men of Prussia, and the answers of the English men, to make and ordaine a friendly reconciliation; or honest recompence betweene such parties: which reconciliation the sayd parties reconciled are bound vndoubtedly and without delay to obserue. But if there be any English man found, who shall rashly contradict or contemne the composition of the foresaid ambassadors: then the sayd ambassadours are to bring the forenamed Prussian plaintifes before the presence of the kings Maiestie: and also to make supplication on the behalfe of such plaintifes, that complete iustice and iudgment may without delayes bee administred, according as those suites are commenced. Moreouer whatsoeuer English man, against whom anie one of Prussia would enter his action, shall absent himselfe at the terme, the said ambassadours are to summon and ascite the foresayd English man to appeare at the terme next insuing, that the plaintifes of Prussia may in no wise seeme to depart or to returne home, without iudgement or the assistance of lawe. Nowe if the sayd English man being summoned shall be found stubborne or disobedient, the forenamed ambassadours are to make their appeale and supplication in manner aforesayd. And in like sorte in all respects shall the English plaintifes be dealt withall in Prussia, namely in the citie of Dantzik, where the deputies of the sayd citie and of the citie of Elburg shal take vnto themselues two other head boroughs, one of Dantzik, and the other of Elburg: which foure commissioners are to haue in al respects, the very like authority of deciding, discussing, and determining all criminall complaints propounded criminally, by English men against any Prussian or Prussians, by friendly reconciliation, or honest recompense, if it be possible. But if it cannot friendly be determined, or if anie Prussian shall not yeeld obedience vnto any such order or composition, but shalbe found to contradict and to contemne the same: from thenceforth the said foure deputies and head-boroughs are to make their appeale and supplication into the Master generall of the land aforesayd, that vnto the sayd English plaintifes speedy iudgement and complete iustice may be administred. But if it shall so fall out that any of the principall offenders shall decease, or already are deceased in either of the sayd countries, that then it shall bee free and lawfull for the plaintife to prosecute his right against the goods or heires of the party deceased. Also, for the executing of the premisses the termes vnder written are appointed: namely the first, from the Sunday whereupon Quasi modo geniti is to be sung next ensuing, vntill the seuenth day following: The second vpon the feast of the holy Trinitie next to come, and for seuen dayes following: The third vpon the eight day after Saint Iohn Baptist next to come, and for seuen daies following: The fourth, last, and peremptory terme shall be vpon the feast of S. Michael next to come, and vpon seuen dayes next following. And from thenceforth all causes which concerne death, or the mayming of a member, with all actions proceeding from them, are to remaine altogether voide and extinct. And if peraduenture any one of the foresayd ambassadours, shall in the meane season dye, then the other two shall haue authoritie to chuse a third vnto them. [Sidenote: An ancient custome.] And if after the date of these presents any cause great or small doth rise or spring forth, it must bee decided in England and in Prussia, as it hath beene accustomed in times past and from ancient times.

[Sidenote: 4. The priuileges of the English marchants in Prussia.] Also, it is farther concluded and agreed vpon, that all lawfull marchants of England whosoeuer shall haue free licence and authority, with all kindes of shippes, goods, and marchandises, to resorte vnto euery port of the land of Prussia, and also to transport all such goods and marchandises vp farther vnto any other place in the sayde land of Prussia, and there with all kindes of persons freely to bargaine and make sale, as heretofore it hath from auncient times bene accustomed. Which priuiledge is granted in all things and by all circumstances vnto the Prussians in England. And if after the date of these presents betweene the sayd kingdome of England, and land of Prussia any dissension or discorde (which God forefend) should arise: then the foresayd souereigne prince and king of England, and the sayd right reuerend lord the Master generall are mutually by their letters and messengers to giue certificate and intimation one vnto another, concerning the matter and cause of such dissension and discord: which intimation, on the behalfe of the foresaid souereigne prince and king of England, shall be deliuered in the forenamed castle of Marienburg: but on the behalfe of the sayd right reuerend lord the Master generall, such intimation shall be giuen in the citie of London aforesayd, vnto the Maior of the said city: that then such a denuntiation or intimation being made, the marchants of England and the subiects of the land of Prussia may, within the space of one yeere next following, freely and safely returne home with al their goods and marchandises: if at the least, in the mean while, some composition, and friendly league betweene the two foresayd countreis be not in some sorte concluded. And that all the premisses may more firmely and faithfully be put in due practise and execution on both partes, for the strong and inuiolable keeping peace and tranquillity: and also for the full confirmation and strengthening of all the sayde premisses, the three foresayd honourable and religious personages being by the said right reuerend lord the Master general appointed as commissioners to deale in the aboue written ordination and composition, haue caused their seales vnto these presents to be put: and the sayd ordination also, and letter in the same tenour word for word, and in all points euen as it is inserted into these presents, they haue mutually receiued from the abouenamed three ambassadours of the right soueraigne king of England vnder their seales. Giuen at the castle of Marienburg in the yeare of our lord aforesayd, vpon the twentieth day of the moneth of August. And we therefore doe accept, approue, ratifie, and by the tenour of these presents doe confirme, the composition, ordination, concorde, and treaty aforesayd. In testimony whereof we haue caused these our letters to be made patents. Witnesse our selues at Westminster the 22. of October, in the thirteenth yeare of our reigne.

By the king and his counsell.

Lincolne.

* * * * *

The letters of Conradas de Iungingen, Master generall of Prussia, written vnto Richard the second, king of England, in the yeere 1398, for the renouncing of a league and composition concluded betweene England and Prussia, in regard of manifold iniuries, offered vnto the Prussians.

Our humble commendations, with our earnest prayers vnto God for your Maiestie, premised. Most renowned prince and mighty lord, it is not (we hope) out of your Maiesties remembrance, how our famous predecessour going immediately before vs sent certaine letters of his vnto your highnesse, effectually contayning sundry complaints of grieuances, iniuries and losses, wherewith the marchants of his lande and Order, being woont in times past to visite your kingdome with their goods and marchandises, haue bene contrary to their liberties and priuiledges annoyed with manifold iniuries and wrongs. Especially sithens they haue beene molested in your realme, being contrary to the friendly composition made and celebrated by the hono: personages, master Nicholas Stocket, Thomas Graa and Walter Sibil, in the yeere 1388, with the assistance of their coarbiters on our part and contrary to God and all iustice, oppressed with manifold damages, losses, and grieuances: as in certaine articles exhibited vnto our predecessors aforesayd it doeth more manifestly appeare. In consideration whereof being vehemently moued by the damnified parties, he humbly besought your highnesse by his messengers and letters, for complement and execution of iustice. About the which affayres your Maiestie returned your letters of answere vnto our sayd predecessor, signifying that the sayd businesse of articles concerned al the communalty of your realme, and that your highnesse purposed, after consultation had in your parliament, to send a more deliberate, answere concerning the premisses, vnto our predecessour aforesayd. Howbeit he being by death translated out of this present world, and our selues by the prouidence of God succeeding in his roome, and also long time expecting an effectuall answere from your highnesse, are not yet informed as we looked for: albeit the complaints of iniuries and losses offered vnto our subiects doe continually increase. But from henceforth, to prouide a remedie and a caueat for the time to come, the sayd complaynt doeth vpon great reasons mooue and inuite me. Sithens therefore in regard of the sayd composition, neither you nor your subiects may be iudged in the empire: and sithens plaine reason requireth that the one be not inriched by the others losse: as vndoubtedly our subiects should sustaine great damage by the composition aforesayd, by vertue whereof your subiects doe enioy all commodities in our lande, and contrariwise our subiects in your realme haue suffered, and as yet sundrie wayes do suffer manifold discommodities, losses and iniuries. Wherefore (most soueraigne prince and mighty lord) being reasonably mooued vpon the causes aforesayd, we doe, by the aduise of our counsellors, reuoke and repeale the sayd composition concluded as is aboue written, together with the effect thereof, purely and simply renouncing the same by these presents: refusing hereafter to haue either our selues or our subiects in any respect to stand bound by the vertue of the sayd composition: but from henceforth, and for the times heretofore also, bee it altogether voide and of none effect.

Prouided notwithstanding, that from the time of the notice of this denunciation giuen vnto the hono: Maior of your citie of London, for the space of a yeare next ensuing, it shall be lawfull for all marchants of your kingdome whatsoeuer, with their goods and marchandises to returne home, according to the forme in the foresayd composition expressed: conditionaly that our subiects may euen so in all respects be permitted to depart, with the safety of their goods and liues out of your dominions: this present renuntiation, reuocation, and retractation of the order and composition aforesayd, notwithstanding. Howbeit in any other affayres whatsoeuer, deuoutly to submit our selues vnto your highnesse pleasure and command, both our selues, and our whole order are right willing and desirous: and also to benefite and promote your subiects we wil indeuour to the vtmost of our ability, Giuen in our castle of Marienburgh in the yeare of our Lord 1398, and vpon the 22. day of February.

Frater Conradus de Iungingen, master generall
  of the Order of the Dutch knights of S.
    Maries hospital at Ierusalem.

* * * * *

A briefe relation of William Esturmy, and Iohn Kington concerning their ambassages into Prussia, and the Hans-townes.

[Sidenote: 1403.] Inprimis, that in the moneth of Iuly, and in the yeare of our Lord 1403, and the fift yeare of the reigne of our souereigne Lord the king that nowe is, there came into England the ambassadours of the mighty lord Fr: Conradus de Iungingen, being then Master general of Prussia, with his letters directed vnto our foresayd souereigne lord the king, requiring amends and recompense for certaine iniuries vniustly offered by English men vnto the subiects of the sayd Master generall, written in 20. articles, which amounted vnto the summe of 19120. nobles and a halfe &c.

Item, that the third day of the moneth of October, in the yeare of our Lord abouewritten, and in the fift yere of the reigne of our soueraigne lord the king, between the reuerend father in God, Henrie then bishop of Lincolne lord chancelor, and William lord de Roos high treasurer of England, on the one party and the sayd ambassadours on the other party, it was (according to their petition) amongst other things ordayned: namely that the liege people of our soueraigne lord the king should freely be permitted, vntill the feast of Easter then next after ensuing to remaine in the land of Prussia, and from thence with their goods and marchandises to returne vnto their own homes, and also, that the subiects of the sayd Master generall in the kingdome of England should haue licence and liberty to doe the like. Prouided alwayes, that after the time aboue limitted, neither the English marchants in the land of Prussia, nor the Prussian marchants in the realme of England should vse any traffique of marchandise at all, vnlesse in the meane space it were otherwise agreed and concluded by the sayd king and the sayd Master general.

Item, immediately after our sayd soueraigne lord the king sent his letters by Iohn Browne marchant of Lin vnto the aforesayd Master generall, for to haue mutuall conuersation and intercourse of dealing to continue some certain space, betweene the marchants of England and of Prussia: promising in the same letters, that he would in the meane season send vnto the foresayd Master his ambassadors to intreat about the pretended iniuries aforesaide: which letters the foresayd Master, for diuers causes, refused to yeelde vnto, as in his letters sent vnto our lord the king, bearing date the 16. day of the moneth of Iuly, in the yeare of our lord 1404. more plainely appeareth.

Item, that after the receit of the letters of the Master aforesaid, which are next aboue mentioned, our sayd king, according to his promise, sent William Esturmy knight, M. Iohn Kington clerke, and William Brampton citizen of London, from his court of parliament holden at Couentrie, very slightly informed, as his ambassadours into Prussia.

Item, before the arriuall of the sayd ambassadours in Prussia, all intercourse of traffique betweene the English and the Prussians, in the realme of England, and in the land of Prussia was altogether restrained and prohibited: and in the same land it was ordayned and put in practise, that in whatsoeuer porte of the land of Prussia any English marchant had arriued with his goods, he was not permitted to conueigh the sayd goods, out of that porte, vnto any other place of the land of Prussia, either by water, or by lande, vnder the payne of the forfeiting of the same: but was enioyned to sell them in the very same porte, vnto the Prussians onely and to none other, to the great preiudice of our English marchants.

[Sidenote: 1405.] Item, that after the arriuall of the sayd English ambassadours in the land of Prussia, it was ordayned, that from the eight day of the moneth of October, in the yeare of our lord 1405, all English marchants whatsoeuer should haue free liberty to arriue with all kindes of their marchandise in whatsoeuer port of the land of Prussia, and to make sale of them in the said land, as hath heretofore from auncient times bene accustomed. Also sundry other commodious priuiledges vnto the realme of

England were then ordayned and established: as in the indentures made for this purpose it doth more manifestly appeare.

Item, the said English ambassadours being arriued in the land of Prussia, demanded of the said Master generall, a reformation and amends, for the damages and iniuries offered by the Prussians vnto the liege people of our souereigne lord and king, written in fifteene articles, which losses amounted vnto summe of 4535. nobles.

Item, the said Master generall, besides the articles exhibited vnto our soueraigne lord the king (as it is aboue mentioned) deliuered vnto the sayd ambassadours diuers other articles of certaine iniuries offered (as he sayth) vniustly by English men, vnto his subiects, which amounted vnto the summe of 5200. nobles.

[Sidenote: 1406.] Item, it was afterward concluded, that vpon the first of May next then insuing, namely in the yeere of our Lord 1406, or within the space of one yeare immediately following there should bee made a conuenient, iust, and reasonable satisfaction, for all molestations vniustly offered on both partes, as well on the behalfe, of our soueraigne lord the king, as of the foresayd Master general. Which satisfaction not being performed, the Prussians with their goods and merchandises, within three moneths after the end of the sayd yere next following, were without molestation or impediment, enioined to depart out of the realme of England with their ships and goods, and the English men likewise, out of the territories and dominions of the said Master general, and both of them, without any further admonition, to abstaine and separate themselues, from both the countreis aforesayd. For the performance of which premisses, the ambassadors on both parts being sufficiently instructed, were appointed to meete the first day of May, at the towne of Dordract in Holland.

Item, that the sayd William Esturmy and Iohn Kington in their returne homewards from Prussia towards England passed through the chiefe cities of the Hans, and treated in such sorte with the Burgomasters of them, that there were sent messengers and agents, in the behalfe of the common society of the Hans marchants, vnto the towne of Dordract, to conferre with the ambassadors of England, about the redressing of iniuries attempted on both parts: where diuers agreements were set downe betweene the sayd ambassadors, and messengers, as in the indentures made for the same purpose it doth more manifestly appeare.

Item, that the meeting appointed at the towne of Dordract, vpon the first of May, was by the letters of the foresayd ambassadors, proroged vnto the first of August then next ensuing, and afterward by vertue of the kings letters vnto the first day of March next following: and there was another day of prorogation also.

Item, that after the prorogations aforesayd, the ambassadors of England, and the messengers and commissioners of Prussia met together at the towne of Hage in Holland, the 28. day of August, in the yere of our lord 1407. And there was a treaty between them concerning the summe 25934. nobles and an halfe, demanded on the behalfe of the sayd Master generall for amends and recompence in consideration of wrongs offered vnto himselfe and vnto his subiects of Prussia, as is aforesayd. Also the sayd Master and his Prussians, besides the summe not yet declared in the articles, which is very small, are to rest contented and satisfied with the summe of 8957. nobles, in lieu of al the damages aforesaid: no times of paiment being then assigned or limited, but afterward to be reasonably limited and assigned, by our sayd soueraigne lord the king. Insomuch, that our said soueraigne lord the king is to write his ful intention and determination concerning this matter, in his letters to be deliuered the 16. day of March, vnto the aldermen of the marchants of the Hans residing at Bruges. Otherwise, that from thenceforth all league of friendship shall bee dissolued betweene the realme of England and the land of Prussia.

Also it is farther to be noted, that in the appointment of the summe next before written to be disbursed out of England, this condition was added in writing, namely, that if by lawful testimonies it may sufficiently and effectually be prooued, concerning the chiefe articles aboue written, or any part of them, that satisfaction was made vnto any of those parties, to whom it was due: or that the goods, of and for the which complaint was made on the behalfe of Prussia, in the sayd articles, did or doe pertayne vnto others, or that any other iust, true, or reasonable cause may lawfully be proued and alledged, why the foresaid sums or any of them ought not to be payed: that then in the summes contained in the articles aboue mentioned, so much only must be cut off, or stopped, as shal be found, either to haue bene payd already, or to appertaine vnto others, or by any true, iust, and reasonable cause alledged, not to be due. Neither is it to be doubted, but for the greater part of the summe due vnto the Prussians, that not our lord the king, but others (which will in time be nominated) are, by all equity and iustice, to be compelled to make satisfaction.

Also, at the day and place aboue mentioned it was appointed and agreed vpon, that our lord the king and his liege subiects, for the said 4535. nobles demanded of the English in consideration of recompence to be made for iniuries offered vnto the Prussians, are to discharge and pay the summe of 764. nobles, which are not as yet disbursed: but they haue reserued a petition to them, vnto whom the sayd summe is due, or if they please, there shalbe made satisfaction: which will be very hard and extreme dealing.

Item, that in the last assembly of the sayd ambassadors of England and messengers of Prussia, holden at Hage, made as is aforesayd, for the behalfe of England, there were exhibited anew certaine articles of iniuries against the Prussians. The value of which losses amounted vnto the summe of 1825. nobles and three shillings.

Item, on the contrary part for the behalfe of the Prussians the summe of 1355. nobles, eight shillings and sixe pence.

Item, forasmuch as diuers articles propounded, as well on the behalfe of England, as of Prussia, and of the cities of the Hans, both heretofore and also at the last conuention holden at Hage, were so obscure, that in regard of their obscurity, there could no resolute answere bee made vnto them: and other of the sayd articles exhibited, for want of sufficient proofes, could not clearely be determined vpon: it was appointed and concluded, that all obscure articles giuen vp by any of the foresayd parties whatsoeuer, ought before the end of Easter then next ensuing, and within one whole yeare after, to be declared before the Chancelour of England, for the time being; and other articles euidently exhibited, but not sufficiently proued, to be proued, vnder paine of perpetuall exclusion. Which being done accordingly, complete iustice shall be administred on both parts.

Item, as concerning the eleuenth article, for the behalfe of the Prussians, first exhibited, which conteined losses amounting vnto the summe of 2445. nobles: as touching the first article on the behalfe of England exhibited in the land of Prussia, containing losses which amounted to the summe of 900. nobles: after many things alleadged on both parts, relation thereof shall be made in the audience of the king and of the master generall: so that they shall set downe, ordaine, and determine such an ende and conclusion of those matters, as shall seeme most expedient vnto them.

Now concerning the Liuonians who are subiect vnto the great Master of Prussia.

Inprimis, that the Master of Prussia demaunded of the sayd English ambassadours, at their being in Prussia, on the behalfe of them of Liuonia, who are the sayd Master his liege people, to haue restitution of their losses, vniustly (as he sayth) offered vnto them by the English, namely, for the robbing and rifling of three ships. [Sidenote: These ships were taken by the English the 20. Iuly 1404.] The value of which ships and of the goods contained in them, according, to the computation of the Liuonian marchants, doeth amount vnto the summe of 8037. pound, 12. shillings 7. pence.

Howbeit afterward the trueth being inquired by the sayd ambassadors of England, the losse of the Liuonians exceedeth not the summe of 7498. pound, 13. shillings, 10. pence halfepeny farthing.

Item, forasmuch as in the sayd ships, on the behalfe of the sayd Master, and of certaine cities of the Hans, there are alleadged aboue 250. men very barbarously to be drowned, of whome some were noble, and others honourable personages, and the rest common marchants and mariners, there was demaunded, in the first dyet or conuention holden at Dordract, a recompense at the handes of the sayd English ambassadors: albeit this complaint was exhibited in the very latter end of al the negotiations, in forme of a scedule, the tenor whereof is in writing at this present, and beginneth in maner following: Cum vita hominum &c. Howbeit in the last conuention holden at Hage, as is aforesaid, it was concluded betweene the ambassadours of England, and the messengers and commissioners of the land of Prussia, and of the cities of the Hans; that our sayd soueraigne lord the king, should, of his great pietie, vouchsafe effectually to deuise some conuenient and wholesome remedie for the soules of such persons as were drowned.

Item, that our sayd soueraigne lord the king will signifie in writing his full purpose and intention as touching this matter, vnto the aldermen of the Hans marchants residing at Bruges, vpon the sixtenth day of March next following. Otherwise, that from henceforth all amity and friendship, betweene the realme of England and the land of Prussia shall be dissolued.

Neither is it to be doubted, but that a great part of the sayd goods, for the which they of Liuonia doe demaund restitution, namely waxe and furres, redounded vnto the vse and commoditie of our soueraigne lord the king. And also our said soueraigne lord the king gaue commandement by his letters, that some of the sayd goods should be deliuered vnto others. And a great part of them is as yet reserued in the towne of Newcastle. One Benteld also hath the best of the sayd three ships in possession. Also it is reported and thought to be true, that certaine Furriers of London, which will be detected in the end, haue had a great part of the sayd goods, namely of the Furres.

Now as concerning the cities of the Hans.

[Sidenote: Hamburgh.] Inprimis the Hamburgers exhibited nine articles, wherein they demaunded restitution for certaine damages offered, as they sayd, by the English men, the value of which losses amounted vnto the summe of 9117. nobles, 20 pence. For the which, after due examination, there was promised restitution to the summe of 416. nobles, 5. shillings. Besides the two articles propounded against them of Scardeburg, the summe whereof was 231. pounds, 15s. 8d. concerning the which there was sentence giuen in England by the commissioners of our lord the king, the execution whereof was promised vnto the said Hamburgers by the ambassadors of England: leaue and licence being reserued vnto the sayd

Hamburgers, of declaring or explaining certaine obscure articles by them exhibited, which declaration was to be made at the feast of Easter then next to come, or within one yeare next ensuing the said feast, vnto the chancelor of England for the time being, and of proouing the sayd articles and others also, which haue not as yet sufficiently bene proued. Which being done they are to haue full complement and execution of iustice.

Also by the Hamburgers there are demaunded 445. nobles from certaine of the inhabitants of Linne in England. Which summe, if it shalbe prooued to be due vnto any English men, the Hamburgers are to rest contented with those goods, which they haue already in their possessions.

[Sidenote: Breme.] Item, they of Breme propounded sixe articles, wherein the summe conteined amounteth vnto 4414. nobles. And there was no satisfaction promised vnto them. But the same libertie and licence was reserued vnto them, in like maner as before vnto the Hamburgers.

[Sidenote: Stralessund] Item, they of Stralessund propounded 23. articles, whereof the summe amounted vnto 7415. nobles, 20. d for the which there was promised satisfaction of 253. nobles, 3. d. Also here is a caueat to be obserued: that they of Stralessund had of English mens goods a great summe particularly to be declared, which will peraduenture suffice for a recompense. And some of their articles are concerning iniuries offered before 20, 22, 23, 24. yeres past. Also their articles are so obscure that they will neuer, or very hardly be able to declare or proue them. Howbeit there is reserued the very same liberty vnto them, that was before vnto the Hamburgers.

[Sidenote: Lubec] Item, they of Lubec propounded 23. articles, the summe whereof extended vnto 8690. nobles and an halfe: whereupon it was agreed, that they should haue paied vnto them 550. nobles. There was reserued the same libertie vnto them, which, was vnto the men of Stralessund.

[Sidenote: Gripeswold] Item, they of Gripeswold exhibited 5. articles, the summe whereof amounted vnto 2092. nobles and an halfe. For the which there was promised satisfaction of 153. nobles and an half. And the said men of Gripeswold haue of the goods of English men in possession, to the value of 22015. nobles, 18. s. as it is reported by them of Linne. And the same libertie is reserued vnto them that was vnto the Hamburgers.

[Sidenote: Campen.] Item, they of Campen propounded ten articles, the summe whereof extended vnto 1405. nobles. There is no satisfaction promised vnto them: but the same liberty is reserued vnto them, which was vnto the other aboue mentioned.

Item, the ambassadors of England demanded of the citizens of Rostok and Wismer, for damages and iniuries by them committed against the subiects of the foresayd souereigne king 32407. nobles. 2. s. 10. d. And albeit euery of the foresayd cities sent one of their burgomasters vnto the towne of Hage in Holland, to treat with the English ambassadours, it was in the end found out, that they had not any authority of negociating or concluding ought at al. And therefore they made their faithfull promises, that euery of the said cities should send vnto our soueraigne Lord the king one or two procurator or procurators sufficiently instructed to treat and conclude with our said souereigne lord the king about the damages and iniuries aforesaid at the feast of the natiuitie of Saint Iohn the Baptist.

* * * * *

Compositions and ordinances concluded between the messengers of Frater Conradus de Iungingen master generall of Prussia: and the chancelor and treasurer of the realme of England 1403.

In the yere of our Lord 1403, vpon the feast of S. Michael the Archangel, the right hono: Henrie bishop of Lincoln, chancelor of England, and the lord de Roos high treasurer of England, and the ambassadors of Prussia, Iohn Godek of Dantzik, and Henry Monek of Elbing, masters of the same cities haue at Westminster treated in maner of composition about the articles vnderwritten: between the most souereigne lord the king of England, and the right reuerend and honorable Conradus de Iungingen Master general of Prussia as concerning the iniuries offered vnto the people of Prussia and Liuonia vpon the sea by the English.

First, that all ships with their appurtenances, and the commodities of the mariners, according vnto the condition of the things, and all other goods taken away by the English, which are actually vndiuided and whole, are incontinently and with al speed to bee restored. And if there bee any defect in ought, the value of the said defect is to be accounted, and with other losses of goods to be restored, at the terme of the restitution to be made and deliuered.

Item, that all ships, damages, and goods (as they are conteined in our bill of accusation) which are not now immediately restored, are to be restored and payd in the land of Prussia, between this and the terme appointed, with full execution and complement of iustice.

Item, concerning the persons throwen ouer boord or slaine in the sea: it shall remayne to bee determined at the will and pleasure of the most mighty prince, the king of England, and of the right reuerend the Master of Prussia.

Item, betweene this and the terme appointed for the restoring of the goods taken away, and vntill there be due payment and restitution of the said goods performed, the marchants of England and of Prussia are in no wise to exercise any traffique of merchandise at all in the foresaid lands.

[Sidenote: 1403.] Memorandum, that the third day of the moneth of October, in the yere of our Lord. 1403. and in the fift yere of the reigne of the most mighty prince and lord, king Henrie the fourth, by the grace of God king of England and France &c. betweene the reuerend father Henrie bishop of Lincoln, chancelor, and the right honorable William lord de Roos, high treasurer of England, both of their counsellers vnto the sayd soueraigne king on the one party, and the right worshipfull Iohn Godeke, and Henrie Moneke, sent as messengers by the right reuerend and religious personage, Frater Gonradus de Iungingen Master generall of the Dutch knights of the Order of S. Mary on the other party: it was, at the request and instancie of the sayd messengers, appoynted, and mutually agreed vpon, that all the liege people and subiects of the sayd soueraigne lord and king shall haue free licence and liberty vntill the feast of Easter next ensuing, safety to trauel vnto the land of Prussia aforesayd, there to remaine, and thence, with their ships, marchandises, and other their goods whatsoeuer, to returne vnto their owne home: which on the other side, all the subiects of the sayd Master general may, within the terme prefixed, likewise doe, in the foresaid realme of England. Prouided alwaies, that after the time aboue limited, neither the sayd marchants of the realme of England may in the land of Prussia, nor the marchants of that land, in the realme of England, exercise any traffique at al: vnles it be otherwise ordained by some composition, betweene the foresaid king of England, and the said Master general in the meane time concluded. In witnesse wherof, one part of this present Indenture is to remaine in the custodie of the foresaid messengers. Giuen in the Chapter-house of the Church of S. Paul at London, the day and yere aboue written.

* * * * *

The letters of the chancelor and treasurer of England, vnto Frater Conradus de Iungingen, master generall of Prussia 1403.

Right reuerend and mighty lord, your honorable messengers Iobn Godeke, and Henry Moneke, the bearers hereof comming of late before the presence of our most souereigne lord the king of England and of France, and being welcomed by our said lord with a chearefull and fauourable countenance, they presented certaine letters on your behalfe vnto the kings Maiestie, with that reuerence which beseemed them: expounding vnto his highnes, sundry piracies and molestations offered of late vpon the sea, by his liege people and subiects vnto yours, contrary to the leagues of peace and amitie, which hitherto (by Gods grace) haue bene maintained and continued on both parts. In consideration of which piracies and molestations, your messengers demanded full restitution and recompense to be made, either vnto the damnified parties, or vnto their procurators. We therefore at that time, especially being in the presence of our soueraigne (who with, his puissant army tooke his progresse towards the remote part of Wales being subiect vnto his dominion, to see iustice executed vpon his people of those parts, who very rashly haue presumed to rebell against him their souereigne, contrary to their allegeance) right well perceiued that it was his highnesse intention, that euery one should haue due iustice faithfully administred vnto him, especially your subiects, and that with all fauour, whom he hath alwayes in times past right graciously intreated, as if they had bene his owne liege subiects and natiue countrey men, whome also hee purposeth hereafter friendly to protect: insomuch that betweene him and his subiects on the one party, and betweene you and yours on the other party, great abundance and perfection of mutuall amity may increase. And therefore we offered vnto your foresayd messengers, after they had particularly declared vnto vs such piracies and wrongs, to sende the kings letters vnto them of whom complaint was made, firmely inioyning them, vnder grieuous penalties, that without delay they restore or cause to bee restored vnto the parties damnified, or vnto their procuratours, all ships, marchandises, wares, and goods, by them taken or violently stolne from your subiects. And that your said messengers may partly attaine their desire, we haue commaunded certaine [Marginal note: Namely the ship of Edward Scof at Caleis, The ship of Tidman Dordewant and Tidman Warowen, at Orwel and Zepiswich.] ships, marchandises, wares and goods, found in certaine hauens, to be deliuered vnto them. Howbeit, as touching other goods, which are perhaps perished or wanting by infortunate dissipation or destruction, and for the which the said messengers of yours demand satisfaction to be made vnto them within a certain time by vs limited: may it please your honor to vnderstand that in the absence of our sayd souereigne lord the king, being as yet farre distant from vs, wee can in no wise limit or set downe any such terme of time. Notwithstanding, at the prosperous returne of our soueraigne, we are determined to commune with him about this matter. Of whose answere so soone as we be certified, we purpose to signifie his intention vnto you by our letters. Sithens also (right reuerend and mighty lord) your sayd messengers are contented, for the present, to accept of our offer aforesayde, as indeede by all reason they ought thereat to rest content, especially whereas by this meanes they shall the more speedily attaine vnto the effect of their purposes (to the shorte and wished execution and performance of which offer, we will, by Gods helpe, endeuour, to the vtmost of our ability) may it be your will and pleasure, that as in the kingdome of England, your marchants and subiects are courteously intreated: euen so the marchants and liege people of our soueraigne lord the king and of his kingdomes peaceably frequenting your parts, either in regard of traffique or of any other iust occasion, may there in like manner friendly bee vsed, and with your marchants and subiects suffered to communicate, and to haue intercourse of traffique, inioying the commodities of the ancient league. By this also the feruent zeale and affection which you beare vnto the royall crowne of England shall vndoubtedly appeare: albeit betweene the famous houses of England and of Prussia, the bandes of vnfained loue and friendship haue bin successiuely confirmed and kept inuiolable in times past And thus (right reuerend and mighty lord) wishing vnto you increase of honour and prosperity, wee take our leaues. [Sidenote: Note well. 1403.] Written at London the fift of October, in the yeare of our lord 1403.

By the chancelor, the treasurer, and other lords of the hono: counsell of the king of England and France, being personally present at London.

* * * * *

The letters of king Henry the 4. vnto Conradus de Iungingen the master general of Prussia, for mutual conuersation and intercourse of traffique to continue between the marchants of England and of Prussia, for a certaine terme of time.

Henry by the grace of God king of England and France, and lord of Ireland, to the noble and mighty personage of sacred religion, Frater Conradus de Iungingen Master generall of the Order of the Dutch knights of S. Marie &c. our most deare and welbeloued friend, greeting, and continuall increase of our auncient and sincere amity. By the grieuous complaynts of our liege subiects concerning traffique, as it were circularwise too and fro both our dominions, we haue often bene aduertised that in regard of diuers iniuries and damages, which as well our as your marchants (who by their dealings in merchandise were woont peaceably to vse mutual conuersation together, whereupon very many commodities are knowen to haue proceeded) haue, by occasion of pirates, rouing vp and down the sea, sometimes heretofore sustayned: both the sayd marchants of our and of your dominions do abstaine themselues from their wonted mutual conuersation and traffique, as they haue likewise carefully abstained at sometimes heretofore, and especially from that time, wherein, at the instant request of your messengers, being of late before our presence, the free accesse of our marchants vnto your territories and dominions, and of your marchants vnto our realmes hath bene forbidden. Sithens therefore (our most deare friend) such iniuries (if any) as haue bene attempted against your subiects, were neuer committed by our will and consent, as we thinke that your selfe on the other side haue done the like: [Sidenote The auncient friendship betweene England and Prussia.] sithens also, so much as in vs lieth, wee are ready to exhibit full iustice with fauour vnto any of your people being desirous to make complaint, so that accordingly iustice may equally be done vnto our marchants by you and your subiects, which marchants haue in like sort bene iniuried, wishing with all our heart, that the ancient friendship and loue, which hath continued a long time between our realme and your territories and dominions, may perseuere in time to come, and that sweet and acceptable peace, which is to be embraced of al Christians, may according to the good pleasure of the author of peace, be nourished and mayntained: we do most heartily require the sayd friendship, exhorting you in the Lord that you would on your behalf consent and ordain (euen as, if you shall so do, we for our part wil consent likewise) that from this present vntil the feast of Easter next insuing (al molestations and iniuries which may be offred ceasing on both parts) our subiects by your territories and dominions, and your subiects by our realms, may peaceably and securely trauel, and that according to their wonted maner, they may friendly conuerse and exercise mutual traffick together: because we are determined to send vnto you and your counsel in the mean time some of our ambassadors, friendly to intreat about, the foresaid pretended iniuries, so far forth as they shal concerne our subiects. At whose arriual we stand in good hope that by the due administration of iustice on both parts, such order (by Gods assistance) shalbe taken, that mutual peace and tranquility may be established between vs in times to come. Also our desire is in particular, that our marchants and liege subiects may haue more free passage granted them vnto the parts of Sconia, for the prouiding of herrings and of other fishes there, that they may there remayne, and from thence also may more securely returne vnto their owne home: and we beseech you in consideration of our owne selues, that you would haue our marchants and liege subiects especially recommended vnto you, safely protecting them (if need shall require) vnder the shadow of your defence: euen as you would haue vs to deale in the like case with your own subiects. Moreouer, whatsoeuer you shall thinke good to put in practise in this behalfe, may it please you of your friendship, by our faythfull subiect Iohn Browne the bearer hereof to giue vs to vnderstand. In the sonne of the glorious virgine fare ye well, with continuall prosperity and felicity according to your owne hearts desire. Giuen vnder our priuie seale, at our palace of Westminster, the fift day of Iune, and in the fift yere of our reigne.

Postscriptum.

Right reuerend and our most deare friend: albeit our welbeloued Arnold de Dassele the procurator of your foresaid messengers, being desirous at this time to make his final returne vnto your parts, by reason of the affayres, for which he hath remained in our realme of England, cannot as yet obtaine his wished expedition: notwithstanding you of your sincere affection ought not to maruel or any whit to be grieued thereat: because troubles of wars arising, which in some sort concerned our selues, and especially in regard of the continuall assaults of the French men and Britons against vs and our kingdome, for the offence of whom, and our owne defence, our liege subiects (especially they, of whom your subiects damnified haue made their complaints) haue armed themselues to combate vpon the sea: we could not grant vnto the foresayd Arnold such and so speedy an expedition, as he earnestly desired to haue. Vnto the which Arnold your procurator we haue offered in as short time as may be, to administer complete iustice with fauour, to the end that for this cause he might dispose himselfe to remaine in our realme of England: and yet notwithstanding wee would do the very same euen in the absence of the sayd procurator. Giuen as aboue.

* * * * *

To the most renowned prince and mighty Lord, Henrie king of England &c. our gracious Lord.

Our humble recommendations, with our most instant and continuall prayers for you being graciously by your Maiestie taken in good part &c. Most soueraigne king, mighty prince, gratious lord, and vnto vs most vnfaynedly beloued, we receiued of late your gracious letters by your Maiesties liege subiect Iohn Brown, the contents wherof seemed to be these following: first that of long time heretofore, there haue bene between the marchants of your realm and of our lands, not only quiet and peaceable accesse one vnto another, but also mutual participation, and common traffique of their wares, being right commodious and auaileable for them both: howbeit, that now the focesaid profitable conuersation, by reason of certain notorious robberies, committed vpon the sea by pyrates against both parts, and the wonted accesse also of your subiects vnto our dominions, were altogether forbidden. Moreouer, you call to remembrance the ancient amity and friendship betweene both our lands, with the inualuable commodity of sweet amiable peace, which are by al faithful Christians, to the vtmost of their endeuour to be imbraced. Wherupon you of your exceeding clemency, do offer your Maiesties ful consent, that the foresaid prohibition being released vntil the feast of Easter next ensuing, the said marchants of your dominions may in our territories, and our marchants likewise may in your realms (al molestations ceasing) exercise their woonted traffique: especially sithens in the mean season your royall wisdome hath determined to direct vnto vs your hono: ambassadors in friendly sort to treat and parle with vs as touching the pretended iniuries, so far forth as they may concerne your subiects. Adding moreouer in particular that when your people shall repayre vnto the parts of Sconia to fish for herrings, hauing consideration and regard vnto your maiestie, we would haue them especially recommended vnto our protection &c. Most soueraigne lord and king, and gracious prince, wee doe with vnfained and hearty affection embrace the oracles of your maiesties most courteous and acceptable offer: wherein you haue vsed most diligent and effectuall perswasions, that complement of iustice should be done vnto the parties iniuried, and that peace and friendship should take place, making no doubt of your own royall person, nor of our selues or of any appertayning vnto vs, but that our inclinations and desires in this regarde are all one and the same: neither would we lightly transgresse the limits of your perswasions without some iust, weighty, and reasonable cause, forasmuch as the matters perswaded are in very deede most happy preseruatiues of a common weale, yea, and of nature, it selfe. Moreouer whereas your highnes hath farther requested vs, that the prohibition of your subiects accesse vnto our dominions might, vntill the feast of Easter next ensuing, be released: we answere (vnder correction of your maiesties more deliberate counsell) that it is farre more expedient for both parts to haue the sayd prohibition continued then released, vntil such time as satisfaction be performed on both sides vnto the parties endamaged, not in words only, but actually and really in deeds, or by some course of law or friendly composition. For there is no equall nor indifferent kinde of consort or trade between the impouerished party and him that is inriched, betweene the partie which hath obtayned iustice and him that hath obtayned none between the offender and the party offended: because they are not mooued with like affections. For the remembrance of iniuries easily stirreth vp inconsiderate motions of anger. Also, such a kind of temperature or permixtion, as it were, by way of contrariety breedeth more bitternes then sweetnes, more hate then loue: whereupon more grieuous complaints aswel vnto your highnes as vnto our selues, might be occasioned. The lord knoweth, that euen now we are too much wearied and disquieted with the importunate and instant complaints of our subiects, insomuch that wee cannot at this present by any conuenient meanes release or dissolue the sayd prohibition, before wee be sufficiently informed by your maiesties ambassadors, of the satisfaction of our endamaged subiects. [Sidenote: Margaret queen of Denmarke.] Furthermore, whereas your maiesties request, concerning your subiects that shal come vnto the parts of Sconia, is that we would defend them vnder our protection: be it knowen vnto your highnes, that for diuers considerations vs reasonably mouing, being prouoked by the queene of Denmarke and her people, being also vrged thereunto full sore against our wils, for the repelling and auoiding of iniuries, we haue sent forth our armie against them. Howbeit for a certaine time a truce is concluded on both parts, so that our people are actually returned home. Farre be it from vs also, that our subiects being occupied in warres, should in any sort willingly molest or reproach any strangers, of what landes or nations soeuer, not being our professed enemies. For this should be to oppresse the innocent in stead of the guilty, to condemne the iust for the uniust: then which nothing can be more cruel, nor a reuenge of greater impietie. In very deede (most gracious prince and lorde) we are moued with right hearty sympathy and compassion for any inconuenience which might happen in your regiment: wishing from the bottome of our hearts, that all affayres may right prosperously and happily succeede, about the royall person and regiment of your most excellent Maiestie, and that continually. The like whereof wee hope from you: most humbly commending our selues, and our whole Order vnto your highnes. Giuen at our castle of Marienburgh, the 16. day, the moneth of iuly, in the yere of our Lord 1404.

* * * * *

An agreement made betweene king Henry the fourth and Conradus de Iungingen
  Master generall of the land of Prussia.

This Indenture made between Sir William Esturmy knight, Iohn Kington clerke, and William Brampton citizen of London the ambassadors, commissioners, and messengers of the most mighty prince and lord, our souereigne lord Henrie by the grace of God king of England and France, and lorde of Ireland, for the repayring, reformation, and amends of whatsoeuer damages, grieuances, excesses, violences, and iniuries in any sort vniustly attempted, done, or offered, by our sayd soueraigne lord the king and his liege people and subiects, vnto the great and mighty lord Conradus de Iungingen Master general of the order of the Dutch knights of S. Maries hospitall of Ierusalem, or his subiects: and for the requiring, demanding, and receiuing of such like reparations, reformations and amends, by the foresayd lord the Master generall, for the behalfe of himselfe or any of his subiects whatsoeuer, from and in the name of our soueraign lord the king and his subiects, vnto the sayd Master general, into his land of Prussia, by our souereigne lord the king, and appointed as ambassadors on the one party: And betweene the hono: Lords and religious personages Conradus de Lichtenstein great commander, Warnberus de Tettingen chiefe hospitalary and commander in Elbing, and Arnold de Hacken treasurer, the procurators and commissioners of the great and mighty lord the Master general, being in like and equal sort and in all respects, as the ambassadours of England are, authorised on the contrary side by the authoritie and power of the sayd Master general on the other part, witnesseth: That diuers treaties and conferences being holden between the said ambassadors, messengers, and procurators or commissioners, of and concerning the reparations, reformations and amends of certaine damages, grieuances, excesses, violences, and iniuries offered and attempted, as wel by the Prussians against the English as by the English against the Prussians, and of other actes vniustly committed on both parts: in conclusion, after the sayd treatise, the foresayd ambassadours, procurators and commissioners by vertue of the authority committed vnto them appoynted, and with one consent agreed vnto the articles vnder written.

Inprimis, that for the consideration of mutuall loue and woonted friendship, and of peace and tranquillity hereafter to be continued and maintained, and also that the articles vnder written may more prosperously be brought vnto a wished effect, betwene our said soueraign lord the king and his liege people and subiects, and the subiects, people, and inhabitants of the territories and dominions of the foresayd lord the Master generall, it is agreed and concluded, that all liege marchants of England whatsoeuer, shall haue free licence and libertie to arriue with their shippes, goods and marchandises whatsoeuer, at any porte of the land of Prussia, and also the sayd goods and marchandises farther vnto any place of the sayd land of Prussia to transport, and these with any person or persons freely to contract and bargaine, euen as heretofore, and from auncient times it hath bene accustomed. Which liberty in all respects is granted vnto the Prussians in England.

[Sidenote: 1403.] Item it is further agreed betwene the sayd ambassadours, procurators, and commissioners, that whereas of late, namely in the yeare of our lord 1403, the sayd Master general by his discreet subiects Iohn Godek of Dantzik, and Henry Monek of Elbing, his ambassadors and messengers, for this purpose hath caused certain articles, (namely 20, in number) containing in them matters of damages, molestations, violences, and iniuries committed and offered against the said Master generall and his subiects, by our sayd soueraigne lord the king his subiects and liege people, to be exhibited, giuen vp and deliuered vnto our lord the king aforesaid in his kingdome of England: it is concluded and agreed about the sayd 20, articles, by the aforesaid ambassadors, commissioners, and procurators, as in the acts and pleas had and made before the sayd ambassadors, commissioners and procurators, and in the records made and written of and about, the examination of such articles, it is more at large contayned (vnto the which the sayd ambassadors, commissioners, and messengers doe here in this place referre themselues) of the which articles also some are receiued by the commissioners aforesayd, and others are proroged vnto a certaine time vnder written, euen as in the foresayd registers it is more fully contayned and put downe in writing.

As touching certaine other articles also exhibited a newe vnto the sayd English ambassadors, in the land of Prussia being 16 in number (whereof one is admitted, and the rest are proroged vntil A terme vnder written) the same course is to be taken and obserued, which was before appoynted and agreed vpon, about the articles deliuered and exhibited vnto our foresayd souraigne lorde the king, as is aforesayd.

Moreouer, as touching the articles exhibited by the English ambassadours in the name and behalfe of their sayd soueraigne lord the king of England, vnto the procuratours and commissioners of the foresayd lord the Master generall (of the which some are declared already, and the declaration of the rest is proroged vntill a certayne terme vndernamed, euen as in the registers made of and vpon the examination of the sayd articles, it is more manifestly prouided) the same course is to be taken, which must be obserued about the articles of the sayd lord the Master general), exhibited, as well vnto the foresayd soueraigne prince in England, as vnto his ambassadors in the land of Prussia, euen as about the sayd articles it is before concluded.

[Sidenote: The complaints of Liuonians.] And whereas on the behalfe of the citizens and marchants of the cities of Rij and Dorp [Footnote: These cities seem to haue been large commercial centres.], and of other townes in the land of Liuonia, many and great complaints haue bene by way of articles exhibited and deliuered vnto the sayd English ambassadours in the land of Prussia, which for diuers causes, could not as then be ended: therefere it is concluded and agreed vpon betweene the ambassadours, and the commissioners aforesayd, that the saide citizens and marchants may in the towne of Dordract in Holland, vpon the first day of the moneth of May next ensuing (at the which time and place, the continuation and prorogation of all other articles not fully declared in the partes of Prussia, shall be put in vre [Footnote: *Ure* i.e., use. Norman or law French (See Kelham's Norman Dict.) This vickering will but keep our arms in *ure*, The holy battles better to endure. —*Four Prentices of London*, VI., 493. In Chaucer's time it also meant fortune, like the French Neure. (NARES' *Glossary*).] by themselues or their lawfull procurators, make their appearance, for the obtayning of a conuenient, iust, and reasonable reformation of all iniuries attempted against them, then, or at some other times within one whole yere next following, and not afterward, being effectually set downe and limited, at the place aforesaid, by the consent of the ambassadours and commissioners of either parte, all lawfull impediments ceasing.

Prouided alwayes, that the value and price of all wares, goods, and marchandises, whereof the said citizens and marchants of Liuonia, in their articles receiued by the sayde English ambassadours, as is aforesayd, doe make mention, shall be iustly esteemed, prized, and approoued, not by any of England, or of Prussia, or of Liuonia, but by some other indifferent marchants of good credite, valuing them at the true rate of marchants, which such like marchandise wonld haue amounted vnto, if, at the time when they were taken, they had bene to be solde at the town of Bruges in Flanders.

Forasmuch also, as diuers and sundry Prussians (who exhibited manifolde Articles of complaints, being receiued by the said English Ambassadonrs, at their abode in Prussia) made not their personall appearance, before the saide English Ambassadours, in the lande of Prussia aforesaide: The prorogation aboue-mentioned was made vnto the first day of the moneth of May: and also it was agreed vpon by the saide Ambassadours, Procurators, and Commissioners, that the saide parties which had not appeared before shall haue libertie graunted them, lawfully to make their appearance, vpon the first of May aforesaide, at the towne of Dordract, either by themselues or by their Procurators, and also to bring with them the letters testimonial, and patents, sealed with the seale of the saide Lord the master generall, (he hauing first of all receiued sound and sufficient information from the cities whereof the parties plaintife are citizens, of the damages and grieuances any way vniustly inflicted vpon them or any of them by the English) to the end that they may there by articles conueniently declare and proue, before the Ambassadours, Procurators, messengers, and Commissioners of both partes, the rate and value of their said goods: and that in so doing they may obtaine conuenient, iust, and reasonable restitution, for all acts vniustly attempted against them, then, or at some other times effectually to bee set downe and limited at the foresaid place by the consent of the Ambassadors and Commissioners of both parts, euen as it was aboue promised vnto the marchants of Liuonia.

But if they of Prussia last aboue-mentioned, shall not vpon the first of May, and at the place appointed, for some cause, make their appearance, that then it shalbe lawfull for them, at any time within one whole yeere next following, to repaire vnto the lord Chancelor of England, at the citie of London, and to insinuate and declare vnto him their complaints before exhibited vnto the saide English Ambassadours in the land of Prussia, or which complaints should haue bene deliuered at the foresaid terme and place, or els, the which were not then and there fully finished and dispatched: and also by articles as is aforesaid, to declare and proue the true worth and estimation of all damages and grieuances any wayes vniustly offered by the English vnto them or any of them: to the ende that they may (as it is aboue mentioned) effectually receiue, and also speedily and easily obtaine conuenient, iust, and reasonable reformation and satisfaction, for al acts vniustly attempted against them, which are contained in the complaints not as yet fully declared and finished.

Moreouer, it is appointed and agreed vpon betweene the foresaide Ambassadours and Commissioners: that the forenamed souereign Lord and the said lord the Master general are to send and set forward their Ambassadours, messengers, and Commissioners, vpon the first of May vnto the place appointed, to treate, parle, agree, and conclude about those affaires, which shal then and there happen to be treated of and handled among them.

Furthermore, betweene the often mentioned Ambassadours, Procurators, and Commissioners, it is enacted and concluded: [Sidenote: Note well.] that vnto all and singular lawfull statutes, ordinations, and prohibitions framed, made, and ordained, by the saide lorde the Master generall, in his land of Prussia, or by his Proconsuls and Consuls, and his gouernours of cities, townes, villages, and of other places in the land of Prussia, vnto the obseruation whereof, aswell the subiectes of the said Master general, as foreners and strangers, are tyed and bound: vnto the very same statutes, ordinations, and prohibitions, al English marchants whatsoeuer resorting vnto the land of Prussia, must be firmely bounden and subiect.

Also it is ordained, that whatsoeuer sale-clothes are already transported, or at any time hereafter to bee transported out of England into Prussia by the English marchants, and shall there be offered to bee solde, whether they be whole cloathes or halfe cloathes, they must containe both their endes.

Lastly, that the matters aboue-mentioned fall not short and voyde of their wished effect; the treaty and conference about all and singular damages and grieuances (whereof there is not as yet done, but there must be, by the vertue of these presents, performed, a reformation and amendment) must be continued and proroged vntill the first of May next ensuing: as by these presents they are continued and proroged with the continuation of the dayes then immediately following, at the towne of Dordract aforesaide: at the which time and place, or at other times and places, in the meane space, as occasion shall serue, by both parties to be limited and assigned, or else within one yeere after the said first day of the moneth of May next ensuing bee expired: the hurt and damaged parties generally before-mentioned, shall haue performed vnto them a conuenient, iust, and reasonable reformation on both partes. Prouided alwayes, if within the terme of the saide yeere, some conuenient, iust, and reasonable reformation bee not performed vnto the parties iniuried, and endamaged, which are generally aboue mentioned: that then, within three whole moneths after the foresaid yere shall haue expired, the Prussians shall depart out of the realmes and dominions of the saide Soueraigne Lord the king of England, together with their marchandize, and with other goods which they shal haue gotten or bought, within the space of the foresaid three moneths: and that the English men also are likewise, in all respects bounden to auoid and (no lawfull impediment hindering them) to withdrawe themselues and to depart out of the territories and dominions of the saide Master generall, without all molestation, perturbation, and impediment whatsoeuer, none other intimation or admonition being necessarie in this regard.

Howbeit least that by the robberies and piracies of some insolent and peruerse people, matter should be ministred vnto the said lord the Master generall, of swaruing from the faithfull obseruation of the foresaid agreements, or (which God forbid) any occasion bee giuen him of not obseruing them: it is also decreed by the often aboue mentioned Ambassadours and messengers, that if the goods and marchandize of any of the saide lorde Master generall his subiectes whatsoeuer shall be from henceforth vniustly taken vpon the Sea, by any English Pirates, and shalbe caried into the realme of England, and there receiued, that the Gouernours and keepers of portes, and of other places (with whatsoeuer names they be called) at the which portes and places such merchandises and goods shall chaunce to arriue, beeing onely informed of the saide goods and marchandises, by sole report, or (other proofes wanting) by probable suspition are bound to arrest and to keep them in safe custodie, fauourably to be restored vnto the owners thereof, whensoeuer they shall be lawfully demaunded: which if they shall omit or deny to performe, from thenceforth the saide gouernours and keepers are bound to make vnto the parties endamaged, a recompense of their losses.

And for fault of iustice to be executed, by the said gouernours and keepers, our soueraign lord the king aboue named, after he shall conueniently be requested by the parties damnified, is bound within three moneths next ensuing (all lawfull impediments being excepted) to make correspondent, iust, and reasonable satisfaction, vnto the saide partes endamaged. Otherwise, that it shal be right lawfull for the saide lorde the Master generall, to arrest, and after the arrest to keepe in safe custodie the goods of the English marchants being in the land of Prussia, to the condigne satisfaction of such iniuries, as haue bene offered vnto his subiects, vntill his said subiects be iustly and reasonably contented.

Likewise also in all respects, the same iustice is to be done vnto the English by the said Lord the Master generall and his subiects in Prussia, euen as it hath bene enacted and decreed in the aboue written clause, beginning, Cæterum ne per &c. In English: Howbeit least that &c. for the said Master general, and his subiects by the foresaide ambassadors of England, and the commissioners of the said lord the Master generall, that in like cases iustice ought to be administred on the behalfe of himselfe, and of his subiects in the realme of England.

And that all and singular the couenants aboue written, may in time to come, by the parties whom they concern, firmly and inuiolably be obserued; the forenamed ambassadors, messengers, and commissioners, all and euery of them, for the full credite, probation, and testimonie of all the premisses, haue vnto these present Indentures, made for the same purpose, caused euerie one of their seales with their owne hands to be put. One part of the which indentures remaineth in the custodie of the English ambassadors, and the other part in the hands of the commissioners of Prussia. Giuen at the castle of Marienburgh in Prussia, in the yeere of our Lorde 1405. vpon the 8. day of the moneth of October.

* * * * *

An agreement made betweene King Henrie the fourth and the common societie of the Marchants of the Hans.

This Indenture made betweene the honourable Sir William Esturmy knight, and Iohn Kington clearke, procurators, messengers, and commissioners sufficiently deputed and authorized by the most mighty Prince, Lord Henry, by the grace of God king of England, and France, and lord of Ireland, for the performation of the things vnderwritten, on the one part: and the hon. personages M. Henry Vredeland, M. Riman Salum chief notaries, Thederic Knesuolt secretary, M. Simon Clouesten chief notary, and Iohn Zotebotter citizen, being sufficiently made and ordained procurators and messengers, on the behalfe of the cities of Lubec, Bremen, Hamburg, Sund, and Gripeswold, for the demanding and obtaining seuerally, of due reformation, and recompense at the hands of our saide souereigne lord the king, and of his messengers and commissioners aforesayde, for all iniuries, damages, grieuances, and manslaughters, any wayes vniustly done, and offred seuerally by the liege people and subiects of our soueraigne lord the king, vnto the common societie of the marchants of the Hans, and vnto any of the Citizens, people and inhabitants of the cities aforesaide whatsoeuer on the other part, Witnesseth: That betweene all and euery of the saide Procurators, messengers, and Commissioners, by vertue of the authoritie committed vnto them, it hath bene and is appointed, concluded, and decreed: that the liege marchants and subiects of our said soueraigne lord the king, and the marchants of the common societie of the Dutch Hans aforesaide, from henceforth for one whole yeere and seuen moneths immediately next ensuing and following, shalbe permitted and licenced friendly, freely, and securely, to exercise mutual traffike, and like marchants to buy and sell together, one of, and vnto another, euen as in times past, [Sidenote: 1400.] namely, in the yeere 1400. and before that time also, they haue bin accustomed to exercise mutuall traffike and marchandise, and to buy and sell.

Also the saide William and Iohn agreed and consented, that they themselues, or some other perhaps to be appointed in this behalfe by their saide lord the king in their stead, shall vpon the first day of the moneth of May next to come, with the continuation of the dayes following, at the towne of Dordract in Holland, or vpon any other terme or termes, then perhaps to bee limited, competently satisfie, and performe conuenient recompence vnto the saide common societie, citizens, people, and inhabitants of the cities aforesaide, and also of other cities, townes and villages of the Hans, of and for all iniuries, damages, grieuances, and drownings, or manslaughters done and committed, as they alleage, against them, deliuered and exhibited in written articles, vnto the aboue named William and Iohn, or els heereafter to bee deliuered and exhibited, either by the same procurators or by some others, which shall perhaps be authorized in their stead, of by the messengers procurators and commissioners of other cities, townes, and places of the Hans, in equall and like maner and forme, euen as at the saide terme limited, or then perhaps to be proroged, there is appointed by the said William and Iohn, reparation, reformation, and recompence vnto the inhabitants of Prussia, and Liuonia, for the iniuries, damages, and grieuances vniustly done and committed against them by the liege people and subiects of the saide soueraigne lord the king, in the presence of the mightie lord the Master general of Prussia, in his land of Prussia, as in certain letters indented, bearing date in the castle of Marienburgh in Prussia the eight day of the moneth of October, in the yeere of our lord 1405. and being made and written about the reparation, reformation, and recompence of such like iniuries &c. (the tenour whereof ought here to be vnderstood as if it were inserted) it is more manifestly contained.

It was furthermore promised by the said William and Iohn, that they should uot inforce nor compell the citizens, people, or inhabitants of the common society of the Hans, or of the aboue named cities, or of any other cities of the Hans aforesaid (hauing receiued sufficient information of their dwelling and place of abode) to more difficult or district proofes of their Articles of complaints alreadie exhibited, and in the foresaide termes to come, to bee exhibited, then vnto the inhabitants of the lands of Prussia and Liuonia, according to the forme of the Indentures aboue mentioned.

Moreouer the saide William and Iohn doe promise, that so soone as they shall come into the kingdome of England, and before the presence of their king, they shal prouide, that all and singular the priuiledges graunted vnto the marchants of the saide Hans by the renowmed kings of England, and confirmed by the said Soueraigne lord the king that now is, must, according to al their contents, be inuiolably obserued by the said soueraigne king and his subiects: and also, that from henceforth nothing is vniustly to be attempted, vpon any occasion, pretense, or colour, by the saide Soueraigne Prince, and the inhabitants, of the realme of England, to the preiudice of the sayde priuiledges. They shall prouide also, that all things heretofore attempted and practised against the saide priuiledges, shall, by reasonable, amendement and iust reformation, vtterly be abolished.

But if after the date of these presents (which God forfend) within the space of the said one yere and seuen moneths prescribed any damages, iniuries or grieuances, in ships, goods, or persons, should, either by the English and the inhabitants of England be vniustly inflicted vpon the cities, and marchants of the cities, townes, and places of the Hans aforesaid, or by any merchants or others of the cities or townes of the saide Hans, either vnto the English, or vnto any of the inhabitants of that Realme, vpon any fained pretense whatsoeuer, all and singular the foresaid messengers, commissioners, ambassadours, and procurators haue promised, that all such damages, iniuries and molestations so inflicted by them who shall offer and commit them, must bee reformed and amended, after the very same forme and manner, that in the like case reformation, reparation and amends of iniuries, damages, and molestations committed by the English against them of Prussia is to be performed, according vnto a certaine clause contained in the letters aboue mentioned, which beginneth: Cæterum ne per &c. In English: Howbeit least that &c. continuing vnto that clause: Et vt præscripta omnia &c. In English: And that all the couenants aboue written &c.

It was also concluded betweene the foresaide messengers, commissioners, and procurators, and with one generall consent agreed vpon, that if from the first day of the moneth of May next to come, within one whole yeere following, some conuenient, iust, and reasonable reformation be not performed vnto the parties iniured and damnified generally aboue mentioned, in regard of their damages, molestations, and iniuries: then, within three moneths after the saide yeere bee expired, the marchants of the Hans cities aforesaid are bound, without any molestation, perturbation, and impediment whatsoeuer (none other intimation or admonition being necessarie in this behalfe) to auoyde (and if no lawfull impediment shall hinder them) to abstaine and depart from the Realmes and Dominions of the said Soueraigne king of England, with their marchandize and other goods bought or gotten within the space of the saide three moneths: and also the English likewise in all respects shall auoide, abstaine, and depart from the territories and dominions of the Hans cities aforesaide.

Also it was promised by the saide William and Iohn, that at the terme appointed, namely upon the first of May next following, or at some other terme or termes then limited or to bee limited, there must be made a due recompense, and a proportionall satisfaction, for all those persons of the land of Prussia, Liuonia, and of the cities, townes, and other places of the Hans who haue uniustly bene drowned, and slaine by the English: and that according to the tenour of a certain schedule written concerning a recompense to be had in regarde of the saide persons drowned and slaine, and presented unto them by Albertus Rode consul of the citie of Thoren, and by the forenamed procurators and messengers of the cities aforesaid, they must faithfully and effectually, to the vtmost of their abilitie indeuour, for the obtaining of the saide recompense and amends. In witnesse whereof (these letters of indenture remaining in the possession of the saide William and Iohn the messengers, procurators, and commissioners of England aforesaid, and left in their custodie, by the aboue named procurotors and messengers Henrie Rimarus, Thedericus, Simon, and Iohn Sotebotter, of their certaine knowledge and assurance) and for the full confirmation and testimonie of al the premisses, the foresaid procurators and messengers haue put to their seales. Giuen in the towne of Dordract the 15. day of December in the yere of our Lord 1405.

William Esturmy knight, and Iohn Kington canon of Lincolne (being in this behalfe sufficiently authorized and deputed as Ambassadours, procurators, messengers and commissioners, by our said soueraigne lord the king, namely in regard of the molestations, iniuries and damages uniustly done and committed against the liege people and subiects of the foresaide most excellent Prince and lord, Lord Henry by the grace of God king of England and France, and Lord of Ireland, by the communalties of the cities of Wismer and Rostok vnderwritten, their common counsel being assembled for the same purpose, and authorized also, and as well closely as expresly maintaincd and ratified, by the whole companie of the common society of the marchants of the Dutch Hans) doe, in this present diet at the towne of Hage situate in the countrey of Holland, being appointed for the very same occasion, demaund of you Syr Iohn de Aa knight, and Hermannus Meyer deputies for the cities of Wismer and Rostok, and sufficiently ordeined by authority requisite in this behalfe, to be the procurators and messengers of the said cities, that conuenient, iust, and reasonable satisfaction and recompense may certainely and effectually be done vnto the iniured and endamaged parties, who are specified in the articles vnder written.

[Sidenote: Newcastle. An English ship of 200 tunnes.] Imprimis, that about the feast of Easter, in the yeere of our Lord 1394. Henry van Pomeren, Godekin Michael, Clays Sheld, Hans Howfoote, Peter Hawfoote, Clays Boniface, Rainbek, and many others, with them of Wismer and of Rostok, being of the societie of the Hans, tooke, by maine force, a ship of Newcastle vpon Tine, called Godezere sailing vpon the sea towards Prussia, being of the burthen of two hundred tunnes, and belonging vnto Roger de Thorneton, Robert Gabiford, Iohn Paulin, and Thomas de Chester: which ship, together with the furniture thereof amounteth vnto the value of foure hundred, pounds: also the woollen cloth, the red wine, the golde, and the summes of money contained in the said ship amounted vnto the value of 200. marks of English money: moreouer they vniustly slew Iohn Patanson and Iohn Russell in the surprising of the shippe and goods aforesaide, and there they imprisoned the sayde parties taken, and, to their vtter vndoing, detayned them in prison for the space of three whole yeeres.

[Sidenote: Hull.] Item, that in the yeere of our Lord 1394 certaine persons of Wismer and Rostok, with others of the Hans their confederates robbed one Richard Horuse of Hull of diuers goods and marchandizes in a ship called the Shipper Berline of Prussia, beeing then valued at 160. nobles.

Item, that in the yeere of our Lorde 1395. Hans van Wethemonkule, Clays Scheld, Godekin Mighel, and one called Strotbeker, by force of armes, and by the assistance of the men of Wismer and Rostok, and others of the Hans, did vpon the Sea neere vnto Norway, wickedly and vniustly take from Iohn Tutteburie, fiue pieces of waxe, foure hundred of werke, and halfe a last of osmundes, and other goods, to the value of foure hundred seuentie six nobles.

Item, in the yeere of our Lorde 1396. one Iohn van Derlowe, Hans van Gelder, and other their complices of the Hans villainously and vniustly tooke a shippe of William Terry of Hul called the Cogge, with thirtie wollen broad clothes, and a thousand narrow clothes, to the value of 200. pounds.

Item, in the yeere of our Lorde 1398. one Iohn van Derlowe, Wilmer, Hans van Gelder, Clays Scheld, Euerade Pilgrimson, and diuers others of the Hans, did vpon the Sea neere vnto Norway villainously and vniustly take a shippe of Iohn Wisedome of Hull called the Trinitie, with diuers goods and marchandizes, namely oyle, waxe, and werke, to the value of 300. pounds.

Item, in the yeere of our Lord 1399. one Clays Scheld, and others aboue written of Wismer and Rostok, with certaine others of the Hans, their confederates, wickedly and vniustly tooke from one William Pound marchant of Hull, two cakes of waxe, to the value of 18. poundes, out of the ship called the Hawkin Derlin of Dantzik.

[Sidenote: Yorke.] Item, in the yeere of our Lord 1394. one Goddekin Mighel, Clays Scheld, Storbiker, and diuers others of Wismer and Rostok, and of the Hans, wickedly and vniustly tooke out of a ship of Elbing (the master whereof was called Henry Puys) of the goods and marchandizes of Henrie Wyman, Iohn Topcliffe, and Henry Lakenswither of Yorke, namely in werke, waxe, osmunds, and bowstaues, to the value of 1060. nobles.

Item, in the yeere of our Lorde 1394. certaine malefactors of Wismer and Rostok, with others of the Hans, their confederats wickedly and vniustly took out of a ship of Holland (the master whereof was called Hinkensman) 140. woollen clothes (the price of one of the which clothes was eight nobles) from Thomas Thester of Yorke, and a chest, with armour, siluer and Golde of the foresaid Thomas, to the value of 9. pounds.

[Sidenote: London.] Item, in the yere of our Lord 1393. certaine malefactors of Wismer and Rostok, and others their complices of the Hans, wickedly and vniustly tooke from one Richard Abel of London woollen cloth, greene cloth, meale and fishes, to the value of 133. li. 6. s.

Item, in the yeere of our Lorde 1405. about the feast of S. Michael, one Nicholas Femeer of Wismer marchant of the Hans, with the assistance of other his complices of the Hans aforesaide, wickedly and vniustly tooke from one Richard Morley citizen of London fiue lasts of herrings, besides 32. pounds, in the sea called Northsound.

[Sidenote: Colchester.] Item, in the yeere of our Lord 1398; about the moneth of September, one Godekin Wisle, and Gerard Sleyre of Wismer and Rostok, with others of the Hans, their confederats wickedly and vniustly took out of a ship of Prussia (wherof the master was named Rorebek) from Iohn Seburgh marchant of Colchester two packs of woollen cloth, to the value of 100. markes: from Stephan Flispe, and Iohn Plumer marchants of the same town two packs of woollen cloth, to the value of 60. pounds: from Robert Wight marchant of the same towne, two packs of woollen cloth to the value of an 100. marks: from William Munde marchant of the same town, two fardels of woollen cloth, worth 40. li. and from Iohn Dawe, and Thomas Cornwaile marchants of the same towne, three packs of woollen cloth, worth 200. marks. Moreouer they tooke and imprisoned certain English men, which were in the said ship, namely William Fubborne seruant vnto Iohn Diere, Thomas Mersh seruant vnto Robert Wight, which Thomas paid for his ransome 20. nobles of English money, William Munde marchant of the towne aforesaide, which William, by reason of the extremity of that imprisonment, lost the sight of his eyes, and Thomas Cornwaile, marchant of the foresaide Towne, which Thomas paide for his raunsome twentie nobles.

[Sidenote: Yermouth. Norwich] Item, in the yeere of our Lorde 1394 certaine malefactors of Wismer and Rostok, vpon the coastes of Denmark and Norway, beneath Scawe, and at Anold, tooke Thomas Adams and Iohn Walters marchants of Yermouth: and Robert Caumbrigge and Reginald Leman marchants of Norwich, in a certaine shippe of Elbing in Prussia (whereof one Clays Goldesmith was master) with diuers woollen clothes of the saide Thomas, Iohn, Robert, and Reginald, to the value of one thousande marks English, and carried the persons and goods aforesaide, away with them: and the said Thomas, Iohn, Robert, and Reginald they imprisoned at Courtbuttressow, and there detained them, vntill they paide an hundred markes for their redemption.

[Sidenote: Yermouth.] Item in the yeere of our Lorde 1401. some of the inhabitants of Wismer and of Rostok wickedly tooke at Longsound in

Norway, a certaine shippe of West-Stowe in Zealand (the Master whereof was one Gerard Dedissen) laden with diuerse goods and marchandises of Iohn Hughson of Yermouth, namely with the hides of oxen and of sheepe, with butter, masts, sparres, boordes, questingstones and wilde werke, to the value of an hundred marks, and do as yet detaine the said things in their possession, some of the Hans being their assistants in the premisses.

Item, in the yeere of our Lorde 1402. certaine of the Hans, of Rostok, and of Wismer, tooke vpon the coast of England, neere vnto Plimmouth a certaine barge called the Michael of Yarmouth (whereof Hugh ap Fen was the owner, and Robert Rigweys the master) laden with bay salt, to the quantitie of 130. wayes, and with a thousand canuasse clothes of Britaine, and doe as yet detaine the saide goods in their possession, the said Hugh being endamaged, by the losse of his ship, and of his goods aforesaid 800. nobles and the foresaid Master and the mariners loosing, in regard of their wages, canuas, and armour, 200. nobles.

Item, in the yeere of our Lord 1405. certain malefactors of Wismer wickedly and vniustly tooke, in a certaine port of Norway called Selaw, a ship of Yarmouth (the owner whereof was William Oxney and the master Thomas Smith) laden with salt, cloth, and salmon, to the value of 40. pound, and doe as yet detaine the said ship and goods in their possession, some of the Hans their confederates ayding and assisting them at the same time.

[Sidenote: Cleye.] Item, in the yeere of our Lord 1395. one Godekin Mighel, Clays Scheld, Stertebeker, and other their accomplices of the Hans, vnlawfully tooke vpon the sea a certaine ship of one Iohn Dulwer of Cley, called the Friday (whereof Laurence Tuk of Cley was master) and conueyed the ship it self vnto Maustrond in Norway, and the saide Master and mariners they robbed of diuers commodities, namely of artillery, furniture, and salt fishes being in the same ship, to the value of 500. nobles.

Item, in the yeere of our Lord 1395. Godekin Mighel, Clays Scheld, Stertebeker, and other their accomplices of the Hans vnlawfully tooke vpon the sea a certaine ship of one William Bets of Cleys called the Margaret (wherein Robert Robines was master) and conueyed the ship it self vnto Mawstrond in Norway, and there robbed the master and his partners of diuers commodities, namely of artillerie, furniture, and salt fishes, to the value of 400. nobles, and one of the said masters mates they maliciously drowned.

Item, in the yeere of our Lord 1395. about the feast of the natiuitie of S. Iohn Baptist, the forenamed Godekin and Stertebeker, with others their accomplices of the Hans, vnlawfully took vpon the sea a certain ship of Nicholas Steyhard and Iohn Letis of Cley called the Nicholas (whereof

Iohn Prest was master) and conueyed the said ship vnto Mawstrond, and there robbed the said master and his companie of diuers commodities, namely of furniture and salt fishes, being in the said ship, to the value of 320. nobles.

Item, in the yeere of our Lord 1395. about the feast aforesaid, the said Godekins and Stertebeker, and their companions of the Hans vniustly took vpon the sea a certaine ship of Thomas Peirs of Cley called the Isabel (whereof William Noie was master) and conueyed it vnto Mawstrond, and there robbed the said master and his company of diuers commidities, as namely of furniture, and salt fishes, being in the said ship, to the value of 406. nobles.

Item, in the yeere next aboue mentioned, vpon the Saterday, about the foresaid feast, the forenamed Godekins and Stertebeker, and other their accomplices of the Hans unlawfully took vpon the sea, a certain ship of one Thomas Lyderpole of Cley, called the Helena, wherein Robert Alwey was master, and also wickedly and vniustly drowned in the bottom of the sea diuers commodities, as namely salt fishes, together with the ship it selfe.

Item, in the yeere of our Lord 1398. about the feast of S. Michael the archangel, the foresaid Godekin and Stertebeker, with other their confederats of the Hans, took at Langsound in Norway a certain crayer of one Thomas Motte of Cley, called the Peter, (wherein Thomas Smith was master) and the foresaid crayer they wickedly and vniustly caried away, being worth 280. nobles.

[Sidenote: Wiueton.] Item, in the yeere of our Lord 1395. about the feast of the natiuitie of S. Iohn Baptist, the forenamed Godekins and Stertebeker, and others of the Hans vniustly tooke a certain ship of Simon Durham, called the Dogger-ship, and the Peter of Wiueton, laden with salt fishes (whereof Iohn Austen was master) vpon the coast of Denmarke. And they caried away the saide Dogger, with the furniture thereof, and the foresaid salt fishes, to the value of 170. pound. Moreouer, the master, and 25. mariners in the same ship they maliciously slewe, and a certaine ladde of the saide Dogger they caried with them vnto Wismer.

Item, in the foresaid yeere, and about the feast aforesaid, the forenamed Godekins and Stertebeker, with other their complices, vniustly tooke vpon the sea a certain ship of Thomas Lyderpole, and Iohn Coote of Wiueton: and the master and mariners which were in the saide shippe, they villanously slue, among whom they put to death one Simon Andrew, the godsonne, nephew, and seruant of the foresaid Simon Durham. Which ship, with the goods and furniture that were therein was worth 410. nobles.

Item, in the very same yeere, about the feast aforesaid, the forenamed Godekins and Stertebeker and other their complices wickedly spoiled a certaine ship of the foresaid Simon Durham called the Dogger, wherein Geruase Cat was master, lying, at an anker, while the companie were occupied about fishing, and likewise vniustly tooke away with them the salt fishes, and furniture of the said ship. Moreouer, the master and his company that were in the said Dogger they beate and wounded, so that they vtterly lost their fishing for that yeere, the master and his said companie being endamaged thereby, to the summe of 200. nobles.

Item, in the yere of our Lord 1396. the foresaid Godekins and Stertebeker, and other their complices vniustly tooke vpon the sea a certain crayer, called the Buss of Zeland, which one Iohn Ligate marchant, and seruant vnto the forenamed Simon Durham had laden in Prussia, on the behalfe of the said Simon, to saile for England, and spoiled the said craier, and also tooke and caried away with them the goods and marchandises of the said Simon, being in the foresaid ship, to the value of 66. pounds.

Item, in the yeere of our Lord 1397. certaine malefactors of Wismer and Rostok, with certaine others of the Hans, tooke a crayer of one Peter Cole of Zeland, called the Bussship, which Alan Barret the seruant and factor of the foresaid Simon Durham had laden with mastes, sparres, and other marchandize, for the behalfe of the said Simon, and vniustly tooke from thence the goods of the said Simon, to the value of 24. pounds, and caried the same away.

[Sidenote: Lenne.] Item, in the yeere of our Lord 1394. certaine malefactors of Wismer and others of the Hans vniustly tooke vpon the sea, and caried away with them a packe of woollen cloth of the foresaid Simon, worth 42. pounds, out of a certain crayer of one Thomas Fowler of Lenne being laden and bound for Dantzik in Prussia.

Item, pitifully complaining the marchants of Lenne doe auouch, verifie, and affirme, that about the feast of S. George the martyr, in the yeere of our Lord 1394. sundry malefactors and robbers of Wismer and Rostok, and others of the Hans, with a great multitude of ships, arriued at the towne of Norbern in Norway, and tooke the said town by strong assault, and also wickedly and vniustly took al the marchants of Lenne there residing with their goods and cattels, and burnt their houses and mansions in the same place, and put their persons vnto great ransoms: [Sidenote: 21. houses of English marchants burnt at Norben in Norway.] euen as by the letters of safeconduct deliuered vnto the said marchants it may more euidently appeare, to the great damage and impouerishment of the marchants of Lenne: namely, Inprimis they burnt there 21. houses belonging vnto the said marchants, to the value of 440. nobles. Item, they tooke from Edmund

Belyetere, Thomas Hunt, Iohn Brandon, and from other marchants of Lenne, to the value of 1815. pounds.

[Concerning this surprise Albertus Krantzius in the sixt book of his history of Norway, [Footnote: *Chronica regnorum Aquiloniorum Dania, Suecia, Norwegia, Argentorati*, 1546. Folio.] and the 8. Chapter writeth in maner following.

In the meane while Norway enioyed peace vnder the gouernment of a woman: vntil Albertus king of Suecia, who had now seuen yeeres continued in captiuity vnder Queen Margaret, was to be set at liberty. [Sidenote: The Vitalians.] Which, when the common souldiers of Rostok and Wismer, called the Vitalians perceiued, (who, whilest their king was holden captiue, in the right of the forenamed cities, for the behalfe of their lord the king being prince of Mekleburg by birth, vndertooke and waged warre al the time of his captiuitie) banding their forces together, they resolued, at their own costs and charges, but in the right of the said cities, to saile into the 3. kingdoms, and to take such spoiles as they could lay hold on. These common souldiers therfore, seeing an end of their tyrannical and violent dealing to approach, sailed into Norway, vnto the towne of Norbern, being a mart town for al the marchants of Germanie: who transporting fishes from thence, doe bring thither marchandises of all kinds; especially corne, vnto the scarcitie whereof, vnlesse it be brought out of other countreys, that kingdome (as we haue said) is very much subiect. Departing out of their ships and going on shore, they set vpon the towne, and by fire and sword they easily compelled the inhabitants dwelling in weake wodden houses, to giue place. Thus these Vitalians entring and surprising the towne conueyed such spoiles vnto their ships as them pleased, and hauing laden their ships with those booties, they returned home frolike vnto the ports of their own cities. Without all respect, they robbed and rifled the goods, aswel of the Germanes, as of the Noruagians: and like lewde companions, wasting and making hauock of all things, prooued themselues neuer the wealthier. For it is not the guise of such good fellowes to store vp or to preserue ought. The citizens, at the first, seemed to be inriched: howbeit afterward, (no man misdoubting any such calamitie) goods ill gotten were worse spent. Thus farre Krantzius.]

Item, pitifully complaining, the foresaide marchants auouch, verifie, and affirme, that vpon the 14. day after the feast of S. George, in the yeere of our Lord next aboue written, as 4. ships of Lenne, laden with cloth, wine, and other marchandises, were sailing vpon the maine sea, with all the goods and wares conteined in them, for Prussia, sundry malefactors of Wismer and Rostok, with others of the Hans, being in diuers ships, came vpon them, and by force of armes and strong hand tooke the said ships, with the goods and marchandises contained in them: and some of the people which were in the saide foure ships, they slew, some they spoyled, and others they put vnto extreame ransomes. And carying away with them those foure ships with the commodities and marchandise therin, they parted stakes therwith, as them listed, to the great impoverishment and losse of the said marchants of Lenne, namely in cloth of William Silesden, Tho. Waterden, Ioh. Brandon, Ioh. Wesenham, and other marchants of Lenne, to the value of 3623. li. 5. s. 11. d.

Item, pitifully complaining, the foresaid marchants doe affirme, that one Henry Lambolt and other his adherents, in the yeere of our Lord 1396. tooke vpon the maine sea betweene Norway and Scaw, one crayer laden with osmunds, and with diuers other marchandises, perteining vnto Iohn Brandon of Lenne, to the summe and value of 443. li. 4. s. 2. d. Moreouer, they tooke from Iohn Lakingay 4. lasts and an halfe of osmunds, to the value Of 220. lib. 10. s.

Item, the foresaid marchants complaine, that certain malefactors of Wismer, with other their complices of the Hans, in the yeere of our Lord 1396. tooke from Thomas Ploket of Lenne, out of a certaine ship sailing vpon the maine sea towards Sconeland (whereof Iames Snycop was master) cloth and other marchandise, to the summe and value of 13. lib. 13. s. 4. d.

Item, the aboue-named marchants complaine saying, that certaine malefactors of Wismer, with others of the Hans society, in the yere of our Lord 1397. wickedly and vniustly took out of a certaine ship of Dantzik (whereof Laurence van Russe was master) from Ralph Bedingam of Lenne, one fardel [Footnote: *Fardel*, a burden. (French, *Fardeau*.)] of cloth worth 52. li. 7. s. 6. d. Also, for the ransome of his seruant, 8. li. 6. s. 8. d. Item, they tooke from Thomas Earle diuers goods, to the value of 24. pounds.

Item, the foresaid marchants complaine, that certaine malefactors of Wismer of Rostok, with others of the Hans, in the yeere of our Lord 1399, wickedly and vniustly tooke one crayer pertayning vnto Iohn Lakinglich of Lenne, laden with diuers goods and marchandise pertaining vnto sundry marchants of Lenne, namely from the forenamed Iohn one fardel of cloth, and one chest full of harneis, and other things, to the value of 90. lib. Item, they took out of the foresaid ship from Roger Hood, one fardel of cloth, and one chest with diuers goods, to the value of 58. lib. Item, from Iohn Pikeron, one fardell of cloth, and one chest with diuers goods, to the value of 440. lib. Item, from Andrew Purser one fardell of cloth, and one chest with diuers commodities therein, to the value of ten pounds.

Item, the aboue named marchants complaine saying, that certaine malefactors of Wismer and Rostok, and others of the Hans, namely, Godekin Mighel, Henrie van Hall de Stertebeker, with other of their confederates, in the yeere of our Lord 1399. wickedly and vniustly took from Iohn Priour of Lenne, out of the ship of Michael van Burgh, namely

160. nests of masers, worth 100. lib. 13. s. 4. d. Item, 30. furres rigges of Kaleber woorth 13. s. 4. d. a piece, the summe totall amounting to 20. li. Item, 20. furres wombys of Kalebre worth &c. Item, one girdle of siluer, and one dagger adorned with siluer worth 30. s. Item, two coates, and one long iacket, and other goods, to the value of 30. s. Item, he paide for his ransome 4. lib. 13 s. 4. d.

[Sidenote: Note the secret treasons of the Hans.] Vnto all and singular the articles aboue-written, the ambassadors of England aforesaid do further adde, that the doers and authors of the damages, iniuries, and robberies set down in the articles aboue written, (of whom some are named in particular, and others in general) performed and committed all those outrages, being hired thereunto at the expenses and charges of the common societies, of the cities aforesaid. And that the inhabitants of euery houshold in the foresaide cities (ech man according to his ability) wittingly and purposely set foorth one, two, or more men, for the very same expedition, wherein all and singular the foresaid trespasses were committed.

The foresaid English ambassadors doe exhibite the articles aboue-written vnto the procurators of the cities of Wismer and Rostok aforesaid: leaue and libertie being alwayes reserued vnto the said ambassadors, to enlarge, or to diminish or to expound all, or euery, or any of the said Articles whatsoeuer, so often as it shall seeme expedient vnto them.

* * * * *

These be the grieuances and offences, whereat the marchants of the Hans of Almaine, comming vnto, and residing in the Realme of England, doe finde themselues aggrieued, contrarie to the Articles and priuileges of the Charter graunted vnto them by the worthy Progenitors of the king of England that now is, and also by the saide soueraigne Lord the King, ratified, and confirmed.

Imprimis, whereas the foresaide marchants haue a priuilege graunted vnto them by Charter, that they may, in cities, boroughs, and in other towns and villages throughout the whole realme of England, exercise traffique in grosse, as wel with the natural inhabitants of the kingdome, as with strangers, and priuate persons: of late, those that are free denizens in the cities, boroughs, and villages within the foresaid kingdome, do hinder and restrain all others that be strangers, foreners, and aliens, that they neither can, nor dare buy and sel with the marchants of the Hans aforesaid, to their great hinderance and losse.

Item, the foresaid by vertue of their charter were wont to haue and to hold Innes and mansions, for the reposing of themselues and of their goods, wheresoeuer they pleased in any cities, boroughs, or villages, throughout the whole kingdome; howbeit of late the foresaide marchants are not suffered to take vp their mansions, contrary to the tenour of their charter.

Item, the foresaid marchants are priuileged not to vndergoe any other burthens or impositions, but onely to pay certaine customs, as it doeth by their charter manifestly appeare. Notwithstanding at the same time when Simon de Moreden was maior of London, the foresaid marchants were constrained, in the ward of Doue-gate at London, to pay fifteenths, tallages, and other subsidies contrary to the liberties of their charter. Whereupon the saide marchants prosecuted the matter before the Councel of our soueraign lord the king, insomuch that they were released from paying afterward any such tallages, fifteenths, and subsidies. Which marchants, a while after, of their owne accord and free will, gaue vnto the gild-hall of London an hundreth markes sterling, conditionally, that they of the citie aforesaid shoulde not at any time after exact or demaund of the said marchants, or of their successors, any tallages, fifteenths, or subsidies, contrary to the tenor of their charter, as by records in the foresaid gild-hall, it doth more plainly appeare. Howbeit of late the officers of our lord the king, in the foresaid ward of Doue-gate, constrained the marchants aforesaid to pay tallages, fifteenths, and other subsidies. And because the saide marchants murmured and refused to pay any such contributions, alleaging their priuileges, the foresaid officers arrested the goods of those said marchants (which are as yet detained vpon the arrest) notwithstanding that they were released before the councel of our soueraigne lord the king, and also that they gaue vnto the said gild-hall one hundreth marks to be released, as it is aforesaid. And also the foresaid marchants were constrained to pay 12. d. in the pound, and of late 6. d. and other subsidies, more then their ancient customes, to the great damage of those marchants.

[Sidenote: The ancient customes of wools.] Item, the foresaid marchants are priuileged as touching customs of wols by them bought within the realm of England, that they are not bound to pay, ouer and besides their ancient customs, but onely xl. d, more then the homeborn marchants of England were wont to pay. [Sidenote: Pence for the towne of Cales.] But now the foresaid marchants are compelled to pay for euery sack of wool (besides the ancient custom and the 40. d. aforesaid) a certain imposition called Pence for the town of Cales, namely for euery sack of wool 19. d more then the marchants of England doe pay, to their great losse, and against the liberty of their charter.

Item, the foresaid marchants are priuileged by their charter, that concerning the quantity of their merchandize brought into the realme of England (in regard whereof they are bound to pay 3. d. for the worth of euery pound of siluer) credit is to be giuen vnto them for the letters of their masters and of their companies, if they were able to shew them. And if so be they had no letters in this behalfe to shew, that then credite should bee giuen vnto themselues, and that their othe, or the othe of their atturney should be taken, without any other proof, as touching the value of their merchandize so brought in, and that thereupon they should be bound to pay customs, namely the customes of 3. d. iustly for that cause to be paid. But nowe the customers of our soueraigne lorde the king put their goods to an higher rate then they ought or were woont to be: and heereupon they compell them to pay custome for their goods, at their pleasure, scanning about their fraight and expenses particularly disbursed in regard of the said goods and marchandize, to the great hinderance of the said marchants, and against the tenor of their charter.

[Sidenote: The great charter of marchants.] Item, the foresaid merchants by way of pitiful complaint do alleage, that, whereas the worthy progenitors of our Lord the king that now is, by vertue of the saide great charter, graunted liberty vnto them to pay the customes of certain clothes, namely of skarlet, and cloth died in grayne, and of other clothes of assise, which were by them to be caried out of the realme of England, euen as by their foresaid Charter it doeth more plainly appeare: and whereas our soueraigne lord the king that now is (ratifying and confirming the saide charter, and being willing that they shoulde haue more especiall fauour shewed vnto them) granted vnto them by their Charter, that the said marchants should be exempted and freed from all custome and imposition of small clothes, as in pieces and in narrow clothes which were not of assise, and in such other clothes of like qualitie: [Sidenote: A speciall charter.] yet of late the Customers of our Lorde the King that nowe is, not allowing their saide speciall Charter so graunted vnto the marchants aforesaid, do compel them to pay for straight clothes and for pieces of clothes which are not of assise, (together with other demands particularly and seuerally made) as great custome as if the clothes were full out of assise. [Sidenote: The customers of the pety custome.] Moreouer also of late, the customers of the smal or pety custome and of the subsidie doe demand of them custome for kersey-clothes equal vnto the custome of those clothes, that be of ful assise, whereas the foresaid marchants were not wont to pay for those kerseys by vertue of their Charter, but onely according to the worth of ech pound of siluer, as namely for other goods which are of golde weight: to the great hinderance of the foresaid parties, and against the manifest graunt of our soueraigne Lord the king, as it appeareth in the said speciall Charter.

Item, the said merchants alleage, that they are priuiledged by their Charter, if they pay custome and subsidy for their goods in the behalfe of our lord the king, at any port of England where those goods haue arriued and afterward would transport the saide goods or any part of them vnto any other port within the realme aforesaid: that then they should be quite released from paying of any other custome for the same goods, if they bring a warrant that they haue paide the saide custome, as is aforesaide. [Sidenote: 1405.] Of late it fortuned, that a certaine man of their societie named Nicholas Crossebaire, being a marchant of the lande of Prussia, immediately after the concord was concluded betwene the English and the Prussians, brought vnto the towne of Sandwich a shippe laden with bowe-staues and other marchandize, and there well and truely paide the custome of our lord the king for all his ware: and selling there part of the same goods, he afterward transported parcel thereof in a small barke vnto London, there to be solde, and caried a warrant also with him, that he had at Sandwich paid the custome due vnto our lord the king: and yet (the said warrant notwithstanding) the customers of the pety custome and subsidy of London came and demanded custome of him at another time contrary to reason, and against the tenor of their charter: and the said Nicholas offred pledges vnto them, yea, euen ready money downe into their hands, vntil the question were discussed and determined, whether he should pay new custome or no: but this they would not doe. Then the said Nicholas brought a brief from our lord the king, to get himselfe discharged from paying the said custome: and for all that, the foresaid customers would not as yet haue regard vnto him, but kept the said goods within shipboord, vpon the riuer of Thames, for the space of 15. dayes, vntil he had paid another custome, to the great losse of the said Nicholas, for that which he sold first at Sandwich to be deliuered at London for seuen nobles, he could not afterward haue for it aboue foure nobles, and yet so was it solde, by reason of the harme which his wares had taken by lying so long vpon the water, contrary to the tenor of their Charter.

Item, the said marchants do alleage, that another of their company called Peter Hertson bought at Bristow certain clothes, and laded the same in a ship, to be transported for Prussia, for the which he truely paide at Bristowe, the customs and subsidies due vnto our soueraign lord the king: which ship with the foresaid goods arriuing at London: the customers of the pety-custome and of the subsidie there would not permit the said ship with the goods to passe vnto the parts aforesaid, vntil the said Peter had paid another custome for the same goods (the warrant, which he brought with him notwithstanding) to his great hindrance, and contrary to the tenour of their Charter.

Item, pitifully complaining the foresaid marchants alleage, that wheras euery marchant, bringing wares into the realm, was wont to haue a schedule wherein his name was written, for a specification and certificat of the quantity of his goods in the said schedule to be found at the arriual of the ship, without paying therfore ought at all, of late, the customers of the pety custome do compel them to pay for ech mans name written a peny, at the arriual of their goods out of euery ship wherin the said goods are found, what commodities and marchandize soeuer they be: whereas notwithstanding, if there be a chest or any other smal matter, there should not therfore be any custome due vnto our lord the king, nor any receiued vnto his Maiesties vse. [Sidenote: The customers of the subsidie.] In like maner do the customers of the subsidy deale. Whereas also the foresaid marchants were not wont to pay for a cocket for the conueyance and transportation of their goods out of the realme (albeit many names were written theirne) more then 4. d. of late the customers of the pety custom do compel them to pay for euery name contained in the same cocket 4. d. and in like sort do the customers of the saide subsidy deale. Which contribution in a yere extendeth it self vnto a great summe, to the vnknown preiudice of our lord the king, more then any man could suppose, (for the customers enioy their fees and commodities from his Maiestie that they may doe him faithfull seruice) and likewise to the great damage of the said marchants.

Item, pitifully complaining the said marchants do alleage that they are constrained to pay for subsidy, sometime 12. d. and somtime 6. d. in the pound, contrary to the tenor of their charter: and yet notwithstanding when their marchandize commeth to the wharf, the customers prolong and delay the time 3. or 4. weeks before they wil take custome for their goods, in the which space other marchants sel their goods, the customers not regarding whether the goods aforesaid take wet or no: to the great damage aswel of our lord the king, as of the said marchants: because, if they had quicke dispatch, they might pay custome vnto his Maiestie oftner then they doe.

Item, the said marchants doe farther alleage, that the customers of the petie custome, and of the subsidie in the port of London haue appointed among themselues certaine men to seale vp the goods of the saide marchants, so soon as they are arriued at the port of safetie, vntil the said goods be customed. By meanes of the which sealing, the foresaide parties doe compell the marchants aboue-named, (vpon an vse and custome whereof themselues haue bene the authors) to paye a certaine summe of money, to the great hinderance of the sayde marchants, and contrarie to iustice and to their charter. Moreouer, the saide customers haue ordained betweene themselues, that the saide marchants shall put or make vp no cloth into fardels, to transport out of the realme, vnlesse certaine men appointed by them for the same purpose bee there present, to see what maner of clothes they bee, vnder paine of the forfeiture of the saide goods. Also of late, when the sayde marchants would haue made up such fardels, the foresayde parties assigned to be ouerseers refused to come, vnlesse they might haue for their comming some certain summe of money, delaying and procrastinating from day to day, so long as themselues listed, to the great losse and vndoing of the foresaide marchants, and contrarie to their liberties: because the foresaide customers are bound by their office to doe this, without any contribution therefore to bee paide vnto them by the saide marchants: for that they doe enioy from our soueraigne Lord the King their fees and commodities, to the ende that they may serue him and euery marchant iustly and faithfully, without any contribution by them to be imposed anewe vpon the sayde marchants, of custome.

Item, the said marchants doe alleage, that the customers and balifs of the town of Southampton do compel them to pay for euery last of herrings, pitch, and sope ashes brought thither by them 2. s. more then the kings custome: and for ech hundreth of bowstaues and boords called Waghenscot, 2. d. for euery hundreth of boords called Richolt, 4. d. and for al other marchandize brought by the foresaid marchants vnto the same towne: which contributions they neuer paid at any time heretofore, being greatly to their hinderance, and contrary to the tenour of their Charter.

Item, the foresaid marchants do alleage, that one of their company; called Albert Redewish of Prussia, bringing diuers goods and marchandizes vnto Newcastle vpon Tine, and there laying the vsual custom of 3. d. in the pound for al his wares, the bailifs of the saide towne, against all reason, exacted 7. pound sterling at his hands more then the custome: whereupon the foresaide marchant got a briefe from the kings maiesty, for the recouery of the saide 7. li. according to equity and reason: howbeit, that at the comming of the said briefe the foresaid balifes would do nothing on his behalfe, but would haue slaine their foresaid associate, contrary to their charter and priuiledges.

William Esturmy knight, and Iohn Kington canon of Lincolne, being by the most mighty prince and lord, L. Henry by Gods grace K. of England and France and lord of Ireland, sufficiently deputed and appointed to parle, treate, and agree with the common society of the marchants of the Hans of Dutchland or Almain, concerning and about the redressing and reformation of vniust attempts happening between our said soueraign L. the king his liege people and subiects on the one part, and between the common society aforesaid, the cities, towns, And particular persons thereof on the other part: do (for the behalf of our said soueraign L. the King, with a mind and intention to haue al and singular the things vnderwritten to come to the knowledge of the said common society) intimate, declare, and make known vnto you (hono. sirs) Henr. Westhoff citizen and deputy of the city of Lubec, Henry Fredelaw, Ioh. van Berk citizen of Colen, Mainard Buxtehude citizen, and deputy of the city of Hamburgh, M. Simon Clawstern clerk, sir Iohn de Aa knight deputie of the citie of Rostok, Herman Meyer deputy of the citie of Wismar, being as the procurators, messengers, and commissioners of the foresaid cities, assembled together at the town of Hage in Holland, with the forenamed Will. and Iohn in regard of the foresaid redres and reformation: that, euen as our said soueraign L. the king his meaning is not to disturb or hinder such priuiledges as haue bin heretofore granted and vouchsafed vnto the common society of the marchants aforesaid, by the renoumed kings of England, and the worthy progenitors of our L. the K. that now is, and by himself also vnder a certain form confirmed: euen so he is determined (without the preiudice of forren lawes) vpon iust mature, and sober deliberation, by his royall authorise to withstand such priuiledges, as by reason of the abuse thereof, haue bene infinitely preiudiciall vnto himselfe and his subiects.

Inprimis the said ambassadours doe affirme as afore, that whereas all and euery the Marchants of the said company, as often as they would, were, both in the Realme of England, and in other territories and dominions subiect vnto our soueraigne lord the king, admitted and suffered (according to the tenor of the forenamed priuiledges granted vnto them) freely, friendly and securely to traffique and conuerse with any of his Maiesties liege people and subiects whatsoeuer, or with other people of whatsoeuer nation liuing in the realme of England, or in the dominions aforesaid: the said common society of marchants by their publike and deliberate common counsel did appoint and ordain, that no society in any cities, townes, or places, neither yet any particular man of any such society (there being no lawfull or reasonable cause why) shoulde in any wise admit any marchants of the realm of England resorting vnto their cities or other places for marchandise, to enioy intercourse of traffike: but that the saide English marchants should bee altogether excluded from all traffike and mutuall conuersation among them, by denouncing and inflicting grieuous penalties of money as well vpon cities as other places, and vpon particular marchants also of the foresaid societie practising the contrary.

Item, that immediately after, the foresaid parties enacting and ordaining published their sayde statute and ordinance, in all kingdomes, prouinces, partes, cities, and townes, wherin any marchants of the said societie were conuersant.

Item, that after that publication, the statute and ordinance aforesaid by euery of the marchants of the forenamed society were inuiolably obserued.

Item, that the said statute and ordinance hath bene so rigorously put in execution, that whereas immediately after certaine English marchants with their ships, mariners, and marchandize beeing in a certaine part of one of the principall cities of the foresaide societie, vtterly destitute of meate, drinke, and money, publikely offred to sell their wollen clothes of England, onely to prouide themselues of necessary victuals: yet the marchants of the saide citie, stoutely persisting in their statute and ordinance aforesaid, straightly prohibited the buying of such clothes, vnchristianly denying meate and drinke vnto the said English marchants.

Item, the foresaid society decreed and ordained, that no marchant of the saide Company should in any place or countrey whatsoeuer, buy any woollen clothes of the realme or dominion of England (albeit offered by others and not by English men) or hauing bought any, should, after the terme prefixed, sel them, imposing grieuous pecuniary mulcts, besides the forfeiture of the clothes so bought or sold, vpon them that would attempt the contrary.

Item, that after the said statute and ordinance, the foresaide societie decreed, that all marchants of the said companie, hauing among their wares and marchandise any woollen clothes made in England, should either sell the saide clothes, or within a short space then limited, should, vnder penaltie of forfeiting the said clothes, utterly renounce the vse and commoditie thereof: Notwithstanding a grieuous penaltie of money being imposed vpon the violators of the same statute.

[Sidenote: The Hans societie determineth the ouerthrow of English merchants.] Item, that the statutes and ordinances aforesaid might with more speed and celerity be put in execution, the said authors and publishers thereof imagining, according to their desire, that by this meanes an vtter extirpation and ouerthrow of English marchants might, yea and of necessity must ensue: upon their serious and long premeditated deliberation, straitely commanded and inioyned, vnder pain of losing the benefit of all priuileges, wheresoeuer, or by the princes of what lands, or the Magistrates of what Cities or townes soeuer vouchsafed vnto the said common societie, that not only the aldermen of that, society in al places throughout the realme of England, but also al other marchants of the said company, after the maner of marchants conuersing in the said Realme, should, without exception of persons, vtterly abstein from all intercourse of traffike with the marchants of the realme aforesaid: yea, and that they shoulde depart out of the said kingdome within a very short space limited. For the dispatching of al which premisses without delay, it was according to their commandement effectually prouided.

[Sidenote: Statutes against the English marchants in Norway and Suedland.] Item, that the society aforesaid hath approued diuers very vnreasonable statutes and ordinances, made and published by the marchants of the same society residing in the kingdoms of Norway and Swedland, to the great preiudice of the kingdome of England, and the marchants thereof: and as yet both couertly and expresly do approue the same, vniustly putting them in daily execution.

Item, wheras in the priuileges and indulgences granted by the renouned princes somtimes kings of England, the worthy progenitors of our souereign lord the king that now is, vnto the society aforesaid, it is prouided, that the said marchants shal not auow any man which is not of their company, nor shal not colour his goods and marchandize vnder their company; whereas also in the confirmation of the sayd priuiledges made up by our soueraigne lord that nowe is, it is manifestly prouided, that the marchants of the Hans towns, vnder the colour of their priuiledges in England, shall not vpon paine of the perpetuall frustration and reuocation of the foresayd priuiledges, receiue any stranger of any other towne in their liberties, by whom the kings custome may in any sort be withholden or diminished: and yet the contrary vnto al these prouisoes hath bin euery yere, for these 20. yeres or thereabout notoriously practised and committed, as well ioyntly by the generall counsell, and toleration of the foresayd society, as also seuerally by the aduise and permission of diuers particular cities of the foresayd Hans company to the great diminution of his maiesties custome, the estimation whereof the foresayd ambassadors are not able at this present fully to declare. [Sidenote: How many and which be the Hans townes.] But that all occasions of the last aboue mentioned diminution may bee preuented for the time to come, the sayd ambassadors doe demand to haue from the foresayd societie a declaration in writing, what and what maner of territories, cities, townes, villages or companies they be, for which the sayd society challengeth and pretendeth, that they ought to enioy the priuiledges granted vnto their marchants, as is aboue mentioned.

Moreouer, it is required by the foresaid ambassadors, if the societie aforesayd hath not decreed nor ordayned the things aboue written, that the names of the cities and places decreeing and ordaining such statutes and ordinances, may by the sayd common society either now or at some other times and places conuenient for the same purpose, be expressed and set downe in writing.

* * * * *

A letter of Henry the fourth king of England &c. unto Frater Conradus de Iungingen the Master generall of Prussia.

Henrie &c. to the most noble and mighty personage of sacred religion F: Conradus de Iungingen Master general of the order of the Dutch knights of S. Marie, our most deare friend, greeting, and continual perfection of amity.

When as your messengers and ambassadors were of late personally present in Holland, and there expected the arriual of our ambassadors vntill the first day of the moneth of Nouember last expired, that there might bee by way of friendly conference a remedie prouided in regard of certaine iniuries pretended to be offered, by both our subiects one against another, for the publique commoditie of both parts, we were determined to haue sent vnto Dordract, at the foresaid daye, our welbeloued and faithfull knight William Sturmy, and our welbeloued clerke Iohn Kington, vpon our ambassage-affayres: hauing as yet in our desires, for a peaceable ending of the matter, (which, our foresayd ambassadors, by reason of the shortnes of time, or the finding out of some other remedie and happy conclusion of all and singular the foresaid attempts concerning the principall busines, could by no meanes at that instant attaine vnto) that vpon some other more conuenient day (to the end your ambassadors might not returne home altogether frustrate of their expectation) there might be, after the wonted friendly maner, a conference and agreement with your foresaid ambassadors, euen as by other letters of ours directed vnto your sayd ambassadors the second day of the moneth of Nouember aforesayd wee haue deliuered our mind vnto them. But it fortuned not long before the departure of your ambassadors into their owne countrey, that no sufficient shipping could be found wherein our sayd ambassadors might haue secure and safe passage vnto Dordract, or Middleburgh, neither was it thought that they should get any passage at all, till the ships at Middleborough were returned into our kingdome, by the force whereof they might be the more strongly wafted ouer. And so by reason of the departure of your ambassadours, all matters remaine in suspense till such time as the sayd ambassadors shall againe meete with ours to adde perfection vnto the busines as yet imperfect. Wherefore (our friend unfainedly beloued) desiring from the bottome of our heart that the integritie of loue, which hath from auncient times taken place betweene our and your subiects, may in time to come also be kept inuiolable, we haue thought good once again to send one of our foresaid ambassadors, namely William Esturmy knight to Dordract, giuing him charge thither to make haste, and there to stay, till some of your messengers, at your commandement doe in time conuenient repayre vnto that place, there (by Gods assistance) to bring the matter vnto an happy conclusion. May it please you therefore of your vnfayned friendship, without all inconuenience of delay, to returne, not vnto vs, but vnto our forenamed knight an answere in writing, what your will and determination is. Neither let it seeme strange vnto you, that we haue not at this present sent our forenamed Iohn Kington clerke together with the sayd William; for the cause of his abode with vs is, that he may in the meane season employ his care and diligence about those matters which muust be preparitues for the finall conclusion of the foresayd busines. Honorable sir, and most deare friend, we doe most heartily wish increase of prosperity and ioy vnto your person. [Sidenote: 1407.] Giuen in our palace of Westminster the 14. day of Feb. in the yeare of our Lord 1407.

* * * * *

To the right noble and valiant knight Sir William Sturmy sent at this present by the most souereigne King of England &c, as his ambassadour vnto Dordract, his most sincere friend.

Honorable sir, our most entier friend, wee receiued the royall letters of the most mighty prince and lord, our lord the king of England and France and lord of Ireland, sent vnto vs vnder the date of the 14. day of February (which we receiued at our castle of Marienburgh the 11. of April) containing, amongst other matters, that his Maiesties purpose was once againe to sende one of his ambassadors, namely your selfe our very sincere friend vnto Dordract, giuing you in charge that you would make haste thither and there stay; vntill some of our subiects might at our commandement, in conuenient time repaire vnto the same place, there (by God's assistance) to bring our matters vnto a happy conclusion. And then he requested that wee should without delay write our determination vnto you, as the conclusion of the said letter importeth. Howbeit (our most deare friend) the treaties and conferences about the redresse or reformation of uniust attempts committed by the subiects of our sayd lord and king and our subiects, one against another, are both on our behalfe, and on the behalfe of the common societie of the Hans marchants, hitherto had, made, and continued common. And so our commissioners vpon our full and absolute commandement, shal, for the managing of these and of other affaires of the foresaid societie, many waies vrgent and difficult, vpon the feast of our Lords Ascension next to come, meet with the said societie at Lubec, there to giue notice what they haue determined to conclude in this present busines and in others for their owne behalfe. For we will giue our ambassadours, which are there to appeare, streightly in charge that according to the kings request aforesayde they doe without delay procure an answere to be written vnto your honour concerning the determination of the foresayd societie. Giuen at the place and vpon the day aboue named, in the yeare of our Lord 1407.

Fr. Wemherus de Tettingen, commander in Elbing, general vice-master and lieutenant in the roome of the master generall of the Dutch knights of the Order of S. Marie &c. of late deceased.

* * * * *

The letters of Henry the 4. king of England &c vnto Vlricus de Iungingen Master generall of Prussia, 1408. wherein he doth ratifie and accept the last agreement made at Hage in Holland.

Henry &c. vnto the honourable and religious personage Fr. Vlricus de Iungingen Master generall of the Dutch knights of S. Marie &c. our most deare friend, greeting and dayly increase of our accustomed amity and friendship. We doe by these presents giue your honour to vnderstand, that our faithfull and welbeloued William Esturmy knight, and Master Iohn Kington clerke, our ambassadours and messengers sent of late on our behalfe, vnto the presence of your predecessour for the redressing of certaine grieuances and damages being contrary to iustice offered against vs and our liege subiects by the people and subiects of your predecessors, and against them also by our subiects as it is aforesayd, in friendly maner to be procured, of late returning out of the parts of Alemain made relation vnto vs and to our counsell, that hauing conferred with your forenamed predecessour about the foresayd affayres, the particulars following were at length concluded: namely first of all, that at a certaine day and place they should meete in Holland with his ambassadors and messengers, to hold a friendly conference betweene them about the redressing and reformation of the grieuances and damages aforesayd: and that they should by equall waight of diligent elimination ponder, and in the balance of iustice discusse and define al and singular the foresaid grieuances and damages inflicted on both parts. [Sidenote: A meeting at Hage the 28. of August 1407.] Howbeit at length after sundry prorogations then made and continued on this behalfe, our ambassadors and messengers aforesaid vpon the 28. of August last past, assembling themselues for our part at the towne of Hage in Holland, the hon. and discreete personages Arnold Heket burgomaster of the towne of Dantzik, and Iohn Crolowe, for the behalf of your subiects of Prussia, and Tidman de Meule, and Iohn Epenscheid for the behalfe of Liuonia, being assembled as messengers and commissioners about the redresse and reformation aforesayd, did then and there demaund in certaine articles, of our ambassadours and messengers aboue named 25034. nobles and half a noble, for the grieuances and damages offered (as it was then said) to your subiects of Prussia, and 24082. nobles 12. s. 8. d. in recompense of the damages offered vnto those your subiects of Liuonia. And when the substance of those articles about the grieuances and losses aforesayd was by the sayd ambassadours and messengers aboue named 25034. nobles and half a noble, for the grieuances and damages offered (as it was then said) to your subiects of Prussia, and 24082. nobles, 12. s. 8. d. in recompence of the damages offered vnto those your subiects of Liuonia. And when the substance of those articles about the grieuances and losses aforesayd was by the sayd ambassadours and messengers throughly examined and discussed, by their generall consent it was finally agreed, that your subiects, in consideration of all and singular the foresayd grieuances and damages offered vnto them by our people, should within three yeares after the feast of Easter next ensuing, at three equall payments receiue from vs, namely they of Prussia, 8957. nobles, and they of Liuonia 22496. nobles, six pence, halfepeny, farthing, and no more, so that we our selues thought good to condescend thereunto. Howbeit, forasmuch as certaine other goods of your subiects of Prussia, and also certaine articles in the behalfe of our subiects containing grieuous complaints in them, being propounded before the ambassadors and messengers aforesaid, for the attaining of reformation in regard of the damages and grieuances offered on both parts, could not as then, for the great obscurity of diuers of the sayd articles, and also for want of sufficient proofe at the last meeting appointed and held by the foresayd ambassadors at the towne of Hage in Holland, sufficiently to be examined, discussed, and defined, it was agreed vpon by the ambassadors and messengers of both partes, that from the 15. day of October then last expired vnto the feast of Easter now next ensuing, and from thenceforth within one whole yere immediately following, the plaintifes of both parts should throughly declare before our chancelour of England for the time being, the foresayd obscurities concerning the substance of their articles, and that they should, for the obtaining of execution, and complement of iustice at our sayd chancelours hands, peremtorily minister necessary probations, vnder paine of perpetuall exclusion from the petition of those things which are contayned in the articles aboue mentioned.

Prouided alwayes, that if at the last it shall be by lawfull proofes made manifest concerning the summes aboue written or any part or parcell thereof, that due satifaction hath beene made, to him or them vnto whom it was due, or that those goods of and for the which complaint hath bene made on the behalfe of your subiects haue pertained or doe appertaine vnto others, or any other iust, true, and reasonable cause may lawfully bee alleaged, why the payment of all the foresayd summes or any of them ought not to be performed: that then so much only is to be cut off or deducted from the sayd summes as shall be found to be already payd or to pertaine vnto others, or else vpon some true, iust, and reasonable cause (as is aforesayd) not to be due. We therefore considering that the sayd friendly conference, and the finall agreement ensuing thereupon are agreeable vnto reason and equitie, doe, for our part ratifie and willingly accept the very same conference and agreement. And forasmuch as it hath bene alwayes our desire, and is as yet our intention, that the league of amity and the integritie of loue, which hath of olde time bene obserued betwene our and your subiects; may in times to come perpetually remaine inuiolable, and that your and our people may hereafter, not onely for the good of our common weale but also for the commodity and peace of both parts, according to their woonted maner, assemble themselues and enioy the faithfull and mutuall conuersation one of another: we will cause in our citie of London, with the Summe of 8957. nobles satisfaction to bee made vnto the Prussians, and with the summe of 22496. nobles, sixe pence, halfe peny, farthing, recompense to be performed vnto the Liuonians, in regard of the damages and iniuries (which in very deede proceeded not of our consent) by our subiects offered vnto them, as it is afore sayd, and within three yeares after the feast of Easter next ensuing the sayd summes of money to bee payed at three payments, and by three equal portions. Conditionally that vnto our subiects which be endamaged correspondent satisfaction be likewise on your part within the terme of the foresayd three yeres performed, with paying the summes of 766. nobles and of 4535. nobles, demaunded on our bchalfe, and also with the payment of such summes as within one yeere immediately ensuing the feast of Easter aforesayd, shallbe found by sufficient declarations and proofes to be made on the behalfe of our subiects (as is aforesayd) to be due. Euen as we in like maner will make satisfaction vnto your subiects within our citie aforesayd. Now as touching the request of your ambassadors and of the Liuonians whereby we were required to procure some holesome remedy for the soules of certaine drowned persons, as conscience and religion seemeth to chalenge (in regard of whom we are moued with compassion, and do for their sakes heartily condole their mishaps) you are (our entier friend), of a certaintie to vnderstand, that after we shall be by your letters aduertized of the number, state, and condition of the sayd parties drowned, we will cause suffrages of prayers and diuers other holesome remedies profitable for the soules of the deceased and acceptable to God and men, religiously to be ordained and prouided: vpon condition, that for the soules of our drowned countrey men there be the like remedie prouided by you. The almighty grant vnto your selfe and vnto your whole Order, that, you may prosperously triumph ouer the enemies of Christ his crosse. Giuen vnder our priuie seale at our palace of Westminster the 26. of March, in the yeere of our lord 1408. and in the ninth yere of our reigne.

* * * * *

The letters of Fr: Vlricus Master of Prussia directed vnto the king of England, signifying that he is contented with the agreements concluded by his messengers at Hage.

To the most renowmed prince and mighty lord L. Henrie king of England and
France, and lord of Ireland, our most gracious lord.

Vnto your highnes pleasure at all assaies humbly recommending my voluntarie seruice &c. Most renowned king, mighty prince, and gracious Lord, we receiued of late with great reuerence as it becommeth vs, by our wellbeloued Arnold de Dassel the bearer of these presents, your Maiesties letters of late directed vnto vs, making mention amongst other matters of certaine appointments first made and concluded between the noble and worthy personages William Esturmy knight, Iohn Kington clerke, and

William Brampton citizen of London your ambassadours and messengers on the one parte, and our honorable and religious brethren, namely Conradus Lichtensten great commander, Warnherus de Tettingen chiefe hospitalary and commander in Elbing, and Arnold de Hacken treasurer, being the procuratours and commissioners of Fra. Conradus de Iungingen our last predecessour of famous memory on the other parte, concerning the redressing, reformation, and amendement of vniust attempts committed on both sides, at our castle of Marienburgh, and also very lately at the towne of Hage in Holland, namely the twenty eight of the moneth August in the yeare immediately past, betweene your foresayde ambassadours William Esturmy knight, and Iohn Kington clerke, for your part, and our trusty and welbeloued commissioners and procurators, namely Arnold Hecht burgomaster of our citie of Dantzik, and Iohn Crolow citizen of the same citie, for our parte. And for our more perfect knowledge in this behalfe, our sayd commissioners made relation vnto vs and vnto our whole counsell, that associating vnto themselues our messengers of Liuonia, namely, Tidman Myeul, and Iohn Epensheid, together with your foresaid ambassadours and messengers, they there finally appoynted and concluded, of and about the aboue mentioned summes of money due on both partes, of the which mention is made in your letters aforesayd. [Sidenote: Here relation is had vnto the king of the Romans.] With this special prouiso that in like manner satisfaction be made in all points, both vnto other of our damnified subiects of Prussia, namely such whose goods or the true value thereof haue bene finally adiudged by the iudges or professors of our lawes, and vnto such who hauing brought their articles of complaints vnto the audience of the most dread and mighty prince and lorde, our lord Rupertus king of the Romans alwayes most soueraigne, were in conclusion to haue the estimations of their goods to be adiudged by the sentence of the sayd lord, with the aduise of two of his counsellors, and also vnto other of our subiects who haue brought in sufficient proofe of damages uniustly inflicted vpon them by your subiects, ouer and besides the premisses. So that in like maner satisfaction be made vnto the common societie of the Hans marchants: and by the arbitrament set downe in the conferences had at Marienburgh, of the which it was aboue prouided and enacted on their behalfe, namely if they will rest contented with our subiects in the courses and meanes then concluded. If not, we intend not at all to adhere vnto them in this behalfe. Afterward our messengers aforesayd, both they of Prussia and of Liuonia demanded conuenient, iust, and speedy satisfaction, with the payment of all and singular the summes aboue mentioned due vnto both parts (so farre foorth as equity and reason would yeeld vnto, for the recompense of the parties iniuried and endamaged on both sides) to be made within one whole yere accompting from the feast of Easter now last expired vnto the very same feast next to come in the yere immediatly following, and that in three seueral termes of payment, by three portions of the said summes equally to be diuided, at the towne of Bruges in Flanders as being a place indifferent for all parties, in maner and forme as it was before at Marienburgh required and stoode vpon: namely that reformation, reparation, and amendement of all uniust attempts committed on both parts ought to bee performed within one yere. Howbeit contrariwise your ambassadors aforesayd decreed that the sayd satisfaction should be performed vnto the parties iniuried of both parts within three yeeres, beginning to accompt from the feast of Easter last past. And when your ambassadours were not contented with the maner of satisfaction set downe by our men, nor our commissioners were willing in any sort to consent vnto that course which was thought conuenient by your ambassadors, the honorable messengers of the sea-townes of the Hans being there at that time present, made a motion that the foresayd satisfaction might be performed within two yeeres and a halfe, accompting from the feast of Easter last past, often before mentioned: yet vnder a certaine protestation, namely if both parties should agree vnto that forme of satisfaction, and if they should thinke good finally and conclusiuely to yeeld their consent vnto it. Which kind of satisfaction also conceiued by the messengers, your sayd ambassadours without giuing notice thereof vnto your royall Maiestie, refused finally to approue; being rather desirous to make a true and faithfull report of the sayd forme of satisfaction last aboue mentioned vnto your kingly highnesse, and that in such sorte, that (as they hoped) effectuall satisfaction and payment of all and singuler the summes due and to bee due on both partes should more conueniently and speedily bee performed. Whereupon we might be put in good hope, that more speedy and conuenient appointments of termes, for the sayd satisfaction friendly on both parts to to be performed in, would haue proceeded from your bountifull and gracious clemencie. And in very deede (most mighty prince) albeit it was neuer the meaning of our foresayd predecessor, so for foorth as these affayres concerned him, to protract and delay the execution of the sayd busines so many and such long distances of time, and that for diuers respects, both because restitution vnto the parties robbed consisted herein, and also because the sayd restitutions and satisfactions are to be made vnto poore people, widowes, orphanes, and other miserable creatures, diuersly and miserably slaine and oppressed: notwithstanding we being moued with hearty and feruent zeale and speciall affection vnto your royall crowne of England, and hauing due regard and consideration of your most excellent Maiestie, upon the aduise of our honourable brethren our counsellors, doe thankfully recieue, and by the tenour of these presents totally ratifie and approue such satisfactions of the foresayd summes howsoeuer due vnto our subiects both Prussians and Liuonians, in friendly sorte to be performed at such times and occasons limited and prefixed by your highnes as are expressed in your maiesties letters, and also of other sammes which within one yeare immediately ensuing after the feast of Easter last past, by sufficient proofes to be madee on their part before your chancelour at your citie of London shall be found due vnto them. Conditionally that without inconuenience of delay and impediment they be performed as they ought to be, according to the premisses. In like maner also we our selues within the termes of payment aboue mentioned will procure satisfaction to be without fayle perfourmed vnto your subiects endamaged, with the summe of 766. nobles being in regard of their losses, of the which they haue giuen vp sufficient informations due vnto them: and with other like summes also which are by sufficient proofes, within the yeare aforesayd, and in maner and forme prescribed to be exhibited before our treasurer at our citie of Dantzik. [Sidenote: Septem. 27. 1408.] The almighty vouchsafe prosperously and longtime to preserue your maieisties royal person. Giuen at our castle of Marienburgh the 27. of September, in the yeare of our Lord 1408.

Fr. Vlricus de Tungingen master generall of the order of the Dutch-knights of S. Maries hospital of Ierusalem.

* * * * *

The letters of king Henry the 4. sent vnto F. Vlricus master general of Prussia, wherein he doth absolutely approue the foresaid conference holden at Hage, and treateth about a perpetual league and amitie to be concluded betweene England and Prussia.

Henry by the grace of God king of England and France and lord of Ireland, vnto the noble and mighty personage of sacred religion Vlricus de Iungingen master generall of the order of the Dutch knights of S. Maries hospitall of Ierusalem, our entirely beloued friend, greeting and increase of vnfained friendship. After diuers conferences had in sundry places beyond the seas betweene the ambassadours and messengers of your late predecessor and of your selfe also, on the one parte, and betweene our especiall ambassadors and messengers on the other parte, concerning reformations, reparations, and restitutions in certaine maner and forme to be performed vnto our subiects of both parts, in regard of manifold iniuries practised against them both, and after that, in the last conference holden by the ambassadours of vs both at the towne of Hage at Holland, there was a motion made concerning a certaine forme of satisfaction, by way of finall conclusion in that behalfe: but not being as then by our ambassadours condescended vnto, because they durst not proceede vnto the same conclusion without our priuitie, relation thereof at length being by them made before vs and our counsel; we returned vnto your honour an answere in writing by our letters vnder our priuie seale, of our full purpose and intention (vnto the which letters we doe at this present referre our selues, as if they were here again expressly written) what we thought good to haue done in this behalfe: so that we also might by your friendly letters be certaynly informed of your will and express consent, being likewise conformable vnto our foresayd intention. Nowe whereas since that time we haue of late receiued the certaintie of the matter by your letters written vnto vs from your castle of Marienburgh, bearing date the 27. of September last past, contayning in effect amongst other matters, that you beeing mooued with a feruent zeale and speciall affection (as you write) vnto the royall crowne of our realme, and hauing due regard and consideration of our royall maiestie, vpon the aduise of your honourable brethren your counsellers, doe with a thankful mind accept, and by the tenour of the said letters of yours totally approue the concord of a certaine satisfaction to be performed with the payment of certaine summes of money howsoeuer due vnto your subiects as well of Prussia as of Liuonia, expressed in our former letters, within the termes prefixed by our consent and limited in our said letters, and also of other summes which within one whole yeare immediately following the feast of Easter last past, be sufficient proofes on their part to bee made before our chauncelour at our citie of London, shall be found due vnto them: conditionally, that without inconuenience of delay and impediments, the premisses be performed as they ought to be. And that your selfe also will without fayle, vpon the termes appointed for the said payments, procure satisfaction to be made accordingly vnto our endamaged subiects with the summes due vnto them by reason of their losses, whereof they haue sufficient information. Wherefore in regard of those your friendly letters, and your courteous answere returned by them vnto vs, as is aforesaid, wee doe yeelde vnto you right vnfained thanks. [Sidenote: A motion for a perpetuall league.] But because it will vndoubtedly be most acceptable and pleasing both vnto vs and vnto our people, and vnto you and your subiects that the zeale and feruencie of loue which hath from auncient times growen and increased betweene our progenitours for them and their subiects, and your predecessors and their subiects, and which by the insolencie of certayne lewde persons, without any consent of the principall lords, hath often bene violated betweene vs and you and mutually betweene the subiects of vs both may be put in perpetuall vre and obtaine full strength in time to come, sithens hereupon (by Gods assistance) it is to be hoped, that vspeakable commodity and quiet will redound vnto both parts: may it seeme good vnto your discretion, as it seemeth expedient vnto vs, that some messengers of yours sufficiently authorised to parle, agree, and conclude with our deputy, about the mutuall contraction of a perpetuall league and confimation of friendship, may with all conuenient speede be sent vnto our presence. At whose arriuall, not onely in this busines so profitable and behoouefull, but also in certaine other affaires concerning the former treaties and conclusions, they may, yea and of necessitie must greatly auayle. Wherefore (our entirely beloued friend) euen as vpon confidence of the premisses we haue thought good to grant vnto the marchants and subiects of our realme full authority to resort vnto your dominions, so we doe in like maner graunt vnto your marchants and subiects free licence and liberty with their marchandises and goods securely to come into our realmes and dominions, there to stay, and at their pleasures thence to returne home. Moreouer, if Arnold Dassel, who last of all presented your foresayd letters vnto vs, shal thinke good in the meane season to make his abode here in our dominions (as in very deede it is expedient) he may both by serious consideration and deliberate consulting with our commissioners more conueniently and prosperously finde out wayes and meanes, for the more speedy expedition of all the premisses. Fare ye well in Christ, Giuen vnder our priuie seale at our palace of Westminster, the seuenth of March, in the yere of our lord 1408. according to the computation of the church of England, and in the tenth yere of our reigne.

* * * * *

A new concord concluded between king Henry the 4. and Vlricus de Iungingen
  Master generall of Prussia in the yeare of our Lord 1409.

By this indenture or letters indented be it euidently knowen (for the perpetual memory of the matter) vnto all faithfull Christians, that the noble and honourable personages Richard Merlowe Maior and citizen of London, Master Iohn Kington clerke, and William Askham citizen and Alderman of the same citie, the commissioners of the most soueraigne prince and lord, L. Henrie by the grace of God king of England and France, and lord of Ireland, and Tidericus de Longenthorpe knight, Lefardus de Hereford burgomaster of Elbing, and Iohn Crolowe citizen of the citie of Dantzik, the procurators, commissioners, deputies, and messengers of the right noble and religious personage Fr. Vlricus de Iungingen Master general of the order of the Dutch knights of S. Maries hospital of Ierusalom, hauing in the names of the sayd king and Master by vertue of the power on both parts committed vnto them, sufficient authority, haue appointed and with one consent agreed vpon all and singular the things vnder written.

1. Imprimis for the conseruation and mutuall loue and wonted amitie, and for the tranquilitie of sweete amiable peace, it is decreed and ordained, that all and singular the liege people and subiects of the Realme of England and the marchants of the territories and dominions of the said Realme and all other persons of what state or condition soeuer, shall and may safely and securely, as well by land as by water enter into the parts of Prussia, and

there mutually conuers and freely after the Maner of marchants exercise traffique aswell with the Prussians as with others, of what nation or qualitie soeuer, there also make their abode, and thence vnto their owne homes and dwelling places returne, and depart vnto any place whither and so often as they shall thinke good, as well by land as by water, with their goods merchandize, and wares whatsoeuer; faithfully paying in the meane time all rights and customes due in regard of their said wares and marchandize. Reserued alwaies vnto the said Master and his sucessours all right and remedie ordained, granted, and vouchsafed in certaine obligations by our Lord the king, whereof mention shall be made in the articles following.

2. It is ordained, that all and singular the subiects of the said Master generall and of his order, of what state and condition soeuer, shall and may, as well by water as by land enter into the kingdome of England and into the territories, and dominions, thereof, and there mutually conuerse, and freely after the maner of Marchants exercise traffique as well with all English people as with others of what nation or qualitie soeuer, and there also make their abode, and thence returne vnto their owne habitations and dwelling places, and to deport whither they will and as oft as they shall thinke good as well by land as by water, with their goods, marchandize and wares whatsoeuer: truely paying in the meane time all rights and customes due in regard of their said wares and Marchandize. Reserued alwayes vnto the said soueraigne king, his heires and successours, all rights and remedies ordained and graunted vnto them in certaine obligations, by the commissioners and procurators of the said Master generall aboue-named, and in the name of the said Master generall.

3. Item it is with one consent agreed upon, promised, and granted that for all and singular damages, grieuances, and robberies howsoeuer done and committed before the date of these presents against the foresaid soueraigne Prince and his subiects whatsoeucr, and all others which at the time of the grieuances, damages, and robberies aforesaid, were, or at this present are the said soueraigne king his subiects; there are due to be payed vnto the said king or his successours by the said Master generall or his successours, in full satisfaction and recompence of the damages, grieuances, and robberies aboue written, certaine summes of English money: euen as in the letters obligatorie made by the said Master generall his procurators and messengers aboue named in this behalfe, and sealed with their seales, and deliuered vnto the forenamed procurators and commissioners of our said Lord the king it is expressed more at large.

4. Item it is couenanted, graunted, and promised, that no subiect of the said Master generall or of his successours, by reason or occasion of the damages, grieuances, and robberies aforesaid, shall, by the said soueraigne king or his successours or by their authoritie or commandement, or by

another person whatsoeuer who in regard of the foresaid losses, grieuances and robberies hath bene molested and damnified, or at the procurement or instant suite of any, be attached, arrested, imprisoned, or detained; nor that the goods of the said Master generall, or of his successors, or of any of them, shal be laid hold on, arrested, or detained.

5. Item it is couenanted and ordained, that if any of the liege people and subiects of the sayde Master generall or of his successors shall, contrary to the forme of the concord and graunt next aboue-written, chance to be molested or endamaged: that then the foresaid soueraigne Lord the King and his successors the kings of England are bound to make full satisfaction for all such losses as the subiects of the said Master generall or of his successours or any of them shall for that cause haue vniustly sustained, vnto the parties endamaged. Which thing if the foresaid soueraigne Prince, or his successours in the Realme of England, being conueniently requested by the letters of the said Master generall or of his successours shall refuse to doe, that then after the terme of sixe moneths immediately following the said deniall or refusall, it shalbe right lawfull for the Master generall that now is and for any of his successours in time to come (hauing first made conuenient proofe that the foresaid request was by him or them exhibited) to arrest so many goods of the foresaid king his subiects found in the land of Prussia, as may suffice for the reasonable satisfaction and recompense of any person or persons whatsoeuer vniustly molested in this behalfe; and also to detaine the said goods under arrestes, vntil condigne satisfaction and amends be made vnto the party or parties molested.

6. Item by the commissioners and procuratours often aboue named it is couenanted, promised, and graunted, that for all and singular the damages, molestations and robberies by the foresayde soueraigne king his liege people and subiects howsoeuer before the date of these presents committed and offred against the said Master general or against any of his subiects whether Prussians or Liuonians, and against all others who at the time of the damages, grieuances and robberies aforesaid were, or at this present are the subiects of the Master generall aforesaid (except notwithstanding certaine damages and grieuances hereafter to be mentioned, whereof also some prouisoes shalbe had in the articles following, which damages were before the date of these presents by the said soueraigne king his liege people and subiects inflicted vpon certaine subiects of the foresaid general Master, especially them of Prussia which hereafter shalbe named) there are certaine summes of money due to be payed vnto the said Master generall or vnto his successours by the said soueraigne Prince or his successours for the full satisfaction of the foresaid damages, molestations and robberies inflicted vpon the Prussians and Liuonians, and the others mentioned, euen as in the leters obligatorie of the said soueraigne Lord the king made in this

behalfe, being giuen and deliuered vnto the said Master generall his procuratours and messengers, it is declared more at large.

7. Item, it is couenanted, granted and promised, that none of the liege people or subiects of the foresaid soueraigne prince or of his heires shall, by reason or occasion of the damages, grieuances and robberies aforesaid, by the sayd Master generall or his successours or by their authoritie and commandement, or by any other who in respect of the said damages, grieuances and robberies aboue mentioned, hath beene molested or damnified, or by any of their procurements or instant suites shalbe attached, arrested, imprisoned or detained: nor that any goods of the subiects of the said soueraigne king or his heires or any of them, shall bee attached, arrested, or detained. Reserued always vnto the forenamed Master generall and his subiects all right and remedie any way requisite or competent vnto them by meanes of the obligations aforesaid.

8. Item it is couenanted and agreed that if any of the liege people or subiects of the sayde soueraigne prince or of his heires and successours shall (contrary to the forme of concord and graunt next aboue-written) chaunce to bee molested or endamaged; that then the saide Master generall and his successours, for all losses and hindrances which the liege people and subiects of the foresayde soueraigne prince or of his heires or successours, shall by that meanes haue vniustly sustained, are bound to make full satisfaction vnto the partie endamage. Which if the Master generall aforesaid or his successors being conueniently requested by the letters of the sayde soueraigne prince or of his heires, shall refuse to doe; that then, after the space of sixe moneths next ensuing the time of the foresayde request, it may bee right lawfull for the forenamed soueraigne prince that nowe is, or that then for that time shall be (conuenient proofe being first brought, that the foresayd request had conueniently beene exhibited) to arrest so many goods of the sayde Master generall his subiects founde in the Realme of England, as may suffice for the reasonable satisfaction and amends of any person or persons vniustly molested in this behalfe; and also to detaine the sayde goods vnder safe custodie, vntill condigne satisfaction and amends be made vnto the partie or parties aggrieued.

9. Item it is couenanted that besides the summes due vnto the sayde Master generall and his successours in the behalfe of his subiects both of Prussia and of Liuonia (whereof mention is made in the former articles) there are due to be payed vnto the sayde Master generall and his successours, for sundry other damaged, grieuances, and robberies against himselfe and diuers other of his subiects of Prussia, namely. Matthewe Ludekensson, Arnold Ashen, Henri Culeman, Iohn Vnkeltop, Iohn Halewater, Egghard Scoffe of Dantzik, and Nicolas Wolmerstene of Elbing, done and

committed by the sayde soueraigne king his liege people and subiects vnder-written, euen before the date of these presents, for the full satisfaction of the sayde damages, grieuances and robberies, certaine summes of nobles hereafter following. Namely Imprimis by Tutburie, and Terry of Hull, 82. nobles, which are due vnto the foresaid Matthew Ludekinson. Item by Nicholas Scot of Caleis the sonne of Tutbury, and Hilg of Hull, 256. nobles, which are due vnto the foresayd Arnold de Aschen. Item by the inhabitants of Scardeburgh, Blakeney, and Crowmer (who had one Iohn Iolly of Blakeney for their captaine) 156. nobles, which are due vnto Henrie Culeman aforesayd. Item by the inhabitants of Bayon (Whose Capitaine was one Pideuille) 125. nobles which are due vnto the said Iohn Vnkeltop. Item by the inhabitants of Plymmouth and Dertmouth (whose Captaines were Henrie Pay, and William Gadeling) 600. nobles which are due vnto the foresayde Iohn Halewater, in respect of his goods by them violently taken away. [Sidenote: A ship of the burthen of 300. tonnes.] Item 334. nobles to be payed by the selfe same parties, being due vnto the sayde Iohn Halewater by reason that they detained his ship from him three moneths and more, which ship was of the burthen of three hundreth tonnes of wine, and had in it all the foresayde time fiue and fourtie seruants maintained at the expenses of the sayde Iohn Halewater. Item that Sir William de Ethingham knight, who was Vice-admirall for the sea, must bee summoned to alleage a reasonable cause (for that the sayd Sir William with his seruants expelled the said Iohn Halewater out of his ship for the space of fifteene dayes together, and tooke of the goods and victuals of the said Iohn to the summe of 114. nobles) why he ought not to pay the said summe of 114. nobles vnto Iohn Halewater aforesaid: which if hee shall not bee willing nor able to alleage before the first of April next ensuing, that then by the kings authoritie hee must be compelled to pay vnto the foresaid Iohn the said 114 nobles. Item by the inhabitants of Caleis (whose captaines were Michael Scot, Bishop, and William Horneby) 1900. nobles, which are due vnto the foresayde Eggard Scoff, because the saide soueraigne king hath giuen them in charge by the said Michael Scot and the rest concerning the payment of the summe aforesaid. Item by Iohn Bilis neere vnto Crowmer, 68. nobles, which are due vnto Nicholas Wolmersten of Elbing. Which summes of nobles must by the kings authority be leuied at the hands of his subiects aboue-mentioned betweene the time that nowe is and the feast of the Purification of the blessed virgine which shall fall in the yeere of our Lord 1411. effectually to bee deliuered and payed vnto the sayd Master generall or his lawfull procurator, or vnto his successours or their lawfull procuratours, at the Citie of London, vpon the feast aforesaid.

Item it is couenanted that besides the summes specified in the foresayde letters obligatorie, made in the behalfe of the said soueraigne prince, there are due to be paied vnto one Iohn Marion of Wersingham lately deceased being in his life-time the liege subiect of the foresaid soueraigne prince 200. nobles of Knglish money in regard of certaine iniuries and robberies done and committed before the date of these presents against the foresayde Iohn, by one Eghard Scoff, subiect vnto the said deceased Iohn, his wife, children, heires, or executors by the said Egghard, his heires or by the administrators of his goods at the time and place aboue mentioned.

10 Item, it is couenanted, confirmed, and promised, that for all the iniuries and robberies done and committed against one Iohn Dordewant of Elbing, being in his life time subiect vnto the sayd Master generall, by the liege people and subiects of the said soueraigne king the inhabitants of the Scardeburgh before the date of these presents; for the full recompense of all such iniuries and robberies, there must bee payed vnto one Iohn Gruk of Dantzik eight hundred nobles of English money, vpon the feast of Easter next following in the Citie of London by them of Scardeburgh being guilty and culpable in this behalfe; who are by definitiue sentence condemned vnto the said Iohn in the summe of 800. nobles by reason of the iniuries and robberies aforesaid, except the lawfull expenses in this behalfe layed out: they are also taxed in due time for the issue. And therefore the foresayde condemned parties (whose names are in the sentence against them pronounced in this behalfe more expresly conteined) must in the meane season by the kings authority be compelled and constrained really and actually to obey the foresayd sentence, namely by deliuering and paying vnto Iohn Gruk the summe of 800. nobles at the time and place aboue mentioned, with reasonable expences, wherein also the said parties stand condemned, their lawfull taxation being reserued.

Item it is couenanted and granted, that the heires of Lord Henrie du Percy the younger after they shall come vnto lawfull age, and shall haue attained vnto the possession and goods of their inheritance, must be compelled by the kings authoritie (iustice going before) to make satisfaction vnto the great procurator of Marienburgh with the summe of 838. nobles in lieu of certaine corne and graine which the foresaid Lord Henrie, in the yeere 1403, bought and receiued of the said great procuratour, for the vse of the castle of Zutberwik. In testimonie and confirmation of all the which premisses, the said Tedericus Lefardus, and Iohn Crolow, of their certaine knowledges haue put their seales vnto these present letters indented, in the presence of the aboue-named Richard Merlow, Iohn Kington, and William Askam, commissioners for the behalfe of England giuen at the Citie of London in England the fourth day of December, in the yeere of our Lord 1409.

* * * * *

That the Brittons were in Italie and Greece with the Cimbrians and Gaules, before the incarnation of Christ. M. Wil. Camden, pag. 33.

[Sidenote: Triadum Liber.] Britannos autem cum Cimbris et Gallis permistos fuisse in expeditionibus illis in Italiam et Græciam videtur. Nam præter nomen commune in Britannico Triadum libro vetustissimo, vbi tres maximi exercitus, qui è Britannis conscripti erant, memorantur, proditum est, exterum quendam ducem longè maximum exercitum hinc contraxisse, qui, populata magna Europæ parte tandem ad Græcum mare (forsitan Galatiam innuit) consederit.

Britomarum item ducem inter illos militarem, cuius meminit Florus et Appianus, Britonem fuisse nomen euincit, quod Britonem magnum significat.
Nec torquebo illud Strabonis, qui Brennum natione Prausum fuisse scribit vt
natione Britonem faciam.

The same in English.

It is not vnlike that the Britons accompanied the Cimbrians and Gaules in those expeditions to Italy and Greece. For besides the common name, it is recorded in that most ancient British booke called Liber Triadum, (wherein also mention is made of three huge armies that were leuied out of Britaine) that a certaine outlandish captaine gathered from hence a mightie armie; who hauing wasted a great part of Europe, at length tooke vp his abode (perhaps the Author meaneth in Gallatia) neere vnto the sea of Greece.

Likewise that the warrelike captaine Britomarus (of whom Floras and Appian doe make report) was himselfe a Briton, his very name doeth testifie, which signifieth A great Briton. Neither will I wrest that testimony of Strabo (who reporteth Brennus to haue bene a Prause by birth) that I may prooue him also to haue bene a Briton borne.

* * * * *

The trauaile of Helena.

Helena Flauia Augusta serenissimi Coeli Britannici Regis Hæres, et vnica filia, Magni Constantini Cæsaris mater, incomparabili decore, fide, religione, bonitate, ac magnificentiâ piâ, Eusebio etiam teste, per totum resplenduit orbem: Inter omnes ætatis suæ foeminas, nulla inueniebatur eâ in liberalibus artibus doctior, nulla in instrumentis musicis peritior, aut in linguis nationum copiosior. Innatam habebat ingenij claritudinem, oris facundiam, ac morum ornatissimam compositionem: Hebraicè, Græcè et Latinè erudita. Caruerat pater alia sobole (inquit Virumnius) quæ Regni solio potiretur. Illam proprerea his instrui fecit per optimos præceptores, vt eò commodius

Regni tractaret negotia. Vnde ob incredibilem eius pulchritudinem, atque alias eximias animi et corporis dotes, Constantius Chlorus Cæsar illam duxit in vxorem, atque ex eâ filium in Britanniâ genuit Constantinum Magnum. Sed eo tandem Eboraci defuncto, cum Annâ illâ Euangelicâ, in sanctâ viduitate perdurauit ad vltimum vitæ diem, tota Christianæ religione dedita. Sunt enim authores, qui narrent per instam, cessante persecutione, pacem Ecclesijs datam: Ad tantam coelestis Philosophiæ; cognitionem cam ferunt post agnitum Euangelium peruenisse, vt olim multos ediderit libros, et carmina quaædam Græca, quæ hucúsque à Pontico superesse perhibentur. Visionibus admonita Hierosolymam petijt, et onmia saluatoris loca perlustrauit. Romæ tandem octogenaria foeliciter in Christo quieuit 15. Kalendas Septembris, filio adhuc superstite, anno salutis humanæ 337. Regnante apud Britannos Octauio. Huius corpus non minimâ nunc curâ Venetijs seruatur.

The same in English.

Helena. Flauia Augusta, the heire and onely daughter of Coelus sometime the most excellent King of Britaine, the mother of the Emperour Constantine the great, by reason of her singular beautie, faith, religion, goodnesse and godly Maiestie (according to the testimonie of Eusebius) was famous in all the world. Amongst all the women of her time, there was none either in the liberall arts more learned, or in instruments of musike more skilfull, or in the diuers languages of nations more abundant than herselfe. She had a naturall quicknesse or excellency of wit, eloquence of speech, and a most notable grace in all her behauiour. She was seene in the Hebrew, Greeke and Latine tongues.

Her father (as Virumnius reporteth) had no other childe to succeed in the kingdome after him but her, and therefore caused her to be instructed in these things by the best teachers, that thereby she might the better in time gouerne the Realme: so that by reason of her passing beautie, and other her excellent giftes of body and minde, Constantius Chlorus the Emperour married her, and had by her a sonne called Constantine the great, while hee remained in Britaine. Who at length deceasing at Yorke, this Helena (no otherwise then Anna of whom mention is made in the new Testament) continued a vertuous and holy widow to the end of her life.

There are some writers which doe affirme, that persecution ceased, and peace was granted to the Christian Churches by her good meanes.

After the light and knowledge of the Gospel, she grewe so skilfull in diuinitie, that shee wrote and composed diuers bookes and certaine Greeke verses also, which (as Ponticus reporteth) are yet extant. Being warned by some visions she went to Ierusalem, and visited all the places there, which Christ had frequented. She liued to the age of fourescore yeeres, and then died at Rome the 15 day of August in the yeere of oure redemption 337. Octauius being then king of Britaine, and her sonne Constantine the Emperour then also liuing, and her body is to this day very carefully preserued at Venice.

* * * * *

The life and trauels of Constantine the great, Emperour and king of Britaine.

Flauius Constantinus cognomento Magnus post Genitorum Constantium Britannorum Rex, ac Romanorum Cæsar Augustus, ex Britannica matre in Britannia natus, et in Britannia creatus Imperator, patriam natalem magnificè suæ gloria; participem fecit, Profligatis Alemanis, Hispanis, et Francis, eorúmque Regibus pro spectaculo bestijs obiectis, Galliam subiectam tenuit: Tres Helenæ matris auunculos Brittanos, Leolinum, Traherum, et Marium, quos cæteris semper fidentiores habuerat in suis fortunis, Italis à Maxentij tyrannide foelicitèr liberatis, in Senatorum ordinem Romæ promouit. Innumeræ in eo (vt Eutropius habet) claruêre tam animi, quàm corporis virtutes, dum appetentissnnus esset gloriæ militaris, successu semper in bellis prospero. Inter literas tam Græcas quàm Latinas, à Christianissima matre Helena Christi fidem edoctus, eos honorabat præcipué [Transcriber's note: 'præciqué' in original] qui in Philosophia Christiana vitam reclinassent. Vnde ab oceani finibus nempe Britannis incipiens, ope fretus diuina, religionis curam in medijs superstitionum tenebris cepit, ab Occiduis ad Indos, innumeras ad æternæ spem vitæ erigens gentes. Animum diuinis exercendo studijs, noctes trahebat insomnes, et quæsita scribendi diuerticula per otium frequentabat: Imperium oratione, ac Sanctis operationibus continendum ratus, Egregius Christianæ disciplinæ præco, filios ac proceres docuit, pietatem diuitijs omnibus, atque adeò ipsi anteferre totius mundi Monarchiæ. Falsorum deorum euersor. Imaginum cultus per Græciam, Ægyptum, Persiam, Asiam, et vniuersam ditionem Romanam, repetitis abrogat legibus, iubens per edicta Christum coli, Euangelium prædicari sacrum, Ministris honores, et alimenta dari, atque idolorum vbíque destrui templa. Et vt fidei forma cunctis videretur, Euangelium Iesu Christi ante se semper ferri fecit, et Biblia sacra ad omnes prouincias destinari, diademáque Monarchicum primus Britannis regibus dedit: Ecclesijs infinita præstitit, agros, annonam, stipem egenis, ægris, viduis, ac orphanis, pro quibusque vt pater sollicitus. Eusebium, Lactantium, et similes, familiarissimos habuit, et hanc ad Deum orationem indiès ipsis in eius vita testibus fudit. Vnum et Deum esse nouimus, vnum te Regem intelligimus, appellamus adiutorem, nobis abs te victoria cecidit, ex te Aduersarium fudimus, &c. Pro delicijs habuit, vt Sextus Aurelianus tradit, literarum studia colere, bonos artes fouere, legere, scribere, meditari: composuit Græcè et Latinè multos libros et Epistolas. E vita Nicomediæ discessit Senex, ætatis suæ Anno 66. et Imperij 32. à Christi verò incarnatione 339. Constantinopoli sepultus, Octauio in Britannijs regnante. Eius vitam in quatuor libris Eusebius Cæsariensis Græcè scripsit, et Ioannes Portesius Gallus in Latinum transtulit sermonem.

The same in English.

Flauius Constantine, surnamed the great, king of the Britaines after his father, and Emperor of the Romanes, borne in Britanie of Helena his mother, and there created Emperour, made his natiue countrey partaker of his singular glory and renoume.

Hauing conquered and put to flight the Almanes, Spaniards, Frenchmen, and their Kings for a spectacle throwen out to wild beasts, he held France it selfe as subiect vnto him: and hauing happily deliuered the Italians from the tyrannie of Maxentius, he preferred three of his mothers vncles, all Britaines, namely, Leoline, Trahere, and Marius, whom in all his actions he had found more faithfull vnto him then any others, to be of the order of the Romane Senators.

Eutropius reporteth, that he infinitely excelled in the vertues both of the mind and body also, and that hauing a pleasure in the practise of warre, and in the iust commendation, of Martiall prowesse, he neuer pitched his field but his successe in the battel was always victorious. His mother Helena hauing instructed him in the faith of Christ, although hee made much of all men that were learned in the Greeke and Latine tongues, yet he yeelded speciall honor to those that spent their time in the studie of Diuinitie, which he called Christian Philosophie: so that beginning at the furthest part of the Ocean sea, which then was taken to be his owne natiue soyle of Britaine, and trusting in the assistance of God, when the darkenes of superstition was most thicke, then hee vndertooke a care of Religion, stirring vp innumerable nations from the West as farre as India it selfe, to the hope of eternall life.

Hee passed many nightes without sleepe, hauing his minde occupied in diuine studies: and whensoeuer his laisure from greater affaires did permit him, his vacant times should be spent in the vse of writing and other good exercises, assuring himselfe that his kingdomes and Empire were to be continued and strengthened to him by prayer and holy workes: and oftentimes taking vpon him as it were the person of a notable preacher of Christian discipline, he would teach his children and nobilitie, that godlinesse was to be preferred before riches, yea, before the Monarchie of all the world.

He ouerthrew the false gods of the heathens, and by many lawes often reuiued, he abrogated the worshipping of Images in all the countries of

Greece, Egypt, Persia, Asia, and the whole Romane Empire, commanding Christ onely by his Edicts to be worshipped, the sacred Gospell to be preached, the Ministers thereof to be honored and relieued, and the temples of Idoles euery where to be destroyed.

Whithersoeuer he went hee caused the booke of the Gospell of Christ to be still caried before him, that thereby it might appeare to be a forme of faith to all men, and to appertaine generally to all nations.

He was the first that appointed an Imperiall Diademe, or Crowne to the Kings of Britaine.

He was most beneficiall to all Churches, bestowing vpon them lands and fields, and vpoh the poore, sicke persons, widowes and orphanes, corne and wood, being as carefull of them as if he had beene their naturall father.

He vsed learned men most familiarly, as Eusebius, Lactantius and others, and they are witnesses that this was his usuall prayer to God. O Lord we know thee to be the onely God, we are sure that thou art the onely King, and wee call vpon thee as our helper: through thee we haue gotten the victorie, and by thee we haue ouerthrowen the enemie.

Sextus Aurelius reporteth, that it was his greatest delight to imbrace the studie of learning, to fauour good Arts, to read, write and meditate, and that he composed many bookes and Epistles both in the Greeke and Latine tongues.

He died at Nicomedia, being then 66. yeres of age, in the 32. yere of his reigne, and in the 339. yeere after the Incarnation of Christ, and was buried at Constantinople, Octauius being then King of Britaine: whose life Eusebius bishop of Cæsarea hath written in Greeke in 4 bookes, which afterwards, were translated into the Latine tongue by Iohn Portes a Frenchman.

* * * * *

Certaine Englishmen sent to Constantinople by the French King to Iustinian the Emperour, about the yeere of Christ, 500. out of the fourth booke of Procopius de Bello Gothico.

Britanniam insulam tres numerosissimæ gentes incolunt: Quorum vnicuique suus Rex imperat. Nominantur hæ gentes Angili, Frisones, et qui eiusdem sunt cum insula cognominis Britones. Tanta vero hominum multitudo esse videtur, vt singulis annis inde magno numero cum vxoribus et liberis ad Francos emigrent. Illi autem in eorum terram, quæ maximè deserta videtur, excipiunt. Vnde insulam sibi vendicare ferunt. Vtique non ita pridem, cum Francorum Rex quosdam è suis Constantinopolim ad Iustinianum legaret,

Anglos etiam misit, ambitiosius vendicans, quasi hæc insula suo subesset imperio.

The same in English.

The Isle of Britaine is inhabited by three most populous nations, euery of which is gouerned by a seuerall king. The sayd nations are named Angili, Frisones, and Britones which last are called after the name of the Island. In this Isle there are such swarmes of people, that euery yeare they goe foorth in great numbers with their wiues and children into France. And the Frenchmen right willingly receiue them into their lande, which seemeth very desolate for want of inhabitants. Whereupon it is sayd that the French doe challenge the foresayde Island vnto themselues. For not long since, when the king of the Frankes sent certaine of his subiects ambassadours to Constantinople vnto Iustinian the Emperour, he sent English men also, ambitiously boasting, as though the sayd Isle had bene vnder his iurisdiction.

* * * * *

The life and trauailes of Iohn Erigena.

Ioannes Erigena Britannus natione, in Meneuia vrbe, seu ad fanum Dauidis; et patricio genitore natus, dum Anglos Daci crudeles bellis ac rapinis molestarent, ac omnia illic essent tumultibus plena, longam ipse peregrinationem Athenas vsque suscepit, annósque quamplures literis Græcis, Chaldaicis, et Arabicis insudauit: omnia illic inuisit Philosophorum loca, ac studia, imo et ipsum oraculum Solis, quod Æsculapius sibi construxerat. Inueniens tandem quod longo quæsierat labore, in Italiam et Galliam est reuersus vbi ob insignem eruditionem, Carolo Caluo, et postea Ludouico Balbo acceptus, Dionysij Areopagitæ libros de coelesti Hierarchia, ex Constantinopoli tunc missos Latinos fecit, Anno Dom. 858. Profectus postea in Britanniam, Alphredi Anglorum Regis, et suorum liberorum factus est præceptor, atque ipso mox adhortante, inter ocia literaria è Græco transtulit in tres linguas, scilicet Chaldaicam, Arabicam, et Latinam, Aristotelis moralia, de secretis secretorum, seu recto regimine Principum, opus certe exquisitum. In Malmsburiensi cænobio tandem, quo recreationis gratia se contulerat, inter legendum a quibusdam discipulis maleuolis interimebatur, Anno Christi, 884.

The same in English.

Iohn Erigene a Britane, descended of honourable parents, and borne in the Towne of S. Dauid in Wales, seeing the Englishmen to be oppressed with the warres and rapines of the cruell Danes, and all the land in a hurlie burlie, he in the meane time vndertooke a long iourney, euen as farre as Athens, and there spent many yeres in the studie of the Greeke, Chaldie, and Arabian tongues: he there frequented all the places and schooles of the Philosophers, and the oracle also of the Sunne, which Æsculapius had built vnto himselfe. And hauing found at length that which he had with long trauell searched, he returned againe into Italie, and France, where for his singular learning, he was much fauoured of the two Kings Charles and Lewes, and in his being there, he translated into Latine the bookes of Dionysius Areopagita concerning the Heauenly Hierarchie, which were sent from Constantinople in the yeere 858. After this hee came backe againe into his owne Countrey, and was schoolemaster vnto Alphred then King of England, and his sonnes: and vpon his request, at his times of leasure, he translated Aristotles Morals, of the Secrets of Secrets, or of the right gouernement of Princes, out of Greeke into these three tongues, Chaldie, Arabian, and Latine, which he did very exquisitely. At the last, being in the Abbie of Malmesburie, whither he went for his recreation, and there according to his manner disputing, and reading to the Students, some of them misliking and hating him, rose against him, and slue him in the yeere of Christ, 884.

* * * * *

English men were the guard of the Emperours of Constantinople in the reigne of Iohn the sonne of Alexius Comnenus. Malmesburiensis, Curopolata and Camden, pag. 96.

Iam inde Anglia non minus belli gloria, quam humanitatis cultu inter Florentissimas orbis Christiani gentes imprimis floruit. Adeo vt ad custodiam corporis Constantinopolitanorum Imperatorum euocati fuerint Angli. Ioannes enim Alexij Comneni filius vt refert noster Malmesburiensis, eorum fidem suspiciens præcipue familiaritati suæ applicabat amorem eorum filio transcribens: Adeo vt iam inde longo tempore fuerint imperatorum illorum satellites, Inglini Bipenniferi Nicetæ Choniatæ, Barangi Curopoatæ dicti. Qui vbique Imperatorem prosequebantur ferentes humeris secures, quas tollebant, cum Imperator ex oratorio spectandum se exhibebat Anglicè vitam diuturnam secures suas collidentes vt sonitum ederent comprecabantur.

The same in English.

From this time forward the kingdome of England was reputed among the most nourishing estates of Christendome, no less in chiualrie then humanitie. So farforth that the English men were sent for to be the guarders of the persons of the Emperours of Constantinople. For Iohn the sonne of Alexius Comnenus, as our countreyman William of Matmesburie reporteth, highly esteeming their fidelity, vsed them very nere about him, recommending them ouer to his sonne: so that long time afterwards the guard of those Emperours were English halberdiers, called by Nicetas

Choniata, Inglini Bipeniferi, and by Curopolata, Barangi, which alwayes accompanied the Emperour with their halberds on their shoulders, which they held vp when the Emperour comming from his Oratorie shewed himselfe to the people; and clashing their halberds together to make a terrible sound, they in the English tongue wished vnto him long life.

* * * * *

The woorthy voiage of Richard the first, K. of England into Asia, for the recouerie of Ierusalem out of the hands of the Saracens, drawen out of the booke of Acts and Monuments of the Church of England, written by M. Iohn Foxe.

King Richard the first of that name, for his great valure surnamed Ceur de Lion, the sonne of Henry the second, after the death of his father remembring the rebellions that he had vndutifully raised against him, sought for absolution of his trespasse, and in part of satisfaction for the same, agreed with Philip the French king to take his voiage with him for the recouerie of Christes patrimonie, which they called the Holy land, whereupon the sayd King Richard immediately after his Coronation, to prepare himselfe the better towards his iourney, vsed diuers meanes to take vp summes of money, and exacted a tenth of the whole Realme, the Christians to make three score and ten thousand pounds, and the Iewes which then dwelt in the Realme threescore thousand.

Hauing thus gotten sufficient money for the exploite, he sent certaine Earles and Barons to Philip the French king in the time of his Parliament at S. Denis, to put him in mind of his promise made for the recouerie of Christs holy patrimonie out of the Saracens hands: To whom he sent againe in the moneth of December, that he had bound himselfe by solemne othe, deposing vpon the Euangelists, that he the yeere next following, about the time of Easter, had certainly prefixed to addresse himselfe toward that iourney, requiring him likewise not to faile, but to bee ready at the terme aboue limited, appointing also the place where both the Kings should meete together.

In the yere therfore 1190. King Richard hauing committed the gouernment of this realme in his absence to the bishop of Ely then Chancellor of England, aduanced forward his iourney, and came to Turon to meet with Philip the French king, and after that went to Vizeliac, where the French king and he ioyning together, for the more continuance of their iourney, assured themselues by solemne othe, swearing fidelitie one to the other: the forme of whose oth was this.

[Sidenote: The oth of fidelity betwixt King Richard and the French King.]
That either of them should defend and maintaine the honour of the other,

and beare true, fidelitie vnto him, of life, members and worldly honor, and that neither of them should faile one the other in their affaires: but the French King should aide the King of England in defending his land and dominions, as he would himselfe defend his owne Citie of Paris if it were besieged: and that Richard King of England likewise should aide the French King in defending his land and Dominions, no otherwise then he would defend his own Citie of Roan if it were besieged, &c.

Concerning the lawes and ordinances appointed by K. Richard for his Nauie, the forme thereof was this.

[Sidenote: The discipline and orders of the King.] 1. That who so killed any person on shipboord, should be tied with him that was slaine, and throwen into the sea.

2. And if he killed him on the land, he should in like manner be tied with the partie slaine, and be buried with him in the earth.

3. He that shalbe conuicted by lawfull witnes to draw out his knife or weapon to the intent to strike any man, or that hath striken any to the drawing of blood, shall loose his hand.

4. Also he that striketh any person with his hand without effusion of blood, shall be plunged three times in the sea.

5. Item, who so speaketh any opprobrious or contumelious wordes in reuiling or cursing one another, for so oftentimes as he hath reuiled, shall pay so many ounces of siluer.

6. Item, a thiefe or felon that hath stollen being lawfully conuicted, shall haue his head shorne, and boyling pitch powred vpon his head, and feathers or downe strawed vpon the same, whereby he may be knowen, and so at the first landing place they shall come to, there to be cast vp.

These things thus ordered, king Richard sending his Nauie by the Spanish seas, and by the streights of Gibraltar, betweene Spaine and Africa, to meete him at Marsilia, hee himselfe went as is said to Vizeliac to the French king. Which two kings from thence went to Lions, where the bridge ouer the flood Rhodanus with preasse of people brake, and many both men and women were drowned: by occasion whereof the two kings for the combrance of their traines, were constrained to disseuer themselues for time of their iourney, appointing both to meet together in Sicily: and so Philip the French king tooke his way to Genua, and king Richard to Marsila, where be remained 8. dayes, appointing there his Nauie to meete him. From thence crossing ouer to Genua where the French king was, he passed forward by the coasts of Italy, and entred into Tiber not farre from Rome.

King Richard staying in Marsilia 8. dayes for his Nauie which came not, he there hired 20. Gallies, and ten great barkes to ship ouer his men, and so came to Naples, and so partly by horse and wagon, and partly by the sea, passing to Falernum, came to Calabria, where after that he had heard that his ships were arriued at Messana in Sicilie, he made the more speed, and so the 23. of September entred Messana with such a noyse of Trumpets and Shalmes, with such a rout and shew, that it was to the great wonderment and terror both of the Frenchmen, and of all other that did heare and behold the sight.

To the said towne of Messana the French king was come before the 16. of the same moneth of September, and had taken vp the pallace of Tancredus king of Sicily for his lodging: to whom king Richard after his arriuall eftsoones resorted, and when the two kings had communed together, immediately the French king tooke shipping and entred the seas, thinking to saile towards the land of Ierusalem: but after he was out of the hauen, the winde rising contrary against him, returned him backe againe to Messana. Then king Richard (whose lodging was prepared in the suburbs without the Citie) after he had resorted againe and talked with the French king, and also had sent to Tancredus king of Sicily, for deliuerance of Ioane his sister (who had beene somtimes Queene of Sicily) and had obtained her to be sent vnto him, the last day of September passed ouer the streight del Fare, and there getting a strong hold called de la Baguare, or le Bamare, and there placing his sister with a sufficient garrison, he returned againe to Messana.

The 2. of October king Richard wan another strong hold, called Monasterium Griffonum, situated in the midst of the streight del Fare, betweene Messana and Calabria, from whence the Monks being expulsed, he reposed there all his store and prouision of victuals, which came from England or other places.

The Citizens of Messana seeing that the king of England had wonne the castle and Island de la Baguare, and also the Monasterie of the Griffons, and doubting least the king would extend his power further to inuade their Citie, and get if he could the whole Isle of Sicilie, began to stirre against the Kings armie, and to shut the Englishmen out of the gates, and kept their walles against them. The Englishmen seeing that, made to the gates, and by force would haue broken them open, insomuch that the King riding amongst them with his staffe, and breaking diuers of their heads, could not asswage their fierceness, such was the rage of the Englishmen agaynst the citizens of Messana. The King seeing the furie of his people to be such that hee could not stay them, tooke boate, and went to the pallace of king Tancred, to talke of the matter with the French king, in which meane time the matter was so taken vp by the wise handling of the ancients of the citie, that both parts laying downe their armour, went home in peace.

The fourth day of the sayd moneth of October, came to king Richard the Archbishop of Messana with two other Archbishops also with the French king, and sundry other Earles, Barons, and Bishops, to intreat of peace, who as they were together consulting, and had almost concluded vpon the peace, the Citizens of Messana issuing out of the towne, some went vp vpon the mountains, some with open force inuaded the mansion or lodging of Hugh Brune, an English captaine. The noyse whereof comming to the eares of the King, hee suddenly breaking off talke with the French king and the rest, departed from them, and comming to his men, commanded them forthwith to arme themselues. Who then with certaine of his souldiours making vp to the top of the mountaine (which seemed to passe their power to climbe) there put the Citizens to flight, chasing them downe the mountaines, vnto the very gates of the citie, whom also certaine of the kings seruants pursued into the citie, of whom fiue valiant souldiers and twentie of the kings seruants were slaine, the French King looking vpon, and not once willing to rescue them, contrary to his othe, and league before made with the king of England: for the French king with his men being there present, rode in the midst of them safely, and without any harme too and fro, and might well haue eased the Kings partie, more then he, if it had so liked him.

[Sidenote: Messana won by the English.] This being knowen to the English hoste how their fellowes were slaine, and the Frenchmen permitted in the citie, and that they were excluded and the gates barred against them, being also stopped from buying of victuall, and other things, they vpon great indignation gathered themselues in armes, brast open the the gates, and scaled the wals, and so winning the citie, set up their flags with the English armes vpon the wals which when the French King did see, he was mightily offended, requiring the King of England that the Armes of France might also be set vp, and ioyned with his: but King Richard to that would in no case agree, notwithstanding to satisfie his minde, he was contented to take downe his Armes, and to commit the custodie of the citie to the Hospitaleries and Templaries of Ierusalem, till the time that Tancred king of Sicily and he should agree together vpon conditions.

These things being done the fift and sixt day of October, it followed then vpon the eight day of the same, that peace was concluded among the kings. In which peace, first King Richard, and Philip the French king renewed againe their oth and league before made, concerning their mutual aide and societie, during the time of that peregrination.

Secondly, peace also was concluded betweene king Richard and Tancred king of Sicily aforesaide, with conditions, that the daughter of Tancrede in case king Richard should die without issue, should be married to Arthur Duke of Britaine the kings Nephew and next heire to his crowne, whereof a formall charte was drawen, and letters sent thereof to Pope Clement being dated the ninth of Nouember.

From this time vntill Februarie the next yeere these two kings kept still at Messana, either for lacke of winde and weather, or for the repairing of their shippes. And in the aforesayde Februarie, in the yeere 1191. King Richard sent ouer his gallies to Naples, there to meete his mother Elinore, and Berengaria the daughter of Zanctius king of Nauarre, whom he was purposed to marry, who by that time were come to Brundusium, vnder the conduct of Philip Earle of Flanders, and so proceeding vnto Naples, they found the kings shippes wherein they sayled to Messana.

In this meane space, king Richard shewed himselfe exceeding bounteous and liberall to all men: to the French king first he gaue diuers shippes, vpon others likewise he bestowed riche rewardes, and of his treasure and goods he distributed largely to his souldiers and seruants about him, of whom it was reported, that he distributed more in one moneth, than any of his predecessors did in a whole yeere: by reason, whereof he purchased great loue and fauour, which not onely redounded to the aduancements of his fame, but also to his singular vse and profite, as the sequele afterwards prooued.

The first day of March following, he left the citie of Messana, where the French King was, and went to Cathneia, a citie where Tancredus king of Sicily then lay, where he was honorably receiued, and there remained with king Tancredus three dayes and three nights. On the fourth day when he should depart, the aforesaid Tancredus offred him many rich presents in gold and siluer, and precious silkes, whereof king Richard would receiue nothing, but one little ring for a token of his good will: for the which king Richard gaue againe vnto him a riche sworde. At length when king Richard should take his leaue, king Tancred would not let him so depart, but needes would giue 4. great shippes, and 15. gallies, and furthermore hee himselfe would needes accompanie him the space of two dayes iourney, to a place called Tauernium.

Then the next morning when they should take their leaue, Tancredus declared vnto him the message, which the French King a little before had sent vnto him by the Duke of Burgundie, the contents whereof were these: That the King of England was a false Traytour, and would neuer keepe the peace that was betweene them: and if the sayd Tancredus would warre against him, or secretly by night would inuade him, he with all his power would assist him, to the destruction of him and all his armie. To whom Richard the King protested againe, that he was no traytour, nor neuer had bene: and as touching the peace, begun betwixt them, the same should neuer be broken through him; neither could he beleeue that the French King being his good lord, and his sworn Compartner in that voyage, would utter any such wordes by him. Which when Tancredus heard, he bringeth foorth the letters of the French King, sent to him by the Duke of Burgundie, affirming moreouer, that if the Duke of Burgundie would denie the bringing of the said letters, he was readie to trie it with him by any of his Dukes. King Richard receiuing the letters, and musing not a little vpon the same, returneth againe to Messana. The same day that King Richard departed, the French king came to Tauernium to speake with Tancred, and there abode with him that night, and on the morrowe returned to Messana againe.

From that time, King Richard mooued in stomacke against King Philip, neuer shewed any gentle countenance of peace and amitie, as he before was woont: whereat the French king greatly marueiling, and enquiring earnestly what should be the cause thereof, word was sent him againe by Philip earle of Flanders from king Richard, what words he had sent to the King of Sicily, and for testimony thereof the letters were shewed, which he wrote by the duke of Burgundie to the king of Sicily: which when the French king vnderstood, first he held his peace as guilty in his conscience, not knowing well what to answere. At length turning his tale to another matter, he began to quarrell with king Richard, pretending as though he sought causes to breake with him, and to maligne him: and therefore he forged (sayd he) these lies vpon him, and all because he by that meanes would auoid to marry with Alise his sister, according as he had promised. Adding moreouer that if he would so do, and would not marry the said Alise his sister according to his oth, he would be an enemy to him, and to his, while he liued.

To this king Richard sayd againe that he could by no meanes marry that woman, forsomuch as his father had carnal copulation with her, and also had by her a sonne: for proofe whereof he had there presently to bring forth diuers and sundry witnesses to the kings face, to testifie with him.

In conclusion, through counsell and perswasion of diuers about the French king, agreement at last was made, so that king Philip did acquite king Richard from this bond of marrying his sister, and king Richard againe should be bound to pay to him euery yeere for the space of fiue yeeres, two thousand markes, with certaine other conditions besides, not greatly materiall for this place. And thus peace being betweene them concluded the 28 day of the sayd moneth of March, the French king launching out of the hauen of Messana, the 22 day after in the Easter weeke, came with his armie to the siege of Achon.

After the departure of the French king from Messana, king Richard with his armie yet remaining behinde, arriued Queene Alinor the kings mother, bringing with her Berengaria the king of Nauars daughter, to be espoused to king Richard: [Sidenote: The Nauie of King Richard.] which being done, king Richard in April following, about the 20 day of the sayd moneth, departed from the hauen Messana with 150 great ships, and 53 great gallies well manned and appointed, and tooke his iourney toward Achon: who being vpon the Seas on Good friday about the ninth houre, rose a mighty South winde, with a tempest, which disseuered and scattered all his Nauie, some to one place and some to another. The king with a few ships was driuen to the Ile of Creta, and there before the hauen of Rhodes cast anker. The ships that caried the kings sister, queene of Sicily, and Berengaria the king of Nauars daughter, with two ships were driuen to the Ile of Cyprus.

The king making great mone for the ships of his sister, and Berengaria his wife that should be, not knowing where they were become, after the tempest was ouerblowen, sent forth his gallies diligently to seeke the rest of his Nauie dispersed, but especially the shippe wherein his sister was, and the maiden whom he should marry, who at length were found safe and merry at the port of Lymszem [Footnote: Lymasol.] in the Ile of Cyprus, notwithstanding the two other ships, which were in their company before in the same hauen, were drowned with diuers of the kings seruants and men of worship, among whom was M. Roger, called Malus Catulus, the kings Vicechancellour, who was found with the kings seale hanging about his necke.

The king of Cyprus was then Isakius [Footnote: Isaac Comnenus who became King in 1184.] (called also the Emperour of the Gryffons) who tooke and imprisoned all Englishmen, which by shipwracke were cast vpon his land, also inuegled into his hands the goods and prises of them which were found drowned about his coastes, neither would suffer the ships wherein the two ladies were to enter within the port.

The tidings of this being brought to king Richard, he in great wrath gathering his gallies and ships together, boordeth the land of Cyprus, where he first in gentle wise signifieth to king Isakius, how he with his English men, comming as strangers to the supportation of the holy land, were by distresse of weather driuen vpon his bounds, and therefore with all humble petition besought him in Gods behalfe, and for reuerence of the holy crosse, to let go such prisoners of his as he had in captiuitie, and to restore againe the goods of them that were drowned, which he deteined in his hands, to be employed for the behoofe of their soules. And this the king once, twise, and thrise desired of the Emperour: but he proudly answering againe, sent the king word, that he neither would let the captiues go, nor render the goods of them which were drowned.

When king Richard heard this, how light the emperour Isakius made of his so humble and honest petition, and how that nothing could be gotten without violent force, eftsoones [Footnote: The Saxon *Eft* properly means *after*. It was beginning to be obsolete in 1400 but Spencer frequently uses it. It occurs rarely after his time.] giueth commandement thorowout all his hoste to put themselues in armour and follow him, to reuenge the iniuries receiued of that proud and cruell king of Cyprus, willling them to put their trust in God, and not to misdoubt but that the Lord would stand with them, and giue them the victory. The Emperour in the meane time with his people stood warding the Sea coasts, where the English men should arriue, with swords, billes, and lances, and such other weapons as they had, setting boordes, stooles, and chestes, before them as a wall: few of them were harnessed, [Footnote: Clad in armour. This apish and unmannerly approach, This *harness'd* masque, and unadvised revel. KING JOHN v. 2.] and for the most part all vnexpert and vnskilfull in the feates of warre.

Then king Richard with his souldiers issuing out of ships, first set his bowemen before, who with their shot made a way for others to folowe. The Englishmen thus winning the land vpon them, so fiercely pressed upon the Gryffons, that after long fighting and many blowes, at last the Emperour was put to flight, whom king Richard valiantly pursued, and slue many, and diuers he tooke aliue, and had gone neere also to take the Emperour, had not the night come on and parted the battell. And thus king Richard with much spoyle, and great victory, returning to the port Towne of Lymszem, which the Townesmen had left for feare, found there great abundance of corne, wine, oyle, and victuals.

The day after the victory gotten, Ioanna the Kings sister, and Berengaria the mayden, entred the Porte and Towne of Lymszem, with 50. great ships, and 14. galliots: so that all the whole Nauie there meeting together, were 254. tall shippes, and aboue threescore galliots. Then Isakius the Emperour, seeing no way for him to escape by Sea, the same night pitched his tentes fiue miles off from the English army, swearing that the third day after, he would surely giue battell to king Richard: but he preuenting him before, suddenly the same morning before the day of battell should be, setteth vpon the tentes of the Gryffons early in the morning, they being vnawares and asleepe, and made of them a great slaughter, insomuch that the Emperour was faine to runne away naked, leauing his tentes and pauilions to the Englishmen, full of horses and rich treasure, also with the Imperial standerd, the lower part whereof with a costly streamer was couered, and wrought all with golde.

King Richard returning with victorie and triumph to his sister and Berengaria, shortly after in the moneth of May next following, and the 12. day of the said moneth, married the said Berengaria daughter of Zanctius, king of Nauarre, in the yle of Cyprus at Lymszem.

The king of Cyprus seeing himselfe ouermatched, was driuen at length to yeelde himselfe with conditions to giue king Richard 20000. markes in golde for amends of such spoyles as he had gotten of them that were drowned, also to restore all the captiues againe to the king: and furthermore, he in his owne person, to attend vpon the king to the lande of Ierusalem, in Gods seruice and his, with 400. horsemen, and 500. footemen: in pledge whereof he would giue to his hands his castles, and his onely daughter, and would hold his kingdome of him.

This done, and the Emperour swearing fidelitie to king Richard before Guido king of Ierusalem, and the prince of Antioche (who were come thither to king Richard a little before) peace was taken, and Isakius committed to the warde of certaine keepers. Notwithstanding shortly after he breaking from his keepers, was againe at defiance with the King: whereupon king Richard besetting the Iland of Cyprus round about with shippes and gallies, did in sucn sort preuaile, that the subiects of the land, were constrained to yeelde themselues to the King, and at last the daughter of the Emperour, and the Emperour himselfe, whom king Richard caused to be kept in fetters of gold and siluer, and to be sent to the citie of Tripolis.

[Sidenote: The Lord Chamberlaine of King Richard left gouernour of Cyprus.] These things thus done, and all set in order touching the possession of the Ile of Cyprus, the keeping whereof he committed to Radulphe sonne of Godfrey Lord Chamberlaine, being then the first day of Iune upon the fift of the saide moneth, king Richard departed from the Ile of Cyprus, [Footnote: Cyprus, the third largest island of the Mediterranean, situated in the N.E. angle, equidistant about 60 miles from the coasts of Syria and Asia Minor. Its form was compared in ancient times to the skin of a deer. Its length, from Cape Andrea to Cape Epiphanias, the ancient Acamas, is 140 miles. Its greatest breadth, from Cape Gatto on the south coast to Cape Kormakiti on the north, is about 50 miles, but it gradually narrows towards the east, being no more than 5 miles wide near Cape Andrea.

The coast of the island consists of a succession of gulfs and bays, many of which, though not sufficiently land-locked to form natural harbours, would be capable, with the addition of some artificial works, such as breakwaters, &c., of affording safe anchorage in all the preuailing winds. On the north-west and north the principal harbours or roadsteads affording shelter from

- 90 -

certain winds are the Bay of Chrysochon and the roads of Pyros and Morpha, the harbour of Kyrenia, and the Bay of Exarkos; on the east and south, the bays and harbours of Salamis and Famagusta, the bay and roads of Larnaka, the roads of Limasol, which latter were greatly improved by the opening of an iron pier in 1882, and the small harbour of Paphos (Kuklia). The great disadvantage of all these harbours and roadsteads is the shallowness of the water for some distance from the land; this has the effect of raising a great deal of surf when the wind blows on shore, and also of compelling vessels of any size to anchor at a considerable distance out, thus making the operations of landing and embarking cargo both tedious and expensiue. It would not, however, be a matter of great expense to construct breakwaters and deepen the old harbours, especially that of Famagusta, which, at the end of the sixteenth century, was sufficiently deep and large to afford safe anchorage to the whole fleet of the Venetian Republic, and when in the outer harbour there is now shelter for about twelve ironclads. Larnaka is the port at present most frequented by trading vessels.

The ancient Olympus, how called Santa Croce, rises in the centre of the island, and two principal ranges of mountains runs in the direction of its length, keeping closer to the north than to the south coast. The highest summit of the range of Santa Croce is mount Troödos, with an elevation of 6590 feet above the sea-level. Here, on the south-east slopes, are the summer quarters of the troops and the summer residence of the high commissioner. The most extensive plain, called Messarea, is in the south-east part of the island, and is watcred by the river Pedæus. The south of the island is watered by several streams, the principal of which is the river Kuris, or Lico, which falls into the sea at Episkopi, the ancient *Curium*. But these streams, which were once rivers of some importance, had very much decreased, owing to the almost complete denudation, in the plains and lower slopes of the mountains, of the forests which anciently covered them. Since the British occupation greater attention has been paid to the forests, and the beneficial results are already apparent. The Pedæus is the chief river. This and the other streams generally overflow their banks in the rainy season, and flood the land; as the waters subside, they leave behind a fertilizing mud, in the same manner as the Nile, but during the rest of the year they give but little if any help in the way of irrigation. The rainy season, although generally occurring from October to February, is not, however, to be absolutely depended upon; thus it is recorded that in 1330, during the reign of Hugo of Lusignan, the rainfall was so heavy and the rivers flooded to such an extent as to spread desolation far and near; and under Constantine there was no rain for thirty-six years, so that most of the inhabitants left the island. Again, in modern times, there was a disastrously small rainfall in 1869.

The soil is naturally fertile, and formerly maintained a population of nearly 1,000,000 but the number of inhabitants in 1881 was only 185,906, of whom the bulk were Greek Christians. Cotton of the finest quality has been raised from American seed; excellent wine and all kinds of fruit are produced, but agriculture is in a most backward state. Besides the productions already named, madder, opium, oranges, lemons, pomegranates, &c., are grown. The carob-tree abounds in some districts; its succulent pods are exported to Egypt and Syria, while the fruit called St. John's Bread is used as an article of food. Of all the agricultural products, cereals hold the most important place. Wheat was largely grown until recently, but of late years, it has been in great measure replaced by barley and oats, which ripen earlier; and are not subject to the attacks of locusts.] with his shippes and gallies toward the seige of Achon, and on the next morrowe came to Tyrus, where by procurement of the French king he was restrained by the Citizens to enter. The next day after, which was the first day of Iune, crossing the seas, he met with a great carak, fraught with souldiers and men of warre to the number of a thousand and fiue hundred, which pretended to be Frenchmen, and setting foorth their flagge with the French armes, were indeede Saracens, [Sidenote: A great ship of Saracens taken by king Richard.] secretly sent with wilde fire [Footnote: Greek Fire was the name given to a composition which was largely used by the Greeks of the Byzantine Empire in their wars with the Mohammedans. Its nature was kept a profound secret for centuries, but the material is now believed to have been a mixture of nitre, sulphur, and naphtha. It burned with terrible fury wherever it fell, and it possessed the property of being inextinguishable by water. Even when poured upon the sea it would float upon the surface and still burn. It was used in warfare for a considerable time after the discovery of gunpowder, but gradually fell into the disuse as artillery became more effective. The name is still sometimes used to designate the inflammable compounds known to modern chemists which have been designed for use in incendiary shells, and for a composition which has been used by the Fenians to set fire to public buildings.] and certaine barrels of unknowen serpents to the defence of the towne of Achon, which king Richard at length perceiuing eftsoones set upon them and so vanquished them, of whom the most were drowned and some taken aliue: which being once knowen in the citie of Achon, as it was a great discomfort to them, so it was a great helpe to the Christians for winning the citie.

[Sidenote: King Richard arriued at Achon.] The next day after which was the seuenth of Iune, king Richard came to Achon, which at that time had bene long besieged by the Christians. After whose comming it was not long, but the Pagans within the citie, seeing their wals to be undermined and towers ouerthrowen, were driuen by composition to escape with life and limme, to surrender the citie to the two kings.

Another great helpe to the Christians in winning the citie, was this. In the said city of Achon there was a secret Christian among the Saracens, who in time of the siege thereof vsed at sundry times to cast ouer the wals into the campe of the Christians, certaine bils written in Hebrue, Greeke, and Latine, wherein he disclosed to the Christians from time to time, the doings and counsels of the enemies, aduertising them how and what way they should worke, and what to beware, and alwayes his letters began thus. In nomine Patris, et Filij, et Spiritus sancti Amen. By reason whereof the Christians were much, aduantaged in their proceedings: but this was a great heauines unto them, that neither he would utter his name, nor when the citie was got did they euer understand who he was.

To make of a long siege a short narration. Vpon the twelfth day of Iuly the yeere aforesaid, the Princes and Captaines of the Pagans, vpon agreement resorted to the tent of the Templaries to commune with the two kings touching peace, and giuing vp of their citie: the forme of which peace was thus.

[Sidenote: The forme of peace concluded between the Kings and Princes of Achon.] 1 That the Kings should haue the citie of Achon freely and fully deliuered vnto them, with all which was therein.

2 That 500. captiues of the Christians should be restored to them, which were in Achon.

3 That the holy crosse should be to them rendred, and a thousand Christian captiues with two hundreth horsemen, whosoeuer they themselues would chose out of all them which were in the power of the Saladine.

4 That they would giue vnto the Kings two hundreth thousand Bysants, so that they themselues should remaine as pledges in the Kings hands, for the performance hereof, that if in fortie daies, the aforesayd couenants were not accomplished, they should abide the Kings mercie touching life and limme.

These couenants being agreed vpon, the Kings sent their souldiers and seruants into the citie, to take a hundreth of the richest and best of the citie, to close them vp in towers vnder strong keeping, and the residue, they committed to be kept in houses and in streetes, ministring vnto them according to their necessities: to whom notwithstanding this they permitted, that so many of them as would be baptized and receiue the faith of Christ, should be free to goe whither they would: wherupon many there were of the Pagans, which for feare of death pretended to be baptized, but afterward so soone as they could, reuolted againe to the Saladine: for the which it was afterward commanded by the Kings that none of them should be baptized against their wils.

The thirteenth day of the said moneth of Iuly, King Philip of France, and King Richard, after they had obteined the possession of Achon, [Footnote: Acre, acca, anciently Ptolemais, in Syria, was taken by the Saracens in 638; by the Crusaders under Baldwin I. in 1104; by Saladin in 1187; and again by Richard I. and other Crusaders 12 July 1191, after a siege of 2 years, with a loss of 6 archbishops, 12 bishops, 40 earls, 500 barons, 300,000 soldiers. It was then named *St. Jean d'Acre*. It was retaken by the Saracens in 1291, when 60,000 Christians perished, and the nuns, who had mangled their faces to preserue their chastity, were put to death.] deuided betweene them all things therein conteined as well the people as golde and siluer, with all other furniture whatsoeuer was remaining in the citie: who in diuiding the spoyle, were so good caruers to themselues that the Knights and Barons had but litle to their share, whereupon they began to shew themselues somewhat discontented, which being knowen of the kings, they sent them answere that their wils should be satisfied.

The twentieth day of Iuly, king Richard speaking with the French king, desired him that they two with their armies, would binde themselues by othe to remaine there stil in the land of Ierusalem the space of 3 yeeres, for the winning and recouering againe of those countreys: but he sayd he would sweare no such othe, and so the next day after king Richard, with his wife and sister entred into the citie of Achon, and there placed himselfe in the kings pallace: The French king remayning in the houses of the Templaries, where he continued till the end of the moneth.

[Sidenote: The French kings shamefull returne home.] About the beginning of the moneth of August, Philip the French king after that he and King Richard had made agreement betweene Guido and Conradus the Marques, about the kingdome of Ierusalem, went from Achon to Tyrus, notwithstanding king Richard and all the Princes of the Christian armie with great intreatie desired him to tary, shewing what a shame it were for him to come so farre, and now to leaue vndone that for which he came, and on the 3. day of August departed from Tyrus, leauing the halfe part of the Citie of Achon in the hands of the aforesayd Conradus Marques.

After his departure the Pagans refused to keepe their couenants made, who neither would restore the holy Crosse nor the money, nor their captiues, sending word to king Richard, that if he beheaded the pledges left with him at Achon, they would choppe off the heads of such captiues of the Christians, as were in their hands.

[Sidenote: The captiues of the Saladine slaine by king Richard.] Shortly after this the Saladine sending great gifts to king Richard, requested the time limited for beheading of the captiues to be proroged, but the king refused to take his gifts, and to graunt his request, whereupon the Saladine caused all the Christian captiues within his possession forthwith to be beheaded, which was the 28. of August: which albeit king Richard vnderstood, yet would not he preuent the time before limitted for the execution of his prisoners, being the 20. day of August: vpon which day he caused the prisoners of the Saracens openly in the sight of the Saladines armie to loose their heads: the number of whom came to two thousand and fiue hundreth, saue onely that certaine of the principal of them he reserued for purposes and considerations, especially to make exchange for the holy Crosse, and certaine other of the Christian captiues.

[Sidenote: A notable victorie against the Saladine.] After this king Richard purposed to besiege the Citie of Ioppe, where by the way beweene Achon and Ioppe, neere to a towne called Assur, Saladine with a great multitude of his Saracens came fiercely against the kings rereward, but through Gods mercifull grace in the same battell, the kings warriers acquited themselues so well, that the Saladine was put to flight, whom the Christians pursued the space of 3 miles, and he lost that same day many of his Nobles and Captaines, in such sort (as it was thought) that the Saladine was not put to such confusion 40 yeres before, and but one Christian Captaine called James Auernus in that conflict was ouerthrowen.

[Sidenote: King Richard in possession of Syria.] From thence king Richard proceeding further went to Ioppe, and then to Ascalon, where he found first the citie of Ioppe forsaken of the Saracens, who durst not abide the kings comming: Ascalon the Saladine threw downe to the ground, and likewise forsooke the whole land of Syria, through all which land the king had free passage without resistance: neither durst the Saracene Prince encounter after that with K. Richard. Of all which his atcheuances the sayd K. Richard sent his letters of certificate as well into England, as also to the Abbot of Clara valle [Footnote: Clairvaux, a famous Cistercian abbey, founded in 1114 by the celebrated Bernard. It increased so rapidly that before his death, in 1153, it contained 700 monks, and had connected with it seventy-six monasteries in various parts of Europe, partly founded by Bernard and partly induced to join the brotherhood. All sorts of handicraft and agricultural operations were carried on by the brethren. After supplying the wants of their community the surplus was disposed of in the nearest markets. It was suppressed at the Revolution.] in France, well hoping that he God willing should be able to make his repaire againe to them by Easter next.

Many other famous acts were done in this voyage by these two Kings, and moe should haue bene, had not they falling into discorde disseuered themselues, by reason whereof Philip the French king returned home againe within short space: who being returned againe eftsoones inuaded the countrey of Normandy, exciting also Iohn the brother of king Richard, to take on him the kingdome of Englande in his brothers absence: [Sidenote: 1193.] who then made league vpon the same with the French king, and did homage vnto him, which was about the fourth yeere of king Richard. [Sidenote: King Richard returneth from Palaestina.] Who then being in Syria, and hearing thereof, made peace with the Turkes for three yeeres: and not long after, king Richard the next Spring following returned also, who in his returne driuen by distresse of weather about the parts of Histria, in a towne called Synaca, was there taken by Lympold, Duke of the same countrey, and so solde to the Emperour for sixtie thousand Markes: who for no small ioy thereof, writeth to Philip the French king, these letters here following.

* * * * *

The letter of the Emperour to Philip the French king, concerning the taking of King Richard.

Henricus Dei gratia Romanorum Imperator, et semper Augustus, Dilecto et speciali amico suo, Philippo illustri Francorum Regi salutem, et sinceræ dilectionis affectum. Quoniam Imperatoria Celsitudo non dubitat Regalem Magnificentiam tuam Iætiorem effici, de vniuersis quibus omnipotentia creatoris nostri nos ipsos, et Romanum Imperium honorauerit et exaltauerit, nobilitati tuæ tenore præsentium declarare duximus, quod inimicus Imperij nostri, et turbator Regni tui Rex Angliæ, quum esset in transeundo mare ad partes suas reuersurus, accidit vt ventus rupta naui sua, in qua ipse erat, induceret eum in partes Histriæ ad locum qui est inter Aquileiam, et Venetias. Vbi Rex, Dei permissione passus naufragium cum paucis euasit.

Quidam itaque fidelis noster Comes, Maynardus de Grooxce, et populus regionis illius, audito quod in terra erat, et considerato diligentius, qualem nominatus Rex in terra promissionis proditionem et traditionem, et perditionis suæ cumulum exercuerat, insecuti sunt, intendentes eum captiuare. Ipso autem Rege in fugam conuerso, ceperunt de suis octo milites: Postmodum processit Rex ad Burgum in Archiepiscopatu Salseburgensi, qui vocatur Frisorum, vbi Fridericus de Betesow, Rege cum tribus tantum versus Austriam properante, noctu sex milites de suis coepit: Dilectus autem Consanguineus noster Lympoldus Dux Austriæ, obseruata strata sæpe dictum Regem iuxta Denam in villa viciniori in domo despecta captiuauit.

Cum itaque in nostra nunc habeatur Potestate, et ipse semper tua molestauit, et turbationis operam præstiterit, ea quæ præmissimus, nobilitati tuæ insinuare curauimus: scientes ea dilectioni tuæ bene placita existere, animo tuo vberrimam importare lætitiam. Datum apud Ritheontum 5. Kalendas Ianua.

King Richard being thus traitorously taken, and solde to the Emperour by the Duke of Austridge for 60000. markes, was there kept in custodie a yeere and 3. moneths.

In some stories it is affirmed, that King Richard returning out of Asia, came to Italy with prosperous winde, where he desired of the Pope to be absolued of an othe made against his will and could not obteine it: and so setting out from thence towards England, passing by the Countrey of Conradus the Marques, whose death (he being, slaine a litle before) was falsly imputed by the French king to the king of England, there traiterously was taken (as is aforesayde) by Limpoldus duke of Austridge.

Albeit in another storie I finde the matter more credibly set forth: which saith thus. That king Richard slewe the brother of this Limpoldus, playing with him at Chesse in the French Kings Court: and Limpoldus taking his vantage, was more cruel against him and deliuered him (as is sayde) to the Emperour. In whose custodie he was deteined during the time aboue mentioned, a yeere and 3. moneths. During which time of the kings endurance, the French king in the meane season stirred warre in Normandie: and Earle Iohn the Kings brother, made stirre and inuaded England, but the Barons and Bishops of the land mightily withstood him.

At length it was agreed and concluded with the Emperour, that king Richard should be released for a hundreth and foure thousand pound: of which money part should remaine to the Duke of Austridge, the rest should be the Emperours. The summe of which money was here gathered and made in England of chalices, crosses, shrines, candlestickes and other Church place, also with publike contribution of Friers, Abbots, and other subiects of the Realme: whereof part was presently paid, and for the residue remaining, hostages and pledges were taken, which was about the fift yeere of his reigne: and then it was obteined of the Pope that Priestes might celebrate with Chalices of latten and tinne.

[Sidenote: The iust iudgment of God vpon the Duke of Austria.] At what time this aforesaide money was payde, and the hostages giuen for the ransome of the King, I haue an olde historie which saith, that the aforesaid Duke of Austridge was shortly after plagued by God, with 5. sundry plagues.

First, with the burning of his chiefe Townes.

2. With drowning of tenne thousand of his men in a flood happening no man can tell how.

3. By turning all the eares of his corne fieldes into wormes.

4. By taking away almost all the Nobles of his land by death.

5. By breaking his owne leg falling from his horse, which leg he was compelled to cut off with his owne hands, and afterwards died of the same: who then at his death is reported to forgiue K. Richard 50000. marks, and sent home the hostages that were with him. And further a certaine booke intituled Eulogium declareth, that the sayd Limpoldus duke of Austrich fell in displeasure with the bishop of Rome and died excommunicate the next yeere after, Anno 1196.

But thus, as you haue heard, Richard the King was ransomed and deliuered from the couetuous captiuitie of the Emperor, and returning home made an ende of his voyage for Asia, which was both honourable to himselfe and to all Christian states, but to the Saracens the enemies of Christianitie, terrible and dishonourable.

[This historie of King Richards voiage to Ierusalem is very excellently and largely written in Latine by Guilielmus Neobrigensis, [Footnote: William Little, died between 1208 and 1220. The best edition of his history is Mr Howlett's, 1884, published in the Rolls Series. It extends from the Conquest to 1197.] and Roger Houeden.] [Footnote: Roger of Hoveden, a fine old English chronicler attached to the household of Henry II. in some capacity of treasurer connected with minor abbeys and their royal dues, was also professor of theology at Oxford. His chronicle was chiefly written under Richard of the Lion Heart, and breaks off at the third year of John, 1201. It is in Latin, and is easily accessible—the *Chronica Rogeri de Hovedene* forming part of the magnificent Rolls Series. It is in four vols. 8vo, edited, by Professor Stubbs (London, 1871) The first part of Roger's chronicle, beginning with the year 732, is really due to Benedict of Peterborough, under which name the king's treasurer, Bishop Richard Fitz Neal, wrote. It professes to continue and complete Bede's History. Roger of Hoveden is of high value for Henry II.'s time, but for that of Richard and the first year of John he is really admirable. No circumstance is too trivial for his pen, and in this garrulous diffuseness many touches are preserved of priceless worth to us, with which better authors would have disdained to cumber their work.]

* * * * *

Epitaphium Richardi primi regis Anglorum apud fontem Ebraldi.

Scribitur hoc auro, rex auree, laus tua tota
aurea, materiæ conueniente nota.
Laus tua prima fuit Siculi, Cyprus altera, Dromo
tertia, Caruanna quarta, suprema Iope. [Marginal note: Ciuitas Ioppe.]

Retrusi Siculi, Cyprus pessundata, Dromo
mersus, Caruanna capta, retenta Iope.

Epitaphium eiusdem vbi viscera eius requiescunt.

> Viscera Kareolum, corpus fons seruat Ebraldi, et cor
> Rothomagus, magne Richarde, tuum.

* * * * *

The trauailes of Gulielmus Peregrinus.

Gulielmus Peregrinus, Poeta quidem per eam ætatem excellens, genere Anglus florebat, literarum, vt multi tunc erant, amator maximus, et qui bona tempora melioribus impenderat studijs. Hic cum accepisset, expeditionem in Saracenos per Regem Richardum parari, accinxit se ad iter illud, non tantum vt miles, sed etiam in peregrinus. Vidit ea quæ in Mari Hispanico fiebant, vidit quæ in Syria et Palæstina commissa fuerunt, in Sultanum Babyloniæ Regem, ac perfidos Sarracenos. Omnia hæc scripsit, et viuis depinxit coloribus, ita vt quasi præ oculis, totum poneret negotium, idémque Argumentum cum Richardo Canonico non infoeliciter, Heroico pertractauit carmine, opúsque iam absolutum Huberto Cantuariorum Archiepiscopo, et Stephano Turnhamo Capitaneo rerum bellicarum expertissimo dedicauit, addito hoc titulo, Odeporicon Richardi Regis. Multáque alia edidisse Poetam talem non dubito, sed num extent illa eius scripta, mihi non constat. Hoc tamen satis constat, eum fuisse in pretio, Anno à saluitfero virginis partu 1200. sub Anglorum Rege Ioanne.

The same in English.

William the Pilgrime, a very excellent Poet in those dayes and an Englishman borne, was of great fame, being much giuen to good letters, (as many then were) and bestowed his good time in the best kinde of studies. Hee vnderstanding of the preparation of king Richard against the Saracens, prepared himselfe also for the same voyage, not onely as a Souldiour, but as a Pilgrime also. He sawe those things which happened in the Spanish Seas, and which were done in Syria and Palestina, against the Sultan the King of Babylon, and the trecherous Saracens. All which things he wrote and expressed them as it were in liuely colours, as if they had bene still in doing before his eyes, and handled the same Argument in Heroicall verse which the forenamed Richard Canonicus did. And hauing finished his worke he dedicated it to Hubert Archbishop of Canterburie, and to Stephen Turneham a most expert Captaine of warres, giuing it this Title, The expedition of King Richard. And I doubt not but that so good a Poet as hee has published many other things, but whether they be extant yea or no, I know not: but this I know, that he was a man well accounted of, and flourished in the yeere after the birth of Christ 1200. vnder king Iohn.

* * * * *

The comming of the Emperour of Constantinople called Baldwine into England in the yere 1247, out of Matth. Paris, and Holensh. page 239. vol. 2.

About the same time, Baldwine naming himselfe emperour of Constantinople, came againe into England, to procure sone new ayd of the king towards the recouery of his empire, out of the which he was expelled by the Greeks.

* * * * *

Confirmatio treugarum inter Regem Angliæ Eduardum quartum, et Ioannem
  secundum Regem Portugalliæ, datarum in oppido montis Maioris 8. Februarij, et apud Westmonasterium 13, Septembris, 1482. anno regni 22. Regis Eduardi quarti, lingua Lusitanica ex opere sequenti excerpta.

Libro das obras de Garcia de Resende, que tracta da vida è feitos del Rey dom Ioham secundo. Embaxada que el Rey mandou à el Rey D'Inglaterra. Cap. 33.

Edaqui de Monte Mor mandou el Rey por embaixadores, à el rey dom Duarte de Inglaterra Ruy de Sousa-pessoa principal è de muyto bon saber é credito; de que el Rey muyto confiua: é ho doutor Ioam d'Eluas, é fernam de Pina por secretario. E foram por mar muy honradamente cum muy boa companhia: hos quaes foram en nome del rey confirmar as ligas antiquas com Inglaterra, que polla-condiçan deltas ho nouo Rey de hum zeyno é do outro era obrigado à mandar confirmar: é tambien pera monstrarem ho titolo que el rey tinha no senhorio de Guinee, pera que depois de visto el rey D'Inglaterra defendesse em todos seus reynos, que ninguen armasse nem podesse mandar à Guinee: é assi mandasse desfazer huna armada que pera laa faziam, per mandado do Duque de Medina Sidonia, hum Ioam Tintam é hum Guilherme fabiam Ingleses. Com ha qual embaixada e, rey D'Inglaterra mostrou receber grande contentamento: é foy delle commuyta honra recebida, é em tudo fez inteiramente ho que pellos embaixadores lhe foy requerido: de que elles trouxeran autenticas escrituras das diligencias que con pubricos pregones fizeram: [Sidenote: These writings are in the Towre.] é assi as prouisones das aprouaçones que eran neccssarias: è com tudo muyto ben acabado, é ha vontade del rey se vieram.

* * * * *

The voyage of Matthew Gourney, a most, valiant English Knight against the
  Moores of Algier in Barbarie and Spaine. M. Camden pag. 159.

Nec tacendum Matthæum Gourney in oppido quodam, vulgari lingua Stoke vnder Hamden in comitatu Somersetensi appellato, sepultum esse, virum bellicosissimum regnante Edwardo tertio: qui 96. ætatis anno diem obiuit, cum (vt ex inscriptione videre licuit) obsidioni d'Algizer contra Saracenos, prælijs Benamazin, Sclusensi, Cressiaco, Ingenos, Pictauiensi, et Nazarano in Hispania dimicasset.

The same in English.

[Sidenote: In the reigne of Edward the third.] It is by no means to be passed ouer in silence, that Matthew Gourney, being a most valiant warriour in the reigne of Edward the third, lyeth buried at a certaine towne, in the countie of Somerset, commonly called Stoke vnder Hamden: who deceased in the 96. yeare of his age: and that (as it is manifest by the inscription of his monument) after he had valiantly behaued himselfe at the siege of Algizer against the Sarazens, and at the battailes of Benamazin, of Sluce, of Cressie, of Ingenos, of Poictou, and of Nazaran in Spaine.

* * * * *

The comming of Lyon King of Armenia into England, in the yeere 1386, and in the ninth yeere of Richard the second, in trust to finde some meanes of peace or good agreement betweene the King of England and the French king. Iohn Froyssart lib. 3. cap. 56.

Thus in abiding for the Duke of Berrie, and for the Constable, who were behind, then king Lyon of Armenia, who was in France, and had assigned him by the king, six thousande frankes by the yeare to maintaine his estate, tooke vpon him for a good intent to goe into England to speake with the king there and his Councell, to see if he might finde any matter of peace to be had, betweene the two Realmes, England and France: And so he departed from his lodging of Saint Albeyne beside Saint Denice, alonely [Footnote: "Merely" "only." (Nare's *Glossary.*) "I speak not this *alonly* for mine owne." MIR. FOR MAGIST., p. 367.] with his owne company, and with no great apparell. So he rode to Boloine, and there he tooke a shippe, and so sayled foorth till he came, to Douer; and there he found the Earle of Cambridge, and the Earle of Buckingham, and moe then a hundreth men of armes, and a two thousand Archers, who lay there to keepe that passage, for the brute [Footnote: Report, *French* BRUIT. (Nare's *Glossary*). Compare 3 Ilen, vi., iv., 7.] ran, that the Frenchmen should lande there or at Sandwich, and the king lay at London, and part of his Councell with him, and daily heard tydings from all the Portes of England. When the king of Armenia was arriued at Douer, he had there good cheere, because he was a stranger, and so he came to the kings vncles there, who sweetly receiued him, and at a time conuenient, they demaunded of him from whence he came and whither he would. The king answered and sayd, that in trust of goodnesse he was come thither to see the king of England, and his Councell, to treate of peace betweene England and France, for he saide that he thought the warre was not meete: for he sayd, by reason of warre betweene these two Realmes, which hath indured so long, the Saracens, Iewes and Turkes are waxed proude, for there is none that make them any warre, and by occasion thereof I haue lost my land and Realme, and am not like to recouer them againe without there were firme peace in all Christendome: and I would gladly shew the matter that toucheth all Christendome to the king of England, and to his Councell, as I haue done to the French king. Then the kings Vncles demaunded of him if the French king sent him thither or no; he answered and sayd, no: there is no man that sent mee, but I am come hither by mine owne motion to see if the king of England and his Councel would any thing leane to any treaty of peace, then was he demaunded where the French king was, he answered I beleeue he be at Sluce, I sawe not him sithence I tooke my leaue of him at Senlize. Then he was demaunded, howe he could make any treatie of peace, and had no charge so to doe, and Sir, if yee be conueyed to the King our Nephew and to his Counsell, and the French king in the meane season enter with his puissance into England; yee may happe thereby to receiue great blame, and your person to be in great ieoperdy with them of the Countrey. Then the King answered and said, I am in suretie of the French king, for I haue sent to him, desiring him till I returne againe, not to remoue from Sluce, and I repute him so noble and so well aduised, that he will graunt my desire, and that hee will not enter into the sea, till I come againe to him. Wherefore, sirs, I pray you in the instance of loue and peace, to conuey me to speake with the King, for I desire greatly to see him: or else yee that be his Vncles, if ye haue authoritie, to giue me answere to all my demaunds. Then the Earle of Buckingham sayd, syr king of Armenia, we be ordayned here to keepe and defend this passage, and the frontiers of England, by the King and his Counsell, and wee haue no charge to meddle any further with the businesse of the Realme, without we be otherwise commanded by the King. But sith ye be come for a good intent into this Countrey, ye be right welcome; but sir, as for any firme answere ye can haue none of vs, for as now we be not of the Councell, but we shall conuey you to the king without perill or danger. The king thanked them, and said: I desire nothing else but to see the king and to speake with him.

How the King of Armenia returned out of England, and of the answere that was made to him.

When the king of Armenia was refreshed at Douer a day, and had spoken with the kings Vncles at good leasure, then he departed towards London, with a good conduct that, the Lords appointed to him, for feare of any recounters: so long he rode that he came to London, and in his ryding through London he was well regarded, because he was a stranger, and he had good cheare made him, and so was brought to the king, who lay at the Royall at the Queenes wardrobe, and his Councell were in London at their lodgings: The Londoners were sore fortefying of their citie. When the comming of the king of Armenia was knowen, the kings Councell drew to the King to heare what tydings the King brought in that troublous season: When the king of Armenia was come into the kings presence, he made his salutation and then beganne his processe to the states, how he was come out of France principally to see the king of England whom he had neuer seene before, and said, how he was right ioyous to be in his presence, trusting that some goodnesse might come thereby. And there he shewed by his words, that to withstande the great pestilence that was likely to be in England; therefore he was come of his owne good will to doe good therein if he might, not sent from the French king, willing to set some accorde and peace betweene the two Realmes England and France. Many faire pleasant words the king of Armenia spake to the king of England, and to his Counsell, then he was shortly answered thus: Syr king, ye be welcome into this Realme, for the king our soueraigne lord, and all we are glad to see you here, but sir, we say that the king hath not here all his Councell, but shortly they shall be here, and then ye shall be answered. The king of Armenia was content therewith, and so returned to his lodging. Within foure dayes after the king was counselled (and I thinke he had sent to his Vncles to know their intents, but they were not present at the answere giuing) to goe to the pallace at Westminster and his Councell with him, such as were about him, and to send for the king of Armenia to come thither. And when he was come into the presence of the king of England and his Councell, the king sate downe, and the king of Armenia by him, and then the Prelates and other of his Councell. There the king of Armenia rehearsed againe his requestes that he made, and also shewed wisely how all Christendome was sore decayed and feeblished by occasion of the warres betweene England and France. And how that all the knights and Squires of both Realmes entended [Footnote: Attend to. It is used in the same sense in the Alleyn papers. "Loe that I will now after Monday, intend your busines carefully." And in *Timon of Athens* ii., 2.] nothing else, but alwayes to be on the one part or of the other: whereby the Empire of Constantinople leeseth, [Footnote: Diminisheth, dwindleth. Nares does not give this meaning, not have I ever come across a precisely similar instance of its use.] and is like to leese; for before this warre the Knights and Squires were wont to aduenture themselues. And also the king of Armenia shewed that by occasion of this warre he had lost his Realme of Armenia, therefore he desired for Gods sake that there might be some treaty of peace had betweene the two Realmes England and France. To these wordes answered the Archbishop of Canterburie, for he had charge so to doe; And he sayd, Sir king of

Armenia, it is not the manner nor neuer was seene betweene two such enemies as the king of England and the French king, that the King my Souereigne lorde should be required of peace, and he to enter his land with a puissant army, wherefore sir, we say to you, that if it please you, ye may returne to the French king, and cause him and all his puissance to returne backe into their owne countreys. And when euery man be at home, then if it please you ye may returne againe hither, and then we shall gladly intende to your treatie.

This was all the answere the king of Armenia could get there, and so he dined with the king of England, and had as great honour as could bee deuised, and the king offered him many great gifts of golde and siluer, but he would take none though he had neede thereof, but alonely a ring to the value of a hundreth Frankes. After dinner he tooke his leaue and returned vnto his lodging, and the next day departed, and was two days at Douer, and there he tooke his leaue of such lords as were there, and so tooke the sea in a passager, [Footnote: Generally spelt *passenger*, as in the letter of the Earl of Leicester 1585. Quoted by Nares.] and arriued at Calais and from thence went to Sluce, and there he spake with the French king and with his Vncles, and shewed them how he had bene in England, and what answere he had: the French king and his Vncles tooke no regard of his saying, but sent him backe againe into France, for their full intention was to enter into England as soone as they might haue winde and weather, and the Duke of Berrie and the Constable came to them: The winde was sore contrary to them, for therewith they could neuer enter into England but the winde was good to goe into Scotland. [Footnote: The King of Armenia here referred to was Leon VI., the last of the Cilicio Armenian dynasty founded by Rupen, a relative of Gagik, the last of the Bagratide Kings: He was taken prisoner by the Mamelukes of Egypt in 1375, and after a long captivity wandered as an exile through Europe, dying at Paris in 1393.]

* * * * *

The memorable victories in diuers parts of Italie of Iohn Hawkwood English man in the reigne of Richard the second, briefly recorded by M. Camden, pag. 339.

Ad alteram ripam fluuij Colne oppositus est Sibble Heningham, locus natalis, vt accepi, Ioannis Hawkwoodi (Itali Aucuthum corruptè vocant) quem illi tantopere ob virtutem militarem suspexerunt, vt Senatus Florentinus propter insignia merita equestri statua et tumuli honore in eximiæ fortitudinis, fidéique testimonium ornauit. Res eius gestas Itali pleno ore praedicant; Et Paulus Iouius in elogijs celebrat: sat mihi sit Iulij Feroldi tetrastichon adijcere.

Hawkwoode Anglorum decus, et decus addite genti
  Italicæ presidiúmque solo,
Vt tumuli quondam Florentia, sic simulachri
  Virtutem Iouius donat honore tuam.

William Thomas in his Historie of the common wealthes of Italy, maketh honorable mention of him twise, to wit, in the commonwealth of Florentia and Ferrara.

* * * * *

The comming of the Emperour of Constantinople into England, to desire the aide of Henry the 4. against the Turkes, 1400.

[Sidenote: Thomas Walsingham.] Sub eodem tempore Imperator Constantinopolitanus venit in Angliam, postulaturus subsidium contra Turcas. Cui occurit rex cum apparatu nobili ad le Blackheath, die sancti Thomae Apostilo, susceptique, prout decuit, tantum Heroem, duxítque Londonias, et per multos dies exhibuit gloriosè, pro expensis hospitij sui soluens, et eum respiciens tanto fastigio donatiuis. Et paulo post: His auditis rumoribus, Imperator laetior recessit ab Anglis, honoratus à rege donarijs preciosis.

The same in English.

About the same time the Emperour of Constantinople came into England, to seek ayde against the Turkes: whom the king accompanied with his nobilitie, met withall vpon Blackheath vpon the day of saint Thomas the Apostle, and receiued him as beseemed so great a prince, and brought him to London, and roially entertained him for a long season, defraying the charges of his diet, and giuing him many honorable presents. And a litle afterward: Vpon the hearing of these newes, the emperor departed with great ioy out of England, whom the king honoured with many precious gifts.

* * * * *

A briefe relation of the siege and taking of the Citie of Rhodes, by Sultan Soliman the great Turke, translated out of French into English at the motion of the Reuerend Lord Thomas Dockwray, great Prior of the order of
  Ierusalem in England, in the yeere, 1524.

Willingly faithfully to write and reduce in veritie Historiall, the great siege, cruel oppugnation, and piteous taking of the noble and renowmed citie of Rhodes, the key of Christendome, the hope of many poore Christian men, withholden in Turkie to saue and keepe them in their faith: the rest and yeerely solace of noble pilgrimes of the holy sepulchre of Iesu Christ and other holy places: the refuge and refreshing of all Christian people: hauing course of marchandise in the parties of Leuant, I promise, to all estates that shall see this present booke, that I haue left nothing for feare of any person, nor preferred it for fauour. And first I shall shewe the occasions that moued this cruell bloodshedder, enemie of our holy Christian faith, Sultan Soliman, now being great Turke, to come with a great hoste by sea and by lande, to besiege and assayle the space of sixe monethes, night and day, the noble and mightie citie of Rhodes, the yere of the incarnation of our Lord Iesu Christ, 1522.

The occasions why the great Turke came to besiege the Citie of Rhodes.

The first and principall cause was that he did consider and sawe by experience, that there was none other Towne nor place in Leuant that warred against him nor kept him in doubt, but this poore rocke of Rhodes. And hearing that continuall complaintes of his subiectes as well of Syria, as of Turkie, for the domages and prises dayly done of their bodies and goods by Christian men of warre receiued into Rhodes: And also of the shippes and gallies of the religion, he tooke conclusion in himselfe, that if he might put the sayde Towne in his power and subiection, that then he should be peaceable lord of all the parties of Leuant, and that his subiects should complaine no more to him.

The second, that he might followe the doings of his noble predecessours, and shewe himselfe very heire of the mightie and victorious lord Sultan Selim his father, willing to put in execution the enterprise by him left the yeere one thousand fiue hundred twentie and one. The which Selim the great Turke put in all redinesse his armie to the number of three hundreth sayles purposing for to send them against Rhodes, if mortalitie had not happened in his host, and he afterwarde by the will of our lorde was surprised and taken with death: wherefore he being in the latter ende of his dayes, (as some Turkes and false christian men that were at this siege shewed me) did charge by his testament, or caused to charge his sonne now being great Turke, that after this death hee should make his two first enterprises, the one against Bellegrado in Hungarie, and the other against Rhodes, for to get him honour, and to set his Countries and subiectes in rest and suretie. The which fatherly motion easilie entered into him and was imprinted in the heart and yoong will of the sayde Solyman, his sonne, the which soone after the death of his father put in effect the first enterprise, and raised an huge hoste both by water and by land, and went himselfe in person against Bellegrado, a right strong place in Hungarie. [Sidenote: The taking of Belgrade.] And after that hee had besieged it the space of two monethes or thereabout, for fault of ordinance and vitailes, it was yeelded to him by composition the eight day of September, in the yeere of our lord, one thousand fiue hundred twentie and one. The sayd Solyman hauing this victory, being swollen and raised in pride and vaineglory, turned his heart agaynst Rhodes. Neuertheless, he not ignorant of the strength of it, and considering the qualities of the people that were within it, of whom he should be well receiued as his predecessours had bene aforetimes, doubted much, and knew not how to furnish his enterprise. For his capitaines and Bashas turned him from it as much as they might by many reasons, they knowing the force of it, saue onely Mustofa Basha his brother in lawe, the which councelled and put him in minde to goe thither. Finally, hee purposed entirely to haue it by treason or by force. [Sidenote: Forren physicians become spies oftentimes.] And also, for the same cause and purpose, his father in his dayes had sent a Iewe physician into Rhode as a spie, to haue the better knowledge of it: the sayd Solyman was informed that he was there yet, wherefore he sent him worde that he should abide there still for the same cause. And gaue in charge to one of the chiefe men in Sio, to send vnto the sayd Iewe all things needefull to maintaine him. And the same Iewe wrote to him of Sio, vnder priuie wordes, all that was done in Rhodes to giue knowledge thereof to the great Turke: and the better to hide his treason, the sayde Iewe made himselfe to bee baptised. And to bee the more named to be expert in Physike, he did some faire cures to such such as were diseased, whereby he began to bee well trusted, and came in fauour with many substantiall folkes of the towne. Among all other things whereof hee aduertised the great Turke, one was of a wall that was taken downe for to be new builded at the bulwarke of Auuergne, certifying him that if hee came hastely with his hoste, hee might easilie and at vnawares surprise the towne in such estate as it was at that time. Many other aduertisements and warnings hee shewed the Turke, which shall bee declared hereafter. [Sidenote: A Portingale traitor.] But beside his aduertisement, the sayd great Turke stirred and prouoked by a false traitour, a Portingale knight of ours, that time Chanceller of the sayd holy Religion, a man of great authoritie, dignitie, and vnderstanding, and one of the principall lordes of the counsell of the same, named Sir Andrew de Merall, by little and little was mooued and kindled to the sayd enterprise of treason, whereof was no maruell, for it was a great hope and comfort to haue such a person for him, that knew all the estate and rule of the religion and of the towne. And for to declare the occasions of the cursed and vnhappy will of the said traitor that had bene occasion of so great losse and damage, and shall be more at the length, if the diuine power set not to his hand.

[Sidenote: Philip de Villiers great master.] And here it is manifestly to bee vnderstood of all men, that after the death of the noble and right prudent lord, Fabrice of Cacetto, great master of Rhodes, the sayd Sir Andrew enflamed with ambition and couetousnesse to bee great master, and seeing himselfe deceiued of his hope, by the election made the two and twentieth day of Ianuary, of the right reuerend and illustrate lord, Philip de Villiers

Lisleadam, before him: from that time hee tooke so great enuie and desperation, enmitie and euil will, not onely against the sayde lord; but against all the holy religion, that hee set all his studie and purpose, to betray and sell his religion and the citie of Rhodes to the cursed misbeleeuers, forgetting the great honours and goodnesse that hee hath had of the religion, and hoped to receiue, with many other particuler pleasures that the sayd lord master had done to him. But the deuill, vnkindnesse, and wickednesse had so blinded the eyes of his thought, that hee in no wise could refraine him, but at euery purpose that was spoken afore him, hee was short and might not dissemble. And one day among other hee sayde before many knights, that hee would that his soule were at the deuill, and that Rhodes and the religion were lost. And many other foolish and dishonest purposes and wordes hee vttered, whereat none tooke heed, nor thought that hee had the courage to doe that thing that hee hath done. Howbeit, obstinate as Iudas, hee put in execution his cursed will: for soone after that the tidings of the election was sent Westward to the sayde noble lord, the sayd de Merall did send a Turke prisoner of his to Constantinople, vnder shadowe to fetch his ransome. By whom he aduertised the great Turke and his counsell, of the maner and degree of Rhodes, and in what state and condicion the towne was in of all maner of things at that time, and what might happen of it, prouoking and stirring him to come with a great hoste to besiege the towne. And after the comming of the sayd reuerend lord great master, he gaue other aduise to the great Turke, shewing him that hee could neuer haue better time to come, seeing that the great master was new come, and part of the wall taken downe, and that all Rhodes was in trouble by occasion of some Italian knights, rebels agaynst the lord great master: of the which rebellion he was causer, the better to bring his cursed mind to passe: and also gaue the sayde great Turke knowledge that all Christian princes were busie, warring each vpon other, and that he should not doubt but if the rebellion lasted among them, the towne should be his without faile, as it is seene by experience. And for lacke of succours of euery part, and especially of such as might easily haue holpen vs beyng our neighbours, with their gallies and men of warre, wherefore it is now in the handes of the enemies of the christian faith. The which monitions and reasons of the false traitor being vnderstood and pondered by the great Turke and his counsell, it was considered of them not to loose so good occasion and time. Wherefore hee made most extreme diligence to rigge and apparell many ships and vessels of diuers sorts, as galliasses, gallies, pallandres, fustes, and brigantines, to the number of 350. sailes and moe. [Footnote: A Galliasse was a 3 masted galley; Pallandres were manned by 20 men and Fustes by 12 to 15.] When the prisoner that the sayd de Merall did send into Turkie had done his commission, hee returned into Rhodes, whereof euery man had maruell. And many folkes deemed euil of his comming againe, as of a thing vnaccustomed, but none durst say any thing, seeing the sayd de Merall of so great authoritie and dignitie, and he cherished the sayd prisoner, more than he was woont to doe. Therefore belike hee had well done his message, and had brought good tidings to the damnable and shamefull mind of the sayd traitor de Merall.

How the great Turke caused the passages to be kept, that none should beare tidings of his hoste to Rhodes.

The great Turke intending with great diligence to make readie his hoste both by sea and by land, the better to come to his purpose, and to take the towne vnwarily as hee was aduertised, thought to keepe his doings as secret as hee might, and commaunded that none of his subiects should goe to Rhodes for any maner of thing. And likewise he tooke all the barkes and brigantines out of the hauens and portes in those coastes, because they should giue no knowledge of his armie. And also hee made the passages by land to bee kept, that none should passe. Howbeit, so great apparell of an armie could not bee long kept close: for the spies which the lord great master had sent into Turkie, brought tidings to the castle of saint Peter, and to Rhodes, of all that was said and done in Turkie. Neuerthelesse, the sayd lord gaue no great credence to all that was brought and told, because that many yeeres before, the predecessours of the great Turke had made great armies: and alway it was sayd that they went to Rhodes, the which came to none effect. And it was holden for a mocke and a by-word in many places, that the Turke would goe to besiege Rhodes. And for this reason doubt was had of this last armie, and some thought that it should haue gone into Cyprus or to Cataro, a land of the lordship of Venice. Howbeit the great master not willing to bee taken vnwarily, but the meane while as carefull and diligent for the wealth of his towne, and his people, vnderstanding these tidings of the Turkes armie, did all his diligence to repaire and strengthen the towne. Amongst all other things to build vp, and raise the bulwarke of Auuergne, and to cleanse and make deeper the ditches. And the more to cause the workemen to haste them in their businesse, the sayd lord ouersawe them twise or thrise euery day.

How the lord great master counselled with the lordes for prouision of the towne.

[Sidenote: Sir Iohn Bourgh the English Turcoplier.] Then the sayd reuerend lord thought to furnish and store the towne with more vitailes for the sustenance thereof, and for the same many times hee spake with the lordes that had the handling and rule of the treasurie, and of the expenses thereof in his absence, and since his comming: That is to wit, with the great Commander Gabriel de pommerolles, lieutenant of the sayd lord: The Turcoplier Sir Iohn Bourgh of the English nation: and the Chancellor Sir

Andrew de Meral, of whom is spoken afore and of his vntruth agaynst his religion. The which three lordes sayd, that hee should take no thought for it, for the towne was well stored with vitailes for a great while, and that there was wheate ynough till new came in: Notwithstanding it were good to haue more, or the siege were laied afore the towne, and therefore it were behoouefull to send for wheate and other necessaries into the West for succours of the towne, and at that time to puruey for euery thing.

Of the prouision for vitailes and ordinance of warre.

As touching the store and ordinance of warre, the sayd lordes affirmed that there was ynough for a yeere and more, whereof the contrary was found, for it failed a moneth or the citie was yeelded. It is of trueth that there was great store, and to haue lasted longer then it did. But it was needful to spend largely at the first comming of the enemies to keepe them from comming neere, and from bringing earth to the ditches sides as they did. And moreouer you are to consider the great number of them, and their power that was spred round about the towne, giuing vs so many assaults and skirmishes in so many places as they did, and by the space of sixe whole moneths day and night assailing vs, that much ordinance and store was wasted to withstand them in all points. And if it failed, it was no maruell. Howbeit the noble lord great master, prouided speedily for it, and sent Brigantines to Lango, to the castle of saint Peter, and to the castels of his isle Feraclous and Lyndo, for to bring powder and saltpeter to strength the towne, but it suffised not.

And for to speake of the purueiance of vitailes, it was aduised by the lord great master and his three lordes, that it was time to send some ships for wheat to places thereabout, before the Turks hoste were come thither. And for this purpose was appointed a ship named the Gallienge, whose captaine hight [Footnote: The participle of the Anglo-Saxon verb *Hatan*, to call: "Full carefully he kept them day and night; In fairest fields, and Astrophel he *hight*." SPENSER Astrophel i., 6.] Brambois, otherwise called Wolfe, of the Almaine nation, an expert man of the sea, the which made so good diligence, that within a moneth he performed his voiage, and brought good store of wheat from Naples and Romania, [Footnote: The territory around Rome, *not* Roumania.] which did vs great comfort.

How a Brigantine was sent to Candie for wine, and of diuers ships that came to helpe the towne.

After this, a motion was made to make prouision of wine for the towne, for the men of Candie durst not saile for to bring wine to Rhodes as they were woont to doe for feare of the Turkes hoste: and also they of the towne would send no ship into Candie, fearing to be taken and enclosed with the sayd hoste by the way. Howbeit some merchants of the towne, were willing to haue aduentured themselues in a good ship of the religion, named the Mary, for to haue laden her with wine in Candie. But they could not agree with the three lordes of the treasure, and their let was but for a little thing: and all the cause came of the sayd traitour de Merall, faining the wealth of the treasure: for he intended another thing, and brake this good and profitable enterprise and will of the sayd merchants, seeing that it was hurtfull to the Turke, whose part the said traitour held in his diuelish heart: that notwithstanding, the reuerend lord great master, that in all things from the beginning to the ende, hath alway shewed his good will, and with all diligence and right that might bee requisite to a soueraigne captaine and head of warre, found other expedience, and sent a Brigantine into Candie, in the which he sent a brother sergeant named Anthonie of Bosus, a well sprighted [Footnote: Loyal.] man and wise, that by his wisedome wrought so well, that, within a small time he brought fifteene vessels called Gripes, laden with wine, and with them men of warre the which came vnder shadow of those wines, because the gouernours of Candie durst let none of their men goe to the succour of Rhodes for feare of the Turke. And beside those fifteene Gripes came a good ship whose capitaine and owner was a rich yong gentleman Venetian, Messire Iohn Antonio de Bonaldi, which of his good will came with his ship laden with 700. buts of wine to succour the towne with his person and folkes, whose good and lowable will I leaue to the consideration of the readers of this present booke. For hee being purposed to haue had his wines to Constantinople, or he was enformed of the busines of Rhodes, and was in the porte du Castell in Candie, would not beare his vitailes to the enemies of the faith, but came out and returned his way toward Rhodes, forgetting all particular profite and aduantage. He being arriued at Rhodes, dispatched and sold his wine, which was a great encrease and comfort for the towne. And when he had so done, he presented his person, his ship, and his folke, to the reuerend great master, the which retained him, and set him in wages of the Religion. And during the siege, the sayd capitaine behaued him woorthily in his person, and put himselfe in such places as woorthy men ought to be, spending his goods largely without demanding any paiment or recompense for his doing, of the Religion.

How the corne was shorne downe halfe ripe and brought into the towne for feare of the Turkes hoste.

During these things, the reuerend lord great master carefull and busie to haue euerything necessary, as men and other strengths, sent vessels called brigantines, for to cause the wafters of the sea to come vnto Rhodes for the keeping and fortifying of the towne, the which at the first sending came and presented their persons and ships to the seruice of the religion.

[Sidenote: Haruest in April and May.] After that the sayd lord caused to shere downe the Rie of his isle, and caused it to bee brought into the towne, which was done in Aprill: and then in May in some places, he made to shere the wheate halfe ripe, howbeit the most part was left in the fields, because the Turkes hoste was come out of the streights of Constantinople. And doubting that any number of ships should come before to take the people of the sayd Isle vnawares, the sayd lord made them to leaue shering of wheate, and caused the people of the furthest part of the Isle to come into the towne.

While that the great master prouided for all things after the course of time and tidings that hee had, there arriued a Carak of Genoa laden with spicerie from Alexandria, the which passed before the port of Rhodes the eight day of Aprill, and rid at anker at the Fosse, 7. or 8. miles from the towne, for to know and heare tidings of the Turkish hoste. Then the lord willing to furnish him with people as most behoouefull for the towne, sent a knight of Prouence named sir Anastase de sancta Camilla, commander de la Tronquiere to the captaine of the Carak, praying him to come into the hauen with his ship for the defence of the towne, profering him what he would, assuring him ship. The captaine excused him, saying, that the merchandise was not his owne, but belonged to diuers merchants to whom he must yeeld account. Howbeit at the last after many words and promises to him made hee came into the hauen, the which captaine was named messire Domingo de Fournati, and hee in his person behaued him valiauntly in the time of the sayd siege.

How the great master caused generall musters to be made, and sent a vessell to the Turkes nauie, of whom he receiued a letter.

After the moneth of April the lord master seeing that the Turkes hoste drew neere, and that he had the most part of the wafters within the towne, he caused generall musters of men of armes to be made. And began at the knights, the which vpon holy Rood day in May made their musters, before the Commissioners ordained by the sayd lord in places deputed to each of them called Aalberge. The which Commissioners made report to the lordes that they had found the knights in good order of harnesse and other things necessary for warre, and their araie faire and proper, with crosses on them. When the muster of the knights was done, the lord master thought to make the musters of them of the towne, and strangers together: but his wisedome perceiued that harme should come thereby, rather then good, doubting, that the number of people should not bee so great as he would, or needed to haue, whereof the great Turke might haue knowledge by goers and commers into Rhodes, and therefore he caused them of the towne to make their musters seuerall by bandes and companies, and the strangers also by themselues, to the end that the number should not bee knowen, notwithstanding that there was good quantitie of good men and well willing to defend themselues. And the more to hearten and giue them courage and good will, some knights of the Crosse, decked their men with colours and deuises, and tooke with them men of the towne and strangers, and with great noyse of trumpets and timbrels, they made many musters, as enuying each other which should keepe best aray and order, and haue the fairest company. It was a great pleasure to see them all so well agree, and so well willing.

The number of the men of the towne amounted and were esteemed, three, or foure thousand, beside men of the villages that might be 1500. or 2000.

The eight day of the same moneth, the Turkes hearing of those tidings, made a fire for a token in a place called le Fisco, in the maine land right against Rhodes. And certaine dayes afore they had made another, that is to weet, when the ship of a knight named Menetow went thither, and had with him the clarke of the gallies named Iaques truchman, the which vnder shadow to speake with him, was withholden of the Turkes. For the great Turke had commanded to take him or some other man of the Rhodes to haue perfect knowledge in what estate the towne was then in euery thing. And they of the towne weening that the second fire was for to deliuer Iaques, the reuerend lord great master sent one of his galliasses, whose patron was called messire Boniface of Prouence, to know the cause thereof. And when hee arriued at the sayd place of le Fisco, he demaunded of the Turkes wherefore they had made the token of fire. And they said that it was because their lord had sent a letter to the great master, but as yet it was not come, and desired him to tary till it were brought. The patron as warie and wise in the businesse of the sea, thought in himselfe that the Turkes made such prolonging to some euill intent, or to surprise his vessell being alone, wherefore hee bade them giue him the letter speedily, or els he would goe his way, and neither tary for letter nor other thing: and told them of the euill and dishonest deed that they had done the dayes afore, to withhold the clarke vnder their words and safeconduct: and therewith he turned his galliasse to haue gone away. The Turkes seeing that, gaue him the letter, the which he tooke, and when he was arriued at Rhodes, he presented it to the lord great master, which assembled the lordes of his counsell, and made it to be red. The tenor whereof was such as foloweth.

The copie of the letter that the great Turke sent to the lord great master, and to the people of the Rhodes.

Sultan Solyman Basha by the grace of God, right mightie emperor of Constantinople, and of himselfe holding both the lands of Persia, Arabia, Syria, Mecha, and Ierusalem; of Asia, Europe, Aegypt, and of all the Sea, lord and possessor: To the reuerend father lord Philip, great master of

Rhodes, to his counsailors, and to all the other citizens great and small, greeting. Sending conuenient and worthy salutations to your reuerances, wee giue you to weet, that we haue receiued your letters sent vnto our imperiall maiestie by George your seruant, the tenor whereof we doe well vnderstand: and for this occasion we send vnto you this our present commaundement, to the end that we will that ye know surely how by our sentence we will haue that Isle of Rhodes for many damages and euill deeds which we haue, and heare from day to day of the sayd place done to vs and our subiects, and ye with your good will shall hold it of vs and doe vs obeisance, and giue the citie to mine imperiall maiestie. And we sweare by God that made heauen and earth, and by 26000. of our prophets, and by the 4. Misafi that fell from the skies, and by our first prophet Mahomet, that if ye doe vs homage, and yeeld you with good will vpon these othes, all you that will abide in the sayd place, great and small, shall not need to feare perill nor damage of mine imperiall maiestie, neither you, your goods, nor your men: and who so will goe to any other place with his goods and houshold, may so doe, and who so will dwell and inhabits in any other places vnder mine Imperiall maiestie, may remaine where they like best, without feare of any person. And if there bee any of the principals and woorthy men among you that is so disposed, wee shall giue him wages and prouision greater then hee hath had. And if any of you will abide in the sayd isle, yee may so doe after your auncient vsages and customes, and much better. And therefore if that Imperiall maiestie, or els know yee that wee will come vpon you with all prouisions of warre, and thereof shall come as it pleaseth God. And this wee doe, to the end that ye may know, and that ye may not say, but we haue giuen you warning. And if ye doe not thus with your good will, wee shall vault and vndermine your foundations in such maner, that they shalbe torne vpside downe, and shal make you slaues, and cause you to die, by the grace of God, as we haue done many, and hereof haue ye no doubt. Written in our court at Constantinople the first day of the moneth of Iune.

How the Turkes came to land in the Isle of Lango, and were driuen to their ships againe by the Prior of S. Giles.

When the lord great master and his counsell had heard the tenor of the letter, they would giue none answere to the great Turke, but that he should be receiued with good strokes of artillerie. So that to a foolish demaund behooued none answere. And it was very like that he would haue nothing. For sixe dayes after, that was the 14. day of the said moneth of Iune, the Brigantines that went toward Sio to know of the said armie, came againe and sayd, that of a trueth the said armie was comming; and that nigh to Lango an Isle of the religion, and 100. mile from Rhodes, they had seene and told 30. sailes that were most part gallies and fustes: the which vessels set men on land in the isle of Lango. Then the prior of S. Giles, Messire pre Iohn de Bidoux commander of the said place, taried not long from horsebacke with his knights and people of the isle, and he met so well with the Turkes, that he droue them to their ships, and slew a certaine number of them: and of the side of Pre Iohn some were hurt, and his horse was slaine. When the enemies were entered into their gallies, they went to a place called castle Iudeo on the maine land, betweene the sayd isle of Lango and the castle of S. Peter.

How part of the nauie and armie of the great Turke came before the citie of Rhodes.

The 18. day of the said moneth of Iune, these 30. gallies went from the sayd place, and passed, by the Cape of Crion, entering the gulfe of Epimes beside Rhodes, and were discoured from the shade of the hill of Salaco, a castle in the isle of Rhodes. On the morrow they came out of the gulfe by plaine day, and sailing along by the coasts, they entered into a hauen on maine land called Malfata, where they abode three dayes. Then they went from thence, and returned to the gulfe of Epimes, where they abode two dayes and two nights.

The 24 day of the same moneth they issued out of Epimes, and trauersing the chanell, they came to the yle of Rhodes in a place before a castle called Faues, and they went to land, and burnt a great field of corne the same day, which was the feast of S. Iohn Baptist our patron. The guard of a castle named Absito in the yle of Rhodes discoured and spied the great hoste, and in great haste brought word to the lord master, and sayd that the sayd hoste, that was in so great number of sailes that they might not be numbred, was entered into the gulfe of Epimes. The 30 sailes that lay in the yle arose in the night, and went to the sayd hoste in the gulfe.

The 26 day of Iune the sayd great hoste arose and went out of Epimes an houre after the sun rising, and trauersing the chanell, they came to a place called the Fosse, eight miles from the towne. And the 30 first sailes turned backe toward the cape of S. Martin and other places to watch for ships of Christian men, if any passed by to Rhodes. The great hoste abode still till noone or one of the clocke, and then arose, not all, but about 80 or 100 ships, as gallies, galliasses, and fusts: and passed one after another before the towne and hauen of Rhodes three miles off, and came to shore in a place nigh to land, called Perambolin, sixe miles from the towne. In the which place the sayd hoste abode from that time to the end of that vnhappy siege.

The number and names of the vessels that came to besiege Rhodes.

The number of the ships were these: 30 galliasses, 103 gallies, aswell bastards as subtill mahonnets, 15 taffours, 20 fusts, 64 great ships, sixe or seuen gallions, and 30 galleres, besides the nauy that waited for Christain men, if any came to succour vs. These were the vessels that came at the first to lay the siege. And sith that sayd host came out of Perambolin, there came from Syria 20 other sailes, aswell gallies as fusts. And many other ships came sith, and ioyned with the sayd army in the time of the sayd siege. And it was sayd that there were 400 sailes and moe.

The same day that part of the host came to the sayd place, the reuerend lord great master ordeined a great brigandine to send into the West, to certifie our holy father the pope, and the Christian princes how the Turks army was afore Rhodes. And in the sayd vessel he sent two knights, one a French man named Sir Claude Dansoyuille called Villiers, and Sir Loys de Sidonia a Spaniard: and they went to the pope and to the emperour.

After the comming of the Turks nauy into the sayd place, if was 14 or 15 dayes or they set any ordinance on land, great or small, or any quantity of men came on shore, whereof we marueiled. And it was tolde vs by some that came out of the campe, and also by the spies that the lord great master had sent abroad arayed as Turks that they, abode the commandement of their great lord, vntill the hoste by land were come into the campe. Howbeit there came some number for to view the towne, but they went priuity, for the ordinance of the towne shot without cease.

All this while the gallies and galliasses went and came to land, bringing vitaile and people. At the which ships passing nigh the town, were shot many strokes with bombards, which made some slaughter of our enemies: and when the most part of them was past, they began to set ordinance on the land with great diligence. Then the lord great master departed from his palace, and lodged him nigh a church called The victory, because that place was most to be doubted: and also that at the other siege [Footnote: This refers to the siege of Rhodes in 1480, by Mohammed II., the conqueror of Constantinople.] the great businesse and assault was there.

How the lord great master made his petition before the image of S. Iohn, and offered him the keyes of the towne.

The day before were made many predications and sermons, and the last was in the church of S. Iohn Baptist. When the sermon was done, a pontificall Masse was celebrate with all solemnities, and all the reliques taken downe, and the lord great master and all his knights with great deuotions and reuerence heard it. And when the Masse was ended, the lord great master made a pitious oration or prayer before Saint Iohn Baptist his protectour: and aboue all other words, which were too long to tell, he besought him meekly that it would please him to take the keyes of that miserable city. The which keyes he presented and layed vpon the altar before the image, beseeching S. Iohn to take the keeping and protection thereof, and of all the religion, as by his grace he had giuen to him vnworthy, the gouerning vnto that day: and by his, holy grace to defend them from the great power of the enemies that had besieged them.

How the women slaues would haue set fire in the towne.

The eight day of Iuly it was knowen that the Turkish women being slaues and seruaunts in many houses of the towne, had appointed to set fire in their masters houses at the first assault that should be made, to the end that the men should leaue their posterns and defenses to go and saue their houses and goods. And it was found that a woman of Marchopota being a slaue, was first moouer thereof, the which was taken and put to execution.

The same day some of our men went out for to skirmish with the Turkes, and many of them were slaine with shot of our artillerie, and of our men but one.

How the Turkes layd their artillerie about the towne, and of the maner and quantitie of their pieces and gunshot.

The 18. day of Iuly, for the beginning and first day they set vp a mantellet, vnder the which they put three or foure meane pieces, as sacres, wherewith they shot against the posterns of England and Prouence. But the mantellet was soone broken and cast downe, and their pieces destroyed with the shot of the wall, and they that shot them were most part slaine. As this first mantellet was broken, by the great and innumerable people that they had they set all their ordinance on land, and caried it to the places where it should be bent, or nigh thereby.

And the 29. day of the same moneth, they set vp two other mantellets. One beside a church of saint Cosme and Damian, and another toward the West. And from these mantellets they shot great pieces, as Culuerings, double gunnes, and great bombards [Footnote: For particulars of the artillery used from the 14th to the 16th Centuries, see Vol. iii, page 207. note.] agaynst the wals of England and Spaine, to the which mantellets the ordinance of the towne gaue many great strokes, and often brake them. And the more to grieue the towne and to feare vs, they set vp many other mantellets in diuers places, almost round about the towne, and they were reckoned foure score: the which number was well lessened by the great quantitie of strokes of artillerie shot out of the towne from many places.

The artillerie of the Turkes was such as followeth.

First there were sixe great gunnes, cannons perriers of brasse, that shot a stone of three foote and a halfe: also there were 15. pieces of iron that shot stones of fiue or sixe spannes about. Also there were 14. great bombards that shot stones of eleuen spans about. Also there were twelue basiliskes, whereof they shot but with 8. that is to weet, foure shot agaynst the posterns of England and Spaine, and two against the gate of Italy: the other two shot sometime against Saint Nicholas tower. Also there were 15. double gunnes casting bullets as basiliskes. The meane shot, as sacres and pasuolans, were in great number. The handgunshot was innumerable and incredible. Also there were twelue potgunnes of brasse that shot vpward, whereof eight were set behind the church of S. Cosme and Damian, and two at saint Iohn de la Fontaine toward the port of Italy, and the other two afore the gate of Auuergne, the which were shot night and day: and there were three sorts of them, whereof the greatest were of sixe or seuen spannes about. And the sayd stones were cast into the towne to make murder of people, which is a thing very inhumane and fearefull, which maner of shooting is little vsed amongst christian men. Howbeit by euident myracle, thanked be God, the sayd pieces did no great harme, and slew not past 24. or 25. persons, and the most part women and children, and they began to shoot with, the said pieces from the 19. day of the same moneth, vnto the end of August, and it was accounted that they shot 2000. times more or lesse.

Then the enemies were warned by the Iewe that wrote letters to them of all that was done and sayd in the towne, that the sayd potgunnes did no harme: wherefore they were angry, for they thought that they had slaine the third part of our people: and they were counselled by him to leaue that shooting, for it was but time lost, and pouder wasted, and then they shot no more with them. It is of a trueth that they shot with the sayd potgunnes 12. or 15. times with bullets of brasse or copper, full of wild fire, and when they were in the ayre, they flamed foorth, and in falling on the ground, they brake, and the fire came out and did some harme: But at the last wee knew the malice thereof, and the people was warie from comming neere to them, and therefore they did hurt no more folke.

How the captaine Gabriel Martiningo camee to the succor of Rhodes, and all the slaues were in danger to be slaine.

The 24. day of the same moneth a brigantine arriued that was sent afore into Candie, wherein came a worthy captaine named Gabriel Martiningo with two other captains. And there went to receiue him messieur prou Iohn prior of S. Giles, and the prior of Nauarre. Then after his honourable receiuing as to him well apperteined, they brought him before the lord great master that louingly receiued him, and he was gladly seene and welcommed of the people, as a man that was named very wise and ingenious in feats of warre. Then came a Spaniard renegado from the host, that gaue vs warning of all that was done in the field, and of the approaching by the trenches that our enemies made.

And in likewise there arose a great noise in the towne, that the slaues Turks that wrought for vs in the diches had slaine their keepers, and would haue fled, which was not so. Neuerthelesse, the rumour was great, and they rang alarme: wherefore the sayd slaues comming to prison, as it was ordeined in al the alarmes, were met of the people, which in great anger put them to death: so that there were slaine an hundred and moe the same day. And if the lord great master had not commanded, that none should hurt them, they had bene all slaine, and there were fifteene hundredth of them: which slaues did great seruice in time of the siege: for they laboured dayly to make our defences, and to cast earth out of the ditches, and in all works they were necessary at our needs.

How the great Turke arriued in person before Rhodes.

The 25 day of the sayd moneth many of our men went out for to skirmish in the field and made great murder of Turks, and in likewise did our artillery. And it is to be noted that the 28 day of the same moneth the great Turke in person passed le Fisco a hauen in the maine land with a galley and a fust, and arriued about noone, where his army lay, the which day may be called vnhappie for Rhodes. For his comming, his presence and continuall abiding in the fielde is and hath beene cause of the victorie that he hath had. When the gallie that he came in was arriued, all the other shippes of the hoste hanged banners aloft in their toppes and on their sayle yerdes.

Soone after that the Turke was arriued, he went to land, and mounted on his horse, and rode to his pauilion which was in a high place called Megalandra, foure or fiue miles fro the towne but of the danger of the gunne shot. And on the morrow, as it was reported to vs, hee came to a Church nigh the towne called Saint Steuen, for to viewe the Towne and fortresses, whereas they had set vp mantellets for to lay their ordinance.

The last day of Iuly, one of our briganidines went out with a good company of men arrayed as Turkes, and some of them could speake Turkish, and went by night to lande through the Turkes hoste, and demaunded if there were any that would passe ouer into Turkie, that they should haste them to come. The Turkes weening that they had beene of Turkie, there entred a 12. persons, the which were carried to Rhodes, by whom we knew what they did in the campe.

The first day of August the Captaine Gabriel Martiningo was made knight of the order of the religion by the lord great Master, and was made the first auncient of the Italian nation, of the first baliage or priorie that should be vacant. And in the meane season the religion should giue him twelue hundred ducates for pension euery yeere, and the same day he was receiued to the Councell in the roome of a baylife.

The fift day of the sayd moneth our master gunner was slaine with a gunne, which was great losse for vs at that time.

The 15. day of the sayd moneth was knowen and taken for a traitor, Messire Iohn Baptista, the physicion aforesayd, which confessed his euill and diuelish doings, and had his head striken of.

Of the marueiloous mounts that the Turks made afore the towne, and how the capitaines were ordered in the trenches.

After the comming of the great Turke, the enemies began to shoote with ordinance of another sort then they did before, and specially with harquebushes and handguns, and also to make their trenches and approches. And also they did more diligence then afore, to bring the earth nigh the towne with spades and pickaxes. And it is to weet, that they mooued the earth from halfe a mile off, and there were shot out of the towne innumerable strokes with ordinance against the sayd earth, and innumerable quantitie of people hid behind the sayd earth, were slaine. Neuerthelesse they neuer left working till they had brought it to the brimmes of the ditches: and when it was there, they raised it higher and higher in strengthning it behind. And in conclusion the sayd earth was higher then the wals of the towne by 10. or 12. foote, and it seemed a hill. And it was agaynst the gate of Auuergne and Spaine, and beat our men that were at the gates and bulwarks, in such wise, that none durst be seene till certaine defences and repaires were made of plankes and boards to couer our people and keepe them from the shot. And at the gate of Italy was made such another heape, and in none other part.

When the trenches were thus made to the ditches, the enemies made holes in the wals of the ditch outward: wherethorow they shot infinitely with handgunnes at our men aswell on the walles as on the bulwarks, and slew many of them. Then the bashas and captaines entred into the trenches, ech to his place after their order and dignity: that is to wit, Mustafa Basha as chiefe captaine entred the trench direct to the bulwarke of England with his people and captaines vnder him. Pery Bassha went to the trenches against the gate of Italy with his folkes and captaines vnder him. Acmek Bassha was in the trenches of Auuergne and Spaine with the Aga of the Ianizaires and the Beglarby of Romany with him. The Beglarby of Natolia was in the trenches of Prouence. Allibey was with his company against the gardins of saint Anthony on the North side, and diuers other captaines with him, and set his ordinance against the wall of the gate of Almaine, which was but weake, and set vp seuen mantellets by the milles toward the West: and by the space of eight or nine dayes they beat vpon the same wall; which put vs in great feare, if they had continued. Howbeit the noble lord great master forthwith caused repairs to be made within, and planks and tables to be set to fortifie the sayde weake wall: and abode there from the morning til night, to cause it to be the more hasted. The artillery of the gate of Almaine, and the Massif of the gate of the campe and of the palais beat so sore and so often vpon the sayd mantellets that it wearied the enemies to make and repaire them so often: and they tooke vp the pieces, and bare them away. And also they could not well beat the sayd wall because the brimmes of the ditch without were almost as hie as the wall that they beat. But or they bare the artillery away, they beat the steeple of S. Iohns church so, that the most part was broken and cast downe. The foresayd mantellets were appointed to beat S. Nicholas tower, and by the space of ten or twelue dayes they shot sore against it: but they had so sharpe and vigorous answere, that there was not one mantellet that abode whole an houre. The captaine of the sayd tower and his folke did such diligence and businesse in shooting off their pieces, that the enemies durst set up no more mantellets by day, nor shoot no more but onely by night, while the Moone did shine, which is a thing worthy of memory, of maruaile, and of praise. At the last when they had beaten against the sayd tower a certaine time, seeing that it furthered nothing, they tooke their ordinance from thence, and bare it where they thought best.

During the shot in the sayd place, the other captaines were not idle nor in a sleepe, but without cease night and day they beat the wall of England and Spaine, and set foureteene mantellets against it, shooting great bombards, whereof some of the stones were fiue or sixe spannes about, and some other of nine or ten: and within a moneth and lesse they cast downe the wall almost euen smooth with the Barbican. And when the sayd wall was so beaten, they set to beat the bulwarke of Spaine for to raise the defences: and in their trenches they set three great bombards, which shot stones of eleuen spannes in compasse, and with the sayd pieces they beat the sayd bulwarke and wall in such wise, that they made great bracks, and the stones and earth that fell, serued the enemies for ladders, so that they might come upon the plaine ground. In like sort they raised the defences from the height of the bulwarke at the posterne of Prouence, and set three great pieces on the brimme of the ditch, which shot stones of eleuen spannes against the wall, and within a while they made a breach as at the posterne of Spaine. The artillery of the towne did shoot without cease against the mantellets, and brake many of them, but they made other as it is said in the nights. For they had all things that belonged to them, and needed. And out of the posterne of England was shot a gunne that brake downe one of the sayde mantellets, and hit upon one of the pieces, and slew foure or fiue men, and bare away both the legs of the master of the ordinance, which died soone after: whereof the great Turke was very ill content, and sayd that he had rather haue lost one of his basshas or captaines then the sayd master. Also it is to be knowen that there were three or foure mantellets addressed against the plain ground of Italy, and by continuall beating of shot that they made, there was also a breach, and by the earth and stones that were fallen, they might come vp to it.

Of the politike repaires and defences that the ingenious captaine Gabriel Martiningo, made within the towne against the breaches in the walles.

The captaine Gabriel Martiningo, prompt, diligent, and expert to giue remedies to the needful places, foorthwith caused to make the trauerses vpon the wall whereas the breach was, with good repaires, and gunnes small and great which were set in the sayd trauerses, the which shot not onely at the breaches but to the trenches, and made great murder of enemies aswell at the assaults that they made as otherwhiles. And beside the trauerses, the sayd captaine planted small artillery, as harquebushes, and handgunnes vpon certaine houses within the towne, that stood open against the breach, with good repaires: and from that place great slaughter of Turks was made at the assaults. Also it is of trueth that beside the sayd mantellets that shot against the wall of England and Spaine with great bombards, were two mantellets in an hie place toward the way to the gardin of Maunas, in the which were certaine double gunnes, as basilisks with holow stones and wild fire in them, which shot against the wall into the towne at all auentures for to make murder of people: howbeit, thanked be God, they did no great harme but to the houses.

After these great and terrible beatings, and that the enemies had way to mount vpon the towne walles, and come to hand with vs by trauersing of their trenches to the fallen earth within the breach more surely, and without hurt of our gunshot, shooting, thorow holes that they made in the walles of the ditch without, they cast vp much stone and earth, because it should couer them from the shot of the bulwarke of Auuergne. And also they shot feruently against the bulwarke of Spaine, for to raise the defences, of the which at the last they raised the most part, reseruing only a few gunners below in the mine of the sayd bulwarke, which litle or nothing damaged them. And this is touching the gunshot, whereof I say not the third part, because it is a thing incredible to them that haue not seene it. For some dayes they shot with those great bombards that were on the brimme of the ditch, and from the mantellets bent against the wall of England and Spaine 20 or 30 times and more. And I beleeue verily that since the creation of the world such artillery, and so great quantity was neuer bent and layed before any towne as hath bene against Rhodes at this siege. Wherefore it is no maruell if the walles be and haue bene beaten downe, and if there be breaches and clifts in many places.

Of the mines that the Turks made: and how they ouerthrew part of the bulwarke of England.

And because as it is sayd before, that the greatest hope that the enemies had to get the towne of Rhodes, was by mining, therefore now after that I haue spoken of the gunshot and beatings, I shall shew of the mines that the Turks made, the which were in so great quantity, and in so many places, that I beleeue the third part of the towne was mined: and it is found by account made, that there were about 60 mines, howbeit, thanked be God, many of them came not to effect, by occasion of the countermines that they within made, and also trenches that the right prudent lord the great master caused to be made deepe within the ditches, vnto two or three foot of water. The which trenches and certaine pits that he had caused in the sayd ditches to be wrought, or the host arriued, serued right well since: for night and day there were men in them to watch and hearken when the enemies mined, for to meet them and cut their way, as was done many times.

And for to speake of the mines that had effect, and damaged vs, it is to wit, that the fourth day of September, about foure houres after noone, the enemies put fire in two mines, one was betweene the posterne of Spaine and Auuergne, which did no hurt but to the Barbican. The other was at the bulwarke of England, which was so fell and strong, that it caused most part of the town to shake, and cast down a great part of the sayd bulwarke at the spring of the day: and by the earth and stones that fell into the ditches, the enemies came vpon the bulwarke with their banners, and fought sore and mightily with our men, not with hands, but with shot handgunnes. The lord great master that was come 15 dayes or more with his succours to the sayd bulwarke, went with his company to helpe them that fought After that they had fought the space of two or three houres, the enemies repelled and driuen backe by our men from the sayd bulwarke, and beaten with ordinance on euery side, withdrew them with their losse, shame, and damage. [A thousand and more Turkes slaine before the English bulwarke.] And this was the first victory that our lord gaue vs, and there abode of our enemies a thousand and more.

When this assault was done, they, made another at the breach in the wall of Spaine, and mounted vpon it, but the ordinance of the trauerses of the walles and of the houses made so faire a riddance, that they were very willing to withdraw themselues: for at the retreat, and also at their comming the sayd ordinance of the bulwarke did them great damage, albeit that they had made some repaire of earth. Of our men died that day 25 or there about, as well knights as other. And the same day in the morning departed out of this world Gabriel de Pomerolles lieutenant to the lord master, which on a certaine day before fell from the wall as he went to see the trenches in the ditches, and hurt his breast, and for fault of good attendance he fell into a feuer, whereof he died.

How the Turks assailed the bulwarke of England, and how they were driuen away.

The ninth day of the sayd moneth, at seuen in the morning the enemies put fire in two mines; one at the posterne of Prouence, which had none effect: the other was at the bulwarke of England, which felled another piece nigh to that that was cast downe afore. And the sayd mine, was as fierce as the other, or more, for it seemed that all the bulwarke went downe, and almost all they that were in it ranne away. And when the standard of the religion came into the sayd bulwarke, the enemies were at the breach ready to haue entered: but when they saw the sayd standard, as people lost and ouercome, they went downe againe. Then the artillery of the bulwarke of Quosquino, and of other places, found them well enough, and slew many of them. Howbeit, their captaines made them to returne with great strokes of swordes and other weapons, and to remount vpon the earth fallen from the sayd bulwarke, and pight seuen banners nigh to our repaire. Then our men fought with morispikes and fixed speares against them the space of three whole houres, till at the last they being well beaten with great ordinance and small on euery side withdrew themselues. And of their banners our men gate one, for it was not possible to get any more: for assoone as any of our men went vp on our repaires, he was slaine with small gunnes of the trenches, and holes made in the walles of our ditches. [Sidenote: Two thousand Turks slaine at the Englis bulwarke.] And there was slaine of our enemies that day at the assault 2000 of meane men, and three persons of estate, which lay dead along in the ditch, with faire and rich harnesse. And it was reported to us from the campe, they were three saniacbeis, that is to say, great seneshalles or stuards. And of Christian men of our part abode about thirty persons. And this was the second victory giuen to us by the grace diuine.

How Sir Iohn Bourgh Turcoplier of England was slaine at an assault of the English bulwarke.

The 17 day of the same moneth, about midday, the enemy came againe to giue another assault to the sayd bulwarke, at the same place aforesayd, without setting of fire in mines, and brought fiue banners with them, nigh to the repaires. Then was there strong fighting on both parts, and there were gotten two of their banners, of the which sir Christopher Valdenare, that time Castelaine of Rhodes, gate one: the other was in the hands of Sir Iohn Bourgh Turcoplier of England, chiefe captaine of the succours of the sayd posterne of England, a valiant man and hardy: and in holding of it he was slaine with the stroke of a hand-gunne, which was great damage. The sayd banner was recouered by one of our men. And after long fighting on both sides, the enemies seeing that they got nothing but stripes, returned into their trenches. At the sayd fray the lord prior of S. Giles pre Iohn was hurt thorow the necke with a handgun, and was in great danger of death, but he escaped and was made whole. The same day, and the same houre of the sayd assault, the enemies mounted to the breach in the wall of Spaine, and came to the repaires to the handes of our men, and fought a great while: but the great quantity of artillery that was shot so busily and so sharply from our trauerses on ech side, and out of the bulwarks of Auuergne and Spaine, skirmished them so well, that there abode as many at that assault as at the other of England, well neere to the number of 5000. And they withdrew themselues with their great losse and confusion, which was the third time that they were chased and ouercome; thanked be our Lord, which gaue vs the force and power so to doe, for they were by estimation a hundred against one.

Also the 22 day of the same moneth of September they fired a mine betweene
Italy and Prouence, which did no harme.

Of the terrible mine at the posterne of Auuergne.

And the 23 day of the same moneth they fired two mines, one at the posterne of Spaine, and the other by the bulwarke of Auuergne, the which mine by Auuergne was so terrible, that it made all the towne to shake, and made the wall to open from aboue to beneath vnto the plaine ground; howbeit, it fell not, for the mine had vent or breath in two places, by one of the countermines, and by a rocke vnder the Barbican, the which did cleaue, and by that cleft the fury and might of the mine had issue. And if the sayd two vents had not bene, the wall had bene turned vpside downe. And for truth, as it was reported to vs out of the campe, the enemies had great hope in the sayd mine, thinking that the wall should haue bene ouerthrowen, and then they might haue entered into the towne at their pleasures: but when they saw the contrary, they were very ill pleased. And the captaines determined to giue assault at foure places at once, to make vs the more adoo, and to haue an entrance into the towne by one of the foure. And the sayd day and night they ceased not to shoot artillery: and there came in hope of the mine threescore thousand men and moe into the trenches.

How the bulwarke of Spaine was lost, and woone againe.

The 24 day of the same moneth, a little before day, they gaue assault at the breach of Spaine, to the bulwarke of England, to the posterne of Prouence, and at the plaine ground of Italy, all at one houre and one time. The first that mounted to the breach of Spaine, was the Aga of the Ianissaries, a valiant man, and of great courage with his company, and bare three score or three score and tenne banners and signes, and pight them in the earth of the breach, and then fought with our men, and mounted on our repaires, making other maner of fray and more rigorous then the other that were passed, and the sayd skirmish lasted about sixe houres. And forthwith, as the assault was giuen, a great sort of Turks entred into the bulwarke of Spaine, and set vp eight or nine signes or banners vpon it, and droue our men out, I can not tell how, vnwares or otherwise. And they were lords of it three houres and more. Howbeit there were of our men beneath in the mine of the sayd bulwarke, the which bulwarke so lost, gaue vs euill hope. But incontinently the lord great master being at the defence of the posterne of England, hauing knowledge of the sayd losse, and that there was great fighting and resistance on both sides at the breach of Spaine, marched thither with the banner of the crucifix, leauing the charge of the sayd bulwarke in the hands of the bailife de la Moree messieur Mery Combant. And the lord mounted on the wall of Spaine, whereas then began a great skirmish, and euery man layed his handes to worke, as well to put the enemies out of the breach, as to recouer the bulwarke that was lost. And the sayde lord sent a company of men into the bulwarke by the gate of the mine, or by the Barbican, the which entred at the sayd gate, and went vp, where they found but few Turkes. For the artillery of the posterne of England, right against the bulwarke of Spaine, had so well met and scattered them, that within a while our men had slaine all them that were left. And thus the sayde bulwarke was gotten and recouered againe, and with all diligence were made new repaires and strengths to the sayd place. And in like sort, the enemies were put from the breach, and few of them escaped, and all their banners and signes were left with vs. Surely it may be sayd, that after the grace of God (the trauerses of Spaine and Auuergne, and the small artillery set on the houses right against the sayd breaches, as it is sayd, with the comming and presence of the lord great master) hath giuen vs this dayes victory.

As touching the murder of the people, done by the artillery of the bulwarkes of England and Spaine, the quantity was such that a man could not perceiue nor see any ground of the ditches. And the stench of the mastifs carions was so grieuous, that we might not suffer it seuen or eight dayes after. And at the last, they that might saue themselues did so, and withdrew themselues to the trenches: and the reuerend lord great master abode victorious of the sayd place, and in like sort of the other three assaults, the which were but little lesse then that of Spaine, for they fought long. But in conclusion, the enemies beaten on all sides, and in so many sorts, with artillery were put backe, and vanquished, that there died that day at all the foure places fifteene or sixteene thousand. And the slaughter was so great at the plaine Italy, of the cursed enemies, that the sea was made redde with their blood. And on our side also died to the number of an hundred men or more. And of men of dignity in the towne, hauing charge, died Sir Francis de Fernolz, commander of Romania, which Sir Francis was chiefe captaine of the great ship of Rhodes, and he was slaine at the plaine of Italy, wounded with two strokes of harquebushes: it was great dammage of his death, for he was a worthy man, perfect, and full of vertues. There died also messieur Nastasy de Sancta Camilla aforenamed, hauing two hundred men vnder him of the lord great masters succours. There died also diuers other worthy men that day, and many were maimed. Among all other that lost any member, messier Iohn de le Touz called Pradines, being at the sayd bulwarke, with a stroke of artillery had his arme smitten away, in great danger to haue lost his life; howbeit by the helpe of God he died not. [Sidenote: Sir Will. Weston captaine of the English posterne hurt.] In like sort the same day was hurt Sir William Weston abouesayd, captaine of the posterne of England, and had one of his fingers stricken away with an harquebush: which knight behaued himselfe right woorthily at all the assaults.

Of the Turkes part, of great men, were two principall captaines slaine vnder the Aga of the Ianissaries, and another captaine that was come out of Surey to the campe certeine dayes before, with six hundred Mamelukes, and two or three thousand Moores. And of them that were hurt of great men the Beglarby of Natolia had a stroke with an arrow as he was in the trench of Prouence. And many other were wounded, whose names be not rehearsed here, because of shortnesse.

How the great Turke for anger that he could not get the towne, would haue put his chiefe captaine to death, and how they made 11 mines vnder the bulwarke of England.

During this assault, the great Turke was by his pauillion in a place that he had caused to be made, and saw all the businesse, and how his people were so sharpely put backe, and the victory lost on his side, and was very sore displeased, and halfe in despaire: and he sent for Mustafa Basha with whom he was angry, and chid him bitterly, saying that he had caused him to come thither, and had made him to beleeue that he should take the towne in fifteene dayes, or a moneth at the furthest and he had beene there already three moneths with his army, and yet they had done nothing. And after these wordes he was purposed to put him to death in the campe: but the other Bashas shewed him that he ought not to do iustice in the land of his enemies, for it would comfort them and giue them courage. Whereby he did moderate his anger, and left him for that time, and thought to send him to Cairo, least the people there would rebell, by occasion of the captain of Cairo which died a few dayes before. Howbeit he departed not so suddenly, and or he went he thought to assay it he might do some thing for to please the Turke, aswell for his honour as to saue his person, and was marueuous diligent to make mines at the bulwarke of England for to ouerthrow it. And by account were made 11 mines aswell to the sayd bulwarke as elsewhere, beside them spoken of before, and that they had fired. But the most part of the sayd mines came to no proofe though they put fire in them, and many were met with countermines, and broken by our men by the good diligence and sollicitude of sir Gabriel Du-chef, steward of the house of the lord great master, which had the charge of the sayd countermines at the same bulwarke. In the which businesse he behaued himselfe well and worthily, and spared not his goods to cause the people to worke and trauell, but spent thereof largely.

How the Turks were minded to haue gone their way, and of the traitours within the towne, and of many great assaults.

The Turks seeing that by mining they were nothing furthered, nor might not come to their intentions, and hauing but small store of gunpowder, were in deliberation and minde to haue raised the siege, and gone their way. And in deed some of them bare their cariages toward the shippes: and also certaine number of people went out of the trenches with their standards straight to the ships. And it was written vnto vs from the campe how the Ianissaries and other of the host would fight no more: and that they were almost all of one opinion for to go away, saue some of the captaines of the foresayd Mustafa Bassha or Acmek Bassha. And in the meane season the false traitours that were in the towne wrote letters to the campe, giuing them knowledge of all that was sayd and done among vs. And also an Albanese fled to the enemies campe, and warned them not to go, for the gunshot was nigh wasted, and that the most part of the knights and people should be theirs shortly.

In like sort then wrote the abouesayd Chanceller Sir Andrew de Merall, whose treason as then was not knowen: but when it commeth to the effect of his treason, I shall shew the knowledge that he gaue to the enemies at diuers times.

When the bashas and captaines of the hoste vnderstood the sayd warnings, they all purposed for to tary, and caused those tidings of the towne to be knowen ouer all the army. And beganne againe to shoot artillery faster then euer they did, for new shot was come into the campe. Then Mustafa Bassha being in despaire that he could do nothing by mines, by gunshot, nor by assaults, he being ready to depart for to goe into Surey by the great Turkes commandement, before his departing hee thought once againe to assay his aduenture, and made three assaults three dayes together. The first was on a Saturday the fourth day of October an houre before night. The other on Sunday in the morning. And the third on Munday after dinner. And the sayd three assaults were made to the bulwarke of England. And it was assailed but with stones and bagges full of artificiall fire. And at these three assaults many of our men were hurt with the sayd fire, and with the stones that came as thicke as raine or haile. But in the end the enemies got nothing but strokes, and returned into their trenches euill contented, and murmuring, and sware by their Mahomet that Mustafa Bassha shoulde not make them to mount any more to the sayd bulwarke. And that it was great folly for them to cause them to be slaine at the will and fantasie of one man. These wordes sayd in Greeke by some of the enemies were heard of our men as they went downe from the bulwarke. And because (as it is sayd) that the enemies at the assaults that were made, came vp by the earth and stones that fell from the breaches, some of our men aduised to clense the barbican, and take the earth out of the ditch, to the end that the enemies should not easily come vpon the wall. And in effect weening that it were well and behoouefull to be done, by great diligence night and day by mines they voided the barbican, and the most part of the earth that lay in the ditch was brought into the towne, the which was hurtfull afterward, and was cause that the enemies got the foot of the wall. Notwithstanding, they had it but scarsely. But this cleansing furthered the time, and caused them to get it sooner then they should haue done if the earth had lien still: but their finall intent was to raise the defence of the bulwarks, and then passe at their pleasure, and enter into the barbican, as they haue done: for the enemies seeing that the barbican was clensed, thought to get into it by the trenches, and so they did, howbeit they were certaine dayes letted by our handgun shot The enemies seeing, that they might not come neere it, couered their trenches with tables to saue themselues: and then they made a mine whereby they might goe to the barbican. So by these two meanes, afterward they were repaired with earth and with a certaine wall that they made for to eschew the shot of the bulwarks of Auuergne and Spain: and in the mine they found but two gunners, which they slew by force of men. By this manor they being couered on all parts and without any danger, passed thorow and lept into the barbican, and got the foot of the wall; which was the 17 day of October, an vnhappy day for the poore towne, and occasion of the ruine thereof, and winning of the same.

At this point they slept not, but lightly and with great delight they began to picke and hew the wall. And weening to make remedy therefore, and to finde meanes to driue them from the sayde barbican with engines of fire and barrels of gunpowder, wee slew many of them, but it auailed nothing: for the quantitie and multitude of people that trauelled there was so great, that they cared not for losse of them. And if we had had men enow within the towne, there might haue bene remedy to haue raised them from thence: but considering that our force and totall hope was in people, wee left to doe many things that might haue beene done, and that should haue bene good then and other times also, for fault of men of warre. At the last it was pondred by Sir Gabriel Martiningo, that there was no remedy but to hew the wall for to meet them; and beat them with ordinance and with engins of fire to burne and vndoe them. Then our men began to hew the wall, and made some holes to shoot at the enemies that slept not, but did as wee did, and shot at vs, and indeed they slew and hurt many of our men. Then Sir Gabriel Martiningo ordeined to make repaires within the towne at the front where they did cut the wall, to the end that after the walles were cut, the enemies should know with whom to meet. The trauerses were made on ech side with good artillery great and small: and the sayd trauerses and repaires were of the length that the enemies had cut the wall, and beganne at the massife of Spaine made by the reuerend lord great master Mery d'Amboise, and ended at the church of Saint Saluador. The which trauerses and repaires the vulgar people call the Mandra, that is to say, the field.

The meane time that the repaires and trauerses were made with all diligence, Sir Gabriel Martiningo neuer ceased going to euery place to puruey for all things: and he being on the bulwarke of Spaine to ordeine all things that were needfull, there came a stroke of a handgun from the trenches that smote out his eye, and put him in danger of his life, but thanked be God, he recouered his health within a moneth and a halfe. His hurt came ill to passe, for the need that we had of him that time in all things, and specially to the repaires of the breaches. Neuertheles the lord priour of S. Giles (not ignorant in all such things) with other men expert in warre, attended to the sayd repaires and trauerses, there and elswhere. The enemies on the other side night and day without rest (for the great number of labourers that they had hourely and newly ready) hewed and vndermined the sayd wall.

And the 20 day of October they put fire in the vndermines, weening to haue cast downe the wall, but they could not: then they would haue pulled it downe with great ropes and ancres, but the artillery of the bulwarke of Auuergne brake their ropes, and sent them away lightly.

At the last they made a mine vnder the sayd wall and breach; and the 26 day of the same moneth they did put fire to the same mine, weening to haue ouerthrowen the wall, which it did not, but raised it, and made it to fall almost straight vpright, which was more disaduantage to the enemies then profit. Then they shot artillery at it, which in fewe dayes beat it downe, and they had opening and way to come into the Towne. Neuerthelesse it was not necessary for them as then to enter: for the artillery of our repaires beat them in the forepart, and the artillery lying at the two milles at the posterne of Quosquino, and in that of England, whereas was a basiliske that beat right vpon the breach with other pieces: and therefore the enemies sought other meanes, and beganne to raise the earth betweene our two walles, drawing toward the bulwarke of England on the one side, and toward

Auuergne on the other side, and would haue cut the wall further then, our trauerses were for to come in vnbeaten of our artillery. Then were the repaires inlarged and made greater with the wall that was cut, of the height of twelue, and 16 foot in bredth: and so the enemies might goe no further forward, but shot great artillery against our repaires, for to breake and cast them downe, and also they made trenches for to come right to the breach, and vnto the repaires: and certeinly we looked day by day, and houre by houre for to haue some assault. The reuerend lord great master, the which, as it is sayd, had left the bulwarke of England the day that the great assault was made, and since that time he moued not from thence while they hewed the wall, and where as the breach was, because that they were most dangerous and most vnquiet places. And continually the sayd lord kept him behinde the sayd repaires with his knights and men of succours, intentiuely ready and prepared to liue and die, and to receiue his enemies as they ought to bee receiued. And he abode three or foure dayes at the sayd breach, continuing since it was made, vnto the end, fighting with his enemies euery day in great perill of his body: for oftentimes hee put himselfe further in the prease then needed for the danger of his person, but he did it for to hearten and strengthen the courage of his people, being so well willing to defend and die for the faith.

How the enemies assailed the posternes of Prouence and Italy, and how they were driuen away.

By the will of our Lord, the enemies alway in feare and dread, would giue none assault, but continually shot against our repaires, and made trenches for to passe forward into the towne: by the which trenches they shot infinitely with harquebushes and handgunnes, and slew many of our folke, and specially of them that wrought and made the repaires that were broken and crased. And they put vs in such extremity, that we had almost no more slaues nor other labouring people for to repaire that which they brake night and day, which was a great hindrance for us, and the beginning of our perdition. And if we had much to doe in that place, there was not lesse at the gate of Prouence, and at the plaine of Italy: for dayly they were doing either with assault or skirmish, and most at the plaine of Italy. Howbeit by the helpe of our Lorde with the good conducting of the captaine of succours of the same place, the priour of Nauarre, that was prompt and intentiue, and could well incourage his men, the enemies had alway the woorst, and were driuen from the sayde plaine, and from the breach of Prouence.

How the treason of Sir Andrew de Merall was knowen, and of the maraellous assaults that the Turks made.

Vpon these termes and assaults, the treason of the chancellour Sir Andrew de Merall, of whom I spake before, was perceiued: for a seruaunt of his, named Blasie, was found shooting a quarrell of a crossebow with a letter, whereof he was accused to the lord great master, which commanded to take him and examine him by iustice, and he confessed the shot of that letter and of other before, at the commandement of his master: and sayd that he had great acquaintance with the Turks bashas, and that it was not long since he had written a letter, to them, warning them that they should not go, for gunshot began to faile, and the men were wasted by slaying and hurting at the assaults in great quantity: and if they abode still and gaue no more assaults, at the last the towne should be theirs. And diuers other things the seruant sayd of his master, of the which I haue spoken part before at the beginning, and of the warning that he gaue to the great Turke for to come.

But to returne to the plaine of Italy. After many battels and assaults done in the said place, by continuall shot of seuenteene great gunnes that beat the sayde plaine, the repaires and trauerses were almost broken and lost. And by trenches the enemies were come ioining to the breach, and neuer ceased to grate the earth and scrape the earth to cause the repaires and trauerses to fall: and at the last the most part fell downe, and our men were constrained to leaue the sayd plaine, saue a camell that was toward the sea, as it were the third part thereof. Certaine dayes afore the enemies, came to the foot of the plaine, and did cut it and rased the earth, and at the last they passed thorow vnto the towne wall: and anon began to hew and cut as they did at that of Spaine. The lord great master seeing that, anon cast down a part of the church of our Lady de la Victoria, and of an other church of S. Panthalion. And within they began to make the repaires and trauerses as at the place of Spaine, whereto was made extreme diligence, but not such as the lord would, and as was needfull, because there were no labourers for to helpe. After that the enemies had woon the most part of the bulwarke of England and the plaine of Italy, they purposed to make assault to the sayde plaine, and to the breach of Spaine, and to enter into our repaires to winne them for to make an end of vs. And for euer to affeeble the repaires and for to abash vs, the 28 day of Nouember all along the day and night they ceased not to shoot great artillery both from the brimmes of the ditches with those great pieces, casting stones of nine and eleuen foot about, and from the mantellets without. And as it was reckoned, they shot the same day and night 150 times or more against our repaires and trauerses of the wall.

And in the morning the 29 day of the same moneth, the vigill of S. Andrew at the spring of the day, the enemies went thorow the breach with their banners, and entred into the repaires with greater number of people then they did at the great battell in September, hardily and furiously for to fight with vs. But at their comming in, the artillery of the trauerses, and the handgunnes, and the gunshot of the milles found them so well and so sharply, that he that came in, was anon dispatched and ouerthrowen, and there abode aboue 2000 of the Turks slaine. The other that came after seeing their fellowes so euill welcomed, as people that were astonied and lost, they turned againe to their trenches: at whome the artillery of the milles shot victoriously, and hasted them to go apace: and by report from the campe there died sixe thousand or mo that day: the which day might be called very happy, and well fortunate for vs, thanked be God, for there was none that thought to escape that day, but to haue died all, and lost the towne: howbeit, the pleasure of our Lord was by euident miracle to haue it otherwise, and the enemies were chased and ouercome. And it is to be noted that the same day the raine was so great and so strong, that it made the earth to sincke a great deal that they had cast into the ditches, for to couer them from the shot of Auuergne. And the sayd earth being so suncken, the artillery of the sayde bulwarke (vnwares to them) smote them going and comming, and made great murder of the sayd dogges. The sayd day also the enemies came to the plaine of Italy for to assault it; but when they vnderstood that their fellowes had bene put backe so rudely, and with so great slaughter, they were afrayd, and so they returned againe to their trenches.

How the Turks got the plaine ground of Spaine.

And that done, Acmek Basha seeing their businesse euery day goe from woorse to woorse, and that at the assaults were but losse of people, without doing of any good, and that there was no man that willingly would go to it any more, he intended to giue no more assaults but to follow his trenches, and by them enter couertly without losse of a man from the breach to the other end of the towne. Semblably he intended for to winne the plaine earth beside Spaine: the which to get, he came at pleasure to the foot of the wall, and began to beat downe the plaine ground, and to giue many skirmishes and conflicts to our folke that kept it. And there were slaine many good men. And at the last, for default of more helpe and of gunshot, it was left and giuen vp of our men, and so lost. That done, the enemies came thither as in other places. And this is the third place where they came nere to the foot of the wall. And whoso wel considereth in what estate the poore towne was at that time, seeing their enemies haue so great aduantage, might well say, and iudge, that at length it should be taken, and a lost towne.

How a Genouois came to the gate of the towne for to speake for a treaty and deliuerance of the same.

A Few dayes after the saide iourney a Christian man that was in the campe, the which by his speech was a Genouois or Siotis, came to the gate of

Auuergne, and demanded to parle, and after that he was demanded what he would haue, he sayd that he had maruell of vs why we would not yeeld our selues, seeing the pitious estate the towne was in: and he as a Christian man counselled vs to yeeld our selues with some agreement; and that if we would looke thereto, that some should be found expedient to do somewhat for our safeguard. And it is very like that he sayd not such words, nor spake so farforth in the matter, without commission from some of the chiefe of the campe, or of the great Turke himselfe. To the which Siotis was answered, that he should go away with an euill hap, and that it needed not to speake of appointment: and that though the enemies had great aduantage, there was yet enough wherewith to receiue and feast them, if they made any assault. These words heard, he went away: and two days after he came again, and demanded to speak with a marchant Genouois of the towne named Mathew de Vra, and he was answered that he which he demanded was sicke, and might not come, but that he should deliuer the letter, and it should be giuen to him. The sayd Siotis sayd nay, and that he would giue it himselfe, and speake with him: and sayd that he had also a letter of the Grand signior, for the lord master. Vpon this he was bidden to go his way: and to set him packing, they shot after him a piece of artillery. The next day after Ballantis Albanese that was fled thorow the breach of Spaine to the campe, came from the sayd Genouois proposing such words, or like as the other had sayd, saying likewise that the Grand signior had sent a letter to the lord master. To whom no words were spoken nor answere made, for the lord great master as wise and prudent considering that a towne that will heare intreatings is halfe lost, defended vpon the paine of death sith that Siotis had spoken these two times, that none should be so hardy to speak nor answere them of the campe, without his knowledge and commandement: but seeing they were such ambassadors, they reported the words of the sayd Albanese, or euer the sayd lord had knowledge of the words of the Siotis. The which words spread thorow the towne put many folke in thought, and would haue vndone that that the Siotis said the which is no maruell whereas is much people, for with good will and most often they regard sooner to saue the liues of them and their children, then they doe to the honour of the residue. Howbeit not one durst speake a word openly of that businesse, but all secretly: and some came and spake to certaine lords of the great crosse for to speake to the lord great master. And in effect some lords spake thereof to him, persuading him that it should be good to thinke thereon, seeing that the towne went to losse. To whom the sayd lord shewed many things for his honour and the Religion: and that no such things ought to be done or thought for any thing in the world, but rather he and they to die. The lords hearing this answere, went their wayes and then returned againe to the sayd lord, aduising him more to thinke well, on all things, and to the saluation of his towne and of his religion. And they said moreouer, that they doubted that the people would rather haue a peace then to die themselues, their wiues and children. The lord seeing that such words were as things inforced, as who should say, if thou do it not, we shall do it as wise men and prudent, willing to make remedies of needfull things by counsell, called the lords of his Councell for to haue aduise in these doings, and other. And when they were assembled, the lord proposed the words that were to him denounced, and sayd: With these terms and wordes came two or three marchants and citizens of the towne that knocked at the doore of the Councell, and presented a supplication to the great master, and lords of the Councel, whereby they required and besought meekely the sayd reuerend lord to haue respect to them and their poore housholds, and to make some appointment with the great Turke, seeing that the sayd matter was already forward in purpose, that he would do it; and that it would please him to consider the pitious and sorrowful estate that the towne was in; and that there was no remedy to saue it: and at the lest way, if the lord would not make appointment, to giue them leaue (of his goodnesse) to haue their wiues and their children out of the Rodes to saue them, for they would not haue them slaine nor made slaues to the enemies. And the conclusion was, that if the sayd lord would not puruey therefore, they would puruey for it themselues. And there was written in the sayd request the names of eight or ten of the richest of the towne. Which words of the sayd supplication being heard, the sayd lord and his councell were abashed and ill content as reason would, seeing that it was but a course game, and thought on many things to make answere to the sayd citizens, for to content and appease them: and also to see if they should intend to the appointment, as they required, and after as the Genouoy had reported: and the better to make the sayd answere, and to know more plainly in what estate the towne was in all things: that is to wit, first of gunpowder, and then of men of warre, and of the batteries. Also were demanded and asked the lord S. Giles pre Iohn, which had the charge of the gunpowder, and then the captaine Sir Gabriel Martiningo, for being ouer their men of warre (as it is said) as to him that knew the truth; if the towne might holde or not, or there were any meanes to saue it. The sayd lord of S. Giles arose, saying and affirming vpon his honour and his conscience that almost all the slaues and labourers were dead and hurt, and that scantly there were folke enow to remoue a piece of artillery from one place to another, and that it was vnpossible without folke any more to make or set vp the repaires the which euery day were broken and crushed by the great, furious, and continuall shot of the enemies artillery. As for gunpowder the sayd lord sayd, that all that was for store in the towne, was spent long agone, and that which was newly brought, was not to serue and furnish two assaults. And he seeing the great aduantage of the enemies being so farre within the towne, without powder to put or chase them away, for default of men, was of opinion that the towne would be lost, and that there was no meanes to saue it. The words of the sayd lord finished, the captaine Gabriel Martiningo for his discharge sayd and declared to the reuerend lord and them of the Councell, that seeing and considering the great beatings of the shot that the towne had suffered, and after seeing the entring which the enemies had so large, and that they were within the towne by their trenches both endlong and ouerthwart; seeing also that in two other places they were at the foot of the wall, and that the most part of our knights and men of warre and other were slaine and hurt, and the gunpowder wasted, and that it was vnpossible for them to resist their enemies any more, that without doubt the towne was lost if there came no succors for to helpe and resist the siege. The which opinions and reasons of these two woorthy men and expert in such feats, vnderstood and pondered by the lord great master and the lords of the Councell, they were most part aduised for to accept and take treaty if it were offered, for the saueguard of the common people, and of the holy reliques of the church, as part of the holy crosse, the holy throne, the hand of S. Iohn, and part of his head, and diuers other reliques. Howbeit the lord great master to whom the businesse belonged very neere, and that tooke it most heauily, and was more sorrowfull then any of the other, as reason required, was alway stedfast in his first purpose, rather willing to die then to consent to such a thing, and sayd againe to the lordes of the Councell: Aduise you, and thinke well on euery thing, and of the end that may happen, and he proposed to them two points: that is to wit, whether it is better for vs to die all, or to saue the people and the holy reliques. The which two points and doubts were long time disputed, and there were diuers opinions: neuerthelesse, at the last they sayd all, that howbeit that it were well and safely done to die for the faith, and most honor for vs, notwithstanding seeing and considering that there is no remedy to resist against our enemies, and meanes to saue the towne: and on the other part, that the great Turke would not oppresse vs to forsake our faith, but only would haue the towne, it were much better then, and tending to greater wealth to saue all the iewels abouesayde, that should be defiled and lost if they came in the handes of the enemies of the faith. And also to keepe so much small people, as women and children, that they would torment and cut some in pieces, other take, and perforce cause them to forsake their faith, with innumerable violences, and shamefull sinnes that should be committed and done, if the towns were put to the sword, as was done at Modon, and lately at Bellegrado. Whereby they did conclude, that it were better, and more agreeable to God, for to take the treaty, if it were proffered, then for to die as people desperate, and without hope.

How the great Turke sent two of his men to the towne, to haue it by intreating. And how the lord great master sent two knights to him, to know his assurance.

Vpon these consultations and words almighty God that saueth them which trust in him, and that would not that so many euils and cruelties should come to the poore city and inhabitants of it, and also that the great Turke might not arise in ouer great pride and vaineglory, put him in minde to seeke to haue the sayd towne by treaty, which he ought not to haue done for his honour, nor by reason, for the towne was in a maner his. And in like sort he ought not to haue let vs goe as he did, seeing that we were his mortall enemies euer, and shall be still in the time comming, considering the great slaughter of his people that we haue made in this siege. Howbeit, the eternall goodnesse hath blinded him, and hath pleased that these things should be thus, for some cause vnknowen of vs. And for conclusion, the great Turke sent to haue a communication and parle in following the words of the Genouese aforesayd. Then was a signe set vpon the churche of the abbey without the towne, to the which was made answere with another at the milles of Quosquino. And forthwith came two Turks to speake with them of the towne. Then the lord great master sent the Priour of S. Giles pre Iohn, and the captaine Gabriel Martiningo to know the cause of their comming. And when they came to them, without holding of long speech, the two Turkes deliuered them a letter for to beare to the lord great master from the great Turke, and then returned safely into their tents. When the two lords had receiued it, they bare and presented it to the reuerend lord great master, which caused it to be read. By the which the great Turke demanded of the lord great master to yeeld the towne to him, and in so doing he was content to let him go and all his knights, and all the other people of what condition soeuer they were, with all their goods and iewels safe without feare of any harme or displeasure of his folks. And also he swore and promised on his faith so to do. The sayd letter was sealed with his signet that he vseth, that is as it were gilded. And he sayde afterward, that if the lord great master would not accept the sayde treaty, that none of the city, of what estate soeuer he were, should thinke to escape, but that they all vnto the cats, should passe by the edge of the sword, and that they should send him an answere forthwith, either yea or nay. After the sight of the contents of the sayd letter of so great weight, and the time so short for to giue so great an answere, and with demand, the sayd lord great master and all the lords of the Councell were in great thought, howbeit they determined to giue an answere, seeing the estate of the towne so ill that it could be no woorse. Hearing the report and opinions a day or two before of the two lords ordeined to view the defects of the towne, saying that the towne was lost without remedy: considering also that the principalles of the towne would haue appointment. And in likewise, at the other counsell all the lords had already willed and declared, that it were better to saue the towne for respect of the poore people, then to put it all whole to the furie of the enemies, whereupon they agreed and concluded for to take the foresayd treatie. After the conclusion taken, answere was made readily for a good respect: that is to weet, to take the Turke at his worde, to the ende that he should not repent him of it, nor change his opinion. For euery houre his people wanne and entered further and further into the towne. And for to goe vnto the great Turke were ordeined these two knights, Sir Passin afore named, and he bare the token of the White crosse: and another of the towne named Robert de Perruse iudge Ordinarie.

When these two ambassadours had made them readie, they went out at the gate of Quosquino, and went to the tent of Acmek basha, capitaine generall. And because it was late, and that they might not goe that day to the great Turke, on the next day in the morning the foresaid captaine Acmek led and conueied our sayd ambassadours to the great Turkes pauillion, that they might haue the more knowledge plainely, and for to heare his will as touching the wordes which were reported to the reuerend lord great master, and after, the contents of his letter and writings.

When the sayd two ambassadours were departed out of the towne, there did enter two men of authoritie of the campe; one was nephew or kinsman of the sayd Acmek, the other was the great Turkes truchman, which the lord master caused to be well receiued, and they were lodged nigh the sayd gate of Quosquino. And then truce was taken for 3. dayes, and the enemies came to our repaires, and spake with our folke and dranke one with another.

How the ambassadours of Rhodes spake with the great Turke, and what answere they had.

When our ambassadours had made reuerence to the great Turke, they sayd that the lord great master of Rhodes had sent them to his Imperiall maiestie to know what he requested and desired that they might talke together, and how the great master had receiued his letter. The great Turke answered them by his truchman, that of demanding to speake together, nor writing of letter to the great master he knew nothing. Howbeit, sith the great master had sent to him for to know his will, he bade say to them that the great master should yeeld him the towne. And in so doing he promised by his faith for to let him goe with all his knights, and all other that would goe with their goods, without receiuing any displeasure of his people of the campe. And if he accepted not the sayd treatie, to certifie him that he would neuer depart from Rhodes till he had taken it, and that all his might of Turkie should die there, rather then hee would faile of it, and that there should neither great nor litle escape, but vnto the cats they should be all cut in pieces, and sayd that within 3. dayes they should giue him an answere, for hee would not that his people should loose time, and that during the sayd truce they should make no repaires nor defences within the towne.

When the great Turke had ended his wordes, our ambassadours tooke their leaue of him, and returned to the towne, and there was giuen to each of them a rich garment of branched veluet, with cloth of gold of the Turkish fashion. Then Acmek basha tooke sir Passin, and led him to his pauillion, and intreating him right well, caused him to abide all that day and night: and in eating and drinking they had many discourses of things done at the siege, questioning each with other. And among all other things our ambassadour demaunded of Acmek, and prayed him to tell for trueth how many men died of the campe while the siege was laied. [Sidenote: 64000. Turks slaine at the siege of Rhodes] The said Basha sware vpon his faithand certified, that there were dead of the campe of violent death, that is to say, of gunshot and other wayes, 64000. men or more, beside them that died of sicknesse, which were about 40. or 50. thousand.

How one of the ambassadours made answere of his message, and how the
  Commons would not agree to yeeld the towne.

Returne we now to our purpose and to the answere that our ambassadours brought to the lord great master. The sayd Robert Perruse made the answere, and told what the great Turke had sayd, certifying that he would haue an answere quickly yea or nay. The which answere after the demaund of the great Turke hath bene purposed and concluded by the whole counsel, and his offer and treatie accepted, howbeit the sayd ambassadours had it not to do so soone nor the first time that they went for good reasons, but yet they would not deferre it, for feare lest he should repent him. And vpon these determinations that they would haue sent the sayd Peruse to beare the answere, came some of the common people of the towne to the lord great master, that was with the lordes of the counsell, and sayd that they were aduertised of the appointment that he had made with the great Turke, and that he would yeeld the towne with couenaunts by him taken, which, they supposed ought not to be done without calling of them. And because they were not called to it, they sayd that they would not agree thereto, and that it were better for them to die, for the great Turke by some way would put them all to death, as was done in Bellegrado in Hungarie.

How the lord great master sent two ambassadors for the Commons to the great
  Turke.

When the reuerend lord great master had heard their wordes, he sayd graciously to them, that as touching the acceptation of the great Turks offer, it was needful so to do in the degree that the towne was, and the causes wherefore he bad done it the counsell had seene and discussed, and that it was a thing that might not, nor ought not to be sayd nor published in common, for reporting of it to the enemies by traitours, but be kept still and secret. And moreouer, that it was concluded to make an answere shortly, for to take the great Turke at his word, lest he repented, him. For if they had bene called, or the answere had bene giuen, it had bene ouerlong businesse, and in the meane time the Turke might haue changed his mind, and that that he had done and concluded with the great Turke, the lordes of the counsell had well regarded and considered in all things, and for their profite and aduantage, as much or more as for that of the Religion. And that they would send to the great Turke againe other ambassadours, the better to know his will, and to be surer of his promise. Then the lord great master ordained two other ambassadours for to goe to the great Turke, which were two Spaniardes, the one named sir Raimon Market, and the other messire Lopez at whose issuing entered Sir Passin the first ambassadour, and the other two went to the tent; of Acmek basha, for to leade them to the great Turke. And when they were within the Turkes pauillion, and had done him reuerence as appertained, our ambassadours sayd that the great master had heard and seen his demaund to yeeld the towne. And for that it is a thing of great weight, and that he had to doe and say with many men of diuers nations, and because the time of answere was so short, hee might not doe that that hee demaunded so soone. Howbeit hee would speake with his people, and then hee would giue him no answere.

How the Turke began the assault, and how the Commons agreed to yeeld the towne.

When the great Turke heard the answere of our ambassadours, he sayd nothing, but commaunded his Bashas that they should begin the battell againe to the towne, the which was done, and then the truce was broken, and the shot of the enemies was sharper then it was afore. And on the other side nothing, or very litle for fault of pouder: for that that there was left, was kept for some great assault or neede. Howbeit the sayd Acmek Basha kept one of the ambassadours, and messire Lopez onely entered. The great master seeing the warre begun, and the shot thicker then it was afore, and the enemies entred hourely by their trenches further into the towne, called them that before had sayde to him, that they would not the towne should be yeelded, but had rather for to die. And therefore the sayd lord sayd that he was content for to die with them, and that they should dispose them to defend themselues well, or to doe their endeuour better then they had done in times past. And to the ende that each one of them should haue knowledge of his will (for as then be spake but to foure or fiue of them that gainesayd him) he made a cry through all the towne, that all they that were holden to be at the posternes or gates should giue attendance, and not to come away day nor night on payne of death: for afore, the Rhodians came but litle there. And that the other that were not of the posternes, or that were of his succours, should goe to the breach of Spaine where the sayd lord was continually, and not to goe away day nor night on the aboue sayd payne. The sayd cry made, each one were obedient for a day or twaine, howbeit a yoong Rhodian left his posterne and went to his house, which on the next day was hanged for breaking of the lordes commaundement. Notwithstanding that, by litle and litle the people annoyed them, and their heartes failed; and left the posternes and breaches: in such wise, that the enemies might come in without finding great resistaunce, but of a fewe that the lord master caused to abide there (that is to weet) knightes of his succours. And in the night he sought out more people for to keep the watch at the said breach, and paied to them as much as they would. The sayd lord seeing himself thus abandoned and left of his people, he sent to aske them againe wherefore they did not their endeuour, and why they came not to day, as they sayd before. Which made answere that they sawe and knew well that the towne was lost for certaine reasons that were told them: by occasion whereof they had gainesaid the ordinance of the sayd lord, and sayd that they had bene wrong enformed of diuers things: and on the other side, that they feared that the Turke would not hold his word. But sithens they sawe that there was none other remedie but to abide the aduenture and fortune, they sayd that they put all to the sayd lord to doe what he thought good, and that hee would see what were best for them. And required the lord, to doe them so much fauour as to let them choose one or two among them for to goe to the great Turke with his ambassadours for to haue suretie of him. The which was granted, and two ordinarie ambassadours were chosen for them; one Nicholas Vergotie, and the other Piero of saint Cretice, and the foresayd Passin should returne with them for to make the sayd answere. Then the great master or they departed (prolonging the time as much as he might) aduised to send a letter to the great Turke, the which his grandfather had written or caused to be written. In the which letter he gaue his malediction or curse to his children and successours, if they enterprised to besiege Rhodes. The sayd Robert Perruse bare the sayd letter, and as he was accustomed, he went to Acmek Basha for to cause him to haue audience, and to present the sayd letter. And the Basha sayd hee would see the letter: for it is the guise in the great Turkes court, that none may speake to him nor giue him a letter, but he be aduertised first what shall be said, or what shall be written. When the Basha had seene the wordes written in the said letter, he brake it and cast it on the ground, and did tread vpon it, saying many iniurious and villanous wordes to the sayd iudge. And bade him returne apace to his great master, and bid him to thinke on his businesses and to make answere to the great lord (as he had sent and commaunded) or els, it should not be long or he sawe his dolorous and wofull ende. And that same day were taken two men of ours that bare earth toward the bulwarke of England. Of whom the sayd Acmek caused an officer to cut off their noses, fingers, and eares, and gaue them a letter to beare to the lord great master, wherein were great wordes and threatnings. After the sayd Perruse was returned, messire Passin was sent againe to the sayde Basha, for to know of him if the great Turke would be content with any summe of money for his costes and expenses, that he had made for his armie. The which answered that such wordes or offers of siluer were not to bee sayd nor presented to the great lord on paine of life, and that hee set more by honour then by siluer. And therefore hee bade him returne and say to the great master that hee should make answere to the great lord after his demaund, to yeeld or not yeeld the towne. The sayd Passin made relation of the wordes of the Basha to the great master: the which for the great sorrow that hee had deterred alwayes, saw himselfe in such pitious estate. Notwithstanding, the sayd lord putting all to the wil of our lord, and considering that there was no remedie to do otherwise, nor to resist any more his enemies: and being constrained on all sides to make the appointment, with great heauinesse, inestimable dolours and bewailings, at the last gaue his voyce to yeeld the towne (with the treatise or offers to him presented) which was the 20. day of December, the yeere of our lord a thousand fiue hundreth and two and twentie.

An answere to such as will make question for the deliuerance of the citie of Rhodes.

And if by any it were demaunded wherefore the sayde lord great master hath yeelded the towne to the great Turke, requesting it with treatie and couenaunts, which was a signe that he feared and would no more fight, but goe his way. To this I answere: Notwithstanding that the great Turke was aduertised by some traitours, and by other that fled into the campe, that the powder almost failed, and that there were but fewe men of warre within the towne, yet he beleeued not, nor gaue credence of all that was reported to him, but thought verily that wee had ynough for a great while, and considered that hee must tary till they were wasted and spent, whereto behooued time. And seeing all his estate entered into strange places, and into the lands of his enemies, and had bene there already sixe moneths, (and not without great danger of his owne person) thinking on the other side, that taking the towne by assault, he should lose many of his folke; and yet when hee had ouercome and wonne the towne, they should fall each vpon other in departing of the bootie or pillage, doubting finally the hazard of warre. For these reasons and other that may be alleaged, the great Turke had much rather to haue the towne by composition and treaty then otherwise. And it suffised him to driue his olde enemies out of the countreys of Leuant, and set the subiects of his countreys in rest and suretie. And we of the towne that knew our weaknesse, and that we might do no more, it seemed better to saue so much small people, then we and they to fall into the furie of our enemies, for otherwise could we not haue done, but tempt God, and died as in dispaire.

How the citie of Rhodes was yeelded to the great Turke, and of the euill behauiour of certaine Turkes.

But to returne to our principall: After that the reuerend great master had giuen his voyce to the yeelding of the towne, he sent the said Passin againe for to beare it to the great Turke. And with him went the two men that were chosen of the Commons, and they went all three together to the tent of Acmek Basha. To whom the sayd Passin first made this pitious answere and conclusion to yeeld the towne. Notwithstanding, he sayd the people had ordained two men among them for to goe to the great Turke, to speake of their particular doings, and to haue some suretie of their persons, wiues, and children, to the ende that it were not done to them, as to those of Bellegrado. The sayd Acmek led the three ambassadours toward the great Turke. And when they were entered into the pauilion, the sayde messire Passin made the report of his ambassade to the sayd lord, and sayd that the great master yeelded him the towne vnder the promise made by his Imperiall maiestie, with the treatie promised. Of the which promise bee held him sure and certaine, and that hee would doe no lesse: howbeit, the people had required him to giue them licence to go to his maiestie for to aske some request of him. Then the two citizens besought the great Turke that he would for suretie remooue his campe from the towne, to the ende that they should haue no maner of harme to their bodies nor goods, and that they that would goe, should goe, and that they that would abide still, might be well entreated. The great Turke answered by his interpreter to messire Passin, that hee accepted the towne, and promised agayne vpon his faith, and on his honour to the lord great master, that he would performe that he had promised, and sent to him by the same Passin that he should not doubt of the contrary: and if he had not ships ynough for to carie his people and their goods, that hee would let them haue of his, and that he would deliuer the artillerie that was woont to be in the ships of the Religion. And as touching the request of the people, he sayd that he would remooue the campe, and that they that would abide, might abide, and they should bee well entreated, and should pay no tribute in fiue yeeres, and their children should not bee touched, and who so would goe within the sayd space of fiue yeeres, they should goe in good time. These worries ended, our ambassadours tooke leaue of him, and when they were departed, they spake againe with the saide Acmed Basba for to haue a letter of the contents of the promise of the sayd lord. And by his commandement the sayd letter was made, whereby he promised to let go the great master with all his knights, strangers and men of the towne that would go with their goods, without hauing displeasure of any of his people of the campe, or by the wayes. When the letter was made, it was deliuered to messire Passin. And as touching withdrawing of the campe, the sayd Basha promised againe that he would do it, since the great lord would so: howbeit he remooued but from the trenches, and some of his people went a litle way off. And the sayd Basha demaunded in the Turkes behalfe, that they should send to him in hostage foure and twentie knights, whereof two should bee of the great Crosse, and two and twentie citizens. And the sayd lord should send onely a captaine with three or foure hundred Ianissaries, for to keepe the towne when the campe were withdrawen. And so it was done; and beside this he gaue twelue dayes respite to the lord great master, to prepare him and depart out of Rhodes. And in conclusion all this done, our ambassadours returned and made the report to the reuerend great master of all that they had done and practised with the great Turke, and the sayd Basha, and gaue him the letter for to goe surely. Then the great master with his counsell ordained the foure and twentie persons, and other of the towne. When they were readie, they went to the campe, where they were well intreated foure dayes. During this time, Ferra Basha passed from the maine land to the campe, with foure and twentie or fiue and twentie thousand Ianissaries, which by the commaundement of the great Turke was gone vpon the borders of the countreis of the Sophie. For the Turke seeing the people of the campe discouraged and willing no more to goe to the assaults, sent to the sayde Basha to come to Rhodes with his people, which would haue withstood vs sore as fresh men. And it was the worke of God and a wonderfull myracle, that they came after that the appointment was made: for if they had come afore, it is to be supposed that the deed had gone otherwise, and there had bene many strokes giuen: but I beleeue that the ende should haue bene pitious for vs, but God would not that the Turke should haue victory vpon vs as hee might haue had, seeing the great aduantage that he had in all things, but he blinded him and would not that he should know his might. And on the other part it may be sayd and marueiled how it was possible alway to haue ouercome our enemies in all assaults and skirmishes, and at the end to loose the towne, it was the will of God that so hath pleased for some cause to vs vnknowen. It is to bee thought, that lacke of men and gunshot, and the enemies so farre within the towne, and ready to enter at other places with the treasons haue caused the towne to be lost. Two or three dayes after the comming of the sayd Basha, his Ianissaries and other of the campe entred into the Towne, which was on Christmas day, within the time giuen to vs, and then the Turkes word was broken, if it were his will or not, I cannot tell. Neuerthelesse there was no sword drawen, and in that respect promise was kept. But they made pillage, and entered by force into the houses of the castle, and tooke all that they might and would. After that they had ransacked the houses, they entered into the churches, and pilled all that they found, and brake the images. And there was no crucifix, nor figure of our lady, nor of other saints, that were left whole. Then with great inhumanitie they went into the hospitall of poore and sicke folke, called the Fermorie, and tooke all the siluer vessell that the sicke folke were serued with, and raised them out of their beds, and droue them away, some with great strokes and staues, and some were cast down from the galleries. When these hounds had done that acte, they went to the church of saint Iohn and tooke downe the tombes of the great masters, and sought if there were any treasure hid in them, and they forced certaine women and maidens. And all they that were christened and had bene Turkes afore, were they men, women or children, and children, that the sayd men had made christians, they led into Turkie, which thing is of greater importance then any of the other. The morrow after Christmas day, the reuerend lord great master went to the great Turkes pauillion for to visite him, and to be better assured of his promise, the which lord he made to be wel and graciously receiued. And he signified vnto him by his interpreter, that the case so happened to him was a thing vsuall and common: as to loose townes and lordships, and that hee should not take ouermuch thought for it: and as for his promise, he bade that he should not doubt in any thing, and that he should not feare any displeasure to his person, and that he should goe with his people without feare. With these wordes the sayd lord thanked him, and tooke his leaue and departed.

FINIS.

Lenuoy of the Translator.

> Go little booke, and woefull Tragedie,
> Of the Rhodian fearefull oppugnation,
> To all estates complaining ruthfully
> Of thine estate, and sudden transmutation:
> Excusing me if in thy translation
> Ought be amisse in language or in werke,
> I me submit with their supportation,
> To be correct, that am so small a clerke.

* * * * *

An ambassage from Don Ferdinando, brother to the emperor Charles 5. vnto king Henry the 8. in the yeere 1527 desiring his aide against Solyman the great Turke. Holinshed. pag. 894.

On the 14. day of March, 1527. were conueied from London to Greenwich by the earle of Rutland and others, the lord Gabriel de Salamanca, earle of Ottonburge, Iohn Burgraue of Sayluerberge, and Iohn Faber a famous clerke, after bishop of Vien, as ambassadours from Don Ferdinando, brother to Charles the emperor, newly elected king of Hungarie and Beame, after the death of his brother in law king Lewes, which was slaine by Solyman the Turke the last Sommer. This company was welcommed of the high officers, and after brought into the kings presence, all the nobilitie being present; and there after great reuerence made, M. Faber made a notable oration, taking his ground out of the Gospell, Exijt seminator seminare semen suum: and of that hee declared how Christ and his disciples went foorth to sowe, and how their seed was good that fel into the good ground, and brought foorth good fruite, which was the Christian faith. And then he declared how contrary to that sowing, Mahomet had sowen seed, which brought foorth euill fruit. He also shewed from the beginning, bow the Turkes haue increased in power, what realmes they had conquered, what people they had subdued euen to that day. He declared further what actes the great Turke then liuing had done; and in especiall, he noted the getting of Belgrade and of the Rhodes, and the slaying of the king of Hungarie, to the great rebuke (as he sayd) of all the kings christened. Hee set foorth also what power the Turke had, what diuersities of companies, what captaines he had, so that he thought, that without a marueilous great number of people, he could not be ouerthrowen. Wherefore he most humbly besought the king as S. Georges knight, and defender of the faith, to assist the king his master in that godly warre and vertuous purpose.

To this oration the king by the mouth of Sir Thomas Moore answered; that much hee lamented the losse that happened in Hungarie, and if it were not for the warres which were betweene the two great princes, [Sidenote: He meaneth the Emperor and the French King.] he thought that the Turke would not haue enterprised that acte: wherefore he with all his studie would take paine, first, to set an vnitie and peace throughout all Christendome, and after that, both with money and men he would be readie to helpe toward that glorious warre, as much as any other prince in Christendome. After this done, the ambassadours were well cherished, and diuers times resorted to the court, and had great cheere and good rewards, and so the third day of May next following, they tooke their leaue and departed homeward.

* * * * *

The antiquitie of the trade with English ships into the Leuant.

In the yeeres of our Lord, 1511. 1512. &c till the yeere 1534. diuers tall ships of London, namely, The Christopher Campion, wherein was Factor one Roger Whitcome: the Mary George, wherein was Factor William Gresham: the great Mary Grace, the Owner whereof was William Gunson, and the master one Iohn Hely: the Trinitie Fitz-williams, whereof was master Laurence Arkey: the Mathew of London, whereof was master William Capling, with certaine other ships of Southampton and Bristow, had an ordinarie and vsuall trade to Sicilia, Candie, Chio, and somewhiles to Cyprus, as also to Tripolis and Barutti in Syria. The commodities which they caried thither were fine Kersies of diuers colours, course Kersies, white Westerne dozens, Cottons, certaine clothes called Statutes, and others called Cardinal whites, and Cauleskins which were well sold in Sicilie, &c. The commodities which they returned backe were Silks, Chamlets, Rubarbe, Malmesies, Muskadels and other wines, sweete oyles, cotten wool, Turkie carpets, Galles, Pepper, Cinamon, and some other spices, &c. Besides the naturall inhabitants of the foresayd places, they had, euen in those dayes, traffique with Iewes, Turkes, and other forreiners. Neither did our merchants onely employ their owne English shipping before mentioned, but sundry strangers also: as namely Candiots, Raguseans, Sicilians, Genouezes, Venetian galliases, Spanish and Portugale ships. All which particulars doe most euidently appeare out of certaine auncient Ligier Bookes of the R. W. Sir William Locke Mercer of London, of Sir William Bowyer Alderman of London, of master Iohn Gresham, and of others; which I Richard Hakluyt haue diligently perused and copied out. And here for authorities sake I doe annexe, as a thing not impertinent to this purpose, a letter of King Henry the eight, vnto Don Iohn the third, king of Portugale.

* * * * *

A letter of the king of England Henry the eight, to Iohn king of Portugale, for a Portingale ship with the goods of Iohn Gresham and Wil. Locke with others, vnladen in Portugale from Chio.

Serenissimo Principi, domino Ioanni Dei gratia Regi Portugalliæ, et Algarbiorum citra et vltra mare in Africa, ac domino Guineæ, et conquistæ, nauigationis, et commercij Æthiopiæ, Arabiæ, Persiæ, atque Indiæ, etc. Fratri, et amico nostro charissimo.

Henricus Dei gratia, Rex Angliæ, et Franciæ, fidei defensor, ac dominus Hiberniæ, Serenissimo Principi; domino Ioanni eadem gratia Regi Portugalliæ et Algarbiorum citra et vltra mare in Africa, ac domino Guineæ, et conquistæ nauigationis, et commercij Æthiopiæ, Arabiæ, Persiæ, atque Indiæ etc. Fratri, et amico nostro charissimo, salutem. Tanto libentius, promptiusque iustas omnes causas vestræ Serenitati commendandas suscipimus, quanto apertiori indiès nostrorum, qui in eiusdem vestræ Serenitatis regno ac ditione negotiantur, subditorum testimonio cognoscimus, ipsam ex optimi principis officio ita accuratè, exactéque ius suum cuíque præbere, vt ad eam nemo iustitiæ consequendæ gratia frustra vnquam confugiat. Cùm itaque dilectus ac fidelis subditus noster Ioannes Gresham mercator Londoniensis nuper nobis humiliter exposuerit, quod quidam Willielmus Heith ipsius Factor, et negotiorum gestor nauim quondam Portugallensem, cui nomen erat Sancto Antonio, præerátque Diego Peres Portugallensis superioribus mensibus in Candia conduxerit, cum nauísque præfecto conuenerit, vt in insulam Chium ad quasdam diuersi generis merces onerandas primò nauigaret, in Candiámque mox aliarum mercium onerandarum gratia rediret, omnes quidem in hoc nostrum regnum postmodùm aduecturus ad valorem circiter duodecim millium ducatorum, quemadmodum ex pactionis, conuentionisque instrumento apertiùs constat, accidit, vt præfatus Diego vestræ Serenitatus subditus, dictis susceptis mercibus, et iam in itinere parùm fidelitèr, et longè præter initas conuentiones, grauissimo certe nostrorum subditorum detrimento, vbi in Portugalliæ portum diuertisset, sententiæ huc nauigandi mutata, in eodem portu commoretur, nostrorúmque etiam subditorum merces detineat: quam iniuriam (quum subditis nostris in vestræ Serenitatis regno, et ab eius subdito illata sit) ex æquitate, ac iustitia ab ipsa corrigi, emendaríque confidimus, nostro quoque potissimùm intuitu, qui vestræ Serenitatis ipsiúsque subditorum causas, mercésque, si quando in hoc nostrum regnum appulerint, semper commendatissimas habemus, id quod superiori anno testati sumus: proinde ipsam vehementer rogamus, vt

Ioannem Ratliffe præsentium latorem, et dicti Ioannis Gresham nouum constitutum procuratorem, huius rei causa istuc venientem, velit in suis agendis, in dictísque bonis recuperandis, impunéque asportandis remittendísque vectigalibus (quod nos in vestros subditos fecimus) quum per nauis præfectum fraude, ac dolo istuc merces fuerint aduectæ, nisi istic vendantur, ac toto denique ex æquitate conficiendo negotio, sic commendatum suscipere, sicque ad suos, quos opus fore intellexerit magistratus missis literis rem omnem iuuare, et expedire, vi perspiciamus ex hac nostra commendatione fuisse nostrorum subditorum iuri, et indemnitati quàm maximè consultum. Quod nobis gratissimum est futurum, et in re consimili, aut grauiori vestra Serenitas nos sibi gratificandi cupidissimos experietur, quæ foeliciter valeat. Ex Regia nostra de Waltham, Die 15. Octobr. 1531.

The same in English.

To the high and mighty prince, Iohn by the grace of God, king of Portugale, and of Algarue on this side and beyond the sea in Africa, lord of Ghinea, and of the conquest, nauigation, and traffique of Æthiopia, Arabia, Persia, India, &c. our most deere and welbeloued brother.

Henry by the grace of God, king of England and of France, defender of the faith, and lord of Ireland; to Iohn by the same grace, king of Portugale and Algarue, on this side and beyond the sea in Africa, and lord of Ghinea, and of the conquest, nauigation, and traffique of Æthiopia, Arabia, Persia, India, &c. our most deare and welbeloued brother, sendeth greeting. So much the more willingly and readily we vndertake the recommending of all iust causes vnto your highnesse, because by the daily testimonie of our subiects which traffike in your kingdoms and dominions, we are informed, that according to the dutie of a most worthy prince, so carefully and exactly you minister iustice vnto euery man, that all men most willingly repaire vnto your highnesse, with full trust to obtaine the same. Whereas therefore our welbeloued and trustie subiect Iohn Gresham merchant of London, of late in humble maner hath signified vnto vs, that one William Heith his Factor and Agent, certaine moneths agoe had hired in Candie a certaine Portugale ship called Santo Antonio, (the patrone whereof is Diego Perez) and couenanted with the patrone of the sayd ship, that he should first saile to the Isle of Sio, to take in merchandize of sundry sortes, and then eftsoones returne to Candie, to be fraighted with other goods, all which he was to bring into our kingdome of England, to the value of 12000 ducats, as by their billes of couenant and agreement more plainly appeareth: it so fel out, that the aforesaid Diego your highnes subiect hauing receiued the said goods, very trecherously and much contrary to his couenant, to the exceeding great losse of our subiects, putting in by the way into an hauen of Portugale, and altering his purpose of comming into England, he remaineth still in that hauen, and likewise detaineth our subiects goods. Which iniury (seeing it is done in your Highnes kingdome) we hope your Highnes will see reformed according to equity and right, the rather at our request, which alwayes haue had a speciall care of the causes and goods of your Highnes, and of your subiects whensoeuer they come into our kingdome, whereof we made proofe the last yeere. Wherefore wee instantly request your Highnes, that you would so receiue Iohn Ratcliffe the bearer of these present letters, and the new appointed agent of Iohn Gresham, which commeth into your dominions about this busines, being thus commended vnto you in this busines, and recouering and freely bringing home of the said goods, and in remitting of the customs, vnlesse they were sold there (the like whereof we did towards your subiects) seeing by the fraud and deceit of the patron of the ship, the wares were brought thither, and finally in dispatching the whole matter, according to iustice, and so further the same by directing your highnes letters to your officers whom it may concerne, that we may perceiue, that our subiects right and liberty hath especially bene maintained vpon this our commendation. Which we will take in most thankful part, and your highnes shal find vs in the like or a greater matter most readie to gratifie you, whom we wish most heartily well to fare. From our court at Waltham the 15. of October 1531.

* * * * *

A voyage made with the shippes called the Holy Crosse, and the Mathew Gonson, to the Iles of Candia and Chio, about the yeere 1534, according to a relation made to Master Richard Hackluit, by Iohn Williamson, Cooper and citizen of London, who liued in the yeere 1592, and went as cooper in the Mathew Gonson the next voyage after.

[Sidenote: The Holy Crosse and the Mathew Gonson depart for Turkie.] The shippes called the Holy Crosse, and the Mathew Gonson, made a voyage to the Islandes of Candia and Chio in Turkie, about the yeere 1534. And in the Mathew Crosse went as Captaine M. Richard Gonson, sonne of old Master William Gonson, paymaster of the kings nauie. In this first voyage went William Holstocke (who afterwards was Controuller of her Maiesties Nauie, lately deceased) as page to M. Richard Gonson aforesaid, which M. Gonson died in Chio in this his first voyage. The ship called the Holy Crosse was a short shippe, and of burden 160 tunnes. And hauing beene a full yeere at the sea in performance of this voyage, with great danger she returned home, where, vpon her arriual at Blackwall, in the riuer of Thames, her wine and oyle caske was found so weake, that they were not able to hoyse them out of the ship, but were constrayned to draw them as they lay, and put their wine and oyle into new vessels, and so to vnlade the shippe. Their chiefe fraight, was very excellent Muscatels and red Malmesie, the like whereof were seeldome seene before in England. They brought home also good quantitie of sweete oyles, cotton wooles, Turkie Carpets, Galles, Cynamon, and some other spices. The saide shippe called the Holy Crosse was so shaken in this voyage, and so weakened, that she was layd vp in the docke, and neuer made voyage after.

* * * * *

Another voyage to the Iles of Candia and Chio made by the shippe the Mathew
  Gonson, about the yeere 1535, according to the relation of Iohn
  Williamson, then Cooper in the same ship, made to M. Richard Hackluit in
  the yeere 1592.

[Sidenote: The Mathew Gonson goeth into Turkie.] The good shippe called the Mathew Gonson, of burden 300 tunnes, whereof was owner old M. William Gonson, pay-master of the kings Nauie, made her voyage in the yeere 1535. In this ship went as Captaine Richard Gray, who long after died in Russia, Master William Holstocke afterward Controuller of the Queenes Nauie went then as purser in the same voyage. The Master was one Iohn Pichet, seruant to old M. William Gonson, Iames Rumnie was mate. The master Cooper was Iohn Williamson citizen of London, liuing in the yeere 1592, and dwelling in Sant Dunstons parish in the East. The M. Gunner was Iohn Godfrey of Bristoll. In this ship were 6 gunners and 4 trumpetters, all which foure trumpetters at our returne hornewards went on land at Messina in the Iland of Sicilia, as our ship road there at anker, and gat them into the Gallies that lay neere vnto vs, and in them went to Rome. The whole number of our companie in this ship were about 100. men, we were also furnished with a great bote, which was able to cary 10 tunnes of water, which at our returne homewards we towed all the way from Chio vntill we came through the straight of Gibraltar into the maine Ocean. We had also a great long boat and a skiff. We were out vpon this voyage eleuen moneths, yet in all this time there died of sicknesse but one man, whose name was George Forrest, being seruant to our Carpenter called Thomas Plummer.

In a great lygier booke of one William Eyms, seruant vnto Sir William Bowyer Alderman of London, bearing date the 15 of Nouember 1533, and continued vntill the 4. of Iuly 1544. I find that the said William Eyms was factor in Chio, not only for his Master, but also for the duke of Norfolkes grace and for many other worshipful marchants of London, among whom I find the accompts of these especially, to wit, of his said Master, sir William Bowyer, of William and Nicholas Wilford Marchant-taylors of London, of Thomas Curtis pewterer, of Iohn Starkey Mercer, of William Ostrige Marchant, and of Richard Field Draper. And further I find in the said ligier booke, a note of the said Eyms, of all such goods as he left in the hands of Robert Bye in Chio, who became his Masters factor in his roome, and another like note of particulers of goods that he left in the hands of Oliuer Lesson, seruant to William and Nicholas Wilford. And for proofe of the continuance of this trade vntill the end of the yeere 1552. I found annexed vnto the former note of the goods left with Robert Bye in Chio, a letter being dated the 27 of Nouember 1552 in London.

* * * * *

The Epitaph of the valiant Esquire M. Peter Read in the south Ile of Saint Peters Church in the citie of Norwich, which was knighted by Charles the fift at the winning of Tunis in the yeere of our Lord 1538.

Here vnder lieth the corpes of Peter Reade Esquire, who hath worthily serued, not onely his Prince and Countrey, but also the Emperour Charles the fift, both at his conquest of Barbarie, and at his siege at Tunis, as also in other places. Who had giuen him by the said Emperour for his valiant deedes the order of Barbary. Who dyed the 29 day of December, in the yeere of our Lord God 1566.

* * * * *

A discourse of the trade to Chio, in the yeere 1569. made by Caspar Campion, vnto master Michael Locke, and vnto master William Winter, as by his letters vnto them both shall appeare. Written the 14. of February.

Worshipfull Sir, &c. As these dayes past I spake vnto you about the procurement of a safeconduct from the great Turke, for a trade to Chio: The way and maner how it may be obtained with great ease shall plainly appeare vnto you in the lines following. Sir, you shall vnderstand that the Island of Chio in time past hath bene a Signiorie or lordship of it selfe, and did belong vnto the Genowaies. There were 24. of them that gouerned the island which were called Mauneses. But in continuance of time the Turke waxed so strong and mightie, that they, considering they were not able to keepe it, vnlesse they should become his tributaries, because the Island had no corne, nor any kind of vitailes to sustaine themselues, but onely that which must of necessitie come out of the Turkes dominions, and the sayd island being inclosed with the Turks round about, and but 12. miles from the Turks Continent, therefore the said Genowaies did compound and agree to be the Turkes tributaries, and to pay him 14000. thousand ducates yeerely. Always prouided, that they should keep their lawes both spirituall and temporall, as they did when the Iland was in their owne hands. Thus he granted them their priuiledge, which they inioyed for many yeeres, so that all strangers, and also many Englishmen did trade thither of long continuance, and went and came in safety. [Sidenote: The Prince Pedro

Doria is captaine of 40 gallies vnder the Emperor.] In this meane time, the prince Pedro Doria (being a Genouois) became a captaine to serue the Emperour with 30 or 40 gallies against the Turke. And since that time diuers other captaines belonging to Genoa haue bene in the seruice of king Philip against the Turke. Moreouer, whensoeuer the Turke made out any army, he perceiued that no nation did him more hurt then those Genouois, who were his tributaries. Likewise at the Turkes siege of Malta, before which place he lay a great while, with losse of his men, and also of his gallies, he found none so troublesome vnto his force, as one Iuanette Doria a Genouois, and diuers others of the Iland of Chio, who were his tributaries. [Sidenote: The Mauneses put out of the Iland of Chio by the Turke.] At which sight, he tooke such displeasure against them of Chio, that he sent certaine of his gallies to the Iland, for to seise vpon all the goods of the 24 Mauneses and to turne them with their wiues and children out of the Iland, but they would let none other depart, because the Iland should not be vnpeopled. So that now the Turke hath sent one of his chiefe men to rule there: whereby now it will be more easie to obtaine our safeconduct then euer it was before. [Sidenote: The custome thorowout all Turkie is ten in euery hundreth.] For if the townesmen of Chio did know that we would trade thither (as we did in times past) they themselues, and also the customer (for the Turke in all his dominions doth rent his customes) would be the chiefest procurer of this our safe conduct, for his owne gaine: which is no small matter: for we can pay no lesse than ten in the hundred thorowout the Turks whole dominion. Insomuch, that if one of our shippes should go thither, it would be for the customers profit 4000 ducats at least, whereas if we should not trade thither, he should lose so much. [Sidenote: English men do buy more commodities of Chio then any other nation.] Also the burgesses, and the common people would be very glad of our trade there, for the Communalty do get more by our countreymen then they do any nation whatsoeuer: for we do vse to buy many of their silke quilts, and of their Scamato and Dimite, that the poore people make in that towne, more then any other nation, so that we would not so gladly trade, but the people of the countrey would be twise so willing. Wherefore they themselues would be a meanes vnto their gouernour, by their petition to bring this trade to passe: giuing him to vnderstand that of all nations in the world we do him least hurt, and that we may do his countrey great good in consuming those commodities which his countrey people make. Furthermore, it were farre more requisite that we should cary our owne commodities, then to suffer a stranger to cary them thither, for that we can affoord them better cheape then a stranger can. I write not this by hearsay of other men, but of mine own experience, for I haue traded in the countrey aboue this 30 yeres, and haue bene maried in the towne of Chio full 24. yeres, so that you may assure yourselfe that I will write nothing but truth. [Sidenote: Great store of sundry commodities to be had in Chio.] Now I will declare vnto you the wares and commodities that are in the countreys neere about Chio. There are very good galles, the best sort whereof are sold in England fiue shillings deerer then any other countrey galles, There is also cotton wooll, tanned hides, hides in the haire, waxe, chamlets, mocayares, grogerams, silke of diuers countreys, cordouan skinnes, tanned white, to be made blacke, of them great quantity, and also course wooll to make beds. The naturall commodities growing in the Iland it selfe are silke rawe, and masticke. Of these commodities there are laden yeerely ten or twelue great ships of Genoa, besides fiue or sixe that do belong to the towne of Chio, which ships are fraughted for Genoa, Messina, and Ancona. And now that the Mauneses and the chiefe merchants of Genoa are banished, the trade is cleane lost, by reason whereof merchandise must now of necessity be better cheape then they haue bene in times past. But yet when all those ships did trade to the countrey, and also our ships, we neuer had lesse then three kintals of galles for a carsie, and in England we sold them for 35 and 36 shillings the hundred. And whereas now they are brought by the Venetians, they sell them vnto vs for three pound tenne shillings, and foure pound the hundred. Also we had three kintals of cotten wooll for a carsie, and solde the wooll in England for 50 shillings or 3 pound at the most, whereas now the Italians sell the some to vs for 4 pound 10 shillings and 5 pound the hundred. In like maner chamlets, whereas we had three pieces, and of the best sort two and a halfe for a carsie, and could not sell them aboue 20 shillings and 22 shillings the piece, they sell them for 30 and 35 shillings the piece. Also grogerams, where we had of the best, two pieces and a halfe for a carsie, they sell them for foure shillings and foure shillings and sixe pence the yard. Carpets the smaller sort which serue for cupboords, we had three for a carsie: whereas we at the most could not sell them but for 26 shillings the piece, they sell them for 35 shillings the piece. And so all other commodities that the Venetians do bring, they sell them to vs for the third part more gaines then we our selues in those dayes that we traded in those parts. Likewise the barrels of oile that they bring from Candia, we neuer could sell them aboue foure nobles the barrell, where they sell them alwayes for 50 shillings and 3 pound the barrell. What great pity is this, that we should loose so good a trade, and may haue it in our owne hands, and be better welcome to that countrey then the Venetians. Moreouer, the Venetians come very little to Chio, for their trade is into Alexandria. And for to assure you that we had these commodities in barter of our carsies, looke into your fathers books, and the books of Sir Iohn Gresham, and his brethren, and you shall finde what I haue sayd to be true.

[Sidenote: Diuers places where we may haue sweete oiles for our clothing farre cheaper then out of Spaine.] Also you know, that we are forced to seeke oiles out of Spaine, and that for these many yeeres they haue bene solde for 25 pound and 30 pound the tunne: whereas, if we can obtaine the foresayd safeconduct from the Turke, there are diuers places in his dominions, where we may lade 500 tunnes, at 5 pound sterling the tunne. The places are Modon, and Coron, which are but twelue miles distant the one from the other, and do stand in our way to Chio, as you may plainly see by the Card. Also these are places where we may vtter our owne commodities, and not onely these two places, but many others, where we may haue oiles, and be better vsed then we are in Spaine, where we pay very deare, and also are very euill intreated many wayes, as to you is hot vnknowen. So that by these meanes (if the marchants will) we may be eased, and haue such a trade as the like is not in Christendome. Now, as for getting the safeconduct, if I were but able to spend one hundred pounds by the yeere, I would be bound to lose it, if that I did not obtaine the foresayd safeconduct. For I know that if the inhabitants of Chio did but thinke that wee would trade thither againe, they at their owne cost would procure to vs a safeconduct, without any peny of charges to the marchants. So that if the marchants will but beare my charges to solicit the cause, I will vndertake it my selfe. Wherefore I pray you speake to M. Winter and the other marchants, that this matter may take effect And let me haue your answere herein assoone as conueniently you may, for that the time of the yeere draweth nigh that this businesse must be done. Thus I commit you to God, and rest alwayes yours to command.

Yours as your seruant Gaspar Campion.

* * * * *

The first voyage of Robert Baker (to Guinie), with the Minion, and Primrose, set out in October, 1562. by Sir William Garrard, Sir William Chester, M. Thomas Lodge, Anthony Hickman, and Edward Castelin.

As men whose heads be fraught. with care, haue seldom rest: (For through the head the body strait with sorowes is opprest:) So I that late on bed lay wake, for that the watch Pursued mine eye, and causde my hed no sleepe at all to catch: To thinke vpon my chaunce which hath me now betide: To lie a prisoner here in France, for raunsome where I bide; And feeling still such thoughts so thicke in head to runne, As in the sommer day the moats doe fall into the Sunne, To walke then vp I rose, fansie to put to flight: And thus a while I doe purpose to passe away the night. Morpheus I perceiu'd [The God of Sleepe.] had small regarde of me, Therefore I should be but deceiu'd on bed longer to lie. And thus without delay rising as voide of sleepe, I horned Cynthia sawe streight way [The Moone.] in at my grate to peepe: Who passing on her way, eke knowing well my case, How I in darke dungeon there lay always looking for grace: To, me then walking tho in darke withouten light, She wipte her face, and straight did show the best countnance she might: Astonneth eke my head and senses for a space, And olde fansies away now fled she putteth new in place. Then leaning in my grate wherein full bright she shinde, And viewing her thus on her gate she mazeth streight my minde: And makes me thinke anon how oft in Ginnie lande She was my friend, when I haue gone all night vpon the sande, Walking and watching efte least any boate or ship At any time, while we had slept perhaps by vs might slip. And streight with ardent fire my head inflameth shee, Eke me inspires with whole desire to put in memorie, Those daungers I haue bid and Laberinth that I Haue past without the clue of threede, eke harder ieopardie. I then gin take in hand straight way to put in rime, Such trauell, as in Ginnie lande I haue past in my time. But hauing writte a while I fall faint by the way, And eke at night I lothe that stile which I haue writte that day. And thinke my doings then vnworthy sure, to be Set forth in print before all men, for eueryone to see. Eke with dispaire therefore my pen I cast away, And did intende this neuer more hereafter to assay. My fellow prisoner then sir Edward Gages sonne [Sir Edward Gages sonne, Willes me to take againe my pen whose name was George Gage.] and ende that I begonne. By this our friends (sayth he) shall right well vnderstande And knowe the great trauels that we haue past in Heathen lande. Take pen therefore againe in hande, I you require, And thinke (saith he) thereof no paine to graunt this my desire. Then once againe my hed my hande a worke doth sette: But first I fall vpon my bed. and there deepe sighes I fette, To see that this to taske is giuen me silly wight: And of Minerua helpe I aske that she me teach aright. Helpe now without delay, helpe, helpe, ye Muses nine, O Cleo, and Calliope, shew me how to define In condigne stile and phrase eche thing in euery line, To you I giue loe all the praise the trauell only mine. Giue care then ye that long to know of my estate, Which am in France in prison strong as I wrote home of late: Against all lawe or right as I doe thinke in deede, Sith that the warre is ended quite, [The warre at Newe hauen.] and pease is well agreed Yet least perchaunce you might much maruell, how that I Into a Frenchmans powre should light In prison here to lie: Giue now attentiue heede, a straunge tale gin I tell, How I this yeare haue bene besteede, scaping the gates of hell, More harde I thinke truly, in more daunger of life, Than olde Orpheus did when he through hell did seeke his wife, Whose musike so did sounde in pleasant play of string, That Cerberus that hellish hounde (who as the poets sing Hauing three huge heads great, which doe continually Still breath out firy flames of heate most horrible to see) Did giue him leaue to passe in at the gates of Hell: Of which gate he chiefe porter was the Poets thus me tell. And how he past alone through great king Plutos Court Yea ferried ouer with Charon [Caron passenger of Hell.] and yet he did no hurt. Well to my purpose now, in Hell what hurt had hee? Perchance he might strange sights inow and vgly spirits there see: Perhaps eke Tantalus, there, making of his mone, Who staru'd always: and Sysiphus still rolling vp the stone. Yet Orpheus passed by, and went still on his way, There was no torment came him nigh or heate to make him stay. And I a Gods name woulde at hazarde play my life In Guinie lande, to seeke for golde, as Orpheus sought his wife. At which saide lande of Guinie [His first voyage 1562.] I was eke once before, And scapt the death as narrowly As Orpheus did and more. Which first ill lucke will I recite, then iudge you plaine, If loue plagued me not now rightly this yeare to goe againe. The other yeere before when Neptune vs had brought Safely vnto that burning shore, for which so long we sought, One day when shippe was fast in sea at anker holde, The sailes vpfirll'd, all businesse past the boteswaine then I tolde, That he forthwith shoulde see the small pinnesse well mande, Eke all things therin prest to be that we shoulde haue a lande, And gunner see that ye want not bowe, pike, or bill. Your ordinance well primed be with lintstocks burning still. With merchandize a shore, we hied to traffike then, Making the sea fome vs before, by force of nine good men. And rowing long, at last a riuer we espie, In at the which we bare full fast to see what there might be. And entring in, we see a number of blacke soules, Whose likelinesse seem'd men to be, but as blacke as coles. Their Captaine comes to me as naked as my naile, Not hauing witte or honestie to couer once his taile. By which I doe here gesse and gather by the way, That he from man and manlinesse was voide and cleane astray. And sitting in a trough, a boate made of a logge, The very same wherein you know we vse to serue a hogge, Aloofe he staide at first, put water to his cheeke, A signe that he would not vs trust vnlesse we did the like. That signe we did likewise, to put him out of feare, And shewd him much braue marchandise to make him come vs neare. The wilde man then did come, by signes nowe crieth the fiend Of those gay things to giue him some and I should be his friend. I traffikt there that time for such things as they had, At night to ship I caried him, where I with clothes him clad, Yea, made him there good cheere, and he by signes againe Tolde vs that he would fraight vs then after a day or twaine. And eene thus as we were in talke, looking about, Our boate he sawe with wares that there was tied at sterne without: Which boate he viewing still, as then well stuft with ware. We thinking he had ment no ill, had thereof little care. And the next morne, againe we caried him a shore, Eke bartred there that day with them as we had done before. But when Phoebus began somewhat for to draw neare To Icarus his Court, the sonne of Dedalus most deare, (Whose chaunce it is to dwell amids the Ocean flood, Because that he obseru'd not well his fathers counsell good) We then with saile and ore to ship began to hie, That we might fetch aboorde, before the day had lost his eye. To ship we come at last, which rid foure leagues from shore Refresht vs after trauaile past taken that day before. Then, as it was our guise, our boate at sterne we tie, Eke therin leaue our marchandise, as they were wont to be. With troughes then two or three [The theft of the Negroes.] this Captaine comes by night Aboord our boate, where he with wares himselfe now fraighteth quight. The watch now hearing this, the boate they hal'd vp fast: But gone was all the marchandise, and they escapte and past. The next morne then by day againe we went to shore, Amends to haue for that which they had stolne the night before. But all in vaine was it, our signes were now too bad, They would not vnderstand a whit of any thing they had. But as though they had wrong [A conflict between the Negros for to reuenged be, and our men.] As we row'd downe the streame along after comes hee and hee. A hundred boats come fro the steremost towne I say, At least meets vs as many mo before, to make vs stay. In euery boat two men, and great long targets twaine: Most of their darts had long strings then to picke and pull againe. Now gunners to your charge, giue fier all arow, Ech slaue for feare forsakes his barge, and ducks in water low. We downe the streame amaine do row to get the sea, They ouertake vs soone againe, and let vs of our way. Then did the slaues draw neere, with dart and target thicke, With diuelish fixed eyes they peere where they their darts may sticke. Now Mariners do push with right good will the pike, The haileshot of the harquebush The naked slaue doth strike. Through targe and body right that downe he falleth dead His fellow then in heauie plight, doth swimme away afraid. To bathe in brutish bloud, then fleeth the graygoose wing. The halberders at hand be good, and hew that all doth ring. Yet gunner play thy part, make haileshot walke againe, And fellowes row with like good heart that we may get the maine. Our arrowes all now spent, the Negroes gan approach: But pikes in hand already hent the blacke beast fast doth broch. Their captaine being wood, a villaine long and large, With pois'ned dart in hand doth shroud himselfe vnder his targe. And hard aboord he comes to enter in our boat, Our maisters mate, his pike eftsoones strikes through his targe and throat. The capteine now past charge of this brutish blacke gard, His pike he halde backe which in targe alas was fixed hard: And wresting it with might, to pull it forth in hast, A deadly dart strikes him too right and in his flesh sticks fast,

He stands still like a man, and shrinkes not once therefore, But strikes him with his owne dart then which shot at him before. Then presse they on, and shake their darts on euery side, Which, in our flesh doth light, and make both deadly wounds and wide. The gunner in that stound with two darts strooke at last, Shrinks not yet though the double wound with streames of bloud out brast. And eke the maisters mate, of stomacke bolde and stout, For all his wound receiu'd of late, yet stirred not a foot. But kept his standing still, till that a deathful dart Did strike him through the ribs so ill that scarce it mist his hart. The dart out hal'd quickly, his guts came out withall, And so great streames of bloud that he for faintnesse downe gan fall. The Negros seeing this, how he for dead doth lie, Who erst so valiant prou'd iwis, they gladly, shout and crie: And then do minde as there to enter in his place, They thinke so many wounded were the rest would yeld for grace. We then stand by the pike, and foure row on our boat, Their darts among vs fast they strike that few were free I wot. In legge and eke in thigh, some wounded eke in th'arme, Yea many darts stucke vs hard by, that mist and did no harme. By little thus at last, in great danger of life We got the sea, and almost past the danger erst so rife. Then gin they all retire sith all their darts were spent They had nought to reuenge their ire, and thus away they went. Our boat to ship doth roe, where two ores make soft way Six of vs nine were wounded so, [Sixe of our men wounded.] the seuenth for dead there lay. Lo, heare how cruelly the fiends ment vs to kill, Causelesse you see, if they truly on vs might had their will. And yet we gaue before much merchandize away, Among those slaues, thinking therefore to haue friendship for aye. And Orpheus past I wot the passage quietly, Among the soules in Charons boat, and yet to say truly I neuer read that he paid for his passage there, Who past and repast for to see. if that his wife there were. Nor yet that he paid ought, or any bribe there gaue To any office, while he sought his wife againe to haue. Whereby I surely gesse these men with whom that we Haue had to do, are fiends more fierce then those in hell that be. Well we now scaping thus the danger I haue tolde, Aboord we come, where few of vs could stand now being colde. Our wounds now being drest, to meat went they that list, But I desired rather rest, for this in minde I wist. That if I might get once a sleepe that were full sound, I should not feele my weary bones nor yet my smarting wound. And lying long aloft vpon my bed in paine, Vnto Morpheus call'd I oft that he would not disdaine To heare me then poore wight, but sende me helpe with speed That I might haue good rest this night of which I had great need. Me thought then by and by. there hung a heauie waight, At ech eye lid, which clos'd mine eye and eke my head was fraight. And being streight sleepe, I fell into a sweauen, That of my wound I tooke no keepe I dream'd I was in heauen. Where as me thought I see god Mars in armor bright, His arming sword naked holdes he in hand, ready to fight. Castor and Pollux there all complet stand him by, Least if that Mars conuinced were they might reuenged be. Then came marching along the great blacke smith Vulcan, Hauing a staffe of yron strong, and thus at last began: O Mars, thou God of might, what is the cause that thou Hast chaleng'd me with thee to fight? lo present am I now. Wherefore if that thou hast any great grudge to me, Before this day be spent and past it shall reuenged be. Then spake god Mars and said, for that thou churlish wight, Thy brutish blacke people hast made with those white men to fight Which cal'd on me for aid, I bid thee warre for this. Then answered Vulcan straight and said that that coast sure was his. And therefore he would still his blacke burnt men defend, And if he might, all other kill which to that coast did wend, Yea thus (said he) in boast that we his men had slaine, And ere that we should passe this coast he would vs kill againe. Now marcheth Mars amaine and fiercely gins to fight, The sturdie smith strikes free againe whose blowes dint where they light. But iupiter that sat in his great royall throne Hearing this noise maruell'd thereat, and streightway sendeth one To know the cause thereof: but hearing them in fight, Commandeth them for to leaue off by vertue of his might, And of Vulcan demands the cause: then answered he, O mightie Loue whose power commands and rules all things that be, Who at a word hast power all things to destroy cleane, And in the moment of an houre, canst them restore againe, The same God licence me to speake now here my minde: It is not, Loue, vnknowne to thee, how that I was assign'd, And pointed king of most of all the Ginnie land, A people lo is on my coast which doth me now withstand. They do my people strike, they do this day them kill, To whom I minde to do the like if I may haue my will. Then Iupiter bespake: O Vulcan then said he, Let this thy rage and anger slake for this time presently, But if at any time these men chance there againe, Doe as thou list, the charge is thine I will not meddle then. I know, them well (said he) these men need not to seeke, They haue so fruitfull a countrey that there is none the like. But if they can not be therewith content, but still Will seeke for golde so couetously worke then with them thy will. And therewith straight doth send. a pursuiuant in post, To whom (saith he) see that thou wend vnto the windie coast, To Eolus, the king command him thus from me, That he straight way without lingring do set at libertie, His seruant Zephirus, which now is lockt so low, Eke that he do command him thus, that he straight way do go To Vulcans coast in hast, a ship where he shall finde, Which ship he must with gentle blast and eke with moderate winde, Conduct safe to that coast which Albion was hight, And that no stormes do them withstand by day or eke by night. I sleeping all this space, as it were in a trance, The noise of them that hail'd apace did waken me by chance. Then looking out to know what winde did blow in skie, The maister straight came to me tho and thus said by and by. All our ill lucke is past, we haue a merie winde, I hope England, if this winde last, yet once againe to finde. When this I vnderstand, to loue I vowed then, Forswearing cleane the Ginnie land for comming there againe. And passing on in post with fauourable windes, We all arriu'd on Englands coast with passing cheerefull mindes.

* * * * *

The second voyage to Guinie, and the riuer of Sesto, set out in the Moneth of Nouember 1563, by Sir William Gerrard, Sir William Chester, Sir Thomas Lodge, Maister Beniamin Gonston, Maister William Winter, Maister Lionel Ducket, Anthonie Hickman, and Edward Castelin, with two ships, the one called the Iohn Baptist, wherein went for Maister, Laurence Rondell: and the other the Marlin, wherein went also for Maister, Robert Reuell, hauing for Factors, Robert Baker, Iustinian Goodwine, Iames Gleidell, and George Gage: and written in verse by the foresaid Robert Baker.

> You heard before, that home I got from Ginnie at the last, But by and by, I quite forgot the sorrowes I had past. And ships rigged also, with speed to ship againe, I being then requir'd to go, did not denie them plaine, But granted them to go, vnhappie foolish wight, When they command, eke there to do the best seruice I might. In fine, to go our way now serueth time and tide. We hauing nothing vs to stay, what should we longer bide? The hempen band with helpe of Mariners doth threat To wey and reare that slouthfull whelpe [The anker.] vp from his mothers teat. The Maister then gan cheere with siluer whistle blast His Mariners, which at the Icere are laboring wondrous fast. Some other then againe, the maineyard vp to hoise, The hard haler doth hale a maine, while other at a trice Cut saile without delay: the rest that be below, Both sheats abaft do hale straitway and boleins all let go. The Helme a Mariner in hand then strait way tooke, The Pilot eke what course to stir within his care did looke. Againe with siluer blast, the Maister doth not faile, To cause his mates fortwith in hast abroad to put more saile. We then lanch from the shore, sith warre we knew it right. And kept in sea aloofe therefore two dayes and eke a night. And, as it is the guise, to toppe a man we send, Who straight a saile or two espies, with whom we then do wend. Aloofe would some with one, and roomeward would the rest: But with the tallest ship we

gone, whom we thinke to be best. At last, in camming neere as captaines vse to do, I hale them, and of whence they were I did desire to know: Of France when they had said, we weaued them a maine, But they nothing therewith dismaid did like to vs againe. We then our selues aduant through hope of purchase here, Amaine say we, ye iolly gallant or you shall buie it deere. To arme the maine top tho the boatswaine goeth eke, His mate to the foretop also makes hast to do the like. To top both stones and darts good fellowes hoise apace: The quarter maisters with glad hearts do know ech one his place. Our topsailes strike we tho and fit our sailes to fight, Our bulwarke at maine mast also is made likewise aright. Vpon our poope eke then right subtilly we lay Pouder, to blow vp all such men, as enter theraway. Our Trumpetter aloft now sounds the feats of war, The brasen pieces roring oft fling forth both chain and bar. Some of the yardes againe do weaue with naked swoord, And crying loud to them amaine they bid vs come aboord. To bath hir feet in bloud the graigoose fleeth in hast: And Mariners as Lions wood, do crie abroad as fast. Now firie Faulkons flie right greedie of their pray, And kils at first stone dead truely ech thing within their way. Alarme ye now my mates I say, see that ye nothing lacke. At euery loope then gins straightway a harquebush to cracke. Their saile to burne, we shoot our arrowes of wilde fire, And pikes burning therewith about lads tosse with like desire. Eke straightway forth for wine the steward call I then, With fiery spice enough therein I drinke vnto my men, And then euen with a woord our lime pot prest to fall, This iolly gallant we clap aboord and enter him withall. Their nettings now gan teare dint of heauie stone. And some mens heads witnesse did beare who neuer could make mone. The harquebush acroke which hie on top doth lie, Discharg'd full of haileshot doth smoke to kill his enemie. Which in his enemies top doth fight, there it to keepe, Yet he at last a deadly lope is made from thence to lepe. Then entreth one withall into this Frenchman's top, Who cuts ech rope, and makes to fall his yard, withouten stop. Then Mariners belowe, as carelesse of the pike, Do hew, and kill still as they goe, and force not where they strike. And still the trumpets sound with pleasant blast doth cheare Ech Mariner, so in that stound that they nothing did feare. The Maister then also, his mates to cheare in fight, His Whistle chearefully doth blow, whereby strait euery wight So fierce begins to be, that Frenchmen gin to stoe, And English men as right worthy do catch for pillage tho. What would you more I say but tell the truth alway: We vsde our matters so this day we caried him away, Vnto a port in Spaine, which sure is call'd the Groine, Whereas we for French lading plaine receiued readie coine. Well thus this good lucke past, we through salt

Seas did scoure, To Ginney coast eke come at last, O that vnhappie houre. My hand alas for feare now shakes, of this to write, Mine eye almost full fraught with teare, eke lets me to indite. What should I here recite the miserie I had, When none of you will scarce credit that ere it was so bad? Well, yet I would assay to let it, if I might, But O Minerua, helpe me aye, my wits astond be quite. Yea helpe, ye muses nine, lot no thought me withstand, Aid me this thing well to define, which here I take in hand. Well, thus it fortuned tho, in Ginney now arriu'd, Nine men in boat to shoe we go, where we traffike espide, And parting at midday from ship, on good intent In hope of traffike there I say to shore away we went. Our ships then riding fast in sea at anker bight, We minded to dispatch in hast, cke to returne that night. But being hard by land, there suddenly doth rise A mightie winde, wherewith it raind and thundred, in such wise, That we by shore did ride, where we best Port might finde, Our ships we thinke from anker slide, a trice before the winde. This night Vulcan begins on vs reueng'd to be, And thunderbolts about he flings most terrible to see, Admixt with fierie flame which cracks about our cares. And thus gins he to play his game, as now to him appeares, He Eolus hath feed herein to be his friend, And all the whirling windes with speed among vs doth he send, Thus hard by shore we lay, this wet and weary night, But on next morne and all the day of ship we had no sight. For Vulcan all this night from fierie forge so fast Sent thunder bolts with such great light, that when the night was passed, The next day there remaind so great smoke all about, Much like a mist, eke therewith raine, that we were wet throughout. And thus in smoke mindes he to part vs from our ship: Thus nere a one ech other see, and so haue we the slip. Our ships then backe againe, thinking we were behinde, Do saile by shore a day or twaine in hope there vs to finde. And we the contrary, do row along the shore Forward thinking our ships to be still sailing vs before. They sailing thus two dayes or three, and could not finde vs than Do thinke in that foule night we were drowned euery man. Our ship then newes doth beare when she to England wends That we nine surely drowned were, and thus doth tell our friends: While we thus being lost, aliue in miserie Do row in hope yet on this coast, our ships to finde truly. Well thus one day we spent, tho next and third likewise, But all in vaine was our intent, no man a saile espies: Three dayes be now cleane past since any of vs nine, Of any kinde of food hath tast, and thus gan we to pine, Till at the last bare need bids vs hale in with land, That we might get some root or weed our hunger to withstand: And being come to shore, with Negros we intreat, That for our wares which we had there they would giue vs to eat. Then fetch they vs of roots, and such things as they had, We gaue to them our wares to boote and were thereof right glad. To sea go we againe, in hope along the shore, To finde our ships, yet thinking plaine that they had beene before. And thus with saile and ore twelue dayes we went hard by The strange vncomfortable shore where we nothing espie, But all thicke woods and bush and mightie wildernesse, Out of the which oft times do rush strange beasts both wilde and fierse, Whereof oft times we see, at going downe of Sunne, Diuers descend in companie, and to the sea they come. Where as vpon the sand they lie, and chew the cud: Sometime in water eke they stand and wallow in the floud. The Elephant we see, a great vnweldie beast, With water fils his troonke right hie and blowes it on the rest. The Hart I saw likewise delighted in the soile, The wilde Boare eke after his guise with snout in earth doth moile. A great strange beast also, the Antelope I weene I there did see, and many mo, which erst I haue not seene. And oftentimes we see a man a shore or twaine, Who strait brings out his Almadie and rowes to vs a maine. Here let we anker fall, of wares a shew we make, We bid him choose among them all, what wares that he will take To bring to vs some fish, and fresh water therefore, Or else of meat some daintie dish, which their cookes dresse ashore. They bring vs by and by great roots and beries eke, Which grow vpon the high palme tree, such meat as they do like. We drinke eke of their wine much like our whey to see: Which is the sappe as I haue seene that runnes out of a tree. Thus do they bring ech thing which they thinke to be good, Sometime wilde hony combes they bring Which they finde in the wood, With roots and baggage eke our corps we thus sustaine From famine though it be so weake, that death was figured plaine In euery ioynt for lacke of sustenance and rest. That still we thinke our hearts would breake with sorrowes so opprest. We now alongst the coast haue saild so many a mile, That sure we be our ships be lost, what should we do this while? In Heathen land we be, impossible it is That we should fetch our owne countrey in such a boat as this. We now gan to perceiue that wee had ouerpast The Melegate coast so much, that we were come at last Vnto the coast of Myne, for Niegros came aboord With weights to poise their golde so fine, yea speaking euery word In Portugesse right well demanding traffike there? If we had any wares to sell, and where our ships then were? We answered them againe, we had two ships at sea, The which would come trafike with them we thought within a day. The cause why we thus said, was hope to be well vsde: But seeing this, as men dismaid away we went and musde Whither our ships were gone, what way were best for vs: Shall we here perish now saith one? no, let vs not do thus: We see all hope is past our ships to finde againe, And here our liues do shorten fast in miserie and paine:

For why the raging heat of Sunne, being so extreme, Consumes our flesh away in sweat, as dayly it is seene. The Ternados againe so often in a weeke, With great lightnings, thunder and raine with such abundance eke, Doe so beat vs by night, that we sleepe not at all, Whereby our strength is vaded quite. no man an ore can hale. How hard liue we, alas? three whole dayes oft be past, Ere we poore men (a heauie case) of any thing doe tast. These twentie dayes ye see, we haue sit still ech one, Which we doe of necessitie, for place to walke is none. Our legs now vs deceiue, swolne euery ioint withall, With this disease, which, by your leaue, the Scuruie men doe call. We cannot long endure in this case as we be, To leaue our boat I am right sure, compeld we must agree. Three wayes for vs there is, and this is my request, That we may of these three deuise, to choose thereof the best. The Castle of the Mine is not farre hence, we know, To morrow morne we there may be, if thither you will goe. There Portingals do lie, are christened men they be: If we dare trust their curtesie, the worst is hanging glee. Our miserie may make them pitie vs the more, Nine such yong men great pains would take for life to hale an ore. Their Gallies may perhaps lacke such yong men as we, And thus it may fall in our laps, all Galeyslaues to be, During our life, and this, we shall be sure to haue, Although we row, such meate as is the allowance of a slaue. But here we rowe and sterue, our misery is so sore: The slaue with meat inough they serue, that he may teare his ore. If this you will not like. the next way is to goe: Vnto the Negros, and to seeke what friendship they will shew. But what fauour would ye of these men looke to haue: Who beastly sauage people be, farre worse then any slaue? If Cannibals they be in kind, we doe not know, But if they be, then welcome we, to pot straightway we goe. They naked goe likewise, for shame we cannot so: We cannot liue after their guise, thus naked for to go. By rootes and leaues they liue, as beasts doe in the wood: Among these heathen who can thriue, with this so wilde a food? The piercing heate againe, that, scorcheth with such strength, Piercing our naked flesh, with paine, will vs consume at length. The third and last is this, (if those two you refuse) To die in miserable wise, here in the boate you chuse. And this iudge by the way, more trust is to be giuen, Vnto the Portingals alway, sith they be christned men, Then to these brutish sort, which beastly are ye see: Who of our death will make a sport, if Canibals they be. We all with one consent, now death despising plaine: (Sith if we die as innocent, the more it is our gaine) Our sayle we hoyse in hast, wih speed we mind to go Vnto the castell, now not past a twentie leagues vs fro. And sayling all this day, we spied late in the night. And we past by thus on our way, vpon the shore a light. Then sayd our Boateswaine thus, by this great light a shore, Trafique there seemes, will you let vs anker this night therefore, And trie if we may get, this next morning by day, Some kind of food for vs to eate, and then to goe our way? We anker there that night, the next morning to shore: And in the place, where we the light did see the night before: A watch house now there stood, vpon a rocke without: Hard by a great blacke crosse of wood, which putteth vs in doubt, What place that this should be, and looking to the shore, A Castell there we gan espie, this made vs doubt the more. Wherein we saw did stand a Portingall or twaine; Who held a white flag in his hand, and waued vs amaine. Our flesh as fraile now shakes, whereby we gan retire, And he at vs a shot then makes, a Negro giuing fire. A piece discharged thus, the hissing pellet lights, I thinke within a yard of vs, but none of vs it hits. We wisht then we had there a good ship, eke or twaine, But helpelesse now, we rowe a shore to know th'end of our paine. The neerer that we went to them vnto the shore, To yeld our selues, as first we ment they still did shoot the more. Now Canons loud gan rore, and Culuerins now crackt, The Castell eke it thundred sore, as though the wals were sackt. Some shot doth light hard by, some ouer vs againe: But though the shot so thicke doth flie, yet rowe we in a maine, That now so neere we be vnto the castell wall, That none of them at vs we see, can make a shot at all. We ment a land to goe, their curtesie to trie: But from the wall great stones they throw, and therewith by and by, The Negros marching downe, in battell ray do come, With dart and target from the towne, and follow all a dromme. A bowe in hand some hent, with poisn'd arrow prest, To strike therewith they be full bent, a pined English brest. But stones come downe so fast on vs on euery side, We thinke our boats bottom would brast if long we thus abide. And arrowes flie so thicke, hissing at euery eare, Which both in clothes and flesh do sticke, that we, as men past feare, Cry now, Launch, launch in hast, hale of the boate amaine: Foure men in banke let them sit fast and rowe to sea againe. The other fiue like men, do manfully in hand, Take vp each kind of weapon then, these wolues here to withstand. A harquebush takes one, another bends his bowe, Among the slaues then downe fals one and other hurt I trowe. At those Portingals then shoot we, vpon the Fort which stand, In long fine white shirts as we see, and lintstocks in their hand. And of these shirts so white we painted some full red, Striking their open corps in sight, with dint of arrow head. For we sawe they had there no Gallies vs to take, Where threatnings them could vs not feare or make vs once to shake. Then Canons loud gan rore, and pellets flie about, And each man haleth his ore and mooued not a foote. Yea, though the poulder sent the pellets thicke away, Yet spite of them cleane through we went at last, and got the sea, And pieces charging fast, they shot after vs so, That wonder was it how we past the furie of our foe, The pinned anne felt not as now, the heauie ore: With foure such ores was neuer boat I thinke, row'd so before. To seaward scaping so, three Negroes we see there, Came rowing after vs to know, what countrey men we were? We answered Englishmen, and that thither we came, With wares to trafique there with them, if they had meant the same. They Portuguse doe speake right naturall iwis: And of our ship to know they seeke, how big and where she is. We answered them again we had two ships at sea, Right well appointed full of men, that streight would take their way Along the coast for gold, they tarry but for vs, Which came with wares there to haue sold but that they vs'd vs thus. Then gan they vs to pray, if we lackt any thing, To anker there all that whole day, and they to vs would bring All things that we doe want, they sory say they be: But we their words yet trusting scant, refuse their curtesie. We aske them of this hold what place that it should be, Then they againe thus straight vs told that Portingals there lie. And how that point they sayd, which there hard by we see, Was one of Cape three points that lay the Westernmost of three. Withouten further speech, we hoise our saile to sea: Minding a friendlier place to seech, and thus we part our way. We mind truly to prooue the Portingals no more: But now t'assay rather what loue Negroes will shew a shore. We then with saile and ore, went backe againe in hast: A thirtie leagues I thinke, and more from thence where we were chast. And here we anker fall, aboord the Negros come: We gaue gay things vnto them all, and thus their hearts we wonne. At last aboord comes one, that was the kings chiefe sonne: To whom by signes I made great mone, how that I was vndone, Had lost our ships, and eke were almost staru'd for meate, And knew not where our ships to seeke, or any thing to eate. I offred him our wares, and bid him take them all: but he perceiuing now the teares, which from our eyes did fall, Had great pitie on vs, and sayd he would haue nought, But streight by signes he will'd vs then, that we should take no thought. As one whom God has sent, and kept for vs in store, To know in hast away he went, the Kings pleasure on shore. And came foorthwith againe, yea, bade vs come a land: Whereof God knowes we were ful faine, when this we vnderstand. Each man bankes to his ore, to hale the boate a land: Where as we see vpon the shore, fiue hundred Negros stand. Our men rowing in a maine, the billow went so hie, That straight a waue ouerwhelms vs cleane and there in sea we lie. The Negros by and by, came swimming vs to saue: And brought vs all to land quickly, not one durst play the knaue. The Kings sonne after this, a stout and valiant man, In whom I thinke Nature iwis, hath wrought all that she can, He then I say commaunds them straight to saue our boate, To worke forthwith goe many hands, and bring the same a floate. Some swimme to saue an ore, some diue for things be lost: I thinke there helpe to hale a shore fiue hundred men almost. Our boate thus halde vp drie, all things streight way were brought The which we mist or could espie, no man that durst keepe ought. Then vs they led away, knowing we wanted meate. And gaue to us, euen such as they themselues do daily eate. Was neuer Owle in wood halfe so much wondered at, As we were then poore men, alas, which there among them sat. We feared yet our part, and wisht a moneth were past, For each man there went with his dart, which made vs oft agast. We lay vpon the ground, with them there all that night: But fearing still a deadly wound, we could not sleepe a whit. Two dayes thus past we well, no man vs offred wrong: The cause thereof I gin you tell, they thought this them among: Our ships had bene at sea, and would come there before Two dayes, to fetch vs thence away, and giue them wares good store. But when they thus heare tell how that our ships be lost, And that we know not very well, when ships will come to coast: They then waxe wearie streight, and they which did before At sundry times giue vs to eate, did giue vs now no more. Our lowance waxt so small, that neuer nine gesse, Were seru'd the like, yet still withall, it waxed lesse and lesse. Some run now in the wood, and there for rootes do seeke, Base meat would here be counted good too bad that we mislike Our clothes now rot with sweat, and from our backs do fall, Saue that whom nature wils for shame, we couer nought at all. One runs to seeke for clay to fashion straight a pot, And hardens it in Sunne all day: another faileth not To fetch home wood for night, and eke for fire sought, That we our roots and things seeth might if any home were brought. The rest the wood doth seeke, eke euery bush and tree For berries and such baggage like, which should seeme meate to bee. Our fingers serue in steed, both of pickaxe and spade, To dig and pull vp euery weed, that grew within the shade. Eke diged for rootes the ground, and searcht on euery brier For berries, which if we had found, then streight way to the fire: Where we rost some of those, the rest seeth in a pot, And of this banket nought we lose, nor fragment resteth not. The night as beasts we lie the bare hard earth, vpon, And round by vs a great fire light to keepe wilde beasts vs from. But what should I recite, or couet to declare My sorrowes past, or eke t'endite of my hard Ginnie fare? I cease here to enlarge my miserie in that land, A toy in head doth now me charge, as here to hold my hand. In fine, what would ye more, the heat did so exceed, That wanting cloths it scorcht so sore no man could it abide. The countrey eke so wilde, and vnhealthfull withall, That hungry stomacks neuer fill'd, doth cause faint bodies fall. Our men fall sicke apace, and cherishing haue none: That now of nine, within short space, we be left three alone, Alas, what great agast to vs three liuing yet, Was it to see, that death so fast away our fellowes fet? And then to loue on hie we call for helpe and grace, And him beseech vnfainedly, to fetch vs from this place. From this wild heathen land, to Christendome againe, Or else to lay on vs his hand, and rid vs from our paine. Lest that we ouerprest with too much miserie, Perhaps as weake breake our behest which we owe God on high. And least we liuing here among this heathen, might Perchance for need do that which were right hainous in his sight. Well, to my purpose then, when we to loue thus crie, To helpe vs hence poore silly men from this our miserie. He hearing vs at length, how we to him doe call, He helps vs with his wonted strength, and straight thither withall, A French ship sends at last, with whom we three go hence: But six in earth there lie full fast, and neuer like come thence. This Frenchman as I say, through salt and surging seas, Vs brought from Ginnie land, away to France, the Lord we praise. And warre he proues it plaine when we entered his ship, A prisner therefore I remaine, and hence I cannot slip Till that my ramsome be agreed vpon, and paid, Which being leuied yet so hie, no agreement cant be made. And such is lo my chance, the meane time to abide A prisner for ransome in France, till God send time and tide. From whence this idle rime to England I doe send: And thus till I haue further time, this Tragedie I end.

R. Baker.

* * * * *

The voyage of M. Roger Bodenham with the great Barke Aucher to Candia and
 Chio, in the yeere 1550.

In the yeere 1550. the 13 of Nouember I Roger Bodenham Captaine of the Barke Aucher entered the said ship at Grauesend, for my voiage to the Ilands of Candia and Chio in the Leuant. The master of my ship was one William Sherwood. [Sidenote: The Barke Aucher goeth for Leuant.] From thence we departed to Tilbery hope, and there remained with contrarie windes vntill the 6. of Ianuarie, 1551. The 6 of Ianuary, the M. came to Tilbery, and I had prouided a skilfull pylot to cary me ouer the lands end, whose name was M. Wood, and with all speede I valed downe that night 10 miles to take the tide in the morning, which happily I did, and that night came to Douer, and there came to an anker, and there remained vntill Tuesday, meeting with the worthy knight sir Anthony Aucher owner of the saide ship.

The 11 day we arriued in Plimoth, and the 13 in the morning we set forward on our voyage with a prosperous winde, and the 16 we had sight of Cape Finister on the coast of Spaine.

The 30 we arriued at Cades, and there discharged certaine marchandise, and tooke others aboord.

[Sidenote: Mallorca.] The 20 of February we departed from Cades, and passed the straights of Gibraltar that night, and the 25 we came to the Ile of Mallorca, and stated there fiue daies with contrary windes.

The first of March, we had sight of Sardenna, and the fift of the said month wee arriued at Messina in Sicilia, and there discharged much goods and remained there vntill good Fryday in Lent.

The chiefe marchant that landed the sayd Barke Aucher was a marchant stranger called Anselm Saluago, and because the time was then very dangerous, and on going into Leuant, especially to Chio, without a safe conduct from the Turke, the said Anselm promised the owner Sir Anthony Aucher, that we should receiue the same at Messina. But I was posted from thence to Candia, and there I was answered that I should send to Chio, and there I should haue my safe conduct. I was forced to send one, and hee had his answere that the Turke would giue none, willing me to looke what was best for me to doe, which was no small trouble to me, considering I was bound to deliuer the goods that were in the ship at Chio, or send them at mine aduenture. [Sidenote: The Turke prepareth an army to besiege Malta] The marchants without care of the losse of the ship would haue compelled me to goe, or send their goods at mine aduenture, the which I denied, and sayd plainely I would not goe, because the Turkes gallies were come foorth to go against Malta, but by the French kings means, he was perswaded to leaue Malta, and to goe to Tripoly in Barbary, which by the French he wan. In this time there were in Candia certaine Turkes vessels called Skyrasas, which had brought wheat thither to sell, and were ready to depart for Turkie. And they departed in the morning be times, carying newes that I would not goe foorth: the same night I prepared beforehande what I thought good, without making any man priuie, vntill I sawe time. Then I had no small businesse to cause my mariners to venture with the ship in such a manifest danger. Neuerthelesse I wan them to goe all with me, except three which I set on land, and with all diligence I was readie to set foorth about eight of the clocke at night, being a faire moone shine night, and went out. Then my 3 marriners made such requests vnto the rest of my men to come aborde, as I was constrained to take them in. [Sidenote: The Barke Ancher at Milcone.] And so with good wind we put into the Archipelago, and being among the Ilands the winde scanted, and I was forced to anker at an Iland called Micone, where I taried 10 or 12 daies, hauing a Greeke Pilot to carrie the ship to Chio. In this meane season, there came many small botes with mysson sayles to go for Chio, with diuerse goods to sell, and the Pilot requested me that I would let them goe in my company, to which I yeelded. After the sayd dayes expired, I wayed and set saile for the Iland of Chio, with which place I fel in the after noone, whereupon I cast to seaward againe to come with the Iland in the morning betimes. The foresaid smal vessels which came in my company, departed from me to win the shore, to get in the night, but vpon a sudden they espied 3 foystes of Turkes comming vpon them to spoyle them. My Pilot, hauing a sonne in one of those small vessels, entreted me to cast about towards them, which at his request I did, and being something farre from them, I caused my Gunner to shoot a demycoluering at a foyst that was readie to enter one of the botes. That was so happy a shot, that it made the Turke to fall a sterne of the bote and to leaue him, by the which meanes hee escaped. Then they all came to me, and requested that they might hang at my sterne vntill day light, by which time I came before the Mole of Chio, and sent my bote on land to the marchants of that place to send for their goods out of hand, or else I would returne back with all to Candia, and they should fetch their goods there. [Sidenote: The towne of Chio is bound in 12000 ducats for the safegard of Barke Aucher.] But in fine, what by perswasion of my merchant English men, and those of Chio, I was entreated to come into the harbour, and had a safe assurance for 20 dayes against the Turkes army, with a bond of the citie in the summe of 12000 ducats. So I made hast and solde such goods as I had to Turkes that came thither, and put all in order, with as much speede as I could, fearing the comming of the Turkes nauie, of the which, the chiefe of the citie knew right wel. So vpon the sudden they called me of great friendship, and in secret told me, I had no way to saue my selfe but to be gone, for said they, we be not able to defend you, that are not able to help our selues, for the Turke where he commeth, taketh what he will, and leaueth what he list, but the chiefe of the Turkes set order that none shal do any harme to the people or to their goods. This was such news to me, that indeed I was at my wits end, and was brought into many imaginations how to do, for that the winde was contrarie. In fine, I determined to goe foorth. [Sidenote: The companie do murmure against their Captaine.] But the marchants English men and other regarding more their gaines then the ship, hindred me very much in my purpose of going foorth, and made the marriners to come to me to demaund their wages to be payed them out of hande, and to haue a time to employ the same there. But God prouided so for me, that I paied them their money that night, and then charged them, that if they would not set the ship foorth, I would make them to answere the same in England, with danger of their heads. Many were married in England, and had somewhat to loose, those did sticke to me. I had twelue gunners: the Master gunner who was a madde brayned fellow, and the owners seruant had a parlament betweene themselues, and he vpon the same came vp to me with his sword drawen, swearing that hee had promised the owner Sir Anthony Aucher, to liue and die in the sayde shippe against all that should offer any harme to the shippe, and that he would fight with the whole armie of the Turkes, and neuer yeelde: with this fellow I had much to doe, but at the last I made him confesse his fault and followe mine aduise. Thus with much labour I gat out of the Mole of Chio, into the sea by warping foorth, with the helpe of Genoueses botes, and a French bote that was in the Mole, and being out God sent mee a speciall gale of winde to goe my way. [Sidenote: The Turkes Gallies come to seeke the Barke Aucher.] Then I caused a peece to be shotte off for some of my men that were yet in the towne, and with much a doe they came aboord, and then I set sayle a little before one of the clocke, and I made all the sayle I could, and about halfe an houre past two of the clocke there came seuen gallies into Chio to stay the shippe: and the admirall of them was in a great rage because she was gone. Whereupon they put some of the best in prison, and tooke all the men of the three ships which I left in the port, and put them into the Gallies. They would haue followed after mee, but that the townes men found meanes they did not The next day came thither a hundred more of Gallies, and there taried for their whole companie, which being together were about two hundred and 50 sayle, taking their voyage for to surprise the Iland of Malta. The next day after I departed, I had the sight of Candia, but I was two dayes after or euer I could get in, where I thought my selfe out of their daunger. There I continued vntill the Turkes armie was past, who came within the sight of the towne. There was preparation made as though the Turks had come thither. [Sidenote: Fiue thousand banished men in Candia.] There be, in that Iland of Candia many banished men, that liue continually in the mountaines, they came down to serue, to the number of foure or fiue thousand, they are good archers, euery one with his bowe and arrowes, a sword and a dagger, with long haire, and bootes that reach vp to their grine, and a shirt of male, hanging the one halfe before, and the other halfe behinde, these were sent away againe assoon as the armie was past. They would drinke wine out of all measure. Then the armie being past, I laded my shippe with wines and other things; and so after I had that which I left in Chio, I departed for Messina. In the way I found about Zante, certaine Galliots of Turkes, laying abord of certaine vessels of Venice laden with Muscatels: I rescued them, and had but a barrell of wine for my powder and shot: and within a few dayes after I came to Messina. I had in my shippe a Spanish pilot called Noblezia, which I tooke in at Cades at my comming foorth: he went with me all this voyage into the Leuant without wages, of good will that he bare me and the shippe, he stoode me in good steede vntill I came backe againe to Cades, and then I needed no Pilot. And so from thence I came to London with the shippe and goods in safetie, God be praysed. And all those Mariners that were in my sayd shippe, which were, besides boyes, three score and tenne, for the most part were within fiue or sixe yeeres after able to take charge, and did. [Sidenote: Master Richard Chancellour. Master Mathew Baker.] Richard Chanceller, who first discouered Russia, was with me in that voyage, and Mathew Baker, who afterward became the Queenes Maiesties chiefe ship-wright.

* * * * *

Another discourse of the trade to Chio in the yeere 1569, made by Gaspar Campion, vnto master M. William Winter.

It may please your worship to vnderstand, that as concerning the voyage to Chio, what great profit would be gotten, both for marchants, and also for owners of shippes (as it was well knowen in those dayes when the Matthew Gonson, the Trinitie Fitzwilliams, and the Sauiour of Bristow, with diuers other ships which traded thither yerely, and made their voyage in ten or twelue monethe, and the longest in a yeere) M. Francis Lambert, M. Iohn Brooke, and M. Drauer can truely informe you heereof at large. And by reason that wee haue not traded into those parts these many yeeres, and the Turke is growen mighty, whereby our ships doe not trade as they were woont, I finde that the Venetians doe bring those commodities hither, and doe sell them for double the value that we our selues were accustomed to fetch them. Wherefore, as I am informed by the aboue named men, that there is none so fit to furnish this voyage as your selfe: my request is that there may be a shippe of conuenient burthen prepared for this voyage, and then I will satisfie you at large what is to be done therein. And because the Turke, as I sayd before, is waxen strong, and hath put out the Christian rulers, and placed his owne subiects, we may doubt whether we may so peaceably trade thither as we were woont: therefore I dare vndertake to obtaine a safeconduct, if my charges may be borne to goe and come. Of the way how this may be done, M. Locke can satisfie you at large. [Sidenote: Gaspar Campion maried in Chio 24 yeeres.] Moreouer, I can informe you more of the trade of that countrey, then any other, for that I haue bene in those parts these thirty yeeres, and haue bene married in the very towne of Chio full foure and twenty yeres. Furthermore, when one of our ships commeth thither, they bring at the least sixe or eight thousand carsies, so that the customs thereof is profitable for the prince, and the returne of them is profitable to the common people: for in barter of our wares, we tooke the commodities which the poore of that towne made in their houses: so that one of our shippes brought the prince and countrey more gaines than sixe ships of other nations. The want of this our trade thither was the onely cause why the Christian rulers were displaced: for when they payd not their yerely tribute, they were put out by force. Touching the ship that must go, she must obserue this order, she must be a ship of countenance, and she must not touch in any part of Spaine, for the times are dangerous, nor take in any lading there: but she must lade in England, either goods of our owne, or els of strangers, and go to Genoa or Legorno, where we may be wel intreated, and from thence she must make her money to buy wines, by exchange to Candia, for there both custom and exchange are reasonable: and not do as the Math. Gonson and other ships did in time past, who made sale of their wares at Messina for the lading of their wines, and payed for turning their white money into guide after foure and fiue in the hundredth, and also did hazzard the losse of shippe and goods by carrying away their money. Thus by the aforesayd course we shall trade quietly, and not be subiect to these dangers. [Sidenote: Store of hoops laden at Castilla de la mare for Candia.] Also from Legorno to Castilla de la mar, which is but 16 milesfrom Naples, and the ready way to Candia, you may lade hoopes, which will cost carolins of Naples 27 and a halfe the thousand, which is ducats two and a halfe of Spaine. And in Candia for euery thousand of hoops you shall haue a but of Malmesey cleare of all charges. Insomuch that a ship of the burden of the Mathew Gonson will cary foure hundredth thousand hoops, so that one thousand ducats will lade her, and this is an vsual trade to Candia, as M. Michael Locke can testifie. Furthermore, it is not vnknowen to you, that the oiles which we do spend in England for our cloth, are brought out of Spaine, and that very deare, and in England we cannot sell them vnder 28 pound and 30 pound the tunne: I say we may haue good oile, and better cheape in diuers places within the streights. Wherefore if you thinke good to take this voyage in hand, I will informe you more particularly when you please. In the meane time I rest your worships to command.

Yours at your pleasure Iasper Campion.

* * * * *

The true report of the siege and taking of Famagusta, of the antique writers called Tamassus, a city in Cyprus 1571. In the which the whole order of all the skirmishes, batteries, mines, and assaults giuen to the sayd fortresse, may plainly appear. Englished out of Italian by William Malim.

To the right honourable and his singular good Lord, and onely Patron the Earle of Leicester, Baron of Denbigh, Knight of the honourable order of the Garter, one of the Queenes Maiesties most honourable priuy Councell &c. William Malim wisheth long health with increase of honour.

It hath bene a naturall instinct (right honourable and mine especiall good lord) ingraffed in noble personages hearts, much approued and confirmed also by custome, for them to seeke from time to time, by some meanes in their life, by the which they after their death might deliuer ouer their name to their posteritie: least otherwise with their body, their fame also altogether might perchance be buried. Vpon the which consideration we reade many notable and famous things to haue bene erected in time past of noble personages (hauing had wealth at will) in such sort, that not onely certaine ruines of the same sumptuous works, builded so many hundred yeres past, do still remaine, but also the most part of those princes, the authours of them, do continually by them dwell in our memories. As the Pyramides made at Memphis, or neere the famous riuer of Nilus, by the great expenses of the kings of Egypt: the tower called Pharia, made in the Iland of Pharos by king Ptolomee: the walles of Babylon, made or at least reedified by queene Semiramis; Dianas church at Ephesus builded by all the noble persons of Asia; Mausolus toome or sepulchre, made by his wife queene of Caria: Colossus Solis placed at Rhodes, I remember not by what Princes charge, but made by the hands of Cares Lindius scholar to Lysippus: and the image of Iupiter, made of Yuory by the hands of the skilful workman Phydias. The which monuments made of barbarous and heathen Princes to redeeme themselues from obliuion deserued both for the magnificence, and perfect workmanship of the same, to be accounted in those dayes as the seuen woonders of the world. Since the which time, an easier, readier, and lighter way, being also of more continuance then the former, hath bene found out, namely, Letters, which were first inuented by the Caldies and Egyptians, as we reade, and augmented since by others, to our great benefit, and now last of all (no long time past) the same to haue bene committed to Printers presses, to the greatest perfection of the same; men being first inforced to write their actes and monuments in beasts skinnes dried, in barkes of trees, or otherwise perchance as vnreadily. By the which benefit of letters (now reduced into print) we see how easie a thing it is and hath bene for noble persons, to liue for euer by the helpe of learned men. For the memory of those two woorthy and valiant captaines Scipio and Hannibal had bene long before this present quite forgotten, except Titus Liuius, or some such learned Historiographer had written of them in time. And Alexander Magnus himselfe that great conquerour had nothing beene spoken of, had not Q. Curtius, or some other like by his learned stile reuiued the remembrance of him, and called backe his doings to his posteritie. For the which cause we see commonly, in all ages learned men to be much made of by noble personages, as that rare paterne of learning Aristotle to haue bene greatly honoured of that former renowmed Monarch Alexander: who affirmed openly, that he was more bound to his Master Aristotle, then to king Philip his father, because the one had well framed his minde, the other onely his body. Many other like examples I could alledge at this present, if I knew not vnto whom I now wrote, or in what: for your honour being skilfull in histories, and so familiarly acquainted with the matter it selfe, that is in still entertaining learned men with all curtesie, I should seeme to light a candle at noone tide, to put you in remembrance of the one, or to exhort you to doe the other, dayly being accustomed to performe the same. Crassus sayth in Tullies first booke, De Oratore: that a Lawyer's house is the oracle of the whole citie. But I can iustly witnesse, that for these fiue yeeres last past, since my returne from my trauell beyond the seas, that your lodging in the Court (where I through your vndeserued goodnesse to my great comfort do dayly frequent) hath bene a continuall receptacle or harbour for all learned men comming from both the eyes of the realme, Cambridge, and Oxford (of the which Vniuersity your lordship is Chanceller) to their great satisfaction of minde, and ready dispatch of their sutes. Especially for Preachers and Ministers of true religion: of the which you haue beene from time to time not onely a great fauourer, but an earnest furtherer, and protectour: so that these two nurseries of learning (in one of the which I haue before this spent part of my time, that I may speake boldly what I thinke) should wrong your honour greatly, and much forget themselues, if by all meanes possible they should not heerafter (as at this present to their smal powers many well learned gentlemen of them do) labour and trauell in shewing of themselues thankefull, to reuerence and honour your lordship, and honest their owne names: whose studies certeinly would suddenly decay and fall flat, if they were not held vp by such noble proppes, and had not some sure ankerholds in their distresse to leane vnto. How ready dayly your trauell is, and hath long beene besides to benefit all other persons, in whom any sparke of vertue or honesty remaineth, I need not labour to expresse, the world knowing already the same. But whosoeuer they be, that in all their life time haue an especiall care by all meanes to profit as many as they be able, and hurt none, do not onely a laudable act, but leade a perfect and very godly life. Whereupon Strabo affirmeth this most truely to be spoken of them: Mortales tum demum Deum imitari, cum benefici fuerint. That is, Mortall men then specially to follow the nature of God, when they are beneficiall and bountifull to others. Great commendation vndoubtedly it bringeth to any noble personage, that as the Moone, that light and brightness which she receiueth of the Sun, is wont presently to spread abroad vpon the face of the earth, to the refreshing and comforting all inferiour and naturall things bearing life: so for him, to bestow all that fauour and credit, which he hath gotten at the princes handes, to the helpe and reliefe of the woorthy and needy. Great is the force (my right honourable lord) of true vertue, which causeth men, as Tully writeth in his booke De Amicitia, to be loued and honoured oft of those persons, which neuer saw them. [Sidenote: Master Malim at Constantinople 1564.] Whereof I neuer had better proofe (I take God and mine one conscience to witnesse, the which I declared also to certaine of my friends assone as I returned) then at my last being at Constantinople, in the yere of our Lord 1564, whereas I oft resorting (as occasion serued) to the right honorable Christian ambassadors, while I made my abode there (namely vnto Monsieur Antonio Petrimol, lieger there for the French king, Sig. M. Victor Bragadino, for the segniory of Venice, Sig. Lorenzo Giustiniano, for the state of Scio, or Chios, and Sig. Albertacio delli Alberti, for the duke of Florence) heard them often report and speake very honourably of your lordship, partly for your other good inclinations of nature, but especially for your liberality, and courteous intreating of diuers of their friends and countrymen, which vpon sundry occasions had bene here in this our realme. So that to conclude, all men iustly fauour your honourable dealings and deserts: and I for my part haue reuerenced and honoured the same euermore both here at home, and elswhere abroad, wishing often to haue had some iust occasion to pay part of that in good will, which my slender abilitie will neuer suffer me fully to discharge. For vnto whom should I sooner present any thing any way, especially concerning matters done abroad, then vnto your lordship, by whom I was much cherished abroad in my trauell, and mainteined since my returne here at home? For the which cause I haue enterprised (hoping greatly of your lordships fauour herein) to clothe and set forth a few Italian newes in our English attire, being first mooued thereunto by the right worshipfull M. D. Wilson Master of her Maiesties Requests, your honours assured trusty friend, a great and painfull furtherer of learning, whom I, and many other for diuers respects ought to reuerence: who remembring that I had bene at Cyprus, was willing that my pen should trauell about the Christian and Turkish affaires, which there lately haue happened: perswading himselfe, that somewhat thereby I might benefit this our natiue countrey. Against whose reasonable motion I could not greatly wrestle, hazzarding rather my slender skill in attempting and performing this his requested taske, then he through my refusall should seeme to want any iot of my good will. In offering vp the which newes, although I shall present no new thing to your honour, because you are so well acquainted with the Italian copy, as I know: yet I trust your lordship will not mislike, that the same which is both pleasant to reade, and so necessary to be knowen for diuers of our captaines and other our countreymen, which are ignorant in the Italian tongue, may thus now shew it selfe abroad, couered vnder the wing of your lordships protection. Certeinly it mooueth me much to remember the losse of those three notable Ilands, to the great discomfort of all Christendome, to those hellish Turkes, horseleeches of Christian blood: [Sidenote: Rhodes lost.] namely Rhodes besieged on S. Iohn Baptists day, and taken on Iohns day the Euangelist, being the 27 of December 1522. [Sidenote: Scio lost.] Scio or Chios being lost since my being there, taken of Piali Basha with 80 gallies, the 17 of April 1566. [Sidenote: Cyprus lost.] And now last or all not only Famagusta the chiefe holde and fortresse in Cyprus to haue bene lost of the Venetians the 15 of August last past 1571 (the chiefe gouernors and captaines of them being hewen in sunder by the commandement of that tyrant Mustafa Basha) but all the whole Iland also to be conquered by those cruell Turks, ancient professed enemies to all Christian religion. In the which euill successe (comming to vs as I take it for our offences) as I lament the generall losse: so I am surely pensiue to vnderstand by this too true a report of the vile death of two particular noble gentlemen of Venice, Sig. M. Lorenzo Tiepolo, and Sig. M. Giouanni Antonio Querini: of both the which I in my trauaile was very courteously vsed, the former of them being then (as now also he was in this ouerthrow) gouernour of Baffo in Cyprus, the other captaine of one of the castels at Corcyra in Greece, now called Corfu. But things past are past amendment, and they could neuer die more honourably, then in the defence of their countrey. Besides that the late blowes, which the Turks haue receiued since this their fury, in token of Gods wrath against them, do much comfort euery Christian heart. Moreouer this uniforme preparation which is certainly concluded, and forthwith looked for, by very many Christian Princes (would God by all generally) against these barbarous Mahometists: whose cruelty and beastly behauiour I partly know, and am able to iudge of, hauing bene in Turky amongst them more than eight moneths together. Whose vnfaithfulnesse also and breach of promise, as the Venetians manly courage in defence of themselues, and their fortresse, your honour may easily reade in this short treatise and small handfull of leaues, I hauing set downe also a short description of the Iland of Cyprus, for the better vnderstanding of the whole matter. The which I not onely must humbly beseech your honour now fauourably to accept as an earnest peny of more to come, and of my present good will: but with your accustomed goodnesse toward me, to defend the same against such persons, whose tongues too readily roule sometime against other mens painfull trauells, perswading themselues to purchase the sooner some credit of learning with the ruder sort, by controlling and ouerdaintie sifting of other mens laboured tasks, for I know in all ages to be found as well Basilisks as Elephants. Thus nothing doubting of your ready ayd herein, as I assuredly trust of your honours fauourable acceptation of this my poore present, wishing long life with the increase of Gods holy spirit to your lordship and to all your most honourable familie (vnto whom I haue wholly dedicated my selfe by mine owne choise and election for euer) I, crauing pardon for my former boldnesse, most humbly thus take my leaue. From Lambhith the 23 of March. Ann. 1572.

Your honours most humble and faithfull seruant for euer, William Malim.

A briefe description of the Iland of Cyprus: by the which not onely the Venetians title why they haue so long enioyed it, but also the Turks, whereby now he claimeth it, may plainly appeare.

The Iland of Cyprus is inuironed with diuers seas: for Westward it is washed with the sea called Pamphilium: Southward, with the sea Ægyptum: on the East part, with the sea Syrium: and Northward, with the sea called Cilicium. The which Iland in time past had diuers names: called once Acamantis, as Sabellicus witnesseth. Philonides maketh mention, that it was called sometime Cerasis. Xenogoras writeth, that it was named Aspelia, Amathusa, and Macaria. There were in times past fifteene cities or famous townes in it, but now very few, amongst the which Famagusta is the chiefest and strongest, situated by the sea side. There is also Nicosia, which was woont, by the traffike of marchants, to be very wealthy: besides the city of Baffo, Arnica, Saline, Limisso, Melipotamo, and Episcopia. Timosthenes affirmeth, that this Iland is in compasse 429 miles and Arthemidorus writeth the length of the same to be 162 miles, measuring of it from the East to the West, betwixt two promontories named Dinaretta and Acamanta. This Iland is thought to be very rich, abundant of Wine, Oile, Graine, Pitch, Rozin, Allum, Salt, and of diuers precious stones, pleasant, profitable, and necessary for mans vse, and much frequented of Marchants of Syria, vnto the which it lieth very nere. It hath bene, as Plinie writeth, ioyned sometime with Syria, as Sicilia hath beene also with Italy. It was a long time subiect vnto the Romans, after to the Persians, and to the Soldan of Ægypt. The selfe same Iland was sometime also English, being conquered by king Richard the first, in his voyage to Hierusalem in the yeere of our Lord 1192. Who (as Polydore writeth in his fourteenth booke of our English historie) being prohibited by the Cypriottes from arriual there, inuaded and conquered the same soone after by force: and hauing left behinde him sufficient garrisons to keepe the same, departed from thence to Ptolemayda: who afterward exchanged the same with Guy of Lusignan, that was the last christened king of Hierusalem, for the same kingdome. For the which cause the kings of England were long time after called kings of Hierusalem. And last of all, the Venetians haue enioyed it of late a long time, in this order following. In the yeere of our Lord 1476, Iohn king of the said Iland, sonne to Ianus of Lusignan, had by Helen his wife, which was of the Emperiall house of Paleologus, one daughter only called Charlotta, and a bastard called Iames: the which Iames was afterward consecrated Bishop of Nicosia. This Charlotta was married first to the king of Portingall, of whom he had no issue, so that he being dead, Lewes Duke of Sauoy (to whom shee was the second time married) sonne to Lewes the second of that name (vnto whom the said Iland by the right of this his wife Charlotta did appertaine) had the possession of the same. Iames the bastard assoone as his father was dead, of a bishop became a souldiour, and with an army wanne the Iland, making it his owne by force. This Duke of Sauoy hearing these newes, with a number of well appointed souldiers, arriued shortly after in Cyprus, and recouering againe the Iland, compelled the bastard to flie forthwith ouer to the Soldan of Ægypt. Who making himselfe his subiect, in time so wrought and tempered the matter, that the Soldan in person at his request passed ouer into Cyprus, besieged Duke Lewes in the castle of Nicosia, and at length compelled him to depart, leauing his kingdome. So that this Bishop became againe King of this Iland: who shortly after cleauing to the Venetians hauing made a league of friendship with them, married by their consent one Catherina the daughter of Marco Cornaro, which Catherin the Senate of Venice adopted vnto them soone after as their daughter. This Bishop not long after sickened, and died, leauing this his wife with child, who liued not long after his fathers death. By the which meanes the Venetians making themselues the next heires to Catherina by the law of adoption, tooke vnto them the possession of this kingdome, and haue kept and enioyed the same almost this hundred yeeres. Now this great Turke called Sultan Selim in the right of the Soldan of Ægypt, whom his grandfather (called also Sultan Selim) conquered, pretendeth a right title vnto it, and now, as you may vnderstand by reading of this short Treatise, hath by conquest obtained the same. Whom I pray the euerliuing God, if it be his holy will, shortly to root out from thence.

To the Reader.

I am not ignorant (gentle Reader) how hard a matter it is for any one man to write that, which should please and satisfie all persons, we being commonly of so diuers opinions and contrary iudgements: againe Tully affirmeth it to be a very difficult thing, to finde out any matter which in his owne kinde may be in all respects perfect. Wherefore I trust by your owne iudgement I ought of reason to be the sooner pardoned (my translation being precisely tied to mine authours meaning) if anything herein besides be thought to be wanting: I haue learned by the way how comberous a thing it is to turne the selfe same matter out of the Italian language into our countrey speech. But who so doeth what he possibly can is bound to no more. And I now at the request of others (who put me in minde, that I was not onely borne vnto my selfe) haue accomplished that in the ende, which I promised and was required. With what paine and diligence, I referre me to them which are skilfull in the Italian tongue, or may the better iudge, if it please them to trie the same, casting aside this exampler. I speake it not arrogantly, I take God to witnesse: but mens painefull trauels ought not lightly to be condemned: nor surely at any time are woont to be of the learned, or discreet. By whose gentle acceptation if these my present doings be now supported, I will perswade my selfe that I haue reaped sufficient fruit of my trauell. Vnto whome with all my heart I wish prosperous successe in all their affaires.

Ann. Dom. 1572. W. M.

In Turchas precatio.

Summe Deus, succurre tuis, miseresce tuorum,
  Et subeat gentis te noua cura tuæ.
Quem das tantorum finem, Rex magne, laborum?
  In nos vibrabit tela quoúsque Sathan?
Antè Rhodum, max indè Chium, nunc denique Cyprum,
  Turcharum cepit sanguinolenta manus.
Mustafa foedifragus partes grassatur in omnes,
  Et Veneta Cypriam strage cruentat humum.
Nec finem imponit sceleri, mollituè furorem,
  Nec nisi potato sanguine pastus abit.
Qualis, quæ nunquam nisi plena tuménsque cruore
  Sanguisuga obsessam mittit hirudo cutem.
Torturam sequitur tortura, cruorque cruorem,
  Et cædem admissam cædis alius amor.
Sæuit inops animi, nec vel se temperat ipse,
  Vel manus indomitum nostra domare potest.
At tu, magne Pater, tumidum disperde Tyrannum,
  Nec sine mactari semper ouile tuum.
Exulet hoc monstrum, ne sanguine terra redundet.
  Excutiántque nouum Cypria regna iugum.
Et quod Christicolæ foedns pepigere Monarchæ,
  Id faustum nobis omnibus esse velis.
Tu pagna illorum pugnas, et bella secundes.
  Captiuósque tibi subde per arma Scythas.
Sic tua per totum fundetur gloria mundum,
  Vnus sic Christus fiet, et vna fides.

Gulielmus Malim.

The true report of all the successe of Famagusta, made by the Earle Nestor Martiningo, vnto the renowmed Prince the Duke of Venice.

The sixteenth day of February, 1571, [Footnote: In Italy and other places the date of the yere of the Lord is alwayes changed the first of Ianuary, or on New yeres day, and from that day reckoned vpon: although wee heere in England, especially the temporall lawyers for certaine causes are not woont to alter the same vntill the Annunciation of our Ladie.] the fleet which had brought the ayde vnto Famagusta, departed from thence, whereas were found in all the army, but foure thousand footmen, eight hundred of them chosen souldiers, and three thousand (accounting the Citizens and other of the Villages) the rest two hundred in number were souldiers of Albania. After the arriuall of the which succour, the fortification of the City went more diligently forward of all hands, then it did before, the whole garison, the Grecian Citizens inhabiting the Towne, the Gouernours and Captaines not withdrawing themselues from any kinde of labour, for the better incouragement and good example of others, both night and day searching the watch, to the intent with more carefull heed taking they might beware of their enemies, against whom they made no sally out of the City to skirmish but very seldome, especially to vnderstand when they might learne the intent of the enemies. Whilest we made this diligent prouision within the Citie, the Turks without made no lesse preparation of all things necessary, fit to batter the fortresse withall, as in bringing out of Caramania and Syria with all speed by the Sea, many wool packs, a great quantitie of wood and timber, diuers pieces of artillery, engins, and other things expedient for their purpose.

At the beginning of April Halli Basha landed there with fourscore gallies or thereabout in his company, who brought thither that, which of our enemies was desired, who soone after departing from thence, and leauing behinde him thirty gallies, which continually transported souldiers, munition, fresh victuals, and necessaries, besides a great number of Caramusalins, [Footnote: Carumusalini be vessels like vnto the French Gabards, sailing dayly vpon the riuer of Bordeaux, which saile with a mizen or triangle saile.] or Brigandines, great Hulkes called Maones, [Footnote: Maone be vessels like vnto the great hulks, which come hither from Denmarke, some of the which cary 7 or 8 hundred tunnes a piece, flat and broad, which saile some of them with seuen misens a piece.] and large broad vessels termed of them Palandrie, [Footnote: Palandrie be great flat vessels made like Feriboats to transport horse.] which continually passed to and fro between Cyprus and Syria, and other places thereabout, which they did with great speed, standing in feare of the Christian army. And about the middest of the same moneth the Turkes caused to be brought out of the Citie of Nicosia, [Footnote: Nicosia, otherwise called Licosia.] which they had wonne a little before, fifteene pieces of artillery, and raising their army from whence they were before, making ditches and trenches necessary, incamped themselues in gardens, and towards the West part of Famagusta neere a place called Precipola.

The fiue and twentieth day of the same moneth they raised vp mounts to plant their artillery vpon, and caused trenches to be made for harquebuzers, one very nigh another, approaching still very neere the Citie, in such order, as was almost impossible to stay the same, fortie thousand of their Pioners continually labouring there the most part of all the night The intent of the enemie being then knowen, and in what part of the Citie he minded most to plant his battery, we tooke diligent heed on the other part, to repaire and fortifie all places necessary within. For the which cause wee placed a great watch in that way, which was couered with a counterscharfe, and in the sallies of their priuy. Posternes, for the defence of the said counterscharfe, there were new flanckers made, also Trauerses called Butterisses made vpon the Cortaine, with one trench of Turues two foot high and broad, the which was made on that side of the wall of the Citie, which was already battered with the shot of the Turkes, with certaine loopes holes for our Harquebuzers, by the which they defended the counterscharfe. Two noble personages Bragadino and Baglione [Footnote: Sig. Bragadino was Proueditore, that is, Gouernour, and Sig. Baglione Generall of the Christian armie.] personally tooke this charge on them, by the which meanes the Christian affaires passed in very good order. All the bread for our Souldiours was made in one storehouse, of the which noble gentleman Lorenzo Tiepolo captaine of Baffo [Footnote: Baffo of the ancient writers named Paphos, in the which Citie there was a sumptuous Church dedicated to Venus.] had charge, who refused no paine, where thought his trauell might preuaile. In the castle was placed that famous gentleman Andrea Bragadino, who with a diligent gard had charge on that part of the castle principally, next vnto the sea side, trimming and digging out new flanckers for the better defence of the Arsenall. [Footnote: Arsenall in Constantinople and Venice is the place for munition and artillery to lie in.]

A valiant knight named Foito was appointed Master of the Ordinance, who was slain within few dayes after in a skirmish, whose garrison the noble Bragadino Proueditore before named presently deliuered ouer to me. Three other captaines were appointed ouer the wilde-fire with twentie footmen for euery one of them, chosen out of the armie, to vse and execute the same as occasion should serue. The best pieces of Ordinance were brought foorth vnto that side of the towne, where the battery was looked for to be made: and they made priuy fences to couer the better their cannon shot withall. There was no want in the Christians to annoy their enemies in issuing often out of euery side against them, as well to hinder their determinations, as to hurt them otherwise at diuers times. They also rendered to vs the like. For three hundred of the inhabitants of Famagusta one time issuing out of the citie, armed onely with their swords and targets, with so many Italian Harquebuzers also in their company, receiued great dammage, because the trenches of the enemies were made about so thicke, although at the same present wee compelled them to flie, and slew also many of them: yet they increased to such number, that they killed presently thirty, and hurt there threescore of our company. For the which cause order was taken, that our men should no more come forth of their holde, committing themselues to manifest perill to bid their enemies the base.

The Turkes in processe of time by little and little with their trenches, came at length to the toppe of the counterscharfe, and hauing furnished their forts the nineteenth day of May, began their battery with ten forts, hauing threescore and foureteene pieces of great artillery within their custody, amongst the which there were four Basilikes (for so they terme them) of an immeasurable greatnesse, and began to batter from the gate Limisso vnto the Arsenall, and layed fiue batteries against the towne, the one against the great high Turret of the Arsenall, which was battered with fiue pieces of Ordinance mounted vpon that fort of the rocke, the other against the Cortaine it selfe of the Arsenall, battered by one fort with eleuen pieces: another against the Keepe of Andruzzi with two commanders, or caualiers, which were aboue with one fort of eleuen other pieces: another battery against the Turret of S. Nappa, the which was battered with foure Basilisks. The gate of Limisso, which had one high commander or caualier alone, and a Brey and Cortaine without was battered by the forts with three and thirty pieces of artillery, whereas Mustafa himselfe Generall of the Turkes army tooke the charge in person. At the first they seemed not to care much to spoile the walles, but shot still into the city, and against our Ordinance, which greatly galled them. Whereupon they, who were within the city, as well our souldiers as the Grecians, assoone as the battery began, withdrawing themselues, came and dwelt by the walles of the citie, whereas they continued from that time to the end of the siege. The noble Bragadino lodged in the Keepe of Andruzzi, Baglioni in that ward of S. Nappa. The honourable Tiepolo in that which was called Campo Santo. Wherefore they being present at all that was done, both encouraged, and punished the souldiers according to their deserts. The right worshipfull Luigi Martiningo was appointed chiefe ouer the Ordinance, who answering all mens expectation of him, with great courage diuided the charge thereof vnto sixe other inferiour captaines, who tooke order and care for that company, and for the prouision of things necessary for the gunners: one company of the Grecians being appointed to euery gate of the Citie for to attend vpon the seruice of the artillery. The valiant captaine Francesco Bagone warded at the Keepe, and at the great Commander of the Arsenall. Captaine Pietro Conte attended the Cortaine, at the Commander of the Volti, and at the Keepe of Campo Santo. I for my part attended vpon the Commander of Campo Santo, and vpon the Commander of Andruzzi, and of the Cortaine, vnto the Turret of Santa Nappa. The Earle Hercole Martiningo attended vpon the Commander of Santa Nappa, and to the whole Cortaine, vnto the gate of Limisso. Horatio Captaine of Veletri attended vpon the Brey and Cortaine, toward the Bulwarke. Vpon the high Commander of Limisso, which was more troubled then all the rest, attended the Captaine Roberto Maluezzi. At the same time, when the battery began (by the commission of the honourable Bragadino) victuals were appointed, and giuen to all the souldiers, as well Grecians, as Italians, and Gunners: namely Wine, Pottage, Cheese, and Bakon: all the which things were brought to the walks as heed did require in very good order, so that no souldier there spent anymore in bread than two souses a day. [Marginal note: Two Venetian souses or Soldi amount but to one peny English.] They were payed at the end of euery thirty dayes with the great trauell of that right worshipfull Venetian gentleman M. Giouanni Antonio Querini, who besides this his ordinary charge was found present in all weighty and dangerous affaires to the great incouragement of our souldiers. And wee make a counterbattery against our enemies for ten dayes space, with so great rage, that we choked and destroyed fifteene of their best pieces, also we killed and dispatched of them about thirty thousand at that season, so that they were disappointed at that time, of their battery in that place, and were greatly dismayed. But we forseeing that we had no great store of powder left, there was made a restraint, and such order taken, that thirty, pieces should not shoot off but thirty shot a piece euery day, and that in the presence of the Captaines, who were still present, because the Souldiers and Gunners should not shoot off in vaine.

The nine and twentieth day of May there came towards vs from Candia a Fregat or Pinnace, the which giuing vs great hope and lightening of ayde, encreased maruellously euery mans courage. The Turks with great trauell and slaughter of both sides, had woone at the last the counterscharfe from vs, with great resistance and mortalitie on both parts. Whereupon they began on the other side of the fift battery to fill vp the ditch, with the earth that they threw downe, which was taken neere the wall of the counterscharfe. But all that earth and falling downe of the wall made by the shot of their artillery, was carried away of vs within the city, all our company labouring continually as well by night as day, vntil our enemies had made certaine loope-holes in the wall, thorow the which they flancking and scouring all the ditch with their harquebussie, stopped our former course of carying, or going that way any more, without certaine and expresse danger. But M. Gioanni Marmori, a fortifier, had deuised a certaine kinde of ioyned boords, the which being caried of the souldiers, defended them from the shot of the harquebuzers, so that some other quantity of earth, but no great store, was caried also away: in the which place this foresayd fortifier was slaine, who had done especiall good seruice in all our necessary affaires. And our enemies hauing cast so much earth into the ditch, as filled it vp againe, and made it a firme way to the wall of the counterscharfe, and casting before them the earth by little and little, they made one trauerse euen vnto the wall on two sides in all their batteries, the which they made thicke and strong with woolpacks; and other fagots, to assure themselues the better of our flanckers.

When they had once possessed the ditch, that they could not be hurt of vs but by chance, they began foorthwith to cast and digge out vndermines to vndermine the Brey, the Turret of Santa Nappa, the Commander of

Andruzzi, the Keepe of Campo Santo, the Cortaine, and the Turrion of the Arsenatl: so that being able no longer to serue our turne and inioy those fewe flanckers, we threw downe wilde-fire into our enemies campe, the which annoyed them very sore, because it fired their woolpacks, and also their fagots. And for the better encouragement of the souldiers, the right honorable Bragadino gaue to euery souldier one duckat, the which could gaine or recouer any of the former woolpackes, making countermines in all places. To the which charge Maggio the fortifier knight was appointed, who in all our businesse serued with such diligence and courage, as he was able, or was requisite. But the countermines met not, sauing those of the Commander of S. Nappa, of Andruzzi, and that of Campo Santo, because they were open, and our men sallied out often both by day and night into the ditch to perceiue better the way of the mines, and to fire the fagots and wooll. Nor we ceassed at any time through the vnspeakable trauell of the Lord Baglione (who had the ouersight of all these matters) to trouble our enemies intents, by all maner of wit and policie, diuiding the companies for the batteries, ioyning and planting in all places a garrison of the Albanois [Footnote: Albanois souldiers, souldiers of Albania, otherwise called Epirus, who commonly serue the Venetians both on horsebacke and foot, very skilfull and painfull.] souldiers, who as well on foot as on horsebacke, shewed always notable courage and manhood.

The first assault.

The one and twentieth day of Iune they put fire to the mine of the Turret of the Arsenall, whereas Giambelat Bey took charge, who with great ruine rent in sunder a most great and thicke wall, and so opened the same, that he threw downe more then halfe thereof, breaking also one part of the vaimure, made before to vpholde the assault. And suddenly a great number of the Turkes skipping vpon the ruines thereof, displayed their Ensignes, euen to the toppe of the same. Captain Pietro Conte with his company was in that ward, the which was much shaken and terrified by that sudden ruine. I with my company came first thither, so that they shortly tooke the repulse, and although they refreshed themselues with new supplies fiue or six times, yet they failed of their purpose. There fought personally the Lord Baglione: Bragadino and Querini [Footnote: Of this noble and painfull Venetian gentleman M. Gio. Antonio Querini (who was afterwardes hewed in sunder by the commandement of Mustafa) I was entertained very courteously in my trauell at Corcyra, now called Corfu, he being then there Mag. Castellano or Captaine of one of the Castles.] being armed stood not farre off to refresh and comfort our Souldiours, and the Captaine of the Castell with the Ordinance, that was planted vpon the Butteries, destroyed many of our enemies, when they gaue the assault, the which endured fiue houres together: so that of Turkes were slaine very many, and of our side betweene them that were slaine and hurt one hundred: most part of the which number were cast away by a mischance of our wilde-fire, the which being vnaduisedly and negligently handled, burnt vp many of our owne company. There died at that present the Earle Gio. Francesco Goro, the Captaine Barnardino Agubio: and by the throwing of stones Hercole Malatesta, Captaine Pietro Conte, with other Captaines and Standerd-bearers, were very sore hurt.

[Sidenote: In extremities men haue no regard to spare trifles.] The night following arriued in Cyprus a Pinasse from Candia, which bringing newes of most certaine ayde, greatly increased both the mirth and courage of vs all, so that we made soone after, with the helpe of the Captaine Marco Criuellatore, and Maggio the knight, certain retreats flancked to all the places beaten downe, and whereas they suspected that the enemy had digged up any mines, with hogheads, Chests, Tikes, and Sacks stuffed full of moist earth (the Grecians with all speed hauing already brought almost all that which they had) because their hauing dispatched their Canueis about necessary vses, they brought their hangings, cortaines, carpets, euen to their very sheets, to make and stuffe vp their foresayd sacks, a very good and ready way to make vp againe their vaimures, the which were throwen downe with the fury of the artillery, which neuer stinted, so that we made vp againe still that in the night, the which was throwen downe and broken in the day, sleeping very seldome: [Footnote: Prouident and carefull gouernours or magistrates seldome sleepe all the night at any time, much lesse in dangerous seasons.] all the souldiers standing alwayes vpon the walles, visited continually of the Gouernors of the Citie, which slept at no time, but in the extreame heat of the day, hauing no other time to take their rest, because the enemie was at hand giuing vs continually alarmes, not suffering vs long to breath.

The second assault.

The nine and twentieth day of the same moneth they set the mine made towards the Brey on fire, the which mine was digged in stone, which brake and cleft all things in pieces, and caused great ruine, making an easie way for the enemy to assault vs, who with an outragious fury came to the toppe, whereas Mustafa their General was altogether present, which assault was receiued, and stayed at the beginning [Footnote: A small thing at the beginning, or in due time done, helpeth much.] of the Earle Hercole Martiningo with his garrison, and so were repulsed by our company, who fought without any aduantage of couert, the vaimure being throwen downe by the mine. There were slaine of our company Captaine Meani the Serieant Maior of our armie, Captaine Celio de Fuochi, Captaine Erasmo da Fermo: and Captaine Soldatello, Antonio d'Ascoli, Captain Gio. d'Istria, Standerd bearers, with many other officers, were sore wounded, there died also 30

other of our common souldiers. At the Arsenall they were beaten backe
with greater dammage of our enemies, and small hurt to vs. Fiue onely of
our part being slaine there, whereas Captaine Giacomo de Fabriano also
was killed, and I was wounded in my left legge with an harquebush shot.
The which assault continued six houres, the Bishop of Limisso standing
vp there, incouraging the Souldiours. Where also were found present stout
women, [Footnote: That certaine women inhabiting this Iland be viragos,
or mankind, I saw sufficient triall at my last being there, in a city called
Saline.] who came thither with weapons, stones, and water, to help the
Souldiours. Our enemies vnderstanding how great hinderance they had
receiued at these two assaults, changed their mindes, and began againe with
greater fury than euer they had before accustomed to lay battery to all
places, and into our retreats, so that they labouring more speedily then euer
they did, made seuen other forts more, vnder the castle, and taking away
the artillery from them which was farther off, planting of it somewhat
neerer, to the number of fourescore, they battered the holde with so great
rage, that on the eighth day of Iuly, with the same night also were numbred
fiue thousand Canon shot, and after that sort they ouerthrew to the ground
the vaimures, that scarsely with great trauell and paine we could repaire
them againe, because our men that laboured about them were continually
slaine by their Ordinance, and by reason of the endlesse tempest of the shot
of their Harquebuzers. And our men beganne to decrease. For the Turkes
caused vs to retire from our Breyes, by the violence of their artillery and
mining, in such sort, that there being no more standing left for our
Souldiours, because we making our vaimures more thicke, our standing
began to waxe narrower, the which presently we of necessitie enlarged with
boords as a scaffolde to the vaimure, whereby we might haue more elbow
room to fight. Captain Maggio also made one mine vnder the sayd Brey, to
the intent, that we being not able any longer to keepe it, the same might be
left to our enemies to their great hinderance. [Footnote: It is accounted a
good warlike shift, to leaue that to our enemies with hinderance, which we
can not any longer keepe, and vse to our owne commodity.]

The third assault.

To the sayd Brey the ninth day of Iuly they gaue the third assault to the
Turrion of Santa Nappa, to that of Andruzzi, to the Cortaine, to the Keepe
of the Arsenall: the which assault hauing continued more then six houres,
they were beaten backe in foure places, but we left the Brey to their great
losse, and ours also: because we being assaulted, our company being not
able to mannage their pikes in good order, by reason of the narrownesse of
the standing where they were, being willing to retire in that order, as the L.
Baglione had prescribed vnto them, and could not, cast themselues at the
last into a confuse order, and retired, they being mingled amongst the

Turks: so that fire being giuen to our mine, the same (with a terrible sight to beholde) slew presently of our enemies more then one thousand, and aboue one hundred of vs. There was slaine Roberto Maluezzi, and Captaine Marchetto de Fermo was grieuously wounded. At the assault of the Arsenall was slaine Captaine Dauid Noce master of the campe, and I myself was hurt by the racing of a cannon shot. This assault continued fiue houres, and the Citizens of Famagusta shewed great courage in euery place, with their women also, and yoong striplings. The Brey was so defaced by reason of this mine set on fire, that no body any more attempted to recouer the same, because there was no apt place remaining to stay vpon. The left flancker onely remained still, whereas another mine was made. The gate of Limisso was ouer against this foresayd Brey, and somewhat lower, which was alwayes open, hauing made to the same a Portall, with a Percollois annexed to it, the which Percollois by the cutting of a small cord, was a present defence to the gate, and our Souldiours gaue their attendance by that gate to bring in the battered earth, which fell in the ditches from the rampaire: and when they saw that their enemies in foure dayes came not thither, they beganne to entrench aboue the Brey, and by the flanckers aboue they suffered no person to passe out of the gate, the which thing brought great suspition vnto our enemies, because they were often times assailed of our company.

The fourth assault.

Wherefore they came to the foureteenth day of Iuly to assault the gate of Limisso, and laying their battery to all other places, they came and planted their Ensignes euen before the gate, whereas the L. Baglione, and Sig. Luigi were in readinesse, who had taken vpon them to defend that gate of the Citie. Who assoone as they had encouraged their Souldiours, [Footnote: The forwardnesse of the captaine at dangerous times not only much comforteth the common souldier, but also increaseth greatly his credit and commendation with all men.] sallying swiftly foorth, killed, and put to flight the greater part of them, and at the last giuing fire to the mine of the flancker slew foure hundred Turkes, and Sig. Baglione at the same time woon an Ensigne of our enemies, wrasting it violently out of one of the Ensigne bearers hands. The day following they gaue fire to the mine of the cortaine, the which thing not falling out greatly to their purpose, they followed not their prepared assault. Wherefore they beganne to fortifie, and aduance higher their trauerses in the ditches, for their better assurance against they should giue the assault: and they had emptied and carried away all the earth neere vnto the counterskarfe, where they lodged in their pauillions, so that we could not descrie them. They shot seuen pieces of artillery vpon the wall of the counterscharfe so couertly, that they were not seene: two from the Brey of the Turrion of Santa Nappa, one from

Andruzzi, and two other all along the battery of the Cortaine. And they came with certaine boordes couered with rawe and greene hides, vnder which they brought their men to digge in the vaimures, we being nothing behinde or forgetfull to cast wilde-fire amongst them, and sometime to issue foorth of our sallies called Posternes, to offend their Pioners, although to our great hindrance. And we still repaired the vaimures by all meanes possible, with Buffe skins, being moist and wet, throwing in also earth, shreads, and cotton with water, being well bound together with cordes: all the women of Famagusta gathering themselues together into companies in euery street (being guided of one of their Monkes called Caloiero) resorted daily to a certaine place appointed to labour, gathering and prouiding for the souldiers, stones and water, the which was kept for all assaults in halfe buts to quench the fire, which the Turks threw amongst them.

Hauing had no great successe in taking of the gate, they found out a newe way, neuer heard of before, in gathering together a great quantity of certaine wood called Teglia, [Footnote: Teglia in Latine called Teda is a certaine wood which burneth easily, and sauoreth vnpleasantly, of the which there is great store in Sicilia: sometime it is vsed for a torch.] which easily burned, and smelt very euill, the which they throwing before the former gate of the Citie, and fagots fastened to the same, with certaine beames besmeered with Pitch, kindled suddenly so great a fire, as was not possible for vs to quench the same, although we threw vpon it whole Buts of water, which were throwen downe from an high Commander, which Buts presently brake in sunder.

[Sidenote: No necessarie thing to bee done was left vnattempted on either part.] This fire continued foure dayes, wherefore we were inforced by reason of the extreame heat and stinch, to withdraw ourselues further inward, and they descended towardes their lower flanckers, beganne other mines, so that the gate was shut vp, because it would be no longer kept open and suddenly (a thing maruellous to be spoken) the standing of the Brey being repaired, and made vp againe, they planted one piece ouer against the gate, the which of vs with stones, earth and other things, was suddenly buried vp.

[Sidenote: Mans courage oft abateth, but hope seldome forsaketh.] By this time we were driuen to an exigent, all our prouision within the citie stooping very lowe, sauing onely hope, the noble courage of the Gouernours and Captaines, and the stout readinesse of the Souldiours: our wine, and flesh as well powdered as vnpowdered was spent, nor there was any Cheese to be gotten, but vpon an vnreasonable price, our company hauing eating vp their Horses, Asses, and Cats, for lacke of other victualls: there was nothing left to be eaten, but a small quantitie of Bread, and Beanes, and we dranke water and Vinegar together, whereof was not much left. When that we perceiued that our enemies had digged and cast vp three mines in the Commander of the gate, they labouring in all places more diligently then euer they did before, bringing into the ditch, ouer against the battery of the Cortaine, a hill of earth, as high as the wall: and already they came to the wall aboue the counterscharfe ouer against the Turrion of the Arsenall, and had made one Commander complete, fenced with shares, like vnto plough shares, in proportion and height correspondent to ours.

Within the Citie were remaining but fiue hundreth Italian Souldiers, who were not hurt, yet very faint and weary by their long watching and paines in fighting in those feruent and burning heates, which are in those parts. [Footnote: In Iuly the heat is so extreme in this Iland, that the inhabitants thereof are not woont to trauell, but by night onely.] [Sidenote: A letter of supplication exhibited by the Cypriotes vnto Sig. Bragadino.] And the greater and better part, also of the Grecians were by this time slaine, whenas the chiefe of those Citizens remaining did fully resolue themselues (the which was about the twentieth day of Iuly) to present a supplication in writing to that noble gentleman Bragadino Proueditore, desiring and beseeching him, that seeing their Citie and Fortresse was thus battered and brought to extremitie, without sufficient ayde to defend the same, without substance or sustenance, hauing no hope of succour, or any newe supply, they hauing spent and consumed not onely their goods, but also their liues for the defence of them, and in testifying of their dutifull seruice towardes the noble and royall state of the Segniorie of Venice, that it might nowe please him, and the rest of the honourable Gouernours, that were present, and put in trust, hauing a carefull eye vnto some honourable conditions, to haue now at the last a respect to the credit and honour of their long trauelled wiues, and the safegard of their poore children, which otherwise were shortly very like to be a pray to their bloodthirsting and rauening enemies. [Sidenote: The answere of the former letter.] To the which letter or supplication speedy answere was made by the forenamed honourable Bragadino, comforting them, that they should by no meanes abate their courage, and that shortly he looked for succour from the Segniorie, diminishing as much as hee might, the feare which they had conceiued in their hearts, dispatching and sending away suddenly from Cyprus into Candia, a Pinnesse to certifie the duke and gouernours there, in what extremitie they were. The Turkes by this time had ended their mines, and set them on fire, the 29. of Iuly; in the which space our men, according as they were woont to doe, renued and made vp againe the vaimures ruined before by the Ordinance, and hauing no other stuffe left to aduance them with, made sackes of Kersie, vnto the which the noble Tiepolo diligently looked. [Sidenote: It standeth with reason, in hope of sauing the greater, to let the lesser go.] The three mines of the Commander did great damage to vs, hauing throwen downe the greater part of the earth, whereas the the gouernour Randacchi was slaine. The mine of the Arsenall ouerthrew all the rest of the Turrion, hauing smoldered and choked one whole garrison of our souldiers, the two flanckers onely still remaining.

The fift assault.

The enemies trauelled much to become masters of those foresayd flankers, and to sally foorth by the other batteries, and this assault lasted from three of the clocke in the after noone vntil night, where, and at what time were slaine very many of our enemies. In this assault Sig. Giacomo Strambali, amongst the rest, shewed much worthinesse, as hee had done before in other conflicts.

The sixt and last assault.

The next morning following, at the breake of the day, they assailed all places, the which assault continued more then sixe houres, with very little hurt on our side, because our enemies fought more coldly then they were wont to doe, annoying of vs continually on the Sea side with their Gallies, shooting in all their assaults and batteries continually Cannon shot in all parts of the Citie, as neere as they might. After we had defended and repulsed this assault, and perceiued things brought to a narrower straite then they were wont to be at, wee hauing left in all the whole Citie but seuen barrels of pouder, the gouernours of the Citie fully determined to yeelde vp themselues and the Citie, with honourable conditions. [Footnote: Necessitie oft times presseth vs in the end to that, which our will continually spurneth against.] Wherefore the first of August in the after noone, they tooke a truce, one being come for that purpose from Mustafa the Generall, with whom they concluded the next morning following to giue two hostages a piece, vntill such time as both armies were agreed. For our hostages (by the appointment of the right honourable Bragadino) were sent foorth the earle Hercole Martinengo, and Signior Matteo Colsi a Citizen of Famagusta, and from our enemies came into the Citie the Lieutenant of Mustafa, and the Aga of the Gianizzers, [Footnote: Giannezeri be the gard of the great Turke, so that Aga de Giannizeri is the captaine of the Turkes gard.] the which were met, euen vnto the gate of the Citie of Signiour Baglione with two hundreth harquebusers: ours also were met in like maner with great pompe with horsemen and harquebusers, with the sonne also of Mustafa in person, who made very much of them.

The Lord Baglione imparld with these hostages, which were then come for that purpose of the articles of peace, requiring by them of their Generall, their liues, armour, and goods, fiue peeces of Ordinance, three of the best horses, and safe passage from thence vnto Candia accompanied with their Gallies, and last of all, that the Grecians inhabiting the Island, might dwell there still quietly, and enioy peaceably their owne goods and possessions, liuing still Christians hereafter, as they had done before. All the which requests and articles were agreed vpon, granted, and subscribed vnto by the hand of Mustafa. [Footnote: Iust Turkish dealing, to speake and not to meane: sodainly to promise, and neuer to perform the same.] Foorthwith were sent Gallies, and other vessels into the hauen, so that our souldiers immediately began to imbarke themselues, of the which the greater part were already gone aboorde, the Nobilitie and our chiefe Captaines also being likewise very desirous to depart.

The 15. of August in the morning, the worthy Bragadino sent me with a letter vnto Mustafa, by the which hee signified, that the same night hee would come vnto him to deliuer vp the keyes of the Citie, and that he would leaue in the holde the honourable gentleman Tiepolo, praying him therefore, that whilest hee should haue iust cause thus to bee abroad, that there might be no harme done at home, and in the Citie. The Turkes from our truce taking vntill that time, practised with vs all familiarly, and without any suspition of sinister or double dealing, they hauing shewed vs much courtesie both in word and deede. Mustafa himselfe by worde of mouth presently answered me to this letter, in this sort, that I should returne, and make relation to this noble man Bragadino, who had sent mee, that he should come ouer to him at his owne pleasure, for hee was very desirous both to see and know him, for his great worthinesse and prowesse, that hee had tried to be in him, and in the other of his Captaines and Souldiers, of whose manhood and courage he would honourably report, where soeuer he came, as occasion should serue thereunto: and to conclude, that hee should nothing doubt of any thing: because in no maner of condition hee would suffer any violence to be done to those, which remained behind within the Citie. So I speedily returning made true report of the same: and towards night about foure of the clocke, the right honourable Bragadino accompanied with the L. Baglione, with Signior Aluigi Martinengo, with the right worshipfull Signior Gio. Antonio Querini, with the right worshipfull Signior Andrea Bragadino, with the knight of Haste, with the captaine Carlo Ragonasco, with captaine Francesco Straco, with captaine Hector of Brescia, with captaine Girolomo di Sacile, and with other gentlemen and fiftie souldiours, the Gouernours and Noble men with their swordes, and the souldiours with their harquebuzes came foorth of their hold, and went vnto the pauillion of Mustafa, of whom, all they at the beginning were curteously receiued, and caused to sit downe by him, he reasoning and discoursing with them of diuers things, a certaine time, and drawing them from one matter to another, at the last vpon a sudden picked a quarell vnto them, especially burdening that noble Bragadino with an vntrueth, laying to his charge that he had caused certaine of his slaues in the time that the truce continued between them, to be put to death. The which thing was most false. So that hee being angry therewith, suddenly stept foorth, and commaunded them to bee bound. Thus they being vnarmed (not suffered at that time to enter into his pauillion, with their former weapons) and bound, were led one by one into the market place, before his pauillion, being presently cut and hewen in sunder in his presence, and last of all from that woorthy and noble Bragadino (who being bound as the rest, and being commaunded twise or thrise to stretch foorth his necke, as though hee should haue bene beheaded, the which most boldly hee did without any sparke of feare) his eares were cut off, and causing him to bee stretched out most vilely vpon the ground, Mustafa talked with him, and blasphemed the holy name of our Sauiour, demaunding him; where is now thy Christ, that hee helpeth thee not? [Footnote: The propertie of true fortitude is, not to be broken with sudden terrors. Mustafa, cosin germaine to the thiefe, which hong on the left side of our Sauiour at his Passion.] To all the which no answere at all was giuen of that honourable gentleman. The earle Hercole Martinengo, which was sent for one of the hostages, who was also bound, was hidden by one of Mustafas eunuches vntill such time as his furie was past, afterward his life being graunted him, hee was made the eunuches slaue. Three Grecians which were vnder his pauillion were left vntouched. All the souldiers which were found in the campe, and all sortes of Christians to the number of three hundred, were suddenly slaine, they nothing mistrusting any such treason, or tirannie. The Christian souldiers which were embarked a litle before, were linked and fettered with iron chaines, made slaues, all things being taken from them; and stripped into their shirtes.

The second day after this murther was committed, which was the 17. of August, Mustafa entred the first time into the Citie, and caused the valiant and wise gouernour Tiepolo to bee hanged, who remained behind, waiting the returne of Signior Bragadino. I being in the citie at that present, when other of my countreymen were thus miserably slaine and made slaues, hid my selfe in certaine of the Grecians houses the space of fiue dayes, and they not being able to keepe mee in couert any longer for feare of the great penaltie, which was proclaimed agaynst such transgressors and concealers, I offred, and gaue my selfe slaue to one Sangiaccho del Bir, promising him fiue hundred Zechins [Footnote: Zechini, be certaine pieces of fine gold coined in Venice, euery one of the which is in value sixe shillings eight pence of our mony, and somewhat better: and equal altogether to a Turkish Byraltom.] for my ransome, with whom I remained in the Campe. The Friday folowing (being the Turkes sabbath day) this woorthy and patient gentlemen Bragadino was led still in the presence of that vnfaithfull tirant Mustafa, to the batteries made vnto the Citie, whereas he being compelled to cary two baskets of earth, the one vpon his backe: the other in his hand slaue-like, to euery sundry battrie, being enforced also to kisse the ground as oft as he passed by him, was afterward brought vnto the sea side, where he being placed in a chaire to leane and stay vpon, was winched vp in that chaire, and fastened vnto the maineyard of a galley, and hoisted vp with a crane, to shew him to all the Christian souldiers and slaues (which were in the hauen already shipped) hee being afterward let downe, and brought to the market place, the tormentors tooke of his clothes from him, and tacked him vnto the pillorie, whereas he was most cruelly flaied quicke; with so great constancie and faith on his part, that be neuer lost or abated any iot of his stedfast courage, being so farre from any fainting, that hee at that present with most stout heart reproched them, and spake much shame of his most traitorous dealing in breaking of his faithfull promise. At the last without any kind of alteration of his constancie, he recommending his soule vnto almightie God, gaue vp the ghost. When hee had thus ended his life (thanks be to God) his skin being taken and filled with strawe, was commanded foorthwith to be hanged vpon the bowsprit of a Foist, [Footnote: A Foist as it were a Brigandine, being somewhat larger then halfe a galley, much vsed of the Turkish Cursaros, or as we call them Pirates or Rouers.] and to be caried alongst the coast of Syria by the sea side, that all the port townes might see, and understand who he was.

This is now so much as I am able to declare to your highnesse by that I sawe my selfe, and can remember whilest that I was in the Fortresse: that also which by true relation of others I could understand, and sawe also my selfe in the campe, whilest I was slaue, I will likewise briefly vtter vnto you. The enemies armie was in number, two hundred thousand persons of all sortes and qualities. Of souldiers which tooke pay there were 80. thousand, besides the which number, there were 14. thousand of Giannizzers taken out from all the holdes of Syria, Caramania, Natolia, and part of them also which came from the gate [Footnote: The gate of the great Turke, is as much to say, as Constantinople: the which they call in the Turkish language Stanboll.] of the great Turke. The venturers with the sword were 60. thousand in number. The reason, why there were so many of this sort, was because Mustafa had dispersed a rumour through the Turkes dominion, that Famagusta was much more wealthy and rich, then the citie of Nicosia was: so for that cause, and by the commodious and easie passage from Syria ouer into Cyprus, these venturers were easily induced to come thither. [Footnote: Gli Venturieri da spada, are a kind of venturing souldiers, who commonly are wont to follow the army in hope of the spoile.] In 75. dayes (all the which time the batterie still continued) 140. thousand iron pellets were shot of, numbred, and seene. The chiefe personages which were in their armie neere vnto Mustafa, were these following; the Bassa of Aleppo, [Footnote: Aleppo, a famous citie neere vnto Antiochia, otherwise called in Greeke, [Greek: haeliopolis], the city of the Sunne.] the Bassa of Natolia, Musafer Bassa of Nicosia, the Bassa of Caramaniai, the Aga of the Giannizzers, Giambelat Bey, [Footnote: Bey in the Turkish language, signifieth knight with vs.] the Sangiaccho of Tripolis, the Begliarbei of Greece, [Footnote: Begliarbei signifieth lord Admirall.] the Bassa of Sciuassi and of Marasco, Ferca Framburaro, the Sangiaccho of Antipo, [Footnote: Sangiaccho, is that person with the Turkes, that gouerneth a prouince or countrey.] Soliman Bey, three Sangiacchos of Arabia, Mustafa Bey generall of the Venturers, Fergat gouernour of Malathia, the Framburaro of Diuerie, the Sangiaccho of Arabia and other Sangiacchos of lesser credite, with the number of fourescore thousand persons beside, as by the muster made by his Commission might well appeare.

The Framburaro which was at Rhodes, was appointed and left gouernour at Famagusta, and the report was that there should bee left in all the Island of Cyprus, twentie thousand persons, with two thousand horses, many of the which I saw, being very leane and euill appoynted for seruice. It seemeth also a thing not impertinent to the matter, to signifie to you, how I, by the especiall grace of God, was deliuered out of their cruell hands, [Footnote: God suffereth much to be done to his seruants, but neuer forsaketh them.] I hauing paied within two and fortie dayes (all the which time I was slaue) fiue hundred Zechins for my ransome to him, whose prisoner I was, by the meanes of the Consul for the French merchants, a Ligier then at Tripolis, who a litle before came from Tripolis in Syria vnto Cyprus, into the Turkes campe. Yet for all that I had paied this summe of money to him, hee would not so set me at libertie, but fed mee vp still with faire wordes, and promised mee that hee would first bring mee vnto his gouernment, which abutted vpon a piece of the famous riuer of Euphrates, and dismisse me. The which malice and falsehood of his I perceiuing, determined with my selfe to giue him the slip, [Footnote: Necessitie oft times sharpeneth mens wits, and causeth boldnes.] and to flie: so I waiting my time, and repairing often to the Citie, at length met with a small Fisher boate, of the which a small saile made of two shirts, I passed ouer from Cyprus vnto Tripolis, being in very great danger of drowning, whereas I remained in couert in the house of certaine Christians, vntill the fiue and twentie of September, at what time I departed from thence in a little French shippe called Santa Vittor, which came into these partes, and as wee rode, wee touched at a part of Cyprus Westward, called Capo delle Gatte, where as I came on land, and talking with certaine of the inhabitants of the Villages, who were then by chaunce a Hauking, demaunded of them, how they were intreated of the Turkes, and after what sort the Island was tilled: to the which they answered, that they could not possiblie bee in worse pickle then they were at that present, not enioying that quietly which was their owne, being made villains and slaues, and almost alwayes carying away the Bastonados, so that now (they sayd) they knew by triall too perfectly the pleasant and peaceable gouernment of the Christians, wishing and praying God that they might shortly returne. [Footnote: The nature of euery commoditie is sooner vnderstood by lacking, then by continuall enioying of the same.] And concerning the tillage of the Island they made answere moreouer, that no part of it was plowed or laboured, sauing onely that mountaine which was towards the West, and that because they were litle troubled with the crueltie of the Turkes, but as for the plaine and east part of the Island, there was small seede sowen therein, but became in a maner desert, there being left but few inhabitants, and lesse store of cattell there. Afterward wee departing from thence we arriued in Candia, [Footnote: Candia of the old writers called Creta in Latin, [Greek: Hekatompolis] in Greek, because it had once a 100. Cities in it, now there remaining but onely 4. thus commonly named, Candia, la Cania, Retima, and Scythia.] I for my part being clothed in sackecloth, whereas soone after by the great curtesie of the right honourable Signior Latino Orsino, I was new apparelled accordingly, friendly welcommed, and my necessitie relieued. From whence I shortly after sayling in a Cypriettes ship (thankes be to almightie God) arriued in this Citie in health, and am safely come home now at the honorable feete of your highnesse.

The Captains of the Christians slaine in Famagusta.

The lord Estor Baglione.
The lord Aluigi Martinengo.
The lord Federico Baglione.
The knight of Asta Vicegouernor.
The Capitaine Dauid Noce Master of the Campe.
The capitaine Meani of Perugia Serieant Maior.
The earle Sigismond of Casoldo.
The earle Francesco of Lobi of Cremona.
The captaine Francesco Troncauilla.
The captaine Hannibal Adama of Fermo.
The captaine Scipio of the citie of Castello.
The captaine Charles Ragonasco of Cremona.
The captaine Francesco Siraco.
The captaine Robeto Maluezzo.
The captaine Cæsar of Aduersa.
The captaine Bernardin of Agubio.
The captaine Francesco Bugon of Verona.
The captaine Iames of Fabiana.
The captaine Sebastian del Sole of Florence.
The captaine Hector of Brescia, the successour to the captaine Cæsar of Aduersa.
The captaine Flaminio of Florence, successor vnto Sebastian del Sole.
The captaine Erasmus of Fermo, successor to the captaine of Cernole.
The captaine Bartholomew of Cernole.

The captaine Iohn Battista of Riuarole.
The captaine Iohn Francesco of Venice.

The names of Christians made slaues.

The Earle Herocles Martinengo, with Iulius Cæsar Ghelfo a Souldiour of Bressa.
The earle Nestor Martinengo, which fled.
The captaine Marco Criuellatore.
The lord Herocles Malatesta.
The captaine Peter Conte of Montalberto.
The captaine Horatio of Veletri.
The captaine Aluigi Pezano.
The Conte Iames of Corbara.
The captaine Iohn of Istria.
The captaine Soldatelli of Agubio.
The captaine Iohn of Ascoli.
The captaine Antonie of the same towne.
The captaine Sebastian of the same towne.
The captaine Salgano of the citie of Castello.
The captaine Marcheso of Fermo.
The captaine Iohn Antonio of Piacenza.
The captaine Carletto Naldo.
The captaine Lorenzo Fornaretti.
The captaine Barnardo of Brescia.
The captaine Barnardino Coco.
The captaine Simon Bagnese, successour to the captaine Dauid Noce.
The captaine Tiberio Ceruto, successor vnto Conte Sigismond.
The captaine Ioseph of Lanciano, successour vnto captaine Francesco Troncauilla.
The captaine Morgante, successor to captain Hannibal.
The Lieutenant, successour vnto the captaine Scipio.
The Standerd bearer, successour to captaine Roberto.
The captaine Ottauia of Rimini, successour to the captaine Francesco Bugon.
The captaine Mario de Fabiano, successour to captaine Iacomo.
The captaine Francesco of Venice, successour vnto captaine Antonio.
The captaine Matteo of Capua.
The captaine Iohn Maria of Verona.
The captaine Mancino.

The Fortifiers.

Iohn Marmori, slaine.
The knight Maggio, slaue.

Turkish Captaines at Famagusta.

Mustafa Generall.
The Bassa of Aleppo.
The Bassa of Natolia, slaine.
Musafer Bassa of Nicosia.
The Bassa of Catamania.
The Aga of the Giannizers.
Giambelat Bey.
The Sangiaccho of Tripolis, slaine.
The Begliarbei of Greece.
The Bassa of Sciuassi and Marasco.
Ferca Framburaro.
The Sangiaccho of Antipo, slaine.
Soliman Bey, slaine.
Three Sangiacchos of Arabia slaine.
Mustafa Bey, General of the Venturers, slain.
Fergat, ruler of Malathia, slaine.
The Framburaro of Diuerie, slaine.

* * * * *

The renuing and increasing of an ancient and commodious trade vnto
diuerse
  places in the Leuant seas, and to the chiefest partes of all the great
  Turks dominions, by the meanes of the Right worsh. citizens Sir Edward
  Osburne Alderman, and M. Richard Staper marchant of London.

This trade into the Leuant (as is elsewhere mentioned) was very vsuall and
much frequented from the yeere of our Lord 1511, till the yeere 1534, and
afterwards also, though not so commonly, vntill the yeere 1550, when as
the barke Aucher vnder the conduct of M. Roger Bodenham made a
prosperous voyage vnto Sicilia, Candia, Sio, and other places within the
Leuant. Since which time the foresaid trade (notwithstanding the Grand
Signiors ample priuilege granted to M. Anthony Ienkenson 1553, and the
strong and weighty reasons of Gaspar Campion for that purpose) was
vtterly discontinued, and in maner quite forgotten, as if it had neuer bene,
for the space of 20 years and more. Howbeit, the discreete and worthy
citizens Sir Edward Osborne and M. Richard Staper seriously considering
what benefite might grow to the common wealth by renuing of the foresaid
discontinued trade, to the inlarging of her Maiesties customes, the
furthering of nauigation, the venting of diuerse generall commodities of this
Realme, and the inriching of the citie of London, determined to vse some
effectuall meanes for the reestablishing and augmenting thereof.

[Sidenote: The voyage of Iohn Wight, and Ioseph Clements to Constantinople.] Wherefore about the yeere 1575 the foresaid R. W. marchants at their charges and expenses sent Iohn Wight and Ioseph Clements by the way of Poland to Constantinople, where the said Ioseph remained 18 monethes to procure a safe conduct from the grand Signior, for M. William Harborne, then factor for Sir Edward Osborne, to haue free accesse into his Highnes dominions, and obtained the same.

[Sidenote: The first voyage of M. William Harborne to Constantinople.] Which businesse after two yeres chargeable trauell and suit being accomplished, the sayd M. Harborne the first of Iuly 1578 departed from London by the sea to Hamburgh, and thence accompanied with Ioseph Clements his guide and a seruant, he trauelled to Leopolis in Poland, and then apparelling himselfe, his guide, and his seruant after the Turkish fashion (hauing first obteyned the king of Poland his safe conduct to passe at Camienijecz the frontier towne of his dominions next vnto Turky) by good means he obteined fauour of one Acmet Chaus the Turks ambassadour then in Poland, and readie to returne to Constantinople, to bee receiued into his companie and carouan. And so the fourth of September 1578 he departed with the said Acmet from Leopolis in Poland, and trauelling through Moldauia, Valachia, Bulgaria, and Romania, gratifying the Voiauodes with certaine courtesies, he arriued at Constantinople the 28 of October next insuing. Where he behaued himselfe so wisely and discreetly, that within few moneths after he obtained not onely the great Turkes large and ample priuiledge for himselfe, and the two worshipfull persons aforesaid, but also procured his honourable and friendly letters vnto her Maiestie in maner following.

* * * * *

The letters sent from the Imperiall Musulmanlike highnesse of Zuldan Murad Can, to the sacred regall Maiestie of Elizabeth Queene of England, the fifteenth of March 1579, conteyning the grant of the first priuileges.

In greatnes and glory most renowmed Elizabeth, most sacred Queene, and noble prince of the most mightie worshippers of Iesus, most wise gouernour of the causes and affaires of the people and family of Nazareth, cloud of most pleasant raine, and sweetest fountaine of noblenesse and vertue, ladie and heire of the perpetuall happinesse and glory of the noble Realme of England (whom all sorts seeke vnto and submit themselues) we wish most prosperous successe and happie ends to all your actions, and do offer vnto you such pleasures and curtesies as are worthy of our mutuall and eternall familiaritie: thus ending (as best beseemeth vs) out former salutations.

In most friendly maner we giue you to vnderstand, that a certaine man hath come vnto vs in the name of your most excellent Regall Maiestie, commending vnto vs from you all kindnesse, curtesie and friendly offices on your part, and did humbly require that our Imperiall highnesse would vouchsafe to giue leaue and libertie to him and vnto two other merchants of your kingdome [Sidenote: These two were Sir Edward Osborne and M. Richard Staper.], to resort hither and returne againe, and that by way of traffike they might be suffered to trade hither with their goods and merchandizes to our Imperiall dominions, and in like sort to make their returne.

Our stately Court and Countrey hath beene euer open for the accesse both of our enemies and friends. But because we are informed that your most excellent Regall Maiesty doth abound with good will, humanitie, and all kind of louing affection towards vs, so much the rather shall the same our Countrey be alwayes open to such of your subiects, as by way of merchandize shall trade hither: and we will neuer faile to aide and succor any of them that are or shal be willing to esteeme of our friendship, fauour, and assistance: but will reckon it some part of our dutie to gratifie them by all good meanes. And forasmuch as our Imperiall highnesse is giuen to vnderstand that your most excellent Regall Maiestie doth excell in bountie and curtesie, we therfore haue sent out our Imperiall commandement to all our kings, iudges, and trauellers by sea, to all our Captaines and voluntarie seafaring men, all condemned persons, and officers of Ports and customes, straightly charging and commanding them, that such foresaid persons as shall resort hither by sea from the Realme of England, either with great or small vessels to trade by way of marchandize, may lawfully come to our imperiall Dominions, and freely returne home againe, and that no man shall dare to molest or trouble them. [Sidenote: He calleth the Germaine emperor but king of Germanie.] And if in like sort they shall come into our dominions by land, either on foote or on horsebacke, no man shall at any time withstand or hinder them: but as our familiars and confederates, the French, Venetians, Polonians, and the king of Germany, with diuers other our neighbours about vs, haue libertie to come hither, and to returne againe into their owne countreys, in like sort the marchants of your most excellent Regall Maiesties kingdome shall haue safe conduct and leaue to repayre hither to our Imperiall dominions, and so to returne againe into their owne Country: straightly charging that they be suffered to vse and trade all kind of marchandize as any other Christians doe, without let or disturbance of any.

[Sidenote: The Turke demandeth like priuiledges for his subiects in the Queenes dominions.] Therefore when these our Imperiall letters shall be brought to your most excellent Maiestie, it shall be meet, according to our beneuolence, humanity, and familiarity toards your most excellent Maiesty, that you likewise bethinke your selfe of your like beneuolence, humanitie and friendshippe towards vs, to open the gate thereof vnto vs, and to nourish by all good meanes this kindnesse and friendship: and that like libertie may be granted by your Highnesse to our subiects and merchants to come with their merchandizes to your dominions, either by sea with their ships, or by land with their wagons or horses, and to returne home againe: and that your most excellent Regall Maiestie do alwayes declare your humanitie, good will, and friendship towards vs, and alwayes keepe open the dore thereof vnto vs.

Giuen at our citie of Constantinople the fifteenth day of March, and in the yeere of our most holy Prophet Mahomet. [Marginal note: With vs the yeere 1579.]

* * * * *

The answere of her Maiestie to the aforesaid Letters of the Great Turke, sent the 15 of October 1579, in the Prudence of London by Master Richard Stanley.

Elizabetha Dei ter maximi, et vnici coeli terræque Conditoris gratia, Angliæ, Franciæ et Hiberniæ regina, fidei Christianæ contra omnes omnium inter Christianos degentium, et Christi nomen falsò profitentium Idololatrias inuictissima et potentissima Defensatrix, augustissimo, inuictissimóque principi Sultan Murad Can, Turcici regni dominatori potentissimo, Imperíjque orientis, Monarchæ supra omnes soli et supremo, salutem, et multos cum rerum optimarum affluentia foelices, et fortunatos annos. Augustissime et inuictissime Cæesar, accepimus inuicttissimæ Cæsareæ vestræ celsitudinis literas, die decimoquinto Martij currentis anni ad nos scriptas Constantinopoli, ex quibus intelligimus quàm benignè quámque clementer, literæ supplices quæ Cæsareæ vestræ celsitudini a quodam subdito nostro Guilielmo Hareborno in Imperiali Celsitudinis vestræ ciuitate Constantinopoli commorante offerebantur, literæ profectionis pro se et socijs eius duobus hominibus mercatoribus subditis nostris cum mercibus suis ad terras ditionésque Imperio vestro subiectas iam per mare quàm per terras, indéque reuersionis veniæ potestatísque humillimam complexæ petitionem, ab inuictissima vestra Cæsarea celsitudine, acceptæ fuerunt. Neque id solùm, sed quàm mira cum facilitate, dignáque augustissima Cæsarea cleméntia, quod erat in dictis literis supplicibus positum, ei socíjsque suis donatum et concessum fuit, pro ea, vti videtur, solùm opinione, quam de nobis, et nostra amicitia vestra celsitudo concepit. Quod singulare beneficium in dictos subditos nostros collatum tam gratè tamque beneuolè accepimus (maximas celsitudini vestræ propterea et agentes, et habentes gratias) nullo vt vnquam patiemur tempore, pro facultatum nostrarum ratione, proque ea quam nobis inseuit ter maximus mundi monarcha Deus (per quem et cuius auspicijs regnamus) naturæ bonitate, qua remotissimas nos esse voluit, et abhorrentes ab ingratitudinis omni vel minima suspitione, docuitque nullorum vnquam vt principum, vllis in nos meritis nos sineremus vinci, aut superari, vt apud ingratam principem tantum beneficium deposuisse, se vestra Celsitudo existimet. Proptereaque animum nostrum inpræsentiarum vestræ celsitudini emetimur, benè sentiendo et prædicando, quantopere nos obstrictas beneficij huius in subditos nostros collati putemus memoriâ sempiternâ: longè vberiorem, et ampliorem gratitudinis erga vestram celsitudinem nostræ testificationem daturæ, cum tempora incident, vt possimus et à nobis desiderabitur. Quoniam autem quæ nostris paucis subditis, eáque suis ipsorum precibus, sine vlla intercessione nostra concessa donatio est, in æquè libera potestate sita est ad omnes terras ditionesque Imperio vestro subiectas, com mercibus suis tam per mare quàm per terras eundi et redeundi, atque inuictissimæ Cæsareæ vestræ celsitudinis confoederatis, Gallis, Polonis, Venetis, atque adeo regis Romanorum subditis largita vnquam aut donata fuit, celsitudinem vestram rogamus ne tam singularis beneficentiæ laus in tam angustis terminis duorum aut trium hominum concludatur, sed ad vniuersos subditos nostrus diffusa, propagatáque, celsitudinis vestræ beneficium eò reddat augustius, quò eiusdem donatio latiùs patebit, et ad plures pertinebit. Cuius tam singularis in nos beneficij meritum, eò erit celsitudini vestræ minùs poenitendum, quò sunt merces illæ, quibus regna nostra abundant, et aliorum principum ditiones egent, tam humanis vsibus comodæ támque necessariæ, nulla gens vt sit, quæ eis carere queat, proptereáque longissimis, difficillimísque itineribus conquisitis non vehementer gaudeat. Cariùs autem distrabunt alijs, quo ex labore suo quisque victum et quæstum quæritat, adeo vt in earum acquisitione vtilitas, in emptione autem ab alijs onus sit. Vtilitas celsitudinis vestræ subditis augebitur liberâ hac paucorum nostrorum hominum ad terras vestras perfectione: onus minuctur, profectionis, quorumcúnque subditorum nostrorum donatione. Accedet præterea quæ à nobis in celsitudinis vestræ subditos proficiscetur, par, æquáque mercium exercendarum libertas, quoties et quando voluerint ad regna dominiáque nostra mercaturæ gratia accedere. Quam celsitudini vestræ pollicemur tam amplam latéque patentem fore, quàm est vlla à confoederatorum vestrorum vllis principibus antedictis, regibus videlicet Romanorum, Gallorum, Polonorum, ac republica Veneta, celsitudinis vestræ subditis vllo vnquam tempore concessa et donata. Qua in re si honestæ petitioni nostræ inuictissima Cæsarea vestra celsitudo dignabitur ausculate, faciétque vt acceptis nostris literis intelligamus gratum nè habitura sit quod ab ea contendibus et rogamus, ea proposita præstitáque securitate, quæ subditos nostros quoscúnque ad dominia sua, terra, maríque proficiscentes, indéque reuerentes tutos et secures reddat ab omni quorumcúnque subditorum suorum iniuria, efficiemus, vt quæ Deus opt. max. in regna dominiáque nostra contulit commoda (quæ tam singularia sunt, omnium vt principum animos pelliceant ad amicitiam, summæque necessitudinis coniunctionem nobiscum contrahendam, stabiliendámque quo liberius tantis summi Dei beneficijs fruantur, quibus carere nequeunt) nostri subditi ad regna dominiáque Celsitudinis vestræ aduehunt tam affluenter támque cumulate, vt vtríque incommodo prædicto necessitatis et oneris plenissimè succurratur. Facit prætereà singularis ista Celsitudinis vestræ in nos Gentémque nostram summæ beneuolentiæ significatio ac fides, vt eandem, in causam quorumdam subditorum nostrorum, qui captiui triremibus vestris detinentur, interpellemus, rogemúsque, vt quoniam nullo in celsitudinem vestram peccato suo, siuè arma in eam ferendo, siuè iniquiùs præter fas et ius gentium se gerendo in suos subditos, in hanc calamitatem inciderint, soluti vinculis, et libertate donati, nobis pro sua fide et obsequio inseruientes, causam vberiorem præbeant vestræ Celsitudinis in nos humanitatem prædicandi: et Deum illum, qui solus, et supra omnia et omnes est acerrimus idololatriæ vindicator, suíque honoris contra Gentium et aliorum falsos Deos Zelotes, præcabimur, vt vestram inuictissimam Cæsaream Celsitudinem omni beatitate eorum donorum fortunet, quæ sola et summè iure merito habentur desideratissima.

Datæ è Regia nostra Grenouici, prope ciuitatem nostram Londinum, quintodecimo Mensis Octobris, Anno Iesu Christi Saluatoris nostri 1579, Regni verò nostri vicessimo primo.

The same in English.

Elizabeth by the grace of the most mightie God, and onely Creatour of heauen and earth, of England, France and Ireland Queene, the most inuincible and most mighty defender of the Christian faith against all kinde of idolatries, of all that liue among the Christians, and fully professe the Name of Christ, vnto the most Imperiall and most inuincible prince, Zaldan Murad Can, the most mightie ruler of the kingdome of Turkie, sole and aboue all, and most souereigne Monarch of the East Empire, greeting, and many happy and fortunate yeeres, with abundance of the best things.

Most Imperiall and most inuincible Emperour, wee haue receiued the letters of your mightie highnesse written to vs from Constantinople the fifteenth day of March this present yere, whereby we vnderstand how gratiously, and how fauourably the humble petitions of one William Hareborne a subiect of ours, resident in the Imperiall citie of your highnes presented vnto your Maiestie for the obteining of accesse for him and two other Marchants more of his company our subiects also, to come with marchandizes both by sea and land, to the countries and territories subiect to your gouernment, and from thence againe to returne home with good leaue and libertie, were accepted of your most inuincible Imperiall highnesse, and not that onely, but with an extraordinarie speed and worthy your Imperiall grace, that which was craued by petition was granted to him, and his company in regard onely (as it seemeth) of the opinion which your highnesse conceiued of vs and our amitie: which singular benefit done to our aforesaid subiects, wee take so thankefully, and so good part (yeelding for the same our greatest thanks to your highnesse) that we will neuer giue occasion to your said highnesse (according as time, and the respect of our affaires will permit) once to thinke so great a pleasure bestowed vpon an vngratefull Prince. For the Almighty God, by whom, and by whose grace we reigne, hath planted in vs this goodnesse of nature, that wee detest and abhorre the least suspition of ingratitude, and hath taught vs not to suffer our selues to bee ouermatched with the good demerits of other Princes. And therefore at this time wee doe extende our good minde vnto your highnesse, by well concerning, and publishing also abroad, how much we repute our selfe bound in an euerlasting remembrance for this good pleasure to our Subiects, meaning to yeelde a much more large and plentifull testification of our thankefulnesse, when time conuenient shall fall out, and the same shall bee looked for at our handes.

But whereas that graunt which was giuen to a fewe of our Subiects, at their onely request without any intercession of ours, standeth in as free a libertie of comming and going to and from all the lands and kingdoms subiect to your Maiestie, both by land and sea with marchandizes, as euer was granted to any of your Imperiall highnesse confederates, as namely to the French, the Polonians, the Venetians, as also to the subiects of the king of the Romanes, wee desire of your highnesse that the commendation of such singular courtesie may not bee so narrowly restrained to two or three men onely, but may be inlarged to all our subiects in generall, that thereby your highnesse goodnesse may appeare the more notable, by reason of the graunting of the same to a greater number of persons. The bestowing of which so singular a benefit your highnesse shall so much the lesse repent you of, by howe much the more fit and necessary for the vse of man those commodities are, wherewith our kingdomes doe abound, and the kingdomes of other princes doe want, so that there is no nation that can be without them, but are glad to come by them, although by very long and difficult trauels: and when they haue them, they sell them much deerer to others, because euery man seeketh to make profite by his labour: so that in the getting of them there is profit, but in the buying of them from others there is losse. But this profite will be increased to the subiects of your highnesse by this free accesse of a few of our subiects to your dominions, as also the losse and burden wilbe eased, by the permission of generall accesse to all our people. And furthermore we will graunt as equall and as free a libertie to the subiects of your highnesse with vs for the vse of traffique, when they wil and as often as they wil, to come, and go to and from vs and our kingdomes. Which libertie wee promise to your highnesse shalbe as ample, and as large as any was euer giuen or granted to your subiects by the aforesaide princes your confederate, as namely the king of the Romanes, of France, of Poland, and the common wealth of Venice. In which matter, if your most inuincible Imperiall highnesse shall vouchsafe to incline to our reasonable request, and shall giue order vpon these our letters, that wee may haue knowledge how the same is accepted of you, and whether it wilbe granted, with sufficient securitie for our subiects to go, and returne safe and secure from all violences and inuiries of your people, we on the other side wil giue order, that those commodities which Almighty God hath bestowed vpon our kingdomes (which are in deed so excellent, that by reason of them all princes are drawen to enter, and confirme leagues of amitie and good neighborhood with vs, by that meanes to enioy these so great blessings of God, which we haue, and they can in no case want) our subiects shall bring them so abundantly and plentifully to the kingdomes and dominions of your highnesse, that both the former inconueniences of necessitie, and losse, shall most sufficiently be taken away.

Moreouer the signification and assurance of your highnesse great affection to vs and our nation, doeth cause vs also to intreat and vse mediation on the behalfe of certain of our subiects, who are deteined as slaues and captiues in your Gallies, for whom we craue, that forasmuch as they are fallen into that misery, not by any offence of theirs, by bearing of armes against your highnesse, or in behauing of themselues contrarie to honestie, and to the law of nations, they may be deliuered from their bondage, and restored to libertie, for their seruice towardes vs, according to their dutie: which thing shall yeeld much more abundant cause to vs of commending your clemencie, and of beseeching that God (who onely is aboue all things, and all men, and is a most seuere reuenger of all idolatrie, and is ielous of his honour against the false gods of the nations) to adorne your most inuincible Imperiall highnesse with all the blessings of those gifts, which onely and deseruedly are accounted most worthy of asking.

Giuen at our palace of Greenwich, neere to our citie of London, the fiue and twentieth day of October, in the yeere of Iesus Christ our Sauiour one thousand, fiue hundreth, seuentie and nine, and of our reigne the one and twentieth.

* * * * *

The charter of the priuileges granted to the English, and the league of the great Turke with the Queenes Maiestie in respect of traffique, dated in Iune 1580.

Immensa et maxima ex potestate potentissimi, terribilibúsque verbis et nunquam finienda innumerabiliue clementia et ineffabili auxilio sanctissimi et pura mente colendissimi tremendissimíque modernæ ætatis monarcha, totius orbis terrarum potentribus sceptra diuidere potens, clementiæ, gratiæque diuinæ vmbra, regnorum prouinciarumue, et vrbium ciuitatumue distributor permultarum: Nos sacratissimus Cæsar Muzulmanicus Mecchæ, id est domus diuinæ, Medinæ, gloriosissimæ et beatissimæ Ierusalem, Aegypti fertilissimæ, Iemen, et Zouan, Eden et Canan, Sami paciferæ et Hebes, Iabza et Pazra, Zerazub et Halepiæ, Caramariæ et Diabekiruan, et Dulkadiriæ, Babyloniæ, et totius triplicis Arabiæ, Euzorum et Georgianorum, Cypri diuitis, et regnorum Asiæ Ozakior, Camporum Maris albi et nigri, Græciæ et Mesopotamiæ, Africæ et Goletæ, Algeris et Tripolis occidentalis, selectissimæque Europæ, Budæ, et Temeswar, et regnorum transalpinorum, et his similium permultorum princeps Cæsarué sacerrimus, potentissimus Murad Can, filius principis Zelim Can, qui fuit Zoleiman Can, qui fuit Zelim Can, qui fuit Paiezid Can, qui fuit Mehemed Can, &c.

Nos princeps potentissimos Murad Can hoc in signum nostræ Cæsareæ amicitiæ significamus, manifestamus, quòd in temporibus modernis Regina Angliæ, Franciæ, et Hiberniæ Elizabetha in Christianitate honoratissima Regina (cuius mercatorum exitus sit foelicissimus) ad nostram excelsam, et iustitiæ plenam, fulgidissimámue portam, quæ omnibus principibus mundi est refugium et requies, per egregium Gulielmum Harebornum literas misit suas, quibus sua maiestas significauit, quod tempore præterito quidam subditi sui venissent ad nostram portam excelsam, et suam obedientiam erga eam demonstrauissent, et ob eam causam illis quoque ad nostras ditiones mercandi gratia venire et redire poscerent venia et potestas fuisset data: et quòd in locis et hospitijs eorum per mare et terram nemo auderet impedire et illis damnum facere, mandatum Cæsareum fuisset datum: et quòd hanc nostram gratiam, quam paucis hominibus suæ maiestatis demonstrauissemus, vniuersis suis subditis concederemus petebat. [Sidenote: Foedus Turcici Imperatoris cum Regina initum.] Quare, quemadmodum cum serenissimis beneuolentiam et obedientiam, seruitiáue sua demonstrantibus erga nostram portam excelsam regibus et principibus confoederatis (vt sunt rex Gallorum. Veneti, et rex Polonorum, et cæteri) pacem et foedus sanctissimum pepigimus: sic etiam cum præfata Regina amicitiam custodiendam, pacem et foedus coniunximus. Illius igitur homines, et vniuersi mercatores, sine aliquo impedimento cum suis mercibus et oneribus cunctis ad nostras ditionis Cæsareas pacificè et securè veniant, et suam exerceant mercaturam, maneant in suis statibus, et secundum suos mores negocientur. Et adhæc, sua maiestas significabat ex hominibus suis aliquos iamdudum captos fuisse, et in captiuitate detineri, et quod hi dimitterentur petebat, et quòd sicut alijs principibus nobiscum confoederatis priuilegia et mandate Cæsarea super foedus sanctissimum dedissemus, sic præfatæ quoque Reginæ priuilegium et mandata Cæsareæ vt daremus, nostræ Cæsareæ celsitudini placeret. Quare secundùm nostram beneuolentiam et gratiam innatam, optata suæ maiestatis apud nos grata fuere: Et hoc nostrum priuilegium iustitijs plenum dedimus maiestata suæ: Et Beglerbegis, Zanziacbegis famulis nostris, et Kazijs, id est, iudicibus, et omnibus teloniatoribus omnium locorum, portuum, et vadorum firmiter mandamus, vt donec ex parte præfatæ reginæ foedus, et pax, et eorum conditiones articulíque (vt conuenit) custodiuntur et seruantur, nostræ quóque Cæsareæ celsitudinis mandata sunt:

[Sidenote: Articuli huius priuilegij.] 1 Vt præfatæ Reginæ homines, et subditi eius quibusuis rebus et mercibus, oneribus et suppellectilibus per mare in magnis et paruis nauibus, per terram autem homines cum oneribus et pecoribus, securè et pacificè ad nostras ditiones Cæsareas veniant, et nemo illis noceat, sed securè et sine aliquo impedimento negocientur, et in suis statibus et conditionibus permaneant.

2 Item, si præfeti homines et mercatores in suis rectis vijs et negociationibus aliquo modo caperentur, sine aliqua tergiuersatione dimittantur liberentúrque.

3 Item, si naues eorum ad aliquos portus et loca venire voluerint, pacificè omni in tempore, et sine impedimento veniant, et discedant in sua loca.

4 Item, si in tempestatibus maris naues eorum essent in periculo et auxilio opus esset illis, naues nostræ Cæsareæ celsitudinis, earúmque homines, et aliornm naues hominésque statim auxilium et opem ferant illis, mandamus.

5 Item, si edulia suis pecunijs emere voluerint, nemo resistat illis, sed sine impedimento edulia emant.

6 Item, si infortunium maris naues eorum in terram proiecerit, Begi et iudices, et cæteri nostri subditi sint auxilio illis, merces et res eorum quæ remanserint iterum reddantur illis, et nemo impediat illos.

7 Item, si præfatæ reginæ homines, eorum interpretes, et mercatores, siue per terram, siue per mare mercandi gratiâ ad nostras ditiones venire velint, legitimo telonio, et vectigali reddito, pacificè vagentur, capitanei et reges maris et nauium, et aliud genus hominum per mare vagantium in personis, et rebus eorum, pecoribúsque, ne noceant illis.

8 Item, si aliquis ex Anglis debitor, aut ære alieno esset obstrictus, inueniríque non possit, ratione debitorum alterius nullus nisi esset fideiussor capiatur aut impediatur.

9 Item, si Anglus testamentum fecerit, et sua bona cuicúnque legauerit, illi dentur bona illius, et si sine testamento moreretur, consul eorum cuicúnque

sociorum mortui hominis dixerit debere dari, illi, dentur bona mortui hominis.

10 Item, si Angli, et ad Angliam pertinentium locorum mercatores et interpretes, in vendendis et emendis mercibus fideiussionibus et rebus aliquid negocij habuerint, ad iudicem veniant, et in librum inscribi faciant negotium, et si voluerint, literas quóque accepiant à iudice, propterea quòd si aliquid inciderit, videant librum et literas, et secundum tenorem eorum perficiantur negocia eorum suspecta: si autem néque in librum inscriberentur, néque literas haberent, iudex falsa testimonia non admittat, sed secundúm iustitiam legem administrans non sinat illos impediri.

11 Item, si aliquis disceret, quod isti Christiani nostræ fidei Muzulmanicæ male dixerint, et eam vituperijs affecerint, in hoc negocio etiam et alijs, testes falsi minimè admittantur.

12 Item, si aliquis eorum aliquod facinus pataret, et fugiens non possit inueniri, nullus nisi esset fideiussor pro alterius facto retineatur.

13 Item, si aliquod mancipium Anglicum inueniretur, et consul eorum peteret illud, examinetur diligenter mancipium, et si inuentum fuerit Anglicum, accipiatur, et reddatur Anglis.

14 Item, si aliquis ex Anglis huc venerit habitandi aut mercandi gratiâ, sine sit vxoratus, siue sit sine vxore, non saluat censum.

15 Item, si in Alexandria, in Damasco, in Samia, in Tunis, in Tripoli occidentali, in Aegypti portubus et in alijs omnibus locis, vbicúnque voluerint facere Consules, faciant: Et iterum si voluerint eos mutare, et in loco priorum consulum alios locare, liberè faciant, et nemo illis resistat.

16 Item, si illorum interpres in arduis negotijs occupatis abesset, donec veniret interpres, expectetur, et interem nemo illos impediat.

17 Item, si Angli inter se aliquam litem haberent et vellent ad suos consules ire, nemo resistat illis, sed liberè veniant ad Consules suos, vt secundùm mores eorum finiatur lis orta.

18 Item, si post tempus aut datum huius priuilegij, piratæ, aut alij aliqui liberi gubernatores nauium per mare vagarites, aliquem ex Anglis ceperint, et trans mare vel cis mare venderint, secundùm iustitiam examinetur: et si Anglus inuentus fuerit, et religionem Muzulmanicam assumpserit, liberè dimittatur: si autem adhuc esset Christianas, Anglis reddatur, et emptores suam pecuniam ab illo petant, à quo emerant.

19 Item, si nostræ Cæsareæ Celsitudinis naues armatæ exiuerint ad mare, et ibi inuenerint naues Anglicas merces portantes, nemo impediat illas, imò amicè tractentur, et nullum damnum faciant illis: Quemadmodum Gallis,

Venetis, et cæteris nobiscum con foederatis regibus, et principibus priuilegium, et articulos priuilegijs dedimus, et concessimus, simili modo his quòque Anglis priuilegium et articulos priuilegijs dedimus et concessimus, et contra legem diuinam, et hoc priuilegium, nemo vnquam aliquid audeat facere.

20 Item, si naues magnæ, et paruæ in itinere et loco vbi stant detinebuntur, nemo illos audeat impedire, sed potius auxilio sint illis.

21 Item, si latrones et fures vi raperent naues illorum nauiumque merces, magna diligentia quærantu latrones et fures, et seuerissimè puniantur.

23 Ad extremum, Beglerbegij, et Zanziaebegi, Capitanei nostri, Mancipia, et per mare nauigantes serui Capitaneorum, et Indices, et Teloniatores nauium Reiz dicti, et liberi Rez, omnes isti præfati, secundum tenorem huius priuilegij, tenorémue articulorum eius, omnia facere teneantur, et debeæt. Et donec hoc in priuilegio descriptum foedus, et pax illius Maiestatis ex parte sanctè seruabitur, et custodietur, ex parte etiam nostra Cæsarea custodiri, et obseruari mandamus.

Datum Constantinopoli, anno nostri prophetæ Sanctissimi 988, in principio mensis Iunij, anno autem Iesu 1580.

The iterpretation of the letters, or priuilege of the most mightie and Musumanlike Emperour Zuldan Murad Can, granted at the request of Elizabeth by the grace of the most mightie God, and only Creator of heauen and earth, of England, France and Ireland Queene, confirming a peace and league betwixt both the said Princes and their subiects.

We most sacred Musolmanlike Emperor, by the infinite and exceeding great power, by the euerlasting and wonderfull clemencie, and by the vnspeakable helpe of the most mighty and most holy God, creator of all things, to be worshipped and feared with all purenesse of minde, and reuerence of speech. The prince of these present times the onely Monarch of this age, able to giue scepters to the potentates of the whole world, the shadow of the diuine mercy and grace, the distributer of many kingdoms, prouinces, townes and cities, Prince, and most sacred Emperour of Mecca, that is to say, of Gods house, of Medina, of the most glorious and blessed Ierusalem, of the most fertile Egypt, Iemen and Iouan, Eden and Canaan, of Samos the peaceable, and of Hebes, of Iabza, and Pazra, of Zeruzub and Halepia, of Caramaria and Diabekiruan, of Dulkadiria, of Babylon, and of all the three Arabias, of the Euzians and Georgians, of Cyprus the rich, and of the kingdomes of Asia, of Ozakior, of the tracts of the white and blacke Sea, of Grecia and Mesopotamia, of Africa and Goleta, of Alger, and of Tripolis in the West, of the most choise and principall Europe, of Buda and Temeswar, and of the kingdomes beyond the Alpes, and many other such like, most mightie Murad Can, the sonne of the Emperour Zelim Can, which was the sonne of Zoleiman Can, which was the sodne of Zelim Can, which was the sonne of Paiizid Can, which was the sonne of Mehemed Can, &c.

We most mightie prince Murad Can, in token of our Imperiall friendship, doe signifie and declare, that now of late Elizabeth Queene of England, France and Ireland, the most honourable Queene of Christendom (to whose marchants we wish happy successe) sent her letters by her worthy seruant William Hareborne vnto our stately and most magnificent Porch replenished with iustice, which is a refuge and Sanctuary to all the prince of the world, by which letters her Maiestie signified, that whereas heretofore certaine of her subiects had repaired to our saide stately Porche, and had shewed their obedience to the same, and for that cause had desired that leaue and libertie might also be granted vnto them, to come and goe for traffiques sake too and from our dominions, and that our Imperial commandement might be giuen, that no man should presume to hurt or hinder them, in any of their abodes or passages by sea or land, and whereas shee requested that we would graunt to all her subiects in generall, this our fauour, which before wee had extended onely to a fewe of her people: therefore as we haue entred into amitie, and most holy league with the most excellent kings and princes our confederates, shewing their deuotion, and obedience or seruices towards our stately Porch (as namely the French king, the Venetians, the king of Polonia and others) so also we haue contracted an inuiolable amitie, peace and league with the aforesaid Queene, Therefore wee giue licence to all her people, and marchants, peaceably and safely to come vnto our imperiall dominions, with all their marchandise and goods without any impeachment, to exercise their traffique, to vse their owne customes, and to buy and sell according to the fashions of their owne countrey.

And further her Maiestie signified vnto vs, that certaine of her people had heretofore bene taken prisoners, and were detained in captiuitie, and required that they might bee set at libertie, and that as we had graunted vnto other Princes our confederats, priuileges, and Imperiall decrees, concerning our most inuiolable league with them, so it would please our Imperial Maiesty to graunt and confirme the like priuiledges, and princely decrees to the aforesaid Queene.

Wherefore according to our humanitie and gracious ingraffed disposition, the requests of her Maiestie we accepted of vs, and we haue granted vnto her Maiestie the priuilege of ours agreeable to reason and equitie. And we straightly command all our Beglerbegs, and Zanziacbegs our seruants, and our Reyz, that is to say, our Iudges, and all our customers in all places, hauens and passages, that as long as this league and amitie with the conditions, and articles thereof, are kept and obserued on the behalfe of the aforesaid Queene. 1 Our Imperiall commandement and pleasure is, that the people and subiects of the same Queene, may safely and securely come to our princely dominions, with their goods and marchandise, and ladings, and other commodities by sea in great and smal vessels, and by land with their carriages and cattels, and that no man shall hurt them, but they may buy and sell without any hinderance, and obserue the customes and orders of their owne countrey.

2 Item, if the aforesaid people and marchants shalbe at any time in the course of their iourneis and dealings by any meanes taken, they shall be deliuered and inlarged, without any excuse or cauillation.

3 Item, if their ships purpose to arriue in any of our ports and hauens, it shalbe lawfull for them so to do in peace, and from thence againe to depart, without any let or impediment.

4 Item, if it shall happen that any of their ships in tempestuous weather shall bee in danger of losse and perishing, and thereupon shall stand in need of our helpe, we will, and commaund that our men and ships be ready to helpe and succour them.

5 Item, if they shalbe willing to buy any victuals for their money, no person shall withstande them, but they shall buy the same without any disturbance to the contrary.

6 Item, if by any casualtie their shippes shall bee driuen on shoare in perill of shipwracke, our Begs and Iudges, and other our Subiects shall succour them, and such wares, and goods of theirs as shall bee recouered from the losse, shall bee restored to them, and no man shall wrong them.

7 Item, if the people of the aforesayd Queene, their interpreters and marchants, shall for traffique sake, either by lande or Sea repaire to our dominions paying our lawfull toll and custome, they shall haue quiet passage, and none of our Captaines or gouernours of the Sea, and shippes, nor any kinde of persons, shall either in their bodies, or in their goods and cattells, any way molest them.

8 Item, If any Englishman shall grow in debt, and so owe money to any other man, and thereupon doth absent himselfe that he can not be found, let no man be arrested or apprehended for any other mans debt, except he be surety.

9 Item, if any Englishman shall make his will and testament to whom soeuer by the same hee shall giue his goods, the partie shall haue them accordingly, and if hee die intestate, hee to whom the Consull or gouernour

of the societie shall say the goods of the dead are to bee giuen, hee shall haue the same.

10 Item, if the Englishmen or the marchants and interpreters of any places vnder the iurisdiction of England shall happen in the buying and selling of wares, by promises or otherwise to come in controuersie, let him go to the Iudge, and cause the matter to be entred into a booke, and if they wil, let them also take letters of the Iudge testifying the same, that men may see the booke and letters, whatsoeuer thing shall happen, and that according to the tenour thereof the matter in controuersie and in doubt may be ended: but if such things be neither entred in booke, nor yet the persons haue taken letters of the Iudge, yet he shall admit no false witnesse, but shall excute the Law according to iustice, and shall not suffer them to be abused.

11 Item, if any man shall say, that these being Christians haue spoken any thing to the derogation of our holy faith and religion, and haue slandered the same, in this matter as in all others, let no false witnesses in any case be admitted.

12 Item, if any one of them shall commit any great crime, and flying thereupon cannot bee found, let no man be arrested, or detained for another mans fact, except he be his suretie.

13 Item, if any slaue shall be found to be an Englishmen and their Consull or gouernour shall sue for his libertie, let the same slaue be diligently examined, and if hee be found in deed to be English, let him be discharged and restored to the Englishmen.

14 Item, if any Englishman shall come hither either to dwel or trafique, whether hee be married or vnmarried, he shall pay no polle or head money.

15 Item, if either in Alexandria, Damasco, Samos, Tunis, Tripolis, in the west, the port townes of Ægypt, or in any other places, they purpose to choose to themselues Consuls or gouernours, let them doe so, and if they will alter them at any time, and in the roome of the former Consuls place others, and let them do so also, and no man shall restraine them.

16 Item, if their interpreter shalbe at any time absent, being occupied in other serious matters, let the thing then in question bee stayed and differed till his comming, and in the meane time no man shall trouble them.

17 Item, if any variance or controuersie shall arise among the Englishmen, and thereupon they shall appeale to their Counsuls or gouernours, let no man molest them, but let them freely doe so, that the controuersie begunne may be finished according to their owne customes.

18 Item, if after the time and date of this priuilege, any pirats or other free gouernours of ships trading the Sea shall take any Englishman, and shall

make sale of him, either beyonde the Sea or on the side of the Sea, the matter shalbe examined to iustice, and if the partie shalbe found to be English, and shall receiue the holy religion, then let him freely be discharged, but if he wil still remaine a Christian, let him then be restored to the Englishmen, and the buyers shall demaund their money againe of them who solde the man.

19. Item, if the ships of warre of our Imperiall highnesse shal at anytime goe forth to Sea, and shall finde any English ships laden with merchandise, no man shall hidder them, but rather shall vse them friendly, and doe them no wrong, euen as wee haue giuen and granted articles, and priuileges to the French, Venetians, and other Kings and princes our confederates, so also wee haue giuen the like to the English: and contrary to this our diuine lawe and priuilege, let no man presume to doe any thing.

20 Item, if either their great or small ships shall in the course of their voyage, or in any place to which they come, bee stayed or arrested, let no man continue the same arrest, but rather helpe and assist them.

21 Item, if any theeues and robbers shall by force take away any of their ships, and marchandise, let the same theeues and robbers be sought and searched for with all diligence, and let them be punished most seuerely.

22 Last of all the Beglerbegs, and Zanziacbegs, our Captaines, our slaues and seruants of Captaines vsing the sea, and our Iudges, customers and gouernours of ships called Reiz, and free Reiz, all these, according to the tenor of this priuilege and articles, shalbe bound to doe accordingly: and as long as the Queene of England on her part shall duely keepe and obserue this league and holy peace, expressed in this priuilege, we also for our Imperial part, do charge and commaund the same so long to be straightly kept and obserued.

Giuen at Constantinople, in the 988. yeere of our most holy prophet, in the beginning of the moneth of Iune, And in the yeere of Iesus 1580.

* * * * *

Her Maiesties, letter to the Turke or Grand Signior 1581. promising redresse of the disorders of Peter Baker of Ratcliffe, committed in the Leuant.

Elizabeth by the diuine grace of the eternall God, of England, France and Ireland most sacred Queene, and of the most Christian faith, against all the prophaners of his most holy Name the zealous and mightie defendour, &c. To the most renowned and emperious Cæsar, Sultan Murad Can, Emperour of all the dominions of Turkie, and of all the East Monarchie chiefe aboue all others whosoeuer, most fortunate yeeres with the successe of al true happinesse. As with very great desire we wish and embrace the loue and amitie of forreine Princes, and in the same by al good dueties and meanes we seeke to bee confirmed: so to vs there may bee nothing more grieuous and disliking, then that any thing should happen through the default of our Subiects, which any way might bring our faith and fidelitie into suspition: Although wee are not ignorant how many good princes, by the like misaduenture be abused, where the doings of the Subiects are imputed to the want of good gouernment. But such mutters of importance and so well approued we may not omit: such is to vs the sacred estimation of our honour, and of our Christian profession, as we would the same should appeare as well in the concluding of our promises and agreements, as in the faithfull performing of the same.

The matter which by these our letters wee specially beholde, is a most iniurious and grieuous wrong which of late came vnto our vnderstanding, that should be done vnto certaine of your subiects by certaine of our Subiects, at yet not apprehended: but with all seueretie vpon their apprehension they are to be awarded for the same. [Footnote: This was Baker of Ratcliffe, who with the barke called the Roe, robbed certaine Grecians in the Leuant.] And as the deede in it selfe is most wicked, so it is much more intollerable, by how much it doeth infringe the credit of our faith, violate the force of our authoritie, and impeach the estimation of our word faithfully giuen vnto your Imperiall dignitie. In which so great a disorder if wee should not manifest our hatred towardes so wicked and euill disposed persons, we might not onely most iustly be reproued in the iudgement of all such as truely fauour Iustice, but also of all Princes the patrones of right and equitie, might no lesse be condemned. That therefore considered, which of our parts is ordained in this cause which may be to the good liking of your highnesse, we are most especially to request of your Imperiall Maiestie, that through the default and disorder of a son of euill and wicked disposed persons, you wil not withdraw your gratious fauour from vs, neither to hinder the traffique of our Subiects, which by virtue of your highnesse sufferance, and power of your licence are permitted to trade into your dominion and countreys or that either in their persons or goods they be preiudiced in their traueyling by land or by water, promising vnto your greatnesse most faithfully, that the goods whereof your subiects by great wrong and violence haue bene spoyled, shall wholly againe be restored, if either by the liues or possessions of the robbers it may any way be brought to passe: And that hereafter (as now being taught by this euill example) wee will haue speciall care that none vnder the title of our authoritie shall be suffered to commit any the like wrongs or iniuries.

Neither they which haue committed these euil parts had any power vnder your highnesse safeconduct graunted vnto our subiects, but from some other safeconduct whether it were true or fained, we knowe not, or whether they bought it of any person within the gouernment of Marseils: but vnder the colour thereof they haue done that, which the trueth of our dealing doeth vtterly abhorre. Notwithstanding howsoeuer it be, wee will surely measure their euill proceedings with most sharpe and iust correction, and that it shall repent them of the impeachment of our honours, as also it shalbe an example of our indignation, that others may dread at all times, to commit the like offence. Wherefore that our amitie might be continued, as if this vnfortunate hap had neuer chanced, and that the singuler affection of our Subiects towardes your Imperiall Maiestie vowed, and dayly more and more desired, might be conserued and defended, we thereunto do make our humble suite vnto your greatnesse: And for so great goodnesse towardes vs and our people granted, doe most humbly pray vnto the Almightie creatour of heauen and earth, euer to maintaine and keepe your most renowned Maiestie in all happinesse and prosperitie.

Dated at our palace of Greenewich the 26. of Iune, Anno 1581.

* * * * *

The letters patents, or priuileges graunted by her Maiestie to Sir Edward Osborne, Master Richard Staper, and certaine other Marchants of London for their trade into the dominions of the great Turke, in the yeere 1581.

Elizabeth by the grace of God Queene of England, France and Ireland, defender of the faith, &c. To all our Officers, ministers, and Subiects, and to all other people as well within this our Realme of England, as else where vnder our obeysance, iurisdiction, or otherwise, vnto whom these our letters shall be seene, shewed or read, greeting. Where our welbeloued Subiects Edward Osborne Alderman of our Citie of London, and Richard Staper of our sayde City Merchant, haue by great aduenture and industrie, with their great costes and charges, by the space of sundry late yeeres, trauailed, and caused trauaile to bee taken, as well by secret and good meanes, as by dangerous wayes and passages both by lande and Sea, to finde out and set open a trade of Marchandize and traffique into the Lands, Islands, dominions, and territories of the great Turke, commonly called the Grand Signior, not heretofore in the memory of any man nowe liuing knowen to be commonly vsed and frequented by way of marchandise, by any the Marchants or any Subiects of vs, or our progenitours; and also haue by their like good meanes and industrie, and great charges procured of the sayde Grand Signior (in our name), amitie, safetie, and freedome, for trade and traffique of Marchandise to bee vsed, and continued by our Subiects within his sayde Dominions, whereby there is good and apparant hope and likelyhoode both that many good offices may bee done for the peace of Christendome, and reliefe of many Christians that bee or may happen to bee in thraldome or necessitie vnder the sayde Grand Signior, his vassals or Subiects, and also good and profitable vent and vtterance may be had of the commodities of our Realme, and sundry other great benefites to the aduancement of our honour, and dignitie Royall, the increase of the reuenues of our Crowne, and generall wealth of our Realme: Knowe ye, that hereupon wee greatly tendering the wealth of our people, and the incouragement of our Subiects in their good enterprises for the aduancement of the Common weale, haue of our speciall grace, certaine knowledge and meere motion, giuen and graunted, and by these presents for vs, our heires and successours, doe giue and graunt vnta our sayd trustie, and welbeloued Subiects Edward Osborne, and vnto Thomas Smith of London Esquier, Richard Staper, and William Garret of London Marchants, their executors, and administrators, and to the executours and administratours of them, and of euery of them, that they, and euery of them, and such other person and persons Englishmen borne, not exceeding the number of twelue, as they the sayde Edward, and Richard shall appoint, nominate, or admit to be parteners, aduenturers, or doers with them the sayde Edward, Thomas, Richard and William, in their societie by themselues, their seruants, Factours or deputies, and to such others as shall bee nominated according to the tenour of these our letters Patents, shall and may during the terme of seuen yeeres from the date of these Patents, freely trade, traffique, and vse feates of Marchandise into, and from the dominions of the sayde Grand Signior, and euery of them, in such order, and maner, forme, liberties and condition to all intents and purposes as shalbe betweene them limitted, and agreed, and not otherwise, without any molestation, impeachment, or disturbance, any Lawe, statute, vsage, diuersitie of religion or faith, or other cause or matter whatsoeuer to the contrary notwithstanding.

And that it shalbe lawful to the said Edward and Richard their executors and administrators, (during the said terme) to appoint or admit to be parteners and aduenturers with them the sayde Edward, Thomas, Richard and William; such persons not exceeding the number of twelue (as afore is said) to trafique and vse the said trade and feat of marchandise according to our saide graunt. And that all and euery such person and persons, as shall hereafter fortune to bee appointed or admitted as parteners in the saide trade or trafique according to these our letters patents, shall and may from the time of such appointment or admittance, haue and enioy the freedome and libertie of the said trade and trafique during the residue of the said terme of seuen yeeres, according to such limitation and agreement as is aforesaide, and that it shall and may be lawfull to and for the saide Edward, Thomas, Richard and William, their executours and administratours, seruants factours and deputies, and all such as shall be so appointed, nominated or admitted, to be parteners or aduenturers in the saide trade, or so many of them as can and will, to assemble themselues for or about any the matters, causes, affaires or businesse of the saide trade, in any place or places for the same conuenient, from time to time during the said terme of 7. yeeres, within our dominions or elsewhere, and to make, ordeine, and constitute reasonable lawes and ordinances, for the good gouernment of the said Company, and for the better aduancement and continuance of the said trade, and trafique, not being contrary or repugnant to the lawes, estatutes or customes of our Realme, and the same lawes or ordinances so made to put in vse, and execute accordingly, and at their pleasures to reuoke the same lawes and ordinances, or any of them, as occasion shall require.

And in consideration that the said Edward Osborne hath bene the principall setter foorth and doer in the opening, and putting in vse of the said trade, we do therefore especially ordeine, constitute, and prouide by these patents, that the saide Edward Osborne shall be gouernour of all such as by vertue of these our letters patents, shall be parteners, aduenturers, or trafiquers in the said trade, during the said terme of seuen yeeres, if he so long liue: And that if the saide Edward shall happen to decease during the saide terme, the saide Richard Staper then liuing, then the said Richard Staper shall likewise be gouernour during the residue of the said terme (if he so long liue) and that if the said Edward and Richard shall both happen to decease during the said terme, then the partners or aduenturers for the time being, or the greatest, part of them, shall from time to time as necessitie shall require, choose and elect a gouernour of the said Company.

Prouided alwayes, that if there shall happen any great or vrgent occasion to remoue or displace any person that shall be gouernour of the saide fellowship, that then it shall, and may be lawfull for vs, our heires and successours, to remooue, and displace euery such gouernour, and to place another of the said fellowship in the same office, during such time as such person should haue enioyed the same, according to this our graunt, if there had bene no cause to the contrary.

And we further for vs, our heires, and successors, of our especiall grace, certaine knowledge, and meere motion, do graunt to the said Edward Osborne, Thomas Smith, Richard Staper, and William Garret, their executors and administrators, that nothing shall bee done to be of force or validitie touching the sayde trade or trafique, or the exercise thereof, without or against the consent of the saide Edward, during such time as hee shall bee Gouernour as afore is saide. And after that time without the consent of the Gouernour for the time being, and the more part of the said Company.

And further, wee of our more ample and abundant grace, meere motion and certame knowledge, haue graunted, and by these patents for vs, our heires and successors, doe graunt to the saide Edward, Thomas, Richard and William, their executors and administrators, that they, the saide Edward, Thomas, Richard and William, their executors and administrators, and the said person and persons, by them the said Edward and Richard to be nominated, or appointed as afore is said, together, with such two other persons, as wee our heires or successors from time to time during the sayd terme shall nominate, shall haue the whole trade and trafique, and the whole entire onely libertie, vse and priuilege of trading, and trafiquing, and vsing feate of marchandise, into, and from the said dominions of the said Grand Signior, and euery of them. And when there shall be no such persons so nominated or appointed by vs, our heires or successors, that then the said Edward Osborne, Thomas Smith, Richard Staper, and William Garret, their executors and administrators, and such persons by them so to be appointed, shall haue the saide whole trade and trafique, and the whole entire, and onely libertie, vse, and priuilege of trading and trafiquing aforesaid. And that they the said Edward, Thomas, Richard and William, their executors and administrators, and also al such as shal so be nominated or appointed to be partners or aduenturers in the said trade, according to such agreement as is abouesaid, and euery of them, their seruants, factors and deputies, shal haue ful and free authoritie, libertie, facultie, licence and power to trade and trafique into and from all and euery of the saide dominions of the saide Grand Signior, and into, and from all places where, by occasion of the said trade, they shall happen to arriue or come, whether they be Christians, Turkes, Gentiles or other, and into, and from all Seas, riuers, ports, regions, territories, dominions, coastes, and places with their ships, barks, pinnesses and other vessels, and with such mariners and men, as they will lead with them or send for the said trade, as they shall thinke good at their owne proper cost and expenses, any law, statute, vsage, or matter whatsoeuer to the contrary notwistanding. And that it shalbe lawful for the said Edward, Thomas, Richard and William, and to the person aforesaid, and to and for the mariners and seamen to bee vsed and employed in the said trade and voyage to set and place in the tops of their ships and other vessels the armes of England with the red crosse ouer the same, as heretofore, they haue vsed the red crosse, any matter or thing to the contrary notwithstanding.

And we of our further royall fauor, and of our especiall grace, certaine knowledge and meere motion haue graunted, and by these presents doe graunt to the said Edward Osburne, Thomas Smith, Richard Staper, and William Garret, their executors and administrators by these presents, that the said lands, territories, and dominions of the said Grand Signior, or any other of them, shall not be visited, frequented, nor haunted by way of marchandise by any other our subiects during the said terme, contrary to the true meaning of these patents.

And by vertue of our high prerogatiue royall (which wee will not haue argued or brought in question) we straightly charge and commaund, and prohibite for vs, our heires, and successours, all our subiects (of what degree or qualitie soeuer they be) that none of them directly, or indirectly, do visite, haunt, frequent or trade, trafique, or aduenture by way of marchandise into, or from any of the Dominions Of the saide Grand Signior, or other places aboue sayde by water or by lande (other then the said Edward, Thomas, Richard and William, their executours or administrators, or such as shalbe admitted, and nominated as is aforesaide) without, expresse licence, agreement, and consent of the saide Gouernour, and company or the more part of them, whereof the said Gouernour alwayes to be one, vpon paine of our high indignation, and of forfeiture and losse, as well of the ship and shippes, with the furniture thereof, as also of the goods, marchandizes, and things whatsoeuer they be of those our Subiects which shall attempt, or presume to saile, trafigue, or aduenture, to or from any the dominions, or places abouesaid, contrary to the prohibition aforesaid: the one halfe of the same forfeiture to be to the vse of vs, our heires and successors, and the other halfe to the vse of the said Edward, Thomas, Richard and William, and the said companie, and further to suffer imprisonment during our pleasure, and such other punishment as to vs, for so high contempt, shal seeme meete and conuenient.

And further of our grace speciall, certaine knowledge and meere motion we haue condescended and graunted, and by these patents for vs, our heires and successors, doe condescend and graunt to the said Edward, Thomas, Richard and William, their executors and administrators, that we our heires and successors during the said terme, will not graunt liberty, licence or power to any person or persons whatsoeuer, contrary to the tenor of these our letters patents, to saile, passe, trade, or trafique into or from the said dominions of the said Grand Signior or any of them, without the consent of the said Edward, Thomas, Richard and William, and such as shalbe named or appointed as afore is said, or the most of them. And that if at any time hereafter during the said terme, the said Edward, Thomas, Richard and William, or the suruiuors of them, shal admit or nominate any of our subiects to be partners and aduenturers in the said trade to the number of 12. or vnder as afore is said, that, then we our heires and successors at the instance and petition of the said Edward, Thomas, Richard and William, or the suruiuors of them in our Chauncerie to be made, and vpon the sight of these presents, will grant and make to the said Edward, Thomas, Richard and William, of to the suruiuors of them, and to such persons as so shall be nominated or appointed by their speciall names, surnames, and additions as is aforesaid, new letters patents vnder the great seale of England in due forme of law with like agreements, clauses, prohibitions, prouisoes and articles (mutatis mutandis) as in these our letters patents are conteined, for, and during the residue of the said terme of seuen yeres then remaining vnexpired. And that the sight of these presents shalbe sufficient warrant to the Lord Chancellour, or Lord keeper of the great seale for the time being, for the making, sealing and passing of such new letters patents, without further writ or warrant for the same to be required, had, or obtained.

And the said Edward Osburne, Thomas Smith, and Richard Staper, and William Garret and such others as shalbe so nominated or appointed, as is aforesaid, to be of their trade or companie; shall yeerely during 6. of the last yeres of the said 7. yeres, lade out of this our Realme, and bring home yeerely, for, and in the feate and trade of marchandizing aforesaid, so much goods and marchandizes, as the custome, and subsidie inwards and outwards, shall amount in the whole to the summe of 500. li. yeerely. So that the said Edward Osburne, Thomas Smith, Richard Staper, and William Garret and the said persons so to be nominated as is aforesaid, or any of them, or their ship or shippes be not barred, stayed, restrained or let by any reasonable occasion from the saide trade or trafique, and so that the said ship or ships do not perish by any misfortune, or bee spoyled by the way in their voyage.

And further, the said Edward Osborne; Thomas Smith, Richard Staper, and William Garret, and such others as shall be appointed as aforesaide to be of their said trade or Company, shall giue notice vnto the Lord Admirall of England, or to some of the principall officers of the Admiraltie for the time being, of such ship or shippes as they shall set foorth in the same voyage, and of the number of Mariners appointed to goe in the same ship or shippes, by the space of fifteene dayes before the setting or going foorth of the same ship or shippes. And also the said Edward Osborne, Thomas Smith, Richard Staper and William Garret, and such other as shall be by them the saide Edward and Richard, nominated to be of the said trade, shall and will at the setting foorth of their ship, or shippes, for the same voyage, permit and suffer the Master of the Ordinance of vs, our heires and successors, or some others, our or their principall officers of the Ordinance, to take a view of the number and quantitie of such Ordinance, power, and munition as shall be caried in the said ship, or shippes, and shall also at the returne of the same ship, or shippes, suffer a view to be taken, and vpon request made, make an accompt to the saide officers of our Ordinance, of the expenses, and wastes of the said Ordinance, power, and munition, so to bee caried in the same ship, or shippes.

Prouided alwayes, that if any of the said trade or Company, or their seruants, factors, or sailers, in any ship by them laden, shall commit any piracie or outrage vpon the seas, and that, if the said Company or societie shall not, or do not, within reasonable time, after complaint made, or notice giuen to the said Company, or to any of them, either satisfie or recompense the parties that so shall fortune to be robbed, or spoiled by any of the said Company, or sailers, in the said ships, or else shall not do their endeuour to the vttermost oftheir reasonable power, to haue the parties so offending punished for the same their offences, that then, and from thencefoorth, these present letters patents shall be vtterly voyd, cease, and determine.

Prouided likewise, that if it shall hereafter appeare vnto vs, our heires, or successors that this grant, or the continuance thereof in the whole, or in any part thereof, shall not be profitable to vs, our heires, our successors, or to this our Realme, that then, and from thencefoorth, vpon, and after one full yeeres warning, to be giuen vnto the said Company, or to the Gouernour thereof, by vs, our heires or successors, this present grant shall cease, be voyd, and determine, to all intents, constructions, and purposes.

Prouided also, that we, our heires and successors, from time to time, during the said 7. yeeres, may lawfully nominate, appoint, and authorise two persons, being fit men, to be of the saide company, and for want or lacke of them, two others to be aduenturers in the said trade, for such stocke and summe of money, as they shall put in, so that the said persons to bee nominated, or authorised, shall be contributorie to all charges of the said trade and aduenture indifferently, according to their stockes: and as other aduenturers of the said trade shall doe for their stockes, and so that likewise they doe obserue the orders of the said Company, allowable by this our graunt, and that such persons so to be appointed by vs, our heires or successors, shall and may, with the saide Company, and fellowship, vse the trade and feate of marchandise aforesaide, and all the liberties and priuileges herein before granted, according to the meaning of these our letters patents, any thing in these our letters patents contained to the contrary notwithstanding.

And further of our speciall grace, certaine knowledge, and meere motion, we haue condescended and granted, and by these presents for vs, our heires and successors, doe condescend, and grant to the said Edward Osborne, Thomas Smith, Richard Staper, and William Garret, their executors, and administrators, that if at the ende of the said terme of seuen yeeres, it shall seeme meete, and conuenient vnto the saide Edward Osborne, Thomas Smith, Richard Staper, and William Garret, or the suruiuer of them, that this present grant shall be continued: and if that also it shall appeare vnto vs, our heires, or successors, that the continuance thereof shall not be preiudiciall, or hurtfull to this our Realme, that then we, our heires, or successors, at the instance and petition of the said Edward Osborne, Thomas Smith, Richard Staper, and William Garret, or the suruiuor of them, to be made to vs, our heires, or successors, wil grant and make to the said Edward, Thomas, Richard and William, or the suruiuor of them, and to such other persons, as so shall be by the said Edward and Richard nominated and appointed, new letters patents, vnder the great seale of England, in due forme of lawe, with like couenants, grants, clauses, and articles, as in these presents are contained, or with addition of other necessary articles, or change of these, in some part, for and during the full terme of seuen yeeres then next following. Willing, and straightly commanding, and charging all and singuler our Admirals, Viceadmirals, Justices, Maiors, Sheriffes Escheaters, Constables, Bailiffes, and all and singuler our other officers, ministers, liege men, and subiects whatsoeuer, to be aiding, fauouring, helping, and assisting vnto the said Gouernour, and company, and their successors, and to their Deputies, officers, seruants, assignes, and ministers, and euery of them, in executing and enioying the premisses, as well on land as on sea, from time to time, and at all times when you, or any of you, shall be thereunto required, any statute, act, ordinance, prouiso, proclamation, or restraint heretofore had, made, set forth, ordained, or prouided, or any other matter, cause or thing to the contrary, in any wise notwithstanding.

In witnesse whereof we haue caused these our letters to be made patents, witnesse our selfe, at Westminster, the 11. day of September, in the 23. yeere of our raigne.

* * * * *

The Queenes Commission vnder the great seale, to her seruant master William
  Hareborne, to be her maiesties Ambassadour or Agent, in the partes of
  Turkie. 1582.

Elizabetha, Dei optimi Maximi, conditoris, et rectoris vnici clementia, Angliæ, Franciæ, et Hiberniæ Regina, veræ fidei contra Idololatras falso Christi nomen profitentes inuicta et potentissima propugnatrix, vniuersis, et singulis præsentes has literas visuris, et inspecturis, salutem. Cùm, augustissimus, et inuictissimus princeps, Zuldan Murad Can, Turcici regni Dominator potentissimus imperiíque Orientis Monarcha, foedus, amicitiámque nobiscum percusserit, iaurauerítque, (quam nos perpetuis futuris temporibus, quantum in nobis erit; inuiolatè seruare destinamus) ad eámque magis ornandam, illustrandámque concesserit idem augustissimus Imperator subditis nostris liberam suas merces excercendi rationem in omnibus Musulmanici imperij sui partibus, cum tam ampla priuilegorum concessione, quàm alijs bonis principibus, socijs, et foederatis nostris largitus est, quoram priuilegiorum donationem nos gratam, acceptámque habentes, pari cum animi gratitudine colere certum habemus deliberatúmque, nihil, in votis, habentes potiùs, quàm bonorum erga nos principum animos beneuolos honoratissima mente fouere, promereríque: Sciatis, nos de singulari erga nos, obsequiúmque nostrum, fide, obseruantia, prudentia, et dextaitate multum nobis chari Guilielmi Hareborne, è custodibus corporis nostri vnius, plurimùm confidentes, eum Oratorem, Nuntium, Procuratorem, et Agentem nostrum certum et indubitatum ordinamus, facimus, et constituimus, per præsentes: dantes ei, et concedentes potestatem, et authoritatem, nomine nostro, et pro nobis prædictum amicitiæ foedus confirmandi, priuilegiorum concessionem in manus suas capiendi, ratámque habendi, omnibus et singulis subditis nostris, Musulmanicis oris terrísque negotiantibus, pro Maiestatis nostræ authoritate præscipiendi, mandaníque, vt sint in suis commercijs, quamdiu, quotiésque cum Mansulmanicis versantur, dictorum, priuilegiorum præscripto obtemperantes in omnibus, ac per omnia, ad obsequia tanta amicitia digna se componentes, ac in delinquentes in foedus nostrum iustitiam exequatur. Potestatem, et authoritatem ei damus in omnes, et singulos subditos nostros in quibuscunque et locis, et partibus Musulmanici Imperij dominationi subiectis negotiantes, constituendi emporiorum suorum sedes in quibus voluerit portubus, et ciuitatibus, in alijs vetandi, in constitutis autem emporiorum sedibus, consules curandi, leges præceptionésque ferendi, condendique, quarum ex præscripto dicti nostri subditi, et eorum quilibet sese publicè, et priuatim gerant, eorum violatores corrigendi, castigandíque omnia denique et singula faciendi, perimplendíque, quæ ad dictorum subditorum nostrorum honestam gubernationem, et commercij exercendi in illis partibus rationem pertinent: promittentes bona fide, et in verbo Regio, nos ratum, gratum, et firmum habituas, quæcunque dictus Orator, et Agens noster, à legibus nostris non abhorrentia in præmissis aut præmissorum aliquo fecerít. In cuius rei testimonium, has literas nostras fieri fecimus patentes, et sigilli nostri impressione iussimus muniri. Datum è castro nostro Windesoriæ, 20. die Mensis Nouembris, Anno Iesu Christi 1582. regni verò nostri, vicesimo quarto.

The same in English.

Elizabeth, by the clemencie of the most good and most great God, the only creator and gouernour of all things, Queene of England, France, and Ireland, inuincible, and most mightie defender of the true faith, against all Idolaters falsly professing the name of Christ, to all and singuler persons, to whose sight and view these our present letters may come, greeting. Whereas the most renowmed, and most inuincible Prince Zuldan Marad Can, the most mighty gouernour of the kingdom of Turkie, and Monarch of the East Empire, hath entered into league and friendship with vs, (which we for our part, as much as lieth in vs, doe purpose solemnly, and inuiolablie to keepe in all times to come) and whereas for the better countenancing and authorizing of the same, the foresayd renowmed Emperour hath graunted vnto our subiects free libertie of traffique, in all the partes of his sacred Empire, with as ample and large a grant of priuileges, as is giuen to other good Princes our neighbours and confederates, the grant of which priuileges, we taking very thankfully, and acceptably, are certainely, and throughly determined to keepe and mainetaine, with the like goodnesse and curtesie of minde, desiring nothing more, then with an honourable respect to nourish, and deserue the beneuolent affections of good Princes toward vs: Know ye, that wee thinking well, and hauing good confidence in the singular trustinesse, obedience, wisedome, and disposition of our welbeloued seruant William Hareborne, one of the Esquiers of our body, towards vs, and our seruice, doe by these presents, make, ordaine and constitute him our true and vndoubted Orator, Messenger, Deputie, and Agent. Giuing and granting vnto him power and authoritie, in our name, and for vs, to confirme the foresaid league of friendship, to take into his hands, and to ratifie the grant of the priuileges, and to command, and enioyne by the authoritie of our Maiestie, all and singular our Subiects trading and dealing in any of the coastes and kingdomes of that Empire, that as long as they remaine in traffique with his subiects, they be obedient to the prescription and order of the foresayd priuileges, applying themselues in all things, and through all things, to such duties and seruices as appertaine to so great a league and friendship, and the offenders agaynst this our league to receiue iustice, and punishment accordingly. We further giue unto him power and authoritie ouer all and singuler our Subiects, dealing, and vsing traffique in any place or part whatsoeuer, subiect to the gouernment of that Empire, to appoint the places of their traffiques, in what Hauen or Citie it shall please him, and to prohibite them from all other places, and wheresoeuer their traffiques are appointed to bee kept, there to make and create Consuls or Gouernors, to enact lawes and statutes, by the vertue and tenor whereof all our foresayd subiects, and euery one of them, shall both publikely and priuately vse and behaue themselues, to correct and punish the breakers of those lawes: and last of all, to doe and fulfill all and singular things whatsoeuer, which shall seeme requisite and conuenient for the honest and orderly gouernment of our said subiects, and of the maner of their trafique in those parts. Promising assuredly, and in the word of a Prince, that whatsoeuer shall be done of our sayd Orator and Agent, in all, or in any of the premisses, not repugnant and contrary to our lawes, shall be accepted, ratified, and confirmed by vs. In witness whereof we haue caused these our letters to be made patents, and our seale thereunto to be appensed. Giuen at our Castle of Windsore, the 20. day of Nouember, in the yeere of Christ 1582. and of our raigne the 24.

* * * * *

The Queenes Letter to the great Turke 1582. written in commendation of Master Hareborne, when he was sent Ambassadour.

Elizabeth &c. Augustissimo inuictissimóque principi, etc Cùm ad postulatum nostrum Cæsarea vestra Maiestas, anno saluatoris nostri Iesu 1580. pacis foedus nobiscum pepigerit, coniunctum cum liberalissima priuilegiorum quorundam concessione, quorum beneficio subditi nostri cum omni securitate tutissimè liberriméque ad vniuersas et singulas Musulmanici imperij vestri partes terra maríque proficisci, in ijsque commercij exercendi gratia, negotiari, habitare, manere, exindéque ire et redire cum volent queant, ab ijs qui sub Cæsarea vestra Maiestate in magistratu sunt vbique locorum protegendi defendendíque sine vlla vel corporum, vel bonorum læsione: nos tantæ concessionis beneficium gratum acceptúmque habentes, quantum in nobis est, approbamus confirmamúsque: pollicentes in verbo regio, quod nos eandem pacem sine vlla violatione sartam tectámque conseruabimus: faciemúsque vt subditi nostri priuilegiorum sibi indultorum concessione ita vtantur, vt Cæsaream vestram Maiestatem magnificentissimæ suæ liberalitatis nunquam poenitere queat. Quoniam autem concessionis huius virtus in vsu potiùs quam verbis, Maiestatis vtriúsque nostrum sententiâ, ponenda videtur, voluimus hunc mandatarium virum Guilielmum Hareborne, ex satellitibus quibus ad corporis nostri tutelam vtimur vnum, virum compluribus virtutibus ornatum, ad Cæsaream vestram, Maiestatem ablegare, qui tum nomine nostro vobis gratias ageret; tum vt eius opera vteremur ad eam subditorum nostrorum mercimoniorum rationem stabiliendam, tam in Imperiali vestra ciuitate Constantinopoli, quàm alijs imperij vestri Musulmanici locis, quæ ex præscripto priuilegiorum, Cæsareæ vestræ Maiestatis benignítate, conceditur, et ex vsu subditorum vtriúsque nostrum erit. Ad quam rem quoniam opus illi erit Cæsareæ vestræ Maiestatis authoritate, summa contentione ab eadem rogarmus, velit id agere apud omnes qui sub se in magistratu sunt, vt quibuscunque poterunt melioribus modis huic nostro mandatario in Cæsareæ vestræ Maiestatis placito exequendo, adiutores sint et esse velint. Ei enim hanc curam demandauimus, in qua quàm fidem suam sit honestè liberaturus erga Maiestatem vtriusque nostrum neutiquam dubitamus: cui etiam, vt in omnibus sint obtemperantes nostri subditi, quantum Cæsareæ vestræ Maiestatis concessio patitur, volumus. [Sidenote: Mustafa interpres.] Præterea, cum præclarus vir Mustaia sacræ Cæsareæ vestræ Maiestatis Musulmanorum interpres egregiam nauarit operam vt hoc inter nos foedus fieret, rogamus summoperè vt in nostram gratiam eum in Mustafaracarum ordinem Cæsarea vestra Maiestas recipere dignetur. Si in his alijsque omnibus honestis causis hic noster agens subitíque nostri Imperatoriæ vestræ sublimitatis æquanimitatem senserint, florebit inter has gentes nobile commercium, et nos omnibus officijs huic vestræ Maiestatis fauori et beneuolentiæ (si vlla ratione rebus vestris commodare poterimus) respondere libentissimè semper paratæ erimus. Deus optimus maximus mundi opifex, etc.

The same in English.

Elizabeth by the grace of the most mightie God and only creator of heauen and earth, of England, France, and Ireland Queene, the most inuincible and most mightie defender of the Christian faith against all kind of idolatries of all that liue among the Christians and falsly professe the name of Christ, vnto the most Imperiall and most inuincible prince, Sultan Murad Can, the most mighty ruler of the kingdom of Turkie, sole aboue all, and most soueraigne Monarch of the East Empire, greeting.

Whereas at our request your Imperiall Maiestie in the yeere of our Sauiour Iesus 1580. hath entered into a league of peace with vs, whereunto was vnited a most large and bountifull grant of certaine priuileges, by benefite whereof our subiects may with all securitie most safely and freely trauell by Sea and land into all and singular parts of your Musulmanlike Empire, and in the same exercising the trade of marchandise, may traffique, dwell, remaine, depart from thence, and returne thither at their pleasure, and in places be maintained and defended from all damage of bodies and goods, by such as are in authoritie vnder your Imperiall Maiestie: we thankfully and gratefully receiuing the benefite of so great a priuilege, as much as in vs lieth doe approue and confirme the same, promising in the worde of a Prince, that we will keepe the saide league perfect and inuiolable, and will cause our subiects so to vse the grant of the priuileges giuen vnto them, as your Imperiall Maiestie shall neuer haue occasion to repent you of your most princely liberalitie. [Sidenote: M. Wil. Hareborne sent ambassador to the Turke.] And because the force of this grant, in the iudgement of both our maiesties, seemeth rather to consist in the vse thereof then in the wordes, we thought good to send vnto your Imperiall maiestie this our ambassadour William Hareborne, one of the Esquiers of our body, which both on our behalfe should yeeld thanks vnto your maiestie, and also that we might vse his good indeauour for the establishing of such order in our subiects trade of merchandise, as well in your Imperiall citie of Constantinople, as in other places of your Musulmanlike Empire, as according to the prescript of the priuileges is granted by your princely maiesties goodnesse, and shall be for the benefite of both our subiects. For performance whereof because hee standeth in neede of your Imperiall Maiesties authoritie, wee earnestly beseech the same, that you would cause all those which bee in authoritie vnder your Highnesse, by all their best meanes to aide and assist this our Ambassadour in executing this your Imperiall Maiesties pleasure, for vnto him wee haue committed this charge: wherein how honestly hee will discharge his credite toward both our Maiesties, I no whit stand in doubt: to whom also our pleasure is, that all our subiects shall bee obedient, as farre as the grant of your Imperiall maiestie doeth permit. [Sidenote: A request for the preferring of Mustafa Beg.] Moreouer, whereas that woorthie personage Mustafa, your Imperiall maiesties Interpretor, hath taken speciall paines for the procuring of this league betweene vs, wee earnestly beseech you that for our sakes your Imperiall Maiestie would vouchsafe to aduance him vnto the degree of the Mustafaraks or chiefe pensioners. If in these and in all other honest causes, our aforesayde Agent and our subiectes shall finde your Imperiall Highnesses fauour, a noble traffique will flourish betweene these nations, and wee (if by any way wee may stand your State in steade) will always most willingly be readie to requite this your Maiesties fauour and good will with all kinde of good offices. Almightie God the maker of the world preserue and keepe your Imperiall Maiestie, &c.

* * * * *

A Letter of the Queenes Maiestie to Alli Bassa the Turkes high Admirall, sent by her ambassadour M. William Hareborne, and deliuered vnto him aboord his gallie in the Arsenal.

Elizabetha, &c. Illustrissimo viro Alli Bassa, magni Musulmanici Cæsaris Admiralio, salutem et successus fortunatos. Non ignotum esse Excellentiæ vestræ arbitramur, priuilegia quædam à potentissimo Cæsare Musulmanico domino vestro clementissimo subditis nostris Anglicis concessa esse, vt illis liceat in omnibus imperij Musulmarnici prouincijs tutò et securé manere ac negotiari: non aliter quàm hoc ipsum Francis, Polonis, Venetis Germanis antea indultum est. Qua ex causa nos Gulielmum Hareborne nobis dilectum, è corporis custodibus vnum, ac multis nominibus ornatum ad inclytam Constantinoplis ciuitatem pro agente misimus: qui, ex priuilegiorum prædictorum præscripto nostras et subditorum nostrorum res in illis locis constitueret. Facere igitur non potimus, quin Excellentiæ vestræ. Guilielmum hunc, pro ea qua apud magnum Cæsarem polles authoritate, commendaremus: petentes summopere vt tutò in mari sine Classiariorum vestrorum violentia, et securè in portibus absque ministrorum rapinis et iniuria, tam ipse quàm omnes Angli subditi nostri possint versori: vti pro tenore literarum patentium à magno Cæsare concessarum illis licere ex illarum conspectione perspicuum esse potest. Gratissimum ergo nobis excellentia vestra facerit, si portuum omnium, aliorúmque locorum, qui vestræ iurisdictioni parent, custodibus, item classium et nauium præfectis omnibus mandare velit, vt Guilielmus iste, aliíque Angli subditi nostri cum in illorum erunt potestate, amicè et humaniter tractarentur. Quemadmodum nos vicissim omnes magni Cæsaris subditos omni humanitatis genere tructabimus, si in Oceani maria, aliáue loca venerint, quæ nostro parent imperio. Postremo excellentiam vestram pro eo quem in nostros extendet fauore ijs omnibus officijs prosequemur, quæ à gratissima principe in optime de semerentes debent proficisci. Benè et foeliciter valeas. Datum è castro nostro Windesorij die vicessimo mensis Nouembris, Anno Iesu Christi saluatoris nostri 1582. Regni verò nostri vicessimo quarto.

* * * * *

A briefe Remembrance of things to be indeuoured at Constantinople, and in other places in Turkie; touching our Clothing and our Dying, and things that bee incident to the same, and touching ample vent of our naturall commodities, and of the labour of our poore people withall, and of the generall enriching of this Realme: drawen by M. Richard Hakluyt of the middle Temple, and giuen to a friend that was sent into Turkie 1582.

1 Anile wherewith we colour Blew to be brought into this realme by seed or roote.

2 And the Arte of compounding of the same.

3 And also all other herbes vsed in dying in like maner to bee brought in.

4 And all Trees whose Leaues, Seedes, or Barkes, or Wood doe serue to that vse, to be brought into this realme by Seed or Roote.

5 All little Plants and Buskes seruing to that vse to be brought in.

6 To learne to know all earths and minerals forren vsed in dying, and their naturall places, for possible the like may here be found vpon sight.

7 Also with the materials vsed in dying to bring in the excellencie of the arte of dying.

8 To procure from Muhaisira a citie in Ægypt to Constantinople, the seed of Sesamum the herbe, and the same into this realme. Common trade is betweene Alexandria and Constantinople, and therefore you may easily procure the seeds. Of this seed much oyle is made, and many mils set on worke about the same in the sayde Muhaisira, and if this seede may prosper in England, infinite benefite to our Clothing trade may rise by the same. This citie is situate vpon Nilus the riuer, and thence this is brought to Venice and to diuers other Cities of Italie, and to Antwerpe.

9 To note all kindes of clothing in Turkie, and all degrees of their labour in the same.

10 To endeanour rather the vent of Kersies, then of other Clothes as a thing more beneficiall to our people.

11 To endeauour the sale of such our clothes as bee coloured with our owne naturall colours as much as you can, rather then such as be coloured with forren colours.

12 To seeke out a vent for our Bonettos, a cap made for Barbarie, for that the poore people may reape great profite by the trade.

13 To endeuour vent of knit Stocks made of Norwich yarne, and of other yarne, which brought to great trade, may turne our poore people to great benefite, besides the vent of the substance, of our colours, and of our diuers labour.

14 To endeuor a vent of our Saffron for the benefit of our poore people: for a large vent found, it setteth many on worke.

* * * * *

Remembrances for master S. to giue him the better occasion to informe himselfe of some things in England, and after of some other things in Turkie, to the great profite of the Common weale of this Countrey. Written by the foresayd master Richard Hakluyt, for a principall English Factor at Constantinople 1582.

Since all men confesse (that be not barbarously bred) that men are borne as well to seeke the common commoditie of their Countrey, as their owne priuate benefite, it may seeme follie to perswade that point, for each man meaneth so to doe. But wherein men should seeke the common commoditie, and what way, and by what meane that is to bee brought about, is the point or summe of the matter, since euery good man is ready to imploy his labour. This is to bee done by an infinite sort of meanes, as the number of things bee infinite that may be done for common benefite of the Realme. And as the chiefe things so to bee done be diuers, so are they to be done by diuers men, as they bee by wit and maner of education more fit, or lesse fit, for this and for that. And for that of many things that tend to the common benefite of the State, some tend more, and some lesse, I finde that no one thing, after one other, is greater then Clothing, and the things incident to the same. And vnderstanding that you are of right good capacitie, and become a Factor at Constantinople, and in other partes in Turkie, I finde no man fitter of all the English Factors there, then you. And therefore I am so bold to put you in minde, and to tell you wherein with some indeuour you may chaunce to doe your Countrey much good, and giue an infinite sorte of the poore people occasion to pray for you here throughout the Realme this that I meane is in matter of Cloth, &c.

1 First, you cannot denie but that this Realme yeeldeth the most fine Wooll, the most soft, the most strong Wooll, the most durable in Cloth, and most apte of nature of all other to receiue Die, and that no Island or any one kingdome so small doeth yeeld so great abundance of the same and that no Wooll is lesse subiect to mothes, or to fretting in presse, then this as the old

Parliament robes of Kings, and of many noble Peeres to be shewed may plainly testifie.

2 There is no commoditie of this Realme that may set so many poore subiects on worke, as this doeth, that doeth bring in so much treasure, and so much enrich the merchant, and so much employ the Nauie of this Realme, as this commoditie of our Wooll doeth.

Ample and full Vent of this noble and rich commoditie is it that the common weale of this realme doeth require.

Spaine nowe aboundeth with Wools, and the same are Clothed. Turkie hath Wools, and so haue diuers prouinces of Christendome and of Heathenesse, and cloth is made of the same in diuers places.

1 But if England haue the most fine, and the most excellent Wools of the world in all respects (as it cannot bee denied, but it hath). 2 If there may bee added to the same, excellent artificiall, and true making, and excellent dying. 3 Then no doubt but that we shall haue vent for our Clothes, although the rest of the world did abound much more with Wool then it doeth, and although their workemanship and their dying were in euery degree equal with ours of England, vnlesse the labour of our people imployed that way, and the materials vsed in dying should be the cause of the contrary by dearth.

But if Forren nations turne their Wools, inferiour to ours, into truer and more excellent made cloth, and shall die the same in truer, surer, and more excellent and more delectable colours, then shall they sell and make ample vent of their Clothes, when the English cloth of better wooll shall rest vnsold, to the spoyle of the Merchant, of the Clothier, and of the breeder of the wooll, and to the turning to bag and wallet of the infinite number of the poore people imploied in clothing in seuerall degrees of labour here in England.

Which things wayed, I am to tell you what things I wish you in this Realme, and after in Turkie, to indeuour from time to time, as your laisure may permit the same.

Before you goe out of the Realme, that you learne:

1 To know wooll, all kind of clothes made in this realme, and all other employments of wooll, home or forren, be the same in Felt clokes, felt hats, in the red knit cap for Barbarie, called Bonettos rugios colorados, or whatsoeuer, &c.

All the deceits in Clothmaking; as the sorting together of Wools of seuerall natures, some of nature to shrink, some to hold out, which causeth cloth to cockle and lie vneuen.

The euill sorting of threed of good or bad wooll, some tootoo [Footnote: Tootoo. The duplication is often used for the sake of emphasis. "A lesson tootoo hard for living clay." *Spenser, Faerie Queen,* iii., iv., 26.] hard spun, some tootoo soft spun deliuered to be wouen.

The faults in Weauing.

The faults in Walking, [Footnote: A "Walker" is a fuller of cloth. "She curst the weaver and the walker." *Boy and Mantle, Percy Rel.,* iii., 5.] Rowing, and Burling and in Racking [Footnote: Stretching. "Two lutes rack's up / To the same pitch." *The Slighted Maid,* p. 53.] the Clothes aboue measure vpon the Teintors: all which faults may be learned of honest men, which faults are to be knowen to the merchant, to be shunned and not to be vsed.

2 Then to learne of the Diers to discerne all kind of colours; as which be good and sure, and which will not hold: which be faire, which not; which colours by the dearth of the substances bee deare, and which by reason of the cheapenesse of the Materials with which they be died, be cheape colours.

3 Then to take the names of all the materials and substaunces vsed in this Citie or in the realme, in dying of cloth or silke.

To learne to know them, as which be good, which bad.

And what colours they die.

And what prices they be of.

And of them which bee the Naturals of this Realme, and in what part of the Realme they are to be had.

And of all the forren materials vsed in dying to know the very naturall places of them, and the plentie or the scarcenesse of each of them.

These things superficially learned in the realme before you goe, you are the fitter in forren parts to serue your Countrey, for by this meanes you haue an enterie into the thing that I wish you to trauell in.

What you shall doe in Turkie, besides the businesse of your Factorship.

1 Forasmuch as it is reported that the Woollen clothes died in Turkie bee most excellently died, you shall send home into this realme certaine Mowsters or pieces of Shew to be brought to the diers hall, there to be shewed, partly to remooue out of their heads, the tootoo great opinion they haue concerned of their owne cunning, and partly to mooue them for shame to endeuour to learne more knowledge to the honour of their countrey of England, and to the vniuersall benefit of the realme.

2 You shall deuise to amend the Dying of England, by carying hence an apte yoong man brought vp in the Arte, or by bringing one or other from thence of skill, or rather to deuise to bring one for Silkes, and another for Wooll and for Woollen cloth, and if you cannot worke this by ordinarie meanes, then to worke it by some great Bassas meane, or if your owne credite there be not sufficient by meane of your small abode in those parties, to worke it by the helpe of the French ambassador there resident, for which purpose you may insinuate your selfe into his acquaintance, and otherwise to leaue no meane vnsought that tendeth to this end, wherein you are to doe as circumstances may permit.

3 Then to learne to know all the materials and substances that the Turkes vse in dying, be they of Herbes, simple or compound, be they plants, Barkes, Wood, Berries, Seedes, Graines, or Minerall matter, or what els soeuer. But before all other, such things as yeeld those famous colours that carrie such speciall report of excellencie, that our Merchaunts may bring them to this realme by ordinarie trade, as a light meane for the better vent of our clothes.

4 To know the vse of those, and where the naturall place of them and of ech of them is, I meane the place where ech of them groweth or is bred.

5 And in any wise, if Anile that coloureth blew be a naturall commodity of those parts, and if it be compounded of an herbe, to send the same into this realme by seed or by root in barrell of earth, with all the whole order of sowing, setting, planting, replanting, and with the compounding of the same, that it may become a naturall commodity in this realme as Woad is, to this end that the high price of forreine Woad (which deuoureth yeerely great treasure) may be brought downe. So shall the marchant buy his cloth lesse deare, and so he shalbe able to occupy with lesse stocke, be able to afoord cloth cheaper, make more ample vent, and also become a greater gainer himselfe, and all this to the benefit of this realme.

6 To do the like with herbe and plant, or tree that in dying is of any excellent vse, as to send the same by seed, berry, root, &c: for by such meanes Saffron was brought first into this realme, which hath sent many poore on worke, and brought great wealth into this realme. Thus may Sumack, the plant wherewith the most excellent blacks be died in Spaine, be brought out of Spaine, and out of the Ilands of the same, if it will grow in this more colde climat. For thus was Woad brought into this realme, and came to good perfection, to the great losse of the French our olde enemies. And it doth maruellously import this realme to make naturall in this realme such things as be special in the dying of our clothes. And to speake of such things as colour blew, they are of greatest vse, and are grounds of the most

excellent colours, and therefore of all other to be brought into this realme, be it Anile or any other materiall of that quality.

7 And because yellowes and greenes are colours of small prices in this realme, by reason that Olde and Greenweed wherewith they be died be naturall here, and in great plenty, therefore to bring our clothes so died to common sale in Turkie were to the great benefit of the merchant, and other poore subiects of this realme, for in sale of such our owne naturall colours we consume not our treasure in forren colours, and yet we sell our owne trifles dearely perhaps.

8 The woolles being naturall, and excellent colours for dying becomming by this meanes here also naturall, in all the arte of Clothing then we want but one onely speciall thing. For in this so temperate a climat our people may labor the yere thorowout, whereas in some regions of the world they cannot worke for extreme heat, as in some other regions they cannot worke for extreme colde a good part of the yere. And the people of this realme by the great and blessed abundance of victuall are cheaply fed, and therefore may afoord their labour cheape. And where the Clothiers in Flanders by the Flatnesse of their riuers cannot make Walkmilles [Footnote: Fulling, or the art of scouring, cleansing, and thickening cloth, &c., in a mill, makes the material more compact and durable. Walkmill is the old name for a fullingmill.] for their clothes, but are forced to thicken and dresse all their clothes by the foot and by the labour of men, whereby their clothes are raised to an higher price, we of England haue in all Shires store of milles vpon falling riuers. And these riuers being in temperate zones are not dried vp in Summer with drought and heat as the riuers be in Spaine and in hotter regions, nor frozen vp in Winter as all the riuers be in all the North regions of the world: so as our milles may go and worke at all times, and dresse clothes cheaply. Then we haue also for scowring our clothes earths and claies, as Walkers clay, [Footnote: Fuller's earth, which attains a thickness of 150 feet near Bath.] and the clay of Oborne little inferior to Sope in scowring and in thicking. Then also haue we some reasonable store of Alum and Copporas here made for dying, and are like to haue increase of the same. Then we haue many good waters apt for dying, and people to spin and to doe the rest of all the labours we want not. [Sidenote: Supply of the want of oile.] So as there wanteth, if colours might be brought in and made naturall, but onely Oile: the want whereof if any man could deuise to supply at the full with any thing that might become naturall in this realme, he whatsoeuer he were that could bring it about, might deserue immortall fame in this our Common wealth, and such a deuise was offered to the Parliament and refused, because they denied to endow him with a certaine liberty, some others hauing obtained the same before, that practised to worke that effect by Radish seed, which onely made a triall of small

quantity, and that went no further, to make that Oile in plenty: and now he that offered this deuise was a marchant, and is dead, and withall the deuise is dead with him.

It is written by one that wrote of Afrike, [Sidenote: Leo Africanus lib. 8.] that in Egypt in a city called Muhaisira there be many milles imployed in making of Oile of the seed of an herbe called Sesamum. Pena and Lobell, Physicians, write in our time, that this herbe is a codded herbe full of oily seed, and that there is plenty of this seede brought out of Egypt to diuers Cities in Italy. If this herbe will prosper in this realme, our marchants may easily bring of it, &c.

9 Hauing heerein thus troubled you by raising to your minde the consideration of certaine things, it shall not be impertinent to tell you that it shall not be amisse that you note all the order of the degrees of labour vsed in Turky, in the arte of Clothing, and to see if any way they excell in that profession our people of these parts, and to bring notice of the same into this realme.

10 And if you shall finde that they make any cloth of any kind not made in this realme, that is there of great vse, then to bring of the same into this realme some Mowsters, that our people may fall into the trade, and prepare the same for Turkie: for the more kinds of cloth we can deuise to make, the more ample vent of our commoditie we shall haue, and the more sale of the labour of our poore subiects that els for lacke of labour become idle and burdenous to the common weale, and hurtfull to many: and in England we are in our clothing trade to frame our selues according to the desires of forren nations, be it that they desire thicke or thinne, broad or narrowe, long or short, white or blacke.

11 But with this prouiso alwayes, that our cloth passe out with as much labour of our people as may be, wherein great consideration ought to be had: for (if vent might so admit it) as it were the greatest madnesse in the world for vs to vent our wooll not clothed, so were it madnesse to vent our wooll in part or in the whole turned into broad cloth, if we might vent the same in Kersies: for there is great difference in profit to our people betweene the clothing of a sacke of wooll in the one, and the like sacke of wooll in the other, of which I wish the marchant of England to haue as great care as he may for the vniuersall benefit of the poore: and the turning of a sacke of wooll into Bonets is better then both &c. And also not to cary out of the realme any cloth white, but died if it may be, that the subiects of this realme may take as much benefit as is possible, and rather to seeke the vent of the clothes died with the naturall colours of England, then such as be died with forren colours.

12 And if of necessity we must be forced to receiue certaine colours from forren parts, for that this climat will not breed them, I wish that our marchants procure Anile and such other things to be planted in like climats where now it growes, in diuers others places, that this realme may haue that brought in for as base prices as is possible, and that falling out with one place we may receiue the same from another, and not buy the same at the second or the third hand &c. For if a commodity that is to be had of meere necessity, be in one hand, it is dearely purchased.

1. How many seuerall colours be died is to be learned of our Diers before you depart.

2 Then how many of those colours England doth die of her owne naturall home materials and substances, and how many not.

3 Then to bring into this realme herbs and plants to become naturall in our soiles, that may die the rest of the colours, that presently of our owne things here growing we can not yet die, and this from all forren places.

4 There is a wood called Logwood or Palo Campechio, it is cheape and yeeldeth a glorious blew, but our workmen can not make it sure. This wood you must take with you, and see whether the Silke diers or Wooll diers in Turky can doe it, with this one you may inrich your selfe very much, and therefore it is to be endeuoured earnestly by you. It may bring downe the price of Woad and of Anile.

Other some things to be remembred.

If you can finde oat at Tripoly in Syria or elsewhere a vent for the Cappes called in Barbarie, Bonettos colorados rugios, which is a red Scottish cap as it were without brims, you should do your countrey much good: for as a sacke of wooll turned into fine Deuonshire kersies doth set many more people on worke then a sacke spunne for broad cloth in a grosser threed, so a sacke of wool turned into those Bonets doth set many more poore people on worke, then a sacke turned into Kersies, by reason of the knitting. And therefore if you can indeuour that, you worke great effect. And no doubt that a maruellous vent may be found out of them into Afrike by the way of Alexandria, and by Alcayer [Footnote: Cairo.] Southeast and Southwest thence.

2 And by the vent of our knit hose of Woollen yarne, Woorsted yarne, and of Linnen thred, great benefit to our people may arise, and a great value in fine Kersies and in those knit wares may be couched in a small roome in the ship. And for these things our people are growen apt, and by indeuour may be drawen to great trade.

3 Saffron the best of the vniuersall world groweth in this realme, and forasmuch as it is a thing that requireth much labour in diuers sorts, and setteth the people on worke so plentifully, I wish you to see whether you can finde out ample vent for the same, since it is gone out of great vse in those parts. It is a spice that is cordiall, and may be vsed in meats, and that is excellent in dying of yellow silks. This commodity of Saffron groweth fifty miles from Tripoli in Syria, on an high hill called in those parts Garian, so as there you may learne at that port of Tripoli the value of the pound, the goodnesse of it, and the places of the vent. But it is sayd that from that hill there passeth yeerly of that commodity fifteene moiles [Footnote: A Mule. "Well, make much of him; I see he was never born to ride upon a moyle."—*Every man out of his humour*, ii., 3.] laden, and that those regions notwithstanding lacke sufficiencie of that commodity. But if a vent might be found, men would in Essex about Saffronwalden [Footnote: Saffron Walden—*Saffron Weal-den*. The woody Saffron Hill.] and in Cambridge shire reuiue the trade for the benefit of the setting of the poore on worke. So would they doe in Hereford shire by Wales, where the best of all England is, in which place the soile yeelds the wilde Saffron commonly, which sheweth the naturall inclination of the same soile to the bearing of the right Saffron, if the soile be manured and that way employed.

[Sidenote: Leo Africanus lib. 4.] 4. There is a walled towne not farre from Barbarie, called Hubbed, toward the South from the famous towne Telensin, [Footnote: Tlemcen, on a tributary of the Tafna, in Algeria.] about six miles: the inhabitants of which towne in effect be all Diers. And it is sayd that thereabout they haue plenty of Anile, and that they occupy that, and also that they vse there in their dyings, of the Saffron aforesayd. [Sidenote: This may be learned at Alger.] The trueth whereof, in the Southerly ports of the Mediteran sea, is easily learned in your passage to Tripoli, or in returne from thence homeward you may vnderstand it. It is reported at Saffronwalden that a Pilgrim purposing to do good to his countrey, stole an head of Saffron, and hid the same in his Palmers staffe, which he had made hollow before of purpose, and so he brought this root into this realme, with venture of his life: for if he had bene taken, by the law of the countrey from whence it came, he had died for the fact. If the like loue in this our age were in our people that now become great trauellers, many knowledges, and many trades, and many herbes and plants might be brought into this realme that might doe the realme good. And the Romans hauing that care, brought from all coasts of the world into Italie all arts and sciences, and all kinds of beasts and fowile, and all herbs, trees, busks and plants that might yeeld profit or pleasure to their countrey of Italie. And if this care had not bene heretofore in our ancestors, then, had our life bene sauage now, for then we had not had Wheat nor Rie, Peaze nor Beanes, Barley nor Oats, Peare nor Apple, Vine nor many other profitable and pleasant plants, Bull nor Cow, Sheepe nor Swine, Horse nor Mare, Cocke nor Hen, nor a number of other things that we inioy, without which our life were to be sayd barbarous: for these things and a thousand that we vse more the first inhabitors of this Iland found not here. And in time of memory things haue bene brought in that were not here before, as the Damaske rose by Doctour Linaker king Henry the seuenth and king Henry the eights Physician, the Turky cocks and hennes about fifty yeres past, the Artichowe in time of king Henry the eight, and of later time was procured out of Italy the Muske rose plant, the plumme called the Perdigwena, and two kindes more by the Lord Cromwell after his trauell, and the Abricot by a French Priest one Wolfe Gardiner to king Henry the eight: and now within these foure yeeres there haue bene brought into England from Vienna in Austria diuers kinds of flowers called Tulipas, and those and other procured thither a little before from Constantinople by an excellent man called M. Carolus Clusius. And it is sayd that since we traded to Zante that the plant that beareth the Coren is also brought into this realme from thence; and although it bring not fruit to perfection, yet it may serue for pleasure and for some vse, like as our vines doe, which we cannot well spare, although the climat so colde will not permit vs to haue good wines of them. And many other things haue bene brought in, that haue degenerated by reason of the colde climat, some other things brought in haue by negligence bene lost. The Archbishop of Canterburie Edmund Grindall, after he returned out of Germany, brought into this realme the plant of Tamariske from thence, and this plant he hath so increased that there be here thousands of them; and many people haue receiued great health by this plant: and if of things brought in such care were had, then could not the first labour be lost. The seed of Tobacco hath bene brought hither out of the West Indies, [Footnote: As these instructions were written in 1582, how can Tobacco have been introduced by Raleigh in 1586, as generally asserted? It is not more probable that it dates from Sir John Hawkin's voyage 1565?] it groweth heere, and with the herbe many haue bene eased of the reumes, &c. Each one of a great number of things were woorthy of a iourney to be made into Spaine, Italy, Barbarie, Egypt, Zante, Constantinople, the West Indies, and to diuers other places neerer and further off then any of these, yet forasmuch as the poore are not able, and for that the rich setled at home in quiet will not, therefore we are to make sute to such as repaire to forren kingdomes, for other businesses, to haue some care heerein, and to set before their eyes the examples of these good men, and to endeuour to do for their parts the like, as their speciall businesses may permit the same. Thus giuing you occasion by way of a little remembrance, to haue a desire to doe your countrey good you shall, if you haue any inclination to such good, do more good to the poore ready to starue for reliefe, then euer any subiect did in this realme by building of

Almes-houses, and by giuing of lands and goods to the reliefe of the poore. Thus may you helpe to driue idlenesse the mother of most mischiefs out of the realme, and winne you perpetuall fame, and the prayer of the poore, which is more woorth then all the golde of Peru, and of all the West Indies.

* * * * *

The voyage of the Susan of London to Constantinople, wherein the worshipfull M. William Harborne was sent first Ambassadour vnto Sultan Murad Can, the great Turke, with whom he continued as her Maiesties Ligier almost sixe yeeres.

The 14 of Nouember 1582, we departed from Blackewall, bound for the Citie of Constantinople, in the tall shippe called the Susan of London: the Master whereof was Richard Parsons, a very excellent and skilfull man in his facultie. But by occasion of contrary weather we spent two moneths before we could recouer the Kowes [Footnote: Cowes.] in the Isle of Wight. [Sidenote: Ianuary the foureteenth.] Where the 14 of Ianuary following we tooke in the worshipfull M. William Hareborne her Maiesties Ambassadour to the Turke, and his company, and sailed thence to Yarmouth in the foresayd Isle of Wight. The 19 we put from Wight. The 26 we did see Capo de Sant Vincente. The same day we were thwart of Capo Santo Maria. The 27 we passed by Tariffa, and Gibraltar. The 28 in the morning we passed by Velez Malaga: and that night were thwart of Capo de Gates. The 29 at night we had sight of Capo de Palos. The 30 in the morning we did see the high land of Denia, [Footnote: Near Cape Antonio.] in the kingdome of Valentia, and that night we had sight of the Iland Formentera. The 31 in the morning appeared the Iland of Cabrera. [Footnote: A small island south of Majorca.] [Sidenote: February the first.] The first of February we put into a Port in Mallorca, [Footnote: Maiorca.] called Porto de Sant Pedro: where they would haue euill intreated vs for comming into the Harbour: we thought we might haue bene as bolde there as in other places of Christendome, but it proued farre otherwise. [Sidenote: The shippes men goe on land at Porto de Sant Pedro.] The first man we met on land was a simple Shepheard, of whom we demanded whether wee might haue a sheepe or such like to refresh our selues, who tolde vs yea. And by such conference had with him, at the last be came aboord once or twise, and had the best cheare that we could make him: and our Ambassadour himselfe talked with him, and still be made vs faire promises, but nothing at all meant to performe the same, as the end shewed. In the meane time came in a shippe of Marseils, the Master whereof did know our Ambassadour very well, with whom our Ambassadour had conference, and with his Marchants also. They came from Alger in Barbarie, which is vnder the gouernement of the Great Turke. They did present our Ambassadour with an Ape, wherefore he made very much of them, and had them often aboord. [Sidenote: The Ambassadour betrayed.] By them I suppose, he, was bewrayed of his purpose as touching his message, but yet still we had faire words of the Shepheard aforesayd, and others. So that vpon their words, our Purser and another man went to a Towne which was three or foure miles from the port, and there were well entertained, and had of the people very faire speeches, and such small things as could be gotten vpon the sudden, and so returned to the shippe that day. Then wee were emboldened, and thought all had bene well, according to their talke. [Sidenote: February the sixth.] The next day, being the sixth day of Februarie, two of our Gentlemen, with one of our Marchants, and the Purser, and one of the Ambassadours men went to the Towne aforesayd, thinking to doe as the Purser and the other had done before, but it prooued contrary: for at their comming thither they had faire wordes a while, and had bread and wine, and such necessaries for their money, vntill such time as they were beset with men, and the Maiorcans neuer shewed in their countenance any such matter, but as the manner of all the people in the dominions of Spaine is, for the most part to be trecherous to vs, if they thinke they haue any aduantage. [Sidenote: The English men are surprised.] For vpon the sudden they layed handes on them, and put them in holde, as sure as might be in such a simple Towne. Then were they well guarded with men both day and night, and still deluded with faire words, and they sayd to our men it was for no hurt, but that the Viceroy of the Iland would come aboard to see the shippe. But they presently sent the Purser to the Towne of Maiorca, where he was examined by the Viceroy very straightly, what their shippe and captaine were, and what voyage they intended, but he confessed nothing at all. In the meane time they in the Towne were likewise straightly examined by a Priest and other officers vpon their othes: who for their othes sake declared the whole estate of their voyage. The Ambassadours man was a French man, and therefore was suffered to goe to the shippe on a message, but he could tell the Ambassadour none other newes, but that the Viceroy would come aboord the shippe, and that our men should come with him, but they had another meaning. For the Marseilian Marchants were stayed in like maner in the Towne, onely to make a better shew vnto vs. But in the meane time, being there three or foure dayes, there came men vnto vs euery day, more or lesse, but one day especially there came two men on horsebacke, whom we tooke to be officers, being lusty men, and very well horsed. These men desired to speake with our Captaine (for all things that passed there were done in the name of our Captaine Iohn Gray) for it was sayd by vs there, that he was Captaine of one of her Maiesties shippes: wherefore all things passed in his name: and the Ambassadour not seene in any thing but rather concealed, and yet did all, because of his tongue and good inditing in that language. For he himselfe went on land clothed in Veluet, and talked with these men, and with him ten or twelue lusty fellowes well weaponed, ech one hauing a Boarespeare or a Caliuer, the Captaine Iohn Gray being one of them, and our boat lying by very warely kept and ready. For then wee began to suspect, because the place was more frequented with men than it was woont. [Sidenote: The Spaniards come to the sea side to speak with the captaine.] The men on horsebacke were in doubt to come neere, because hee came so well weaponed. But they bade him welcome, and gaue him great salutations, in words as their maner is: and demanded why he came so strong, for they sayd he needed not to feare any man in the Iland. Answere was made, that it was the maner of English Captaines to goe with their guard in strange places. Then they tolde our Ambassador (thinking him to be the Captaine) that they were sent from the Viceroy to know what they did lacke, for they promised him beefe or mutton, or any thing that was in the Iland to be had, but their purpose was to haue gotten more of our men if they could, and they sayde that wee should haue our men againe the next day: with such pretty delusions they fed vs still. Then our Ambassadour did write a letter to the Viceroy in her Maiesties name, and in our Captaine Iohn Grayes name, and not in his owne, and sent it by them, desiring him to send his men, and not to trouble him in his voyage, for he had giuen him no such cause, nor any of his. So these men departed with great courtesie in words on both parts. And in all this time we did see men on horsebacke and on foot in the woods and trees more then they were accustomed to be, but we could perceiue nothing thereby. [Sidenote: The Spaniards come again to parle.] The next day, or the second, came either foure or sixe of the best of them as wee thought (the Viceroy excepted) and very many men besides in the fieldes, both on foot and on horse, but came not neere the water side. And those in like order desired to speake with the Captaine and that when he came on land the trumpets might sound: but then the Ambassadour, whom they thought to be Captaine, would not goe, nor suffer the trumpets to be sounded, for that he thought it was a trappe to take himselfe, and more of his company. But did send one of the principall of the Marchants to talke with them. And the Captaine Iohn Gray went also with him, not being knowen of the Spaniards, for he went as a souldiour. Thus they receiued of those men the like wordes as they had of the other before mentioned, who sayd we should haue our men againe, for they meant vs no hurt. [Sidenote: The Ambassadour writeth to the Viceroy.] Then our Ambassadour did write another letter, and sent it by them to the Viceroy, in like order as he did before, but he receiued no answere of any of them. In all this time they had priuily gathered together the principall men of the iland, and had laboured day and night to bring downe ordinance, not making any shew of their trecherie towards vs. But the same night following, we saw very many lights passe in the woods among the trees. [Sidenote: The ninth of February.] And in the morning when the watch was broken vp, being Saturday the ninth of Februarie, at faire day light, one of our men looked foorth, and saw standing on land the cariage of a piece: then was one commanded to goe into the toppe, and there he did descrie two or three pieces and also many men on the shore, with diuers weapons that they brought. Then they suddenly tooke foure or fiue brasse pieces, and placed them on either side of the harborough where we should go out, and hid them with stones and bushes that we should not see them. Now I think the harborough not to be aboue the eight part of a mile ouer. Thus perceiuing their meaning which was most plaine: wee agreed to take vp our anker and goe out, and leaue our men there, hauing none other way to take. Then our Ambassadour intreated the Master of the Marseilian, his friend, to goe on land with his boat, and to know the trueth: who satisfied his request. And at his returne he tolde vs that it was very true, that they would lay holde of vs if they could. Then we weighed our ankers: but hauing little winde, we towed the ship forward with the boat. The Viceroy himselfe was at the water side with more then fiue hundred men on both sides of the harbour as we thought. [Sidenote: The ship Susan prepareth to defend herselfe.] And when we came out with our shippe as far as their ordinance, our Ambassadour and the Captaine being in their armour, the Master commanding of the company, and trimming of the sailes, the Pilot standing on the poope, attending to his charge, with other very well furnished, and euery man in order about their businesse very ready, they on land on the contrary part hauing a very faire piece mounted on the North side openly in all our sights, as the shippe passed by, they trauersed that piece right with the maine mast or after-quarter of the shippe, and a Gunner standing by, with a lint-stocke in his hand, about foureteene or fifteene foot long, being (as we thought) ready to giue fire. Our whole noise of trumpets were sounding on the poope with drumme and flute, and a Minion of brasse on the summer decke, with two or three other pieces, always by our Gunners trauersed mouth to mouth with theirs on land, still looking when they on land should shoot, for to answere them againe. The Pilot standing on the poope, seeing this readinesse, and the shippe going very softly, because of the calmenesse of the winde, he called to them on the South side, where the Viceroy was, and sayd vnto him: Haue you warres with vs? If you haue, it is more then we know; but by your prouision it seemeth so: if you haue, shoot in Gods name, and spare not, but they held all fast and shot not. Then the Viceroy himselfe held vp a paper, and sayd he, had a letter for our Captaine, and desired vs to stay for it. Then we answered and sayd we would not; but willed him to send it by the Marseilians boat, and our men also, All this while, our trumpets, drum and flute sounded, and so we passed out in the face of them all. When they perceiued that they could lay no holde on vs, they presently sent to the Towne for our men, whom within lesse then three houres after they sent aboord with the sayd letter, wherein he desired our Captaine and his company not to take it in ill part, for he meant them no harme, but would haue seene our shippe. His letter did import these and such like faire speeches: for it altogether contained courteous salutations, saying that he might boldly come into any port within his Iland, and that he and his would shew him what friendship they might: and that the iniury that was offered was done at the requst of the Shepheards; and poore people of the countrey, for the more safegard of their flockes, and because it was not a thing vsuall to haue any such shippe to come into that port, with many other deceitfull words in the sayd letter. [Sidenote: The effect of the Ambassadours answere.] Then our Ambassadour wrote vnto him another letter to answer that, and gaue him thanks for his men that he had sent him, and also for his good will, and sent him a present. This done, we shot off halfe a dozen pieces, hoised our sailes, and departed on our voyage. Then the Purser and the rest of our men that had beene in holde, tolde vs that they did see the Captaine, and other gentlemen of the Iland, hauing their buskins and stockings torne from their legges, with labouring in the bushes day and night to make that sudden prouision. The 12 of February we saw an Iland of Africa side called Galata, [Footnote: Galita, off Cape Serrat, in Tunis.] where they vse to drag out of the Sea much Corall, and we saw likewise Sardinia, which is an Iland subiect to Spaine. The 13 in the morning we were hard by Sardinia. The 15 we did see an Iland neere Sicilia, and an Iland on Africa side called Cysimbre. [Footnote: Zembra, off Cape Bon.] The same day likewise we saw an Iland called Pantalaria, and that night we were thwart the middle of Sicilia. The 16 at night we were as farre as Capo Passaro, which is the Southeast part of Sicilia., The 24 we were put into a port called Porte de Conte, in an Iland called Cephalonia: it is an out Iland in the dominions of Grecia, and now at this present gouerned by the Signory of Venice, as the rest of Grecia is vnder the Turke, for the most part. The 27 we came from thence, and that day arriued at Zante which is also in Grecia: for at this present wee entred the parts of Grecia. The second of March we came from Zante; and the same day were thwart of an Iland called Prodeno [Footnote: Probably Strivali.] and the 4 we were thwart of an Iland called Sapientia [Footnote: Off Cape Gallo.] againe. There standeth a faire Towne and a Castle on the maine ouer against it, called Modon. The same day by reason of contrary windes we put backe againe to Prodeno, because we could not fetch Sapientia. The ninth we came from thence, and were as farre as Sapientia againe. The tenth we were as farre shot as Capo Matapan; and that day we entered the Archipelago, and passed thorow betweene Cerigo and Capo Malio. [Footnote: Cape Malea.] This Cerigo is an Iland where one Menelaus did sometimes reigne, from whome was stollen by Paris faire Helena, and carried to Troy, as ancient Recordes doe declare. The same day we had sight of a little Iland called Bellapola, and did likewise see both the Milos, [Footnote: Milo and

Anti-Milo, the latter a rocky islet, six miles north-west of Milo.] being Ilands in the Archipelago. The 11 in the morning we were hard by an Iland called Falconara, [Footnote: Falconers.] and the Iland of the Antemila. [Footnote: Ante-Milo.] The 12 in the morning we were betweene Fermenia [Footnote: Thermia, so called from the warm springs at the foot of Santa Irene.] and Zea, being both Ilands. That night wee were betweene Negroponte and Andri, being likewise Ilands. The 13 in the morning we were hard by Parsa [Footnote: Probably Psara.] and Sarafo, being Ilands nine or tenne miles from Chio, and could not fetch Chio. [Sidenote: Sigra, a port in Metelin.] So we put roome with a port in Metelin [Footnote: Mitylene, the ancient Lesbos.] called Sigra, and about nine of the clocke at night we ankered there. The 15 we came from thence, the sixteenth we put into Porto Delfi. This port is 9 English miles to the Northward of the City of Chio, (and it may be twelue of their miles) this night we stayed in the sayd port, being in the Iland of Chio. Then went our Marchant and one or two with him to the City of Chio. [Sidenote: Ermin, or Customer.] And when the By, who is the gouernour of the Iland (and is in their language a Duke) had communed with the Marchant, and those that were with him, and vnderstood of our arriuall within his dominion, the day following he armed his gallies, and came to welcome our Ambassadour, accompanied with the Ermine, that is, the Kings Customer, and also the French Consull, with diuers of the chiefe of the City, and offered him as much friendship as he could or would desire: for he did offer to attend vpon vs, and towe vs if need were to the Castles. The 21 we departed from thence, and thar day passed by port Sigra againe. This Iland of Metelin is part of Asia, and is neere to Natolia. The 22 we passed by a head land called Baberno, [Footnote: Cape Baba.] and is also in Asia. And that day at night we passed by the Isle of Tenedo, part of Asia, and by another Iland called Maure. And the same day we passed thorow the straights of Galipoli, and by the Castles, and also by the Towne of Galipoli it selfe, which standeth in Europa. And that night we were in sight of Marmora which is neere Natolia, and part of Asia. The 23 in the morning, we were thwart of Araclia, [Footnote: Erekli.] and that night we ankered in Silauria. [Footnote: Silivri.] The 24 in the morning the Marchant and the Pilot were set on land to goe to the City about the Ambassadours businesse, but there they could not land because we had the winde faire. That place of some is called Ponte grande, and is foure and twenty miles on this side of Constantinople, and because of the winde, they followed in the skiffe vntill they came to a place called Ponte picola, and there is a little bridge; it standeth eight Turkish miles from Constantinople, there the Marchant and the Pilot landed. At this bridge is an house of the great Turkes with a faire Garden belonging vnto it, neere the which is a point called Ponte S. Stephano, and there the shippe ankered that day. The 26 day the ship came to the seuen Towers, and the 27 we came neerer. The 29 there came three gallies to bring vs vp further: and when the shippe came against the great Turks palace, we shot off all our ordinance to the number of foure and thirty pieces. [Sidenote: The arriuall of the Susan at Constantinople.] Then landed our Ambassadour, and then we discharged foure and twentie pieces, who was receiued with more then fifty or threescore men on horsebacke. [Sidenote: The Ambassadour giueth a present to the great Bassa.] The ninth of April he presented the great bassa with sixe clothes, foure canes of siluer double gilt, and one piece of fine holland, and to three other Bassas, that is to say, the second Bassa which is a gelded man, and his name is Mahomet Bassa, to the third who maried the great Turks sister, and to the fourth whom they call Abraham Bassa, to euery one of these he gaue foure clothes. [Sidenote: A man halfe naked goeth before the greaat Bassa.] Now, before the great Bassa, and Abraham Bassa, at their returne from the Court (and as we thinke at other times, but at that time for a certaine) there came a man in maner of a foole, who gaue a great shout three or foure times, crying very hollowly, the place rebounded with the sound, and this man, say they, is a prophet of Mahomet, his armes and legges naked, on his feet he did weare woodden pattens of two sorts, in his hand, a flagge, or streamer set on a short speare painted, he carried a mat and bottels, and other trumpery at his backe, and sometimes vnder his arme, on his head he had a cappe of white Camels haire, flat like an helmet, written about with letters, and about his head a linnen rowle. Other seruingmen there were with the sayd Bassas, with red attire on their heads, much like French hoods, but the long flappe somewhat smaller towardes the end, with scuffes or plates of mettall, like vnto the chape of an ancient arming sword, standing on their foreheads like other Ianisaries. [The Ambassadours entertainment with the Bassas.] These Bassas entertained vs as followeth: First, they brought vs into a hall, there to stand on one side, and our Ambassadour and gentlemen on the other side, who sate them downe on a bench couered with carpets, the Ambassadour in the midst; on his left hand sate our gentlemen, and on his right hand the Turkes, next to the doore where their master goeth in and out: the common sort of Turkes stayed in the Court yard, not suffered to come neere vs. When our Ambassadour had sitten halfe an houre, the Bassas (who sate by themselues in an inner small roome) sent for him; to whom the Ambassadour and his gentlemen went: they all kissed his hand, and presently returned (the Ambassadour only excepted, who stayed there, and a Turks chaus [Footnote: Interpreter.] with him) with the Ambassadour and his gentlemen went in also so many of our men as there were presents to cary in, but these neither kissed his hand nor taried. After this I went to visit the church of Santa Sophia, which was the chiefe church when it was the Christians, and now is the chiefe see and church of primacie of this Turke present: before I entred I was willed to put off my shoes, to the end I should not prophane their church, I being a Christian. [Sidenote: A description of their church.] The pillers on both sides of the church are very costly and rich, their Pulpets seemely and handsome, two are common to preach in, the third reserued onely for their Paschall. The ground is couered with Mats, and the walles hanged with Tapistry. They haue also Lamps in their churches, one in the middle of the church of exceeding greatnesse, and another in another part of the church of cleane golde, or double gilded, full as bigge as a barrel. Round about the church there is a gallery builded vpon rich and stately pillers. That day I was in both the chappels, in one of the which lieth the Turkes father, and fiue of his sonnes in tombes right costly, with their turbents very white and cleane, shifted (as they say) euery Friday, they be not on their heads, but stand on mouldes made for that purpose. At the endes, ouer, and about their tombes are belts, like girdles, beset with iewels. In the other chappell are foure other of his sonnes, and one daughter, in like order. In the first chappell is a thing foure foot high, couered with greene, beset with mother of pearle very richly. This is a relique of Mahomet, and standeth on the left side of the head of the great Turks tombe. These chappels haue their floores couered, and their walles hanged with Tapistrie of great price, I could value the couering and hangings of one of the chappels, at no lesse then fiue hundred poundes, besides their lamps hanging richly gilded. These chappels haue their roofes curiously wrought with rich stone, and gilded. And there lie the bookes of their Lawes for euery man to reade. [Sidenote: The ship cometh to the custome house.] The 11 day of April the shippe came to the Key of the Custome house. [Sidenote: The Ambassadour presenteth the Admirall Vchali.] The 16 the Ambassadour and we his men went to the Captaine Bassa, who is Admirall of the seas, his name is Vchali, he would not receiue vs into his house, but into his gallie, to deliuer our present, which was as followeth: Foure pieces of cloth, and two siluer pots gilt and grauen. The poope or sterne of his gally was gilded both within and without, and vnder his feet, and where he sate was all couered with very rich Tapistry. Our Ambassadour and his gentlemen kissed his hand, and then the gentlemen were commanded out, and our Ambassadour sate downe by him on his left hand, and the chaus stood before him. Our men might walke in the gally fore and after, some of vs taried, and some went out againe. The gally had seuen pieces of brasse in her prowe, small and great, she had thirty bankes or oares on either side, and at euery banke or oare seuen men to rowe. [Sidenote: The Susan goeth from the Custome house. The Admirall departeth to the sea.] The 18 day the shippe went from the Key. And 21 the Admirall tooke his leaue of the great Turke, being bound to the Sea with sixe and thirty gallies, very fairely beautified with gilding and painting, and beset with flags and streamers, all the which gallies discharged their ordinance: and we for his farewell gaue him one and twentie pieces. Then he went to his house with his gallies, and the 22 he went to the Sea, and the Castle that standeth in the water gaue him foureteene or sixteene pieces: and when he came against the Turks Seraglio he shot off all his caliuers and his great pieces, and so hee went his way. [Sidenote: The Ambassadour repaireth to the great Turks court.] The 24 our Ambassadour went to the Court, whose entertainement with the order therof followeth. When wee came first on land there was way made for vs by two or three Bassaes and diuers chauses on horsebacke with their men on foot, to accompany our Ambassadour to the Court. Also they brought horses for him and his gentlemen for to ride, which were very richly furnished: and by the way there met with vs other chauses to accompany vs to the Court. When we came there wee passed thorow two gates, at the second gate there stood very many men with horses attending on their masters. When we came within that gate we were within a very faire Court yard, in compasse twise so bigge as Pauls Church-yard. On the right hand of the sayd Court was a faire gallerie like an Alley, and within it were placed railes and such other prouision. On the left side was the like, halfe the Court ouer: it was diuided into two parts, the innermost fairer then the other. The other part of that side is the place where the Councell doe vsually sit, and at the inner end of that is a faire place to sit in, much like vnto that place in Pauls Church-yard, where the Maior and his brethren vse to sit, thither was our Ambassador brought, and set in that place. Within that sayde place is another like open roome, where hee did eate. [Sidenote: The entertainment at dinner of the Ambassadours men.] Assoone as wee came in, wee were placed in the innermost alley of the second roome, on the left side of the Court, which was spread with carpets on the ground fourescore or fourescore and tenne foot long, with an hundred and fiftie seuerall dishes set thereon, that is to say, Mutton boiled and rosted, Rice diuersly dressed, Fritters of the finest fashion, and dishes daintily dight with pritty pappe, with infinite others, I know not how to expresse them. We had also rosted Hennes with sundry sorts of fowles to me vnknowen. The gentlemen and we sate downe on the ground, for it is their maner so to feede. There were also Greekes and others set to furnish out the roome. Our drinke was made with Rose water and Sugar and spices brewed together. Those that did serue vs with it had a great bagge tied ouer their showlders, with a broad belt like an arming belt full of plates of copper and gilt, with part of the sayd bagge vnder his arme, and the mouth in his hand: then he had a deuise to let it out when he would into cuppes, when we called for drinke. The Ambassadour when hee had eaten, passed by vs, with the chauses aforesayd, and sate him downe in an inner roome. This place where he sate was against the gate where we came in, and hard by the Councell chamber end, somewhat on the left side of the Court, this was at the East end of the Court, for we came in at the West. All this time our presents stood by vs vntill we had dined, and diner once ended, this was their order of taking vp the dishes. Certaine were called in, like those of the Blacke gard in the Court of England, the Turks call them Moglans. These came in like rude and rauening Mastifs, without order or fashion, and made cleane riddance: for he whose hungry eye one dish could not fill turned two, one into the other, and thus euen on the sudden was made a cleane riddance of all. Then came certaine chauses and brought our gentlemen to sit with the Ambassadour. Immediately came officers and appointed Ianisers to beare from vs our presents, who caried them on the right side of the Court, and set them hard by the doore of the Priuy chamber, as we call it: there all things stoode for the space of an houre. Thus the Ambassadour and his gentlemen sate still, and to the Southward of them was a doore whereas the great Turke himselfe went in and out at, and on the South side of that doore sate on a bench all his chiefe lordes and gentlemen, and on the North side of the West gate stood his gard, in number as I gesse them a thousand men. These men haue on their heads round cappes of mettall like sculles, but sharpe in the toppe, in this they haue a bunch of Ostridge feathers, as bigge as a brush, with the corner or edge forward: at the lower end of these feathers was there a smaller feather, like those that are commonly worn here. Some of his gard had smal staues, and most of them were weaponed with bowes and arrowes. Here they waited, during our abode at the Court, to gard their Lord. After the Ambassadour with his gentlemen had sitten an houre and more, there came three or foure chauses, and brought them into the great Turkes presence. At the Priuy chamber doore two noble men tooke the Ambassadour by ech arme one, and put their fingers within his sleeues, and so brought him to the great Turke where he sumptuously sate alone. He kissed his hand and stood by vntill all the gentlemen were brought before him in like maner, one by one, and ledde backewards againe his face towards the Turke; for they might neither tarry nor turne their backs, and in like maner returned the Ambassadour. The salutation that the Noble men did, was taking them by the hands. All this time they trode on cloth of golde, most of the Noble men that sate on the South side of the Priuy chamber sate likewise on cloth of golde. Many officers or Ianisaries there were with staues, who kept very good order, for no Turke whatsoeuer might goe any further than they willed him. [Sidenote: The Turke is presented with a rich present.] At our Ambassadours entring they followed that bare his presents, to say, twelue fine broad clothes, two pieces of fine holland, tenne pieces of plate double gilt, one case of candlesticks, the case whereof was very large, and three foot high and more, two very great Cannes or pots, and one lesser, one basin and ewer, two poppiniayes of siluer, the one with two beads: they were to drinke in: two bottles with chaines, three faire mastifs in coats of redde cloth, three spaniels, two bloodhounds, one common hunting hound, two greyhounds, two little dogges in coats of silke: one clocke valued at fiue hundred pounds sterling: ouer it was a forrest with trees of siluer, among the which were deere chased with dogs, and men on horsebacke following, men drawing of water, others carrying mine oare on barrowes: on the toppe of the clocke stood a castle, and on the castle a mill. All these were of siluer. And the clocke was round beset with iewels. All the time that we stayed at the Councell chamber doore they were telling or weighing of money to send into Persia for his Souldiours pay. There were carried out an hundred and three and thirty bags, and in euery bagge, as it was tolde vs, one thousand ducats, which amounteth to three hundred and thirty thousand, [Footnote: Blank in original.] and in sterling English money to fourescore and nineteene thousand pounds. The Captaine of the guard in the meane time went to the great Turke, and returned againe, then they of the Court made obeisance to him, bowing downe their heads, and their hands on their breasts, and he in like order resaluted them: he was in cloth of siluer, he went and came with two or three with him and no more. Then wee went out at the first gate, and there we were commanded to stay vntill the Captaine of the guard was passed by and all his guard with him, part before him and part behinde him, some on horsebacke and some on foot, but the most part on foot carrying on their shoulders the money before mentioned, and so we passed home. There was in the Court during our abode there, for the most part a foole resembling the first, but not naked as was the other at the Bassas: but he turned him continually, and cried Hough very hollowly. The third of May I saw the Turke go to the church: he had more then two hundred and fifty horses before and behinde him, but most before him. There were many empty horses that came in no order. Many of his Nobilitie were in cloth of golde, but himselfe in white sattin. There did ride behinde him sixe or seuen youthes, one or two whereof carried water for him to drinke as they sayd. There were many of his guard running before him and behinde him, and when he alighted, they cried Hough very hollowly, as the aforesayd fooles.

* * * * *

A letter of Mustapha Chaus to the Queenes most excellent Maiestie.

Serenissima, prudentissima, et sacra Regia Maiestas, domina mihi semper clementissima, meorum fidelium officiorum promptam paratissimámque commendationem. Generosus et virtuosus Gulielmus Hareborne legatus vestræ sacræ Maiestatis venit ad portam excelsissimam potentissimi et inuictissimi, et semper Augustissimi Cæsaris Sultan Murad Can, cui Deus omnipotens benedicat. Et quanto honore, quanta dignitate, quantáque humanitate aliorum confoederatorum legati accipiuntur, præfatus quoque legatus vester tanta reuerentia, tantáque amplitudine acceptus et collocatus est in porta excelsissima. Et posthac subditi et homines vestræ sacræ Maiestatis ad ditiones omnes Cæsareas venire, et sua negocia tractare, et ad suam patriam redire sine impedimento, vt in literis excelsissimi, potentissimi, et inuictissimi et semper Augustissimi Cæsaris ad vestram sacram Regiam Maiestatem datis facile patet, tranquillè et pacificè possunt. Ego autem imprimis diligentem operam et fidele studium et nunc eodem confirmando nauaui, et in futurum quoque vsque in vltimum vitæ spiritum in negotijs potentissimi et inuictissimi Cæsaris et vestræ sacræ Regiæ Maiestatis egregiam nauabo operam. Quod Deus omnipotens ad emolumentum et vtilitatem vtriúsque Reipublicæ secundet. Amen. Sacram Regiam Maiestatem foelicissimè valere exopto. Datum Constantinopoli anno 1583, die octauo Maij.

* * * * *

A letter of M. Harborne to Mustapha, challenging him for his dishonest dealing in translating of three of the Grand Signior his commandements.

Domine Mustapha, nescimus quid sihi velit, cum nobis mandata ad finem vtilem concessa perperàm reddas, quæ male scripta, plus damni, quàm vtilitatis adferant: quemadmodum constat ex tribus receptis mandatis, in quibus summum aut principale deest aut aufertur. In posterum noli ita nobiscum agere. Ita enim ludibrio erimus omnibus in nostrum et tuum dedecus. Cum nos multarum actionum spem Turcicè scriptarum in tua prudentia reponimus, ita prouidere debes, vt non eueniant huius modi mala. Quocirca deinceps cum mandatum aut scriptum aliquod accipias, verbura ad verbum conuertatur in Latinum sermonem, ne damnum insequatur. Nosti multos habere nos inimicos conatibus nostris inuidentes, quoram malitiæ vestræ est prudentiæ aduersari. Hi nostri, Secretarius et minimus interpres ex nostra parte dicent in tribus illis receptis mandateis errata. Vt deinceps similes errores non eueniant precamur. Ista emendes, et cætera Serenissimæ regiæ Maiestatis negocia, vti decet vestræ conditionis hominem, meliùs cures. Nam vnicuique suo officio strenuè est laborandum vt debito tramite omnia succedant: quod spero te facturtum. Bene vale.

* * * * *

A petition exhibited to the viceroy for reformation of sundry iniuries offered our nation in Morea, as also for sundry demaundes needefull for the establishing of the traffike in those parts.

1 First that our people may be freed of such wonted molestation, as the Ianisers of Patrasso haue alwayes from time to time offered them, not regarding the kings commandements to the contrary. That they be remoued and called away from thence, and none other remaine in their place.

2 That where heretofore the kings commandements haue beene graunted to ours, that no person whatsoeuer shall forceably take from them any of their commodities, otherwise then paying them before the deliuerie thereof, for

the same in readie money, at such price as they themselues will, and sell ordinarily to others, as also that no officer whatsoeuer, of the kings or any other, shall force them to buy any commodities of that countrey, otherwise then the needfull, at their owne will and pleasure, that the said commandements not heretofore obeyed may be renued with such straight charge for the execution of the same, as is requisite for their due effect.

3 That whereas sundry exactions and oppressions be offered ours by such Byes, Saniacbies, iustices and Cadies, Ianizaries, Capagies, and others, officers of the kings comming downe into those parts, who finding there resident no other nation but only ours, will vnder the name of presents forceable take from them what they please: We do require to obuent these harmes, it may be specified by a commandement from the king to which of such his officers, presents may be giuen, and their sundry values, whereby both they and ours may rest contented, seuerely prohibiting in the said Commandement, that they take no more then that appointed them, and that no other officers but those onely specified in that commaundement, doe forcibly require of them any thing whatsoeuer.

4. That the Nadir and Customer of the port, hauing permitted our ship to lade, doe not after demand of the marchants any other then the outward custome due to the king for the same goods. And being so laden, may by them and the Cadie with other their inferiour officers be visited, requiring for the visiting no more then formerly they were accustomed to pay at their first comming. After which the said ship to depart at the Consul's pleasure, without any molestation of them, or any other officer whatsoeuer.

5. That Mahomet Chaus, sometime Nadir of Lepanto, and Azon Agon his substitute being with him may be seuerely punished to the example of others, for often and vniustly molesting our nation, contrarie to the kings commandement, which they disdainefully contemned, as also that the said Mahomet restore and pay vnto ours thirtie [Footnote: Blank in original.] for 300 sackes of currants nowe taken forcibly out of a barke, comming thither from the hither partes of Morea, to pay the king his custome, and that from hence forth; neither the said Mahomet, Azon Agon, nor any other officer or person whatsoeuer doe hinder or trouble any of ours going thither or to any other place about their affaires.

6. That whereas certaine Iews of Lepanto owing money to our marchants for commodities solde them, haue not hitherto satisfied them, notwithstanding ours had from the king a commandement for the recouery of the same debts, but fled and absented themselues out of the Towne at the comming of the same, another more forcible commaundement may be graunted ours, that for nonpaiement, whatsoeuer may be found of theirs in

goods, houses, vineyards, or any other thing, may be sold, and ours satisfied of their said debt, according to equitie and reason.

* * * * *

A commandement to Patrasso in Morea.

When this commandement shall come vnto you, know you, that the Consull of the English Nation in our port of Patrasso, hath giuen vs to vnderstand, that formerly we granted him a commandement that hauing paied once custome for the currants bought to lade in their ships, they shall not pay it again: according to which they bringing it to the port of Patrasso, informing thereof Mahomet the Nadir of Lepanto, he contrary to the tenor thereof and former order, doth againe take another custome of him, and requiring him to know why he so did contrary to our commandement, he answered vs, he tooke it not for custome, but for a present. Moreouer the sayd Consull certified vs how that the said Nadir contrary to ancient custome doth not take for the kings right as he ought currents, but will haue of the poore men money at his pleasure, and therewith buyeth currents at a very low price, which after he doth forcibly sell to vs at a much higher price, saying it is remainder of the goods of the king, and by this meanes doth hurt the poore men and do them wrong. Wherefore I command you by this my commandement, that you looke to this matter betweene this Consull, the Nadir, and this people, and do therein equally according to right. And see that our commandement in this matter be obserued in such sort, as they hauing once in the port paied full custome, do not pay it againe, neither that this Nadir do take any more money of them by the way of present, for that therein it is most certaine he doth them iniurie contrarie to the Canon. And if with you shall be found to the value of one Asper taken heretofore wrongfully of them, see it presently restored to them, without any default. And from hencefoorth see that he doe neither him nor his people wrong, but that he deale with them in all things according to our Canon, that the Consull and his hereafter haue no occasion any more to complaine here in our Court, and that the Nadir proceed in gathering corants of the people after the old order and not otherwise. This know you for certaine, and giue credit to this my commaundement, which hauing read deliuer againe into the Consuls handes. From Constantinople the yeere of Mahomet 993.

* * * * *

A commandement for Chio.

Vobis, Beg et Cadi et Ermini, qui estis in Chio, significamus: quòd serenissimæ Reginæ Maiestatis Angliæ orator, qui est in excelsa porta per literas significauit nobis, quod ex nauibus Anglicis vna nauis venisset ad portum Chio, et illinc Constantinopolim recto cursu voluisset venire, et contra priuilegium detinuistis, et non siuistis venire. Hæc prædictus orator significauit nobis; et petiuit a nobis in hoc negocio hoc mandatum, vt naues Anglicæ veniant et redeant in nostras ditiones Cæsareas. Priuilegium datum et concessum est ex parte Serenitatis Cæsareæ nostræ: et huius priuilegij copia data est sub insigni nostro: Et contra nostrum priuilegium Cæsareum quod ita agitur, quæ est causa? Quando cum hoc mandato nostro homines illorum ad vos venerint ex prædicta Anglia, si nauis venerit ad portum vestrum, et si res et merces ex naue exemerint, et vendiderint, et tricessimam secumdam partem rediderint, et res quæ manserint Constantinopolim auferre velint, patiantur: Et si aliquis contra priuilegium et articulos eius aliquid ageret, non sinatis, nec vos facite: et impediri non sinatis eos, vt rectà Constantinopolim venientes in suis negotiationibus sine molestia esse possint. Et quicunque contra hoc mandatum et priuilegium nostrum aliquid fecerit, nobis significate. Huic mandato nostro et insigni fidem adhibete. In principio mensis Decembris.

* * * * *

A commandement for Baliabadram.

Serenissimæ Reginæ Angliæ orator literis supplicatorijs in porta nostra fulgida significauit, quod Baliabadram venientes mercatores, naues et homines eorum, contra priuilegium impedirentur et molestarentur. Inter nos enim et Reginam cum foedus sit, vt mercatores, homines et naues eorum contra priuilegium impediantur aut molestentur, nullo vnquam pacto concedimus. Mandamus igitur, vt literæ nostræ Cæsareæ, quàm primum tibi exhibitæ fuerint, has in persona propria cures, secundum quod conuenit, videasque ex Anglia Baliabadram cum mercibus venientibus mercatoribus, et alias ob causas venientibus hominibus, in summa Angliensibus et nauibus eorum, et in nauibus existentibus mercibus et rebus contra foedus et priuilegium, iniuria, vis aut damnum non inferatur: sed, vt conuenit, defendas, vt naues, mercatores, et homines, nostri velut proprij subditi, liberi ab omni vi et iniuria permaneant; et negotijs suis incumbant. Et quod ilius loci Ianisseri illos impedirent, significatum est: vt illi illis nocumento sint nullo modo concedimus. Iuxta tenorem mandata huius illos commonefacias, vt nihil quicquam contra foedas faciant, ita vt nunquam huiusmodi querela huc veniat, quia quicquid acciderit, a te expostulabimus. Negligentiam postponito, et insigni Cæsareo fidem adhibeto.

* * * * *

A commaundement for Egypt.

Scito quod orator Reginæ Angliæ in porta mea existens libellum supplicem ad portam nostram mittens significauit, quod cum ex Ægypto Consul eorum abesset, Consul illic Gallicus existens, Vento nuncupatus, quamuis ante hæc tempora ne manus in Anglos mitteret mandatum nostrum fuerit datum, Angli sub vexillo et tutela nostra sunt inquiens, mandatum Cæsareum vili existimans, non cessauit perturbare Anglos. Quare scito quod Reginæ Angliæ priuilegium nostrum est datum. Iuxta illud priuilegium Anglis nulla ratione Consul Gallicus Consulatum agat, neue manus immittat, mandatum nostrum postulauit eius legatus. Quare mando, vt contra priuilegium nostrum Consul Gallicus Anglis iniuriam non inferat, neue Consulatum agat. Iudici Ægypti literæ nostræ sunt datæ: hanc ob causam mando tibi quoque, vt iuxta illud mandatum nostrum, contra priuilegium nostrum Anglis Gallum Consulatum agere nunquam patiare. Sic scito, et insigni meo fidem adhibeto.

* * * * *

A commaundement of the Grand Signior to the Cadie or Iudge of Alexandria.

The Embassadour for the Queenes most excellent Maiestie of England certified vs howe that at the death of one of their marchants in Alexandria called Edward Chamberlaine, the French Consul Vento sealing vp his fondego and chamber, tooke vnder his seale al his goods and merchandise into his power, and required our commandement that all the goods might be restored againe according to iustice vnto the Englishmen: wherefore we commaund you that hauing receiued this our commandement, you assemble those of the one part and of the other together, and if it be not passed fiue yeeres, if you haue not looked to it heretofore, now carefully looke to it, and if it be according to their Arz or certificate presented vnto vs, that the foresaid French Consull Vento hath wrongfully taken into his power the goods of the deceased English marchant vnder his seale, that then you cause him to restore all the said goods and marchandise sealed by him, and make good that which is thereof wanting vnto the English marchants: doe in this matter according to iustice, and credite this our seale.

* * * * *

A commandement to the Bassa of Alexandria.

The Embassadour for the Queenes most excellent Maiesty of England by supplication certified vs, how that notwithstanding our priuilege granted them to make Consuls in al parts of our dominions to gouerne their nation according to their owne custome and law, to defend them against all wrongs and iniuries whatsoeuer: yet that the French Consull affirming to thee that art Bassa, that they were vnder his banner, and that he should gouerne them, and ouersee their businesse, and hauing got a new priuilege, mentioning therein the English men to be vnder his banner, did by all meanes molest and trouble them, insomuch that their Consull oppressed with many iniuries fled away, and that thou which art Beglerbie didst maintaine the French Consul herein: whereupon the Embassadour required our commandement, that they might haue iustice for these iniuries: wherefore we commaunde thee that hauing receiued this our commandement, you examine diligently that this priuilege, and send the copie thereof hither, and if it be found that the French Consull Vento hath by subtilitie got the aforesaid priuilege written, that you then see him punished, and suffer not hereafter the French or Venetian Consuls to intermeddle with their businesse. Obey this our commaundement, and giue credit to the seale.

* * * * *

A commaundement to the Byes, and Cadies of Metelin and Rhodes, and to all the Cadies and Byes in the way to Constantinople.

To the Saniakbies of Rhodes and Metelin, to the Saniacbies bordering on the sea coast, and to the Cadies in Rhodes and Metelin, and to the Ermins in the other ports and coastes. This commaundement comming to you, know that the Embassadour of England required of vs our commaundement that their ships comming to Chio, and from thence to Constantinople; no man should hurt them or offer any violence, either in the way on the sea or on the land, or in the portes. I haue commaunded, that their ships comming to any of the said places or ports with marchandise, if they themselues will, they may sell their commodities, and as much, and as little as they will, and if it be in a place where custome was not woont to be taken, hauing taken the custome due by the olde Canon you suffer them not to bee iniuried, either in the way, portes, or other places, but that they may come in quietnesse to Constantinople, and certifie vs of those that be disobedient to our commaundement, and giue credite to our seale. And hauing read this our commandement, giue it to them againe.

* * * * *

A commaundement for Aleppo.

When my letters shal come vnto you, know that the Queene of England her Embassador by supplication certified how that before this time we had giuen our commaundement that the summe of 70 ducats, and other marchandize belonging to one William Barret in Aleppo, now dead, saying he was a Venetian, should be giuen to the Venetians. And if they did find that he was not a Venetian, my will was that they should send all his goods and marchandize to our port into my treasuries. But because that man was an Englishman, the Embassadour required that the sayde goods might not be diminished, but that they might be restored to one of their Englishmen.

This businesse was signified vnto vs in the nine hundred ninety and fourth yere of Mahomet, and in the moneth of May the 10. day. This businesse pertaineth to the Englishmen, who haue in their handes our priuilege, according to which priuilege being in their hands let this matter be done. Against this priuilege do nothing, aske nothing of them, but restore to euery one his goods. And I command that when my commandement shall come vnto you, you doe according to it. And if it be according as the Ambassadour certified, that they haue the priuilege, peruse the same, looke that nothing be committed against it and our league, and let none trouble them contrarie to it, restore them their goods according to iustice, and take heede diligently in this businesse: if another strange marchant be dead, and his goods and marchandize be taken, if he be neither Venetian, nor Englishman, let not his goods perish among you. Before this time one of our Chauses called Cerkes Mahomet chaus was sent with our commaundement to sende the money and marchandize of a dead marchant to our port, and hitherto no letters or newes is come of this matter, for which you shall be punished. Wherefore beware, and if he that is dead be neither Venetian nor Englishman in veritie, doe not loose the goods of the said dead marchant, vnder the name of a Venetian or Englishman, doe not to the discommoditie of my treasurie, for after it will be hard to recouer it.

* * * * *

The voyage of Master Henry Austell by Venice and thence to Ragusa ouer land, and so to Constantinople: and from thence by Moldauia, Polonia, Silesia and Germanie to Hamburg, &c.

The 9. of Iune we tooke shipping at Harewich and the next day landed at the Ramekins in the Isle of Walcheren with very stormy weather, and that night went to Middleburch in the same Island.

The twelft we tooke shipping for Holland, and the 13. we landed at Schiedam: and the same day went to Delft by boat, and so that night to the Hage.

The 17. we tooke shipping at Amsterdam, and the 18. we landed at Enckhuysen.

The 19. we tooke shipping and by the Zuydersee we passed that day the Vlie, and so into the maine sea; And the next day we entred into the riuer of Hamburg called the Elbe.

The 21. we came to anker in the same riuer before a towne of the bishop of Breme called Staden, where they pay a certaine toll, and specially for wine, and so that night wee landed at Hamburg, where we stayde three dayes.

The 24. wee departed from Hamburg in the company of Edward Parish Marchant, and that day wee baited at Wyntson, and so ouer the heathes we left Lunenburg on the left hand, and trauailed all that night.

The 25. we met with Master Sanders vpon the heathes, and passed by a towne
of the duke of Lunenburg called Geftherne, [Footnote: Gifhorn, on the river
Aller.] and from thence through many waters, wee lay that night within an English mile of Brunswig.

The 27. we lay at Halberstat, which is a great towne subiect to the bishop of that towne.

The 28. we baited at Erinsleiben: and there wee entred into the duke of Saxon his countrey: and the same night we lay at a town called Eisleben, where Martine Luther was borne. [Footnote: 10th November, 1483.]

The 29. we passed by Mansfield, where there are many Copper mines: and so that night went to Neuburg vpon the riuer of Sala; [Footnote: Saale.] and at that time there was a great faire.

30. we baited at a proper towne called Iena vpon the same riuer and the same night wee lay at Cone vpon that riuer.

The first of Iuly we baited at Salfeld: and the same day we entred first into the great woods of fine trees, and that night to Greuandal.

The second to dinner to Neustat.

The 3. day to dinner at Bamberg: and before wee came to the towne wee passed the riuer of Mayne that runneth towards Arnfurt, and that night to Forchaim.

The 4. we came to Nurenberg, and there stayed two dayes.

The 6. to bed to Blayfield. [Footnote: Pleinfeld.]

The 7. we passed without Weissenburg to dinner at Monhaim, and that night we passed the riuer of Danubius at Tonewertd, [Footnote: Donauwerth.] and so to be to Nurendof.

The 8. we came to Augspurg, otherwise called Augusta, vpon the riuer of Lech.

The 9. we lay at Landsberg vpon the said riuer, in the duke of Bauars countrey,

The 10. to dinner at Suanego, [Footnote: Shongau.] and that night to Hambers [Footnote: Amergan.] against the mountains, where the small toyes be made.

The 11. to dinner to Parcberk, [Footnote: Partenkirch.] and that night to Sefelt in the Archduke of Austria his countrey.

The 12. to dinner at Inspruck, and that night to bed at Landeck, where there is a toll, and it is the place where Charles the fift and his brother Ferdinand did meet. And there is a table of brasse with Latine letters in memorie thereof.

The 13. we passed by Stizen, and dined at Prisena, and so that night to Clusen. [Footnote: Autstell thus crossed the Alps by Trent and not by the Brenner, which would seem the most direct route to Venice.]

The 14. to dinner at Bolsan and to bed at Neumark, and by the way we passed the dangerous place, where so many murthers haue bene committed.

The 15. to dinner at Trent: That day we entred the borders of Italy, that night to Lenigo. [Footnote: Probably a misprint for Levigo.]

The 16. to dinner at Grigno, where the last toll of the Emperour is: and so we came by Chursa, which is a streight passage. And the keeper thereof is drawne vp by a cord into his holde. And that night we went to Capana to bed in the countrey of the Venetians.

The 17. to dinner at castle Franco: by the way we stayed at Taruiso, and there tooke coche, and that night came to Mestre to bed.

The 18. in the morning we came to Venice, and there we stayed 15. dayes. In which time the duke of Venice called Nicholas de Ponte died, and we saw his burial. The Senators were continually shut vp together, as the maner is, to chuse a new duke, which was not yet chosen when we departed from thence.

The 2. of August at night wee did embarke our selues vpon the Frigate of Cattaro, an hauen neere Ragusa.

The 3. we came to a towne in Istria called Citta noua.

The 4. we came to Parenzo, and so that night to Forcera of the bishop.

The 5. we passed by Rouigno: and a litle beyond we met with 3. Galies of the Venetians: we passed in the sight of Pola; and the same day passed the gulfe that parteth Istria from Dalmatia. [Footnote: Gulf of Quarnero.]

The 6. of August we came to Zara in Dalmatia, a strong towne of the Venetians: and so that night to Sebenico, which standeth in a marueilous goodly hauen, with a strong castle at the entrie thereof.

The 7. we came to Lezina, and went not on shoore, but traueiled all night.

The 8. we passed by a very well seated towne called Curzola, which standeth in an island of that name.

The 9. in the morning betimes we landed at Ragusa, and there stayed three daies, where we found many friendly gentlemen.

The 11 being prouided of a Ianizarie we departed from Ragusa in the company of halfe a dosen Marchants of that towne: and within 6 miles we entred into the countrey of Seruia. So trauailing in barren and craggie mountaines for the space of foure dayes, wee came by a small Towne of the Turkes called Chiernisa, being the 14. of the moneth; and there wee parted from the Marchants.

The 16. we dined in a Cauarsara hi a Towne called Focea, [Marginal note: Or, Fochia.] [Footnote: Fotchia.] being then greatly infected with the plague.

The 17. we lay by a Towne called Taslizea. [Footnote: Tachlidcha.]

The 20. we came to Nouibazar.

The 21. we parted from thence, trauailing stil in a countrey very ill inhabited, and lying in the fields.

The 22. we passed within sight of Nicea. [Sidenote: Or, Nissa.]

The 23. we passed in sight of another towne called Circui: [Footnote: Sharkei.] and about those places wee began to leaue the mountaines, and to enter into a very faire and fertile countrey, but as euill inhabited as the other, or worse.

The 27. we came to Sophia, where wee stayed three dayes, being our Ianizaries home: and by good chance we lay in a Marchants house of Ragusa, that came in company with vs from Nouibazar; and also wee had in company, euer since wee came from Focea, a Turke which was a very good fellow, and he kept with vs till we came very neere Constantinople.

The first of September we came to Philippopoli, which seemeth to be an ancient towne, and standeth vpon the riuer of Stanuch. [Footnote: The Maritza.]

The 4. we came to Andrinopoli, a very great and ancient towne, which standeth in a very large and champion [Footnote: Flat—"the Champion fields with corn are seen," (Poor Robin, 1694).] countrey, and there the great Turks mother doth lye, being a place, where the Emperours of the Turkes were wont to lye very much.

The 5. we lay in one of the great Cauarzaras that were built by Mahomet Bassha with so many goodly commodities.

The 6. we lay in another of them.

The 8. we came to Siliueri, [Footnote: Silivri.] which by report was the last towne that remained Christian.

The 9. of September wee arriued at the great and most stately Citie of Constantinople, which for the situation and proude seate thereof, for the beautifull and commodious hauens, and for the great and sumptuous buildings of their Temples, which they call Moschea, is to be preferred before all the Cities of Europe. And there the Emperour of the Turkes then liuing, whose name was Amurat, kept his Court and residence, in a marueilous goodly place, with diuers gardens and houses of pleasure, which is at the least two English miles in compasse, and the three parts thereof ioyne vpon the sea: and on the Northeast part of the Citie on the other side of the water ouer against the Citie is the Towne of Pera, where the most part of the Christians do lye. And there also wee did lye. And on the North part of the saide Towne is the Arsenal, where the Galies are built and doe remaine: And on the Southside is all the Ordinance, artilerie, and houses of munition. Note that by the way as wee came from Ragusa to Constantinople, wee left on our right hand the Countreys of Albania, and Macedonia, and on the left hande the countreys of Bosnia, Bulgaria, and the riuer of Danubius.

The 14. of September was the Turkes Beyram [Footnote: Bairam is the designation of the only two festivals annually celebrated by the Turks and other Mohammedan nations. The first is also called *Id-at-Fitr*, "the festival of the interruption," alluding to the breaking of the universal fast which is rigorously observed during the month Ramazan. It commences from the moment when the new moon of the month Shewel becomes visible, the appearance of which, as marking the termination of four weeks of abstinence and restraint is looked for and watched with great eagerness. The second festival, denominated *Id-al-Asha* or *Kurban Bairam*, "the festival of the sacrifices," is instituted in commemoration of Abraham offering his son Isaac and is celebrated seventy days after the former, on the 10th of Zulhijjah, the day appointed for slaying the victims by the pilgrims at Mecca. The festival lasts four days. At Constantinople the two bairams are celebrated with much pomp. Amurath III, son of Selim II.] that is, one of their chiefest feastes.

The 16. we went to the blacke Sea called Pontus Euxinus, and there vpon a rocke we sawe a piller of white Marble that was set vp by Pompeius: and from thence we passed to the other side of the water, vpon the shore of Asia and there we dined.

The 25. we departed from Constantinople.

The 29. we came to an ancient Towne called Cherchisea, that is to say, fourtie Churches, which in the olde time was a very great City, now full of scattered buildiugs.

The 4. of October wee came to Prouaz, one dayes iourney distant from Varna vpon the Blacke Sea.

The 9. we came to Saxi [Footnote: Tsakchi, S. E. of Galatz.] vpon the riuer of Danubius.

The 10. we passed the said riuer which in that place is about a mile ouer, and then we entered into the countrey Bogdania [Marginal note: Or, Moldauia]: they are Christians but subiects to the Turkes.

The 12. we came to Palsin vpon the riuer Prut. [Footnote: Faltsi.]

The 14: wee came to Yas [Footnote: Jassy.] the principall Towne of Bogdania, where Peter the Vayuoda prince of that Countrey keepeth his residence, of whom wee receuied great courtesie, and of the gentlemen of his Court: And he caused vs to be safe conducted through his said Countrey, and conueyed without coste.

The 17. we came to Stepanitze. [Footnote: Stephanesti, on the frontier between Moldavia and Bessarabia.]

The 19. we came to Zotschen, [Footnote: Chotin.] which is the last towne of
Bogdania vpon the riuer of Neister, that parteth the said countrey from Podolia.

The 20. we passed the riuer of Nyester and came to Camyenetz [Footnote: on the river Smokriz.] in the countrey of Podolia, subiect to the king of Poland: this is one of the strongest Townes by nature and situation that can be seene.

The 21. we came to Skala. [Footnote: A market town on the Podhoree, S. of
Zeryz.]

The 22. to Slothone, or Scloczow. [Footnote: Czorkorw, on the Sered.]

The 24. to Leopolis [Footnote: Lemberg, also called Leopol.] which is in Russia alba, and so is the most part of the countrey betwixt Camyenetz and it. And it is a towne very well built, well gouerned, full of trafique and plentifull: and there we stayed fiue dayes.

The 30. we baited at Grodecz, and that night at Vilna [Footnote: Probably Sandova—Wisznia.]

The 31. we dined at Mostiska, [Footnote: Mosciska.] and that night at Rodmena. [Footnote: Radymno.]

The first of Nouember in the morning before day wee passed without the Towne of Iaroslaw, where they say is one of the greatest faires in all Poland, and chiefly of horses, and that night to Rosdnoska. [Footnote: Rosnialov.]

The second to diner at Lanczut, [Footnote: Lanaif.] at night to Retsbou. [Footnote: Rzeszow.]

The thirde to Sendxizow, [Footnote: Sedziszow.] at night to Tarnow, and that night wee mette with the Palatine Laski.

The fourth to Vonuez, [Footnote: Woinicz.] and that night to Brytska. [Footnote: Brzesko.]

The fift to Kuhena. [Footnote: Perhaps, Kozmice.]

The 6. to Cracouia the principall Citie of all Poland: at which time the King was gone to Lituania: for he doeth make his residence one yeere in Poland, and the other in Lituania. Cracouia standeth on the riuer of Vistula.

The 9. wee departed from Cracouia, and that night wee came to a village hard by a Towne called Ilkusch, [Footnote: Olkusz.] where the leade Mines are.

The 10. wee passed by a Towne called Slawkow: where there are also leade Mines, and baited that day at Bendzin, [Footnote: Bedzin.] which is the last tome of Poland towards Silesia; and there is a toll.

[Sidenote: Salt digged out of mountaines in Poland] Note that all the Countreys of Poland, Russia alba, Podolia, Bogdania, and diuers other Countreys adioyning vnto them, doe consume no other salt but such as is digged in Sorstyn mountaine neere to Cracouia which is as hard as any stone; it is very good, and goeth further then any other salt. That night we lay at Bitom, [Footnote: Beuthen.] which is the first Towne of Silesia.

The 12. we passed by a great towne called Strelitz, and that night we lay at Oppelen vpon the riuer of Odera.

The 13. we passed by Schurgasse, [Footnote: Schurgast.] and that night wee lay without the towne of Brigk: [Footnote: Brieg.] for wee coulde not bee suffered to come in by reason of the plague which was in those partes in diuers Townes.

The 14. we passed by Olaw, [Footnote: Oblau.] and that night we came to the Citie of Breslaw, which is a faire towne, great, well built and well seated vpon the riuer of Odera.

The 16. we baited at Neumargt. [Footnote: Neumark.]

The 17. wee passed by Lignizt and by Hayn, [Footnote: Hainau.] and that night to Buntzel. [Footnote: Buntzlau.]

The 18. we passed by Naumburg through Gorlitz vpon the riuer of Neiss, and that night lay without Reichenbach.

The 19. wee passed by Baudzen and Cannitz, [Footnote: Camenz.] and that night to Rensperg.

The 20. we passed by Hayn, by Strelen, were we should haue passed the riuer of Elbe, but the boate was not there, so that night we lay at a towne called Mulberg.

The 21. we passed the said riuer, wee went by Belgern, by Torga, by Dumitch: and at night to Bretch.

The 22. wee passed the Elbe againe at Wittenberg, which is a very strong towne, with a good Vniuersitie: and that day we passed by Coswig.

The 23. wee passed through Zerbst in the morning, and that night at Magdeburg, a very strong Towne, and well gouerned as wee did heare. The most part of the Countrey, after wee were come one dayes iourney on this side Breslawe to this place, belongeth to the Duke of Saxon.

The 24. wee passed by a castle of the Marques of Brandenburg called Wolmerstat, and that night we lay at Garleben.

The 25. wee lay at Soltwedel.

The 26. at Berg.

The 27. we baited at Lunenborg, and that night we lay at Winson.

The 28. we came to Homborg, and there stayed one weeke.

The 5. of December wee departed from Hamborg, and passed the Elbe by boate being much frosen, and from the riuer went on foote to Boxtchoede, being a long Dutch mile off, and there we lay; and from thence passed ouer land to Emden.

Thence hauing passed through Friseland and Holland, the 25. being Christmas day in the morning we came to Delft: where wee found the right honourable the Earle of Leicester with a goodly company of Lords, knights, gentlemen, and souldiers.

The 28. at night to Roterodam.

The 29. to the Briel, and there stayed eight dayes for passage.

The fift of Ianuary we tooke shipping.

The 7. we landed at Grauesend, and so that night at London with the helpe of almightie God.

* * * * *

The Turkes passeport or safeconduct for Captaine Austell, and Iacomo Manuchio.

Know thou which art Voyuoda of Bogdania, and Valachia, and other our officers abiding and dwelling on the way by which men commonly passe into Bogdania, and Valachia, that the Embassador of England hauing two English gentlemen desirous to depart for England, the one named Henry Austel, and the other Iacomo de Manuchio, requested our hignesse letters of Safeconduct to passe through our dominions with one seruant to attende on them. Wherefore wee straightly charge you and all other our seruants by whom they shall passe, that hauing receiued this our commandement, you haue diligent care and regard that they may haue prouided for them in this their iourney (for their money) all such necessary prouision as shalbe necessary for themselues and their horses, in such sort as they may haue no cause hereafter to complaine of you. And if by chaunce they come vnto any place, where they shal stand in feare either of their persons or goods, that then you carefully cause them to bee guarded with your men, and to be conducted through all suspected places, with sufficient company; But haue great regard that they conuey not out of our countrey any of pur seruiceable horses. Obey our commandement, and giue credite to this our Seale.

* * * * *

A Passeport of the Earle of Leicester for Thomas Foster gentleman trauailing to Constantinople.

Robertus Comes Leicestriæ, baro de Denbigh, ordinum Garterij et Sancti Michaelis eques auratus, Serenissimæ Reginæ Angliæ a Secretioribus consilijs, et magister equorum, dux et capitaneus generalis exercitus eiusdem Regiæ maiestatis in Belgio, et gubernator generalis Hollandiæ, Zelandiæ, et prouinciarum vnitarum et associatarum, omnibus, ad quos præsentes literæ peruenerint, salutem. Cùm lator præsentium Thomas Foster nobilis Anglus necessarijs de causis hinc Constantinopolim profecturus sit, et inde ad nos quanta potest celeritate reuersurus: petimus ab omnibus et singulis Regibus, principibus, nobilibus, magistratibus, et alijs, mandent et permittant dicto Thomæ cum duobus famulis liberum transitum per eorum ditiones et territoria sine detentione aut impedimento iniusto, et prouideri sibi de necessarijs iustum precium reddenti, ac aliter conuenienter et humaniter tractari, vt occasiones eius eundi et redeundi requirent: Sicut nos Maiestates, Serenitates, Celsitudines, et dominationes vestræ paratos inuenietis, vt vestratibus in similibus casibus gratum similiter faciamus.

Datum in castris nostris Duisburgi, decimo die Septembris, anno 1586. stylo veteri.

* * * * *

The returne of Master William Harborne from Constantinople ouer land to London 1588.

I departed from Constantinople with 30. persons of my suit and family the 3. of August. Passing through the Countries of Thracia, now called Romania the great, Valachia and Moldauia, where ariuing the 5. of September I was according to the Grand Signior his commandement very courteously interteined by Peter his positiue prince, a Greeke by profession, with whom was concluded that her Maiesties subiects there trafiquing should pay but three vpon the hundreth, which as well his owne Subiects as all other nations answere: [Sidenote: The letters of the Prince of Moldauia to the Queene. Letters of the Chanceler of Poland to the Queene.] whose letters to her Maiestie be extant. Whence I proceeded into Poland, where the high Chanceler sent for mee the 27. of the same moneth. And after most honorable intertainment imparted with me in secret maner the late passed and present occurrents of that kingdome, and also he writ to her Maiestie.

Thence I hasted vnto Elbing, where the 12. of October I was most friendly welcomed by the Senate of that City, whom I finde and iudge to be faithfully deuoted to her Maiesties seruice, whose letters likewise vnto the same were presented me. No lesse at Dantzik the 27. of that moneth I was courteously receiued by one of the Buroughmasters accompanied with two others of the Senate, and a Ciuil doctor their Secretarie. After going through the land of Pomer I rested one day at Stetin, where, for that the duke was absent, nothing ensued. At Rostoke I passed through the Citie without any stay, and at Wismar receiued like friendly greeting as in the other places: but at Lubeck, for that I came late and departed early in the morning, I was not visited. At Hamburg the 19. of Nouember, and at Stoad the ninth of December in like maner I was saluted by a Boroughmaster and the Secretarie, and in all these places they presented mee sundry sorts of their best wine and fresh fish, euery of them with a long discourse, congratulating, in the names of their whole Senate, her Maiesties victory ouer the Spaniard, and my safe returne, concluding with offer of their ready seruice to her future disposing. Yet the Dantziks after my departure thence caused the Marchants to pay custome for the goods they brought with them in my company, which none other towne neither Infidels nor Christians on the way euer demanded. And notwithstanding the premisses, I was most certainly informed of sundry of our nation there resident that most of the Hansetowns vpon the sea coasts, especially Dantzik, Lubeck, and Hamborough haue laden and were shipping for Spaine, great prouision of corne, cables, ropes, powder, saltpeter, hargubusses, armour, iron, leade, copper, and all other munition seruing for the warre. Whereupon I gather their fained courtesie proceeded rather for feare then of any good affection vnto her Maiesties seruice, Elbing and Stoad onely excepted, which of duetie for their commoditie I esteemed well affected.

* * * * *

The priuilege of Peter the Prince of Moldauia graunted to the English Marchants.

Petrus Dei gratia princeps Valachiæ et Moldauiæ; significamus præsentibus, vniuersis et singulis quorum interest ac intererit, quòd cum magnifico domino Guilielmo Hareborne oratore Serenissimæ ac potentissimæ dominæ, dominæ Elizabethæ Dei gratia Angliæ, Franciæ, ac Hiberniæ Reginæ apud Serenissimum ac potentissimum Turcarum Imperatorem hanc constitutionem fecerimus: Nimirùm vt dehinc suæ Serenitatis subditis, omnibúsque mercatoribus integrum sit hîc in prouincia nostra commorandi, conuersandi, mercandi, vendendi, contrahendíque, imo omnia exercendi, quæ mercaturæ ac vitæ humanæ societas vsúsque requirit, sine vlla alicuius contradictione, aut inhibitione: saluo ac integro tamen iure Telonij nostri: hoc est, vt a singulis rebus centum ducatorum pretij, tres numerent. Quod ratum ac firmum constitutione nostra haberi volumus. In cuius rei firmius testimonium, sigillum nostrum appressum est. Actum in castris nostris die 27. mensis Augusti, anno Domini 1588.

The same in English.

Peter by the grace of God prince of Valachia and Moldauia; we signifie by these presents to all and singuler persons, whom it doth or shall concerne, that we haue made this agreement with the worthy gentleman William Hareborne Ambassador of the right high and mighty prince, the Lady Elizabeth by the grace of God Queene of England, France and Ireland, with the most puissant and mightie Emperour of the Turkes: To witte, that from hencefoorth it shalbe lawfull for her highnesse subiects and all her Marchants, to remaine, conuerse, buy, sel, bargaine and exercise all such things, as the trade of marchandise, and humane societie and vse requireth, without any hinderance or let: the right of our Custome alwayes reserued; That is, that they pay three ducats vpon all such things as amount to the price of one hundred ducats. Which by this our ordinance we command to be surely and firmely obserued; For the more assured testimony whereof our seale is hereunto annexed. Giuen in our Campe the 27. of the moneth of August in the yeere of our Lord 1588.

* * * * *

The letters of Sinan Bassa chiefe counsellour to Sultan Murad Can the Grand Signior, to the sacred Maiestie of Elizabeth Queene of England, shewing that vpon her request, and for her sake especially, hee graunted peace vnto the King and kingdome Of Poland.

Gloriosissima et splendore fulgidissima foeminarum, selectíssima Princeps magnanimorum IESVM sectantium, regni inclyti Angliæ Regina Serenissima Elizibetha, moderatrix rerum et negotiorum omnium plebis et familiæ Nazarenorum sapientissima; Origo splendoris et gloriæ dulcissima; nebes pluuiarum gratissima, heres et domina beatitudinis et gloriæ regni inclyti Angliæ; ad quam omnes supplices confugiunt, incrementum omnium rerum et actionum Serenitatis vestræ beatissimum, exitusque foelicissimos à Creatore omnipotente optantes, mutuáque et perpetua familiaritate nostra digna vota et laudes sempiternas offerentes: Significamus Ser. vestræ amicissimè; Quia sunt anni aliquot, à quibus annis potentissima Cæsarea celsitudo bella ineffabilia cum Casul-bas, Principe nempe Persarum gessit; ratione quorum bellorum in partes alias bellum mouere noluit, ob eamque causam in partibus Poloniæ latrones quidam Cosaci nuncupati, et alij facinorosi in partibus illis existentes, subditos Cæsaris potentissimi turbare et infestare non desierunt. Nunc autem partibus Persicis compositis et absolutis, in partibus Poloniæ et alijs partibus exurgentes facinorosos punire constituens, Beglerbego Græciæ exercitu aliquo adiuncto, et Principi Tartarorum madato Cæsaris misso, anno proximè præterito pars aliqua Regni Poloniæ infestata, turbata et deuastata fuit, et Cosaci alijque facinorosi iuxta merita sua puniti fuerunt. Quo rex Poloniæ viso duos legatos ad Cæsaream celsitudinem mittens, quòd facinorosos exquirere, et poena perfecta punire, et ab annis multis ad portam Cæsareæ celsitudinis missum munus augere vellet, significauit. Cæsarea autem celsitudo (cui Creator omnipotens tantam suppeditauit potentiam, et quæ omnes supplices exaudire dignata est) supplicatione Regis Poloniæ non accepta, iterùm in regem Poloniæ exercitum suum mittere, et Creatoris omnipotentis auxilio regnum eius subuertere constituerat. Verum Legato Serenitatis vestræ in porta beata et fulgida Cæsareæ celsitudinis residente sese interponente. Et quòd Serenitati vestræ ex partibus Poloniæ, fruges, puluis, arbores nauium, tormenta, et alia necessaria suppediterantur significante, et pacem pro regno et rege Poloniæ petente, neuè regnum Poloniæ ex parte Cæsareæ celsitudinis turbaretur vel infestaretur intercedente, Serenitatisque vestræ hanc singularem esse voluntatem exponente, Legati serenitatis vestræ significatio et intercessio cùm Cæsareæ celsitudini significata fuisset, In fauorem serenitatis vestræ, cui omnis honos et gratia debetur, iuxta modum prædictum, vt Cosaci facinoros exquirantur et poena perfecta puniantur, aut ratione muneris aliquantuli eorum delicta condonentur, hac inquam conditione literæ Cæsareæ celsitudinis ad Regem Poloniæ sunt datæ. Si autem ex parte Serenitatis vestræ foedus et pax sollicitata non fuisset, nulla ratione Cæsara celsitudo foedus cum regno Poloniæ inijsset. In fauorem autem Serenitatis vestræ regno et Regi Poloniæ singularem gratiam Cæsarea celsitudo exhibuit. Quod tàm Serenitas vestra, quàm etiam Rex et regnum Poloniæ sibi certò persuadere debent. Serenitatem vestram benè foelicissiméque valere cupimus. Datum Constantinopoli in fine mensis Sabaum nuncupati, Anno prophetæ nostri sacrati Mahumeddi nongentesimo, nonagesimo, octauo. IESV vero Anno millesimo quingentesimo nonagesimo, die duodecimo mensis Iunij.

The same in English.

Most glorious, and the most resplendent of women, most select Princesse, most gratious Elizabeth Queene of the valiant followers of Iesus in the famous kingdom of England, most wise gouernesse of all the affaires and bussinesses of the people and family of the Nazarens, most sweet fountaine of brightnesse and glory, most acceptable cloud of raine, inheritresse and Ladie of the blessednesse and glory of the renowmed kingdome of England, to whom in humble wise all men offer their petitions: wishing of the almightie Creator most happie increase and prosperous successe vnto all your Maiesties affaires and actions, and offering vp mutuall and perpetuall vowes worthy of our familiarity; with eternall prayses: In most friendly manner we signifie vnto your princely Highnesse, that certaine yeeres past the most mightie Cesarlike maiestie of the Grand Signor waged vnspeakeable warres with Casul-bas the Prince of the Persians, in regarde of which warres he would not goe in battell against any other places; and for that cause certaine theeues in the partes of Polonia called Cosacks, and other notorious persons liuing in the same partes ceased not to trouble and molest the subiects of our most mightie Emperour. But now hauing finished and brought to some good issue his affaires in Persia, determining to punish the saide malefactors of Poland, and for that purpose committing an army vnto the Beglerbeg of Grecia, and the yeere last past, sending his imperiall commaundement vnto the Prince of the Tartars, he hath forraged, molested, and layed waste some part of the kingdome of Poland, and the Cosacks and other notorious offenders haue receiued condigne punishment. Which the king of Poland perceiuing sent two Embassadours to his imperiall Highnesse signifying, that he would hunt out the said malefactors, and inflict most seuere punishments vpon them, and also that he would better his gift, which he hath for many yeeres heretofore ordinarily sent vnto the porch of his imperiall Highnesse. Howbeit his imperiall maiestie (vpon whom the almightie creator hath bestowed so great power, and who vouchsafeth to giue eare vnto all humble suppliants) reiecting the supplication of the King of Poland, determined againe to send his armie against the said king, and by the helpe of the Almightie creator, vtterly to subuert and ouerthrowe his kingdome. But your Maiesties Embassadour resident in the blessed and glorious porch of his imperiall Highnesse interposing himselfe as a mediatour, signifying that from the partes of Poland you were furnished with corne, gun-powder, mastes of ships, guns, and other necessaries, and crauing peace on the behalfe of the kingdome and king of Poland, and making intercession, that the said king might not be molested nor troubled by the meanes of the Grand Signior, and declaring that this was your Maiesties most earnest desire; so soone as the report and intercession of your Maiesties Embassadour was signified vnto the Grand Signor, for your sake, vnto whom all honour and fauourable regard is due, vpon the condition aforesaid, namely, that the wicked Cosacks might be sought out and grieuously punished, or that their offences might be remitted for the value of some small gift, vpon this condition (I say) the letters of his imperiall Highnesse were sent vnto the king of Poland. Howbeit had not this conclusion of league and amitie beene sollicited on the behalfe of your Maiestie, his imperiall Highnesse would neuer haue vouchsafed the same vnto the kingdome of Poland. But for your Maiesties sake his imperiall Higrrnesse hath exhibited this so singular a fauour vnto the said king and kingdome of Poland. And hereof your Maiestie and the king of Poland ought cenainely to be perswaded. We wish your Maiestie most happily and well to fare. Giuen at Constantinople in the ende of the moneth called Sabaum, in the yeere of our sacred prophet Mahomet 998, and in the yeere of Iesus 1590, the 12 of Iune.

* * * * *

A letter written by the most high and mighty Empresse the wife of the Grand Signior Sultan Murad Can to the Queenes Maiesty of England, in the yeere of our Lord, 1594.

Il principio del ragionamento nostro sia scrittura perfetta nelle quatro parte del mondo, in nome di quello che ha creato indifferentemente tante infinite creature, che non haueuano anima ni persona, e di quello che fa girar gli noue cieli, e che la terra sette volte vna sopra l'altra fa firmar; Signor e Re senza vicere, e che non ha comparacion alla sua creatione ne opera, e vno senza precio, adorato incomparabilmente, l'altissimo Dio creatore; che non ha similitudine, si come è descrito dalli propheti: a la cui grandessa non si arriue, e alla perfettione sua compiuta non si oppone, e quel omnipotente creatore e cooperatore; alla grandessa del quale inchinano tutti li propheti; fra quali il maggior e che ha ottenuto gracia, horto del paradiso, ragi dal sole, amato del altssimo Dio e Mahomet Mustaffa, al qual e suoi adherenti e imitatori sia perpetua pace: alla cui sepultura odorifera si fa ogni honore.

Quello che è imperator de sette climati, e delle quatro parti del mondo, inuincibile Re di Græcia, Agiamia, Vngeria, Tartaria, Valachia, Rossia, Turchia, Arabia, Bagdet, Caramania, Abessis, Giouasir, Siruan, Barbaria, Algieri, Franchia, Coruacia, Belgrado, &c. sempre felicissimo e de dodeci Auoli possessor della corona, e della stirpe di Adam, fin hora Imperator, figliolo del'Imperatore, conseruato de la diuina prouidenza, Re di ogni dignita e honore, Sultan Murat, che Il Signor Dio sempre augmenti le sue forzze, e padre di quello a cui aspetta la corona imperiale, horto e cypresso mirabile, degno della sedia regale, e vero herede del commando imperiale, dignissimo Mehemet Can, filiol de Sultan Murat Can, che dio compisca li suoi dissegni, e alunga li suoi giorni felici: Dalla parte della madre del qual si scriue la presente alla serenissima e gloriosissima fra le prudentissime Donne, e eletta fra li triomlanti sotto il standardo di Iesu Christo, potentissima e ricchissima regitrice, e al mondo singularissima fra il feminil sesso, la serenissima Regina d'Ingilterra, che segue le vestigie de Maria virgine, il fine della qoale sia con bene e perfettione, secondo il suo desiderio. Le mando vna salutacion di pace, cosi honorata, che non basta tutta la copia di rosignoli con le loro musiche ariuare, non che con questa carta: l'amore singulare che e conciputo fra noi, e simile a vn'horto di Vccelli vagi; che il Signor Dio la faci degna di saluacione, e il fine suo sia tale, che in questo mondo e nel' futuro sia con pace. Doppo comparsi li suoi honorati presenti da la sedia de la Serenita vostra, sapera che sono capitati in vna hora che ogni punto e stato vna consolation di lungo tempo, per occasione del Ambassadore di vostra serenita venuto alla felice porta del Imperatore, con tanto nostro contento, quanto si posso desiderare, e con quello vna lettera di vostra serenetà, che ci estata presentata dalli nostri Eunuchi con gran honore; liccarta de la quale odoraua di camfora e ambracano, et l'inchiostro di musco perfetto, et quella peruenuta in nostro mano tutta la continenza di essa a parte ho ascoltato intentamente. Quello che hora si conuiene e, che correspondente alla nostra affecione, in tutto quello che si aspetta allie cose attenente alli paesi che sono sotto il commando di vostra serenità, lei non manchi di sempre tenermi, dato noticia, che in tutto quello che li occorerà, Io possi compiacerla; de quello che fra le nostre serenità e conueniente, accioche quelle cose che si interprenderano, habino il desiderato buon fine; perche Io saro sempre ricordeuole al altissimo Imperatore delle occorenze di vostra serenita, per che sia in ogni occasione compiaciuta. La pace sia con vostra serenita, e con quelli che seguitano dretamente la via di Dio. Scritta al primi dell luna di Rabie Liuol, anno del profeta 1002, et di Iesu 1594.

The same in English.

Let the beginning of our discourse be a perfect writing in the foure parts of the world, in the name of him which hath indifferently created such infinite numbers of creatures, which had neither soule nor body, and of him which mooueth the nine heauens, and stablisheth the earth seuen times one aboue another, which is Lord and king without any deputy, who hath no comparison to his creation and worke, and is one inestimable, worshipped without all comparison, the most high God, the creator, which hath nothing like vnto him, according as he is described by the Prophets, to whose power no man can attaine, and whose absolute perfection no man may controll; and that omnipotent creatour and fellow-worker, to whose Maiesty all the Prophets submit themselues, among whom the greatest, and which hath obtained greatest fauour, the garden of Paradise, the beame of the Sunne, the beloued of the most high God is Mahomet Mustafa, to whom and to his adherents and followers be perpetuall peace, to whose fragrant sepulture all honour is performed. He which is emperour of the seuen climats and of the foure parts of the world, the inuincible king of Graecia, Agiamia, Hungaria, Tartaria, Valachia, Rossia, Turchia, Arabia, Bagdet, Caramania, Abessis, Giouasir, Siruan, Barbaria, Alger, Franchia, Coruacia, Belgrade, &c. alwayes most happy, and possessour of the crowne from twelue of his ancestours; and of the seed of Adam, at this present emperour, the sonne of an emperour, preserued by the diuine prouidence, a king woorthy of all glory and honour, Sultan Murad, whose forces the Lord God alwayes increase, and father of him to whom the imperiall crowne is to descend, the paradise and woonderfull tall cypresse, worthy of the royall throne, and true heire of the imperiall authority, most woorthy Mehemet Can, the sonne of Sultan Murad Can, whose enterprise God vouchsafe to accomplish, and to prolong his happy dayes: on the behalfe of whose mother [Marginal note: This Sultana is mother to Mahumet which now reigneth a Emperour.] this present letter is written to the most gracious and most glorious, the wisest among women, and chosen among those which triumph vnder the standard of Iesus Christ, the most mighty and most rich gouernour, and most rare among womankinde in the world, the most gracious Queene of England, which follow the steps of the virgine Mary, whose end be prosperous and perfect, according to your hearts desire. I send your Maiesty so honorable and sweet a salutation of peace, that al the flocke of Nightingales with their melody cannot attaine to the like, much lesse this simple letter of mine. The singular loue which we haue conceiued one toward the other is like to a garden of pleasant birds: and the Lord God vouchsafe to saue and keepe you, and send your Maiesty an happy end both in this world and in the world to come. After the arriuall of your honourable presents, from the Court of your Maiesty, your Highnesse shall vnderstand that they came in such a season, that euery minute ministred occasion of long consolation by reason of the comming of your Maiesties Ambassadour to the triumphant Court of the Emperour, to our so great contentment as we could possibly wish, who brought a letter from your

Maiestie, which with great honour was presented vnto vs by our eunuks, the paper whereof did smell most fragrantly of camfor and ambargriese, and the incke of perfect muske; the contents whereof we haue heard very attentiuely from point to point. I thinke it therefore expedient, that, according to our mutuall affection, in any thing whatsoeuer may concerne the countreys which are subiect to your Maiesty, I neuer faile, hauing information giuen vnto me, in whatsoeuer occasion shall be ministred, to gratifie your Maiesty to my power in any reesonable and conuenient matter, that all your subiects businesses and affaires may haue a wished and happy end. For I will alwayes be a sollicitour to the most mighty Emperour for your Maiesties affaires, that your Maiesty at all times may be fully satisfied. Peace be to your Maiesty, and to all such as follow rightly the way of God. [Sidenote: Ann. Dom. 1594] Written the first day of the Moone of Rabie Liuol in the yere of the Prophet, 1002.

END OF VOL. V.

Milton Keynes UK
Ingram Content Group UK Ltd.
UKHW030622061024
449204UK00004B/396